# Buddhism
## in
# America

# Emma McCloy Layman

# Buddhism in America

Nelson-Hall · Chicago

LIBRARY OF CONGRESS CATALOGING IN PUBLICATION DATA
Layman, Emma McCloy, 1910–
    Buddhism in America.

    Bibliography: p.
    Includes index.
    1. Buddhism—United States.    I.   Title.
BQ732.L39        294.3'0973        76-4566
ISBN 0-88229-166-1 (cloth)
ISBN 0-88229-436-9 (paper)

Manufactured in the United States of America.

To my Buddhist teachers
and friends
this book is gratefully dedicated

# Contents

# Acknowledgments

The author wishes to thank the many individuals who made this book possible; the administrative officers and trustees of Iowa Wesleyan College, who granted the sabbatical leave during which much of the research was done; her husband, Dr. James W. Layman, who was neglected during the research and writing; the numerous Buddhist priests, teachers, and lay adherents who gave so generously of their time to help bring the book to fruition; and the editors of Nelson-Hall, for their patient guidance. She acknowledges with gratitude permission given by the following publishers to quote excerpts from their publications: Newsweek, Inc., New York; Zen Center, San Francisco (excerpts from *Wind Bell*) ; *The Eastern Buddhist,* Kyoto; Buddhist Churches of America, San Francisco; Darma Press, Berkeley (excerpts from *Gesar* and *Crystal Mirror*) ; Karma Dzong, Boulder, Colorado (excerpts from *Garuda*) ; First Zen Institute, New York (excerpts from *Zen Notes*); The Buddhist Society, London (excerpts from *The Middle Way*) ; and Rider Company, London. Lastly, she thanks the following groups for permission to reproduce photographs: Zen Buddhist Temple, Chicago; San Jose Betsuin, San Jose, California; Cleveland Buddhist Temple, Cleveland, Ohio; Eastern States Buddhist Association, New York; and Buddha's Universal Church, San Francisco.

# Preface

This book was written with a two-fold purpose in mind: (1) to meet the need for a work on Buddhism in America which would include a survey of all major Buddhist schools and sects found in the United States; (2) to present an analysis of the American Buddhist scene and American Buddhist adherents from the point of view of a psychologist and social scientist.

A large part of this book is based on observation made during the spring and summer of 1972, when I was on sabbatical leave. During that time I visited Buddhist groups from coast to coast, participating in rituals, meditation, and other aspects of life in Buddhist centers. I also interviewed Buddhist priests representing different sects and about three hundred American lay Buddhists. Since then I have continued with meditational practice, using methods taught me by Buddhist teachers. In the summer of 1973 I participated in Tarthang Tulku's institute on human development, and visited other West Coast Buddhist groups.

In a work of this kind, it is inevitable that some of the material will be out of date before it appears in print because of the time lag between completion of a manuscript and its final publication. It is to be hoped, however, that this has not resulted in any serious distortions in the picture of American Buddhism and Buddhists.

In non-English names and terms, I have omitted all diacritical marks.

# Introduction

For the average American, mention of Buddhism evokes an image of huge, Oriental temples. Statues of enigmatic Buddhas sit or stand in semidarkness; the fragrance of burning incense permeates the otherwise musty atmosphere. Mellow temple bells sound through the cold, clear air before dawn. Brown-skinned, black-robed priests gather to chant scriptures in a barely audible monotone, punctuated by the beat of wooden clappers and reverberating gong. For some, the image includes saffron-clad monks with begging-bowls, walking down a dusty street in a village of India or southeast Asia. Others picture slant-eyed novices with shaven heads, sitting cross-legged in meditation.

Most Americans would be astonished to see a white-faced, black-cassocked monk on the streets of Tokyo, or a yellow-robed American in a Rangoon pagoda. Equally unexpected would be such a sight in Chicago. The usual image of Buddhism does not include temples located in converted warehouses, nor does it include Sunday School rooms, wall-to-wall carpeting, hymns sung in English, and coffee after church. Yet all of this is a part of modern Buddhism, which in the United States has adapted itself to Western architecture and to the American way of life.

Is there a characteristically American style of Buddhism? In a monolithic sense, there is no more an American Buddhism than there is an Indian Buddhism, a Chinese Buddhism, or a Japanese Buddhism. Wherever it is found, Buddhism presents a varied picture. Modern Buddhism probably has even more denominations and sects than does Christianity, with the doctrines and practices of each Buddhist sect differing from those of other sects in major or minor ways. Even within a given sect, there is a tremendous variation from one temple or church to another.

In the Buddhism of America, sectarian and intrasectarian variations also are found. In addition, we find American Buddhist groups differing from one another on the basis of whether their priests or gurus are Chinese, Japanese, Korean, Vietnamese, Ceylonese, Tibetan, or American. At least eight languages in addition to English are used in the rituals and services of different temples and meditation centers in the United States. There is also variety in the manner in which different groups adapt themselves to the American lifestyle. Adaptations range from modifications in clothing and sitting postures to changes in ritual and scheduling. Yet, despite the diversity on the American Buddhist scene, most Buddhist scholars would point out that this is all in the Buddhist tradition—that one of the beauties of Buddhism is its flexibility, so that it can adapt itself to the demands of any lifestyle or culture without sacrificing its identity.

How many Buddhists are there in America? I have asked many American Buddhists this question and have sought information from the American headquarters of different Buddhist sects. Estimates made have ranged from about 50,000 to 500,000 or more, and one Buddhist clergyman even indicated that the membership of his church was "the universe"! The 1973 *Britannica Book of the Year*, basing its report on figures supplied by UNESCO, estimated the Buddhist population in North America to be approximately 300,000, but the author of the report concedes that the accuracy of this figure is in question.[1]

There are several reasons for the difficulty in estimating the number of Buddhists in America:

1. Although most sects have ceremonies in which individuals make their commitment to Buddhism, most nominal Buddhists have made no such formal commitment

2. It is a common practice to consider membership in terms of the number who have made financial contributions to the church or temple

3. Membership figures for many Buddhist groups include "inquirers" who are transients at the temple or meditation center, as well as interested non-Buddhist scholars and Christian clergymen who may be on several Buddhist mailing lists

4. Because Buddhists have a tendency to regard religion as a private matter, many self-styled Buddhists have no affiliation with any Buddhist church, temple, or society.

Some twenty years ago the American secretary of the Buddhist Society in London listed over one hundred Buddhist organizations in the United States.[2] In 1972, the Abbot of a Zen temple in an eastern state suggested to me that there were possibly as many as three hundred Zen groups in America.[3] It would be difficult to estimate how many Buddhist organizations there are in the United States because new groups are constantly being formed while others fade from the scene.

Some organizations, such as the Buddhist Churches of America, the Buddhist Vihara Society, Zen Center of San Francisco, the Cambridge

Buddhist Association, Nichiren Shoshu Academy, the First Zen Institute of America, Rinzaiji, and the Zen Center of Rochester are incorporated, and have a well-defined structure. The structure differs from one organization to another, with some being quite elaborate and hierarchical and others having not more than three or four elected officers. Some of these groups are in the nature of "churches," with boards of directors, whereas others are primarily for training and/or meditation.

In addition to the formally organized groups, some of which are further divided into "chapter" and/or "district" subgroups, there are many informal groups consisting of a few people wanting to learn more about Buddhism or to engage in meditation together. Frequently these groups are organized about some spiritual leader, usually from the Orient. Sometimes they disband as members lose interest or when their leader is called back to his home temple, but they may take on a definable structure and become permanent organizations. Still another possibility is that the group may remain intact but may turn from Buddhism to some different identification, such as affiliation with the Jesus Movement.

The question of how many Buddhists there are in the United States is an academic one, and not too important. Of greater significance are the trends of Buddhism in America. Is its influence increasing or decreasing? Is it making any meaningful impact on American society? Is it being changed by that society?

As pointed out by Donald Swearer, both sociologists and theologians in recent years have been concerned with the dialectical relationship between religion and the cultural society.[4] When society is undergoing change, religion may respond in three ways: it may remain unchanged and rigid, isolating itself from the culture; it may adapt itself creatively to conditions existing within the society while at the same time retaining its basic values and character; it may undergo such radical changes that it is no longer recognizable for what it was. When we look at current developments within the Christian church in the United States, we see examples of all three of these. We also see that what Robert Bellah has called "creative tension" between religious ideals and the world is the only viable alternative if religious values are to influence society.[5]

The dialectical relationship between religion and society is readily apparent in those Asian nations where Buddhism has been intimately linked with government, politics, and education as well as art, literature, and general orientation to life. It is less apparent in the nations of the West in which it has taken root. Britian's most articulate and voluble Buddhist, Christmas Humphreys, while stating that "the

West will never be 'Buddhist,' and only the most unthinking zealot would strive to make it so,"[6] at the same time expresses the conviction that the principles of Buddhism will increasingly meet our Western spiritual needs, but only if these principles are expressed in forms which are consonant with the Western style of life.[7] For many years, in discussing Zen Buddhism,[8] he has insisted that Zen in Britain cannot be "Chinese Zen" or "Japanese Zen," but must be *Western* Zen. And he has taken steps to see that, at the Buddhist Society in London, it is a type of practice in which Westerners—or at least Britons—can feel comfortable.[9]

Buddhism has always been the preferred religion of a large percentage of the Asian immigrants who have settled in the United States. Frequently, their children and grandchildren adopt it as well. In the early years of the twentieth century, a handful of Caucasian Americans begin to practice Zen meditation. Later, others took up the practice, but their numbers were small. In the late 1950s, the "beat" generation showed a flurry of interest in Zen philosophy and practice. However, it was not until the sixties that Buddhism began to attract substantial numbers of adherents from the non-Oriental population of America. Since about 1965 its growth has been rapid, and in the middle seventies it shows no signs of abating.

Now that Buddhism in the United States is no longer considered a religion just for Asians, American Buddhists are directing attention to how they may fashion an *American* Buddhism. They also are trying to apply Buddhist principles in finding answers to the problems of American society. How successful they are in making such applications will possibly determine in part the future of Buddhism on the North American continent. That future, however, will also be influenced by developments within Judaism and Christianity in the decades to come.

Perhaps more interesting than the present characteristics of Buddhism or its future in the United States are two questions of a sociopsychological nature. First, who are the American Buddhists, as far as ethnic, racial, social, and personality characteristics are concerned? Second, why do persons who have grown up in the Judaeo-Christian tradition make the decision to reject that tradition for one which has always been considered alien to the American way of life? The answers to these questions cannot be based primarily on demographic data, which are available to only a limited degree. Rather, they are based on information derived from the following sources: a careful study of newsletters, journals, leaflets, pamphlets, and books prepared and published by Buddhist groups in America; perusal of publications dealing with Zen and/or other types of Buddhist meditation in relation to psychotherapy; my personal participation in Buddhist rituals and meditation sessions; attendance at lectures and discussions sponsored by Buddhist groups; interviews with professors and students from colleges and universities where Buddhism is part of the campus scene; interviews with American Buddhists representing different denominations and sects and affiliated with different groups, from San Francisco to New York; and examination of primary source materials of a documentary nature from individual and organization files made available to me.

This work is divided into four parts. Part 1 consists of a simplified exposition of the essential nature of Buddhism and its principal variants. It is included because it is necessary to know something of Buddhism generally before there can be an understanding of American Buddhism and Buddhists.

Part 2 examines Buddhism in America. Following a brief overview, it devotes a chapter to each of the major schools of Buddhist thought and practice found in the United States. It also includes chapters on Buddhism's approach to the problems of American society, Buddhism in relation to American psychology and psychotherapy, and Buddhism in relation to the Judaeo-Christian tradition.

Part 3 deals with the characteristics of the American Buddhists and their motivations in embracing Buddhism. Part 4 offers some speculations about the future of Buddhism in the United States.

In looking at the various Buddhist sects in America, each is presented in historical context, with a brief presentation of the Asian background preceding the discussion of developments in the United States. In every case, also, attention is given to the various individuals involved in the historical development. This sort of approach has been necessary to give an adequate perspective of Buddhists in America, who are generally more oriented toward the teachings of the founders of the sect and the spiritual heritage of the guru than they are toward the teachings of the Buddha.

Where available, quantitative data have been used to supplement historical information and personal observations. These are included as an additional source of information about the present Buddhist scene, and as an aid in determining trends of growth and decline.

My approach to Buddhism is that of the psychologist and social scientist rather than the philosopher or theologian. It is not my intention that readers of this work should attain a deeper understanding of the philosophical and theological aspects of Buddhism. Rather, it is my hope that this study will contribute to a better understanding of one or several segments of American society.

part **1**

# The Nature of Buddhism

# 1

# The Buddha, the Dharma, and the Sangha

## ORIGINS AND BASIC BELIEFS OF BUDDHISM

### The Vedic Background

In order to understand Buddhism, it is necessary to be familiar with the religious thinking and social conditions which existed in India when the Buddha began his preaching.

The basic religious literature of Hinduism consists of the *Vedas,* written in Vedic, an early form of Sanskrit. There are four Vedas—*Rig, Sama, Yajur,* and *Atharva.* Each consits of two main parts, called "work" and "knowledge" (*Upanishads*). The "work" portions, written between the eleventh and eighth centuries B.C., contained hymns, poems, chants, rituals, and discussions of the significance of ceremonies.[1] The mystical revelations and metaphysical treatises called Upanishads were written later—probably between the sixth and second centuries B.C.

In the Buddha's day, religious rituals had become complex and numerous, and had to be presided over by many priests. Since priests were assumed to have the power to coerce the gods, the former came more and more to dominate Indian society.

It was largely as a protest against the constraining effect of ritual as a way of life that scholars began to postulate that knowledge rather than rituals could be the source of emancipation. This reaction culminated in the writing of the Upanishads, which form the foundation of modern Hindu thinking and contain much that is found in Buddhism.

There are said to be 108 Upanishads which, while not entirely consistent in ideology, contain several concepts basic to advanced Upanishadic thinking:

1. Behind the world as we experience it is one supreme universal principle, *Brahman* (God). All comes from Brahman and is one with Brahman

2. The universal Self (*Atman*) or innermost soul of the individual is one with Brahman

3. The individual self (*otman*) derives its being from the universal Self. It is one with the Self, and Brahman

4. The secret of salvation lies not in rituals, but in meditation, leading to realization of the identity of the Self with Brahman

5. For most men, life is an endless chain of birth, sorrow, death, and rebirth, with the nature of the new life being determined by the deeds in the old one. But the sage who has become one with Brahman is released from this endless cycle of birth, death, and rebirth.[2]

In the sixth century B.C. when the Buddha lived, a rigid hereditary caste system had developed in India, with the *brahmans* (priests and scholars) at the top. However, although the brahmans dominated society, a number of dissident voices were beginning to be heard in the countryside of northern India. At least six important contemporaries of the Buddha had sizable groups of followers who opposed the system, as well as the prevalent ideologies and practices. The people were ready for new ideas and new ways.[3]

Buddhists generally regard Buddhism as a break with Vedic tradition. Hindus and some independent scholars, however, see the Buddha's message as consistent with the more advanced Upanishadic thinking.[4] It has been suggested, also, that later Upanishadic writing showed Buddhistic influences.[5] Whatever view one accepts, the impact of Vedic thought on Buddhism is apparent.

The Buddha rejected the claims of the brahmans that the Vedas were the sole and infallible source of religious truth. He also rejected the idea of the correct performance of rituals as the means to salvation, and the Upanishadic emphasis on intellectualization as the path to wisdom. He developed what Buddhists view as a different concept of the Self. He strongly objected to the caste system. Yet he retained many Hindu concepts. The Buddhist accepts the idea of rebirth and the corollary notion that what one becomes in the next life will be determined by his deeds in this life and past lives. And the Buddhist emphasis on the importance of meditation has its origin in Hinduism. The Buddhist's interpretation of the meaning of "enlightenment" is somewhat different from that of most Hindus, but the experience itself seems to be similar in the two groups.

## The Life of the Buddha

There are in existence more than ten thousand Buddhist scriptures, and a number of these contain stories of the life of the Buddha. However, no biography of the Buddha nor report of his teachings was written during his lifetime, and the earliest account of his life was written some four hundred years after his death. Some of the reports are straightforward; some are more elaborate and dramatic, apparently interweaving facts with surmises, myths, and fantasies.

The earliest accounts of the life of the Buddha treat him as a most unusual man whose life can be an inspiration and model to all men, but who did not perform miracles and is not to be considered a god, in any sense. In some of the later accounts we find reports suggesting an immaculate conception, miracles performed by him and in connection with his birth and death, and struggles with a tempter (*Mara*), who appears to be sort of a devil. No one can say what is fact and what is not.

Historically, Buddhism originated in northeastern India toward the latter part of the sixth century B.C. The founder of Buddhism was a noble of the Sakya clan, whose personal name was Siddhartha Gautama, Siddhartha meaning "he who has accomplished his objectives." Devout Buddhists avoid use of his personal name and have referred to him as the *Buddha* ("enlightened one"), *Sakyamuni* ("teacher of the Sakyas"), *Tathagata* ("one who has reached the reality"), or *Bhagavan* ("revered one"). Frequently he is referred as the "historical Buddha," to differentiate him from the many mythological or symbolic Buddhas. Actually, to refer to him as the Buddha is somewhat misleading, because Sakyamuni himself mentioned that there were many Buddhas before him. According to Buddhist doctrine anyone who achieves complete enlightenment becomes eligible for Buddhahood.

The most usually accepted story of the life of the Buddha says: The Buddha was born around 563 B.C., the son of Suddhodana Gautama, a chief of the Sakya clan located in the southern foothills of the Himalayas. His parents had tried for twenty years to have children, but to no avail. Then following a dream of an elephant entering her side, the chief's wife, Maya, became pregnant, and after ten months Siddhartha was born. Legend has it that the birth of this child was accompanied by flowers blooming out of season, the cessation of illness and suffering, and great happiness throughout the world. Mythology also states that, on the day of Siddhartha's birth, a sage who had a divine revelation predicted that this baby would become either a great monarch or the Buddha.

The rejoicing attending Siddhartha's birth was short-lived, for a few days after his birth his mother died. But he was reared by a kindly and devoted maternal aunt, who was his father's second wife. Since his father was a clan chief, Siddhartha was reared in relative wealth and luxury, which continued after his marriage to his beautiful cousin at age sixteen, and subsequent birth of a son, Rahula. However, so the story goes, despite all this ease and luxury, the young man was troubled by the sorrow and suffering in the world and became increasingly preoccupied with the causes of suffering and how to remove them. Finally, at the age of twenty-nine, on successive trips from the palace with his charioteer, he came across an old man, a sick man, and a dead man. He asked the charioteer about the meaning of what he had seen, and was told, "This comes to all men." After thinking about these experiences, he made the decision to leave his wife and son, renouncing all family ties, and retired to the forest to seek the answers to questions concerning the meaning of life and its suffering.

After Siddhartha decided to renounce the pleasures of life and the satisfactions provided by his family, he joined two hermits who were known for their lives of contemplation and skill in the art of inducing trance states. He soon learned, however, that he could not agree with the theories propounded by his teachers and felt that they had little to offer in the way of deeper insight into life's values and meaning. He therefore left them and joined a group of five ascetics. Admiring their earnestness, for six years he practiced the most severe self-mortification, starving himself, going without sleep, walking or standing without letting himself sit or lie down, and going naked when he needed protection of clothing. He did this until he became so weak that he could scarcely walk or crawl. Seeing that this life did not yield any spiritual enrichment, but resulted in a weakening of both mind and body, he decided to give up the ascetic practices. He continued to seek for the answers to the puzzles of life.

Remembering how he had once experienced a flash of inspiration while sitting in meditation, Siddhartha decided to try that line.

Accordingly, he found a quiet spot under a tree (known as the *bodhi* tree), where he was free from distractions. As he sat in silent meditation the experience which would become known as the "enlightenment" occurred: he felt that he had suddenly discovered the meaning of life and a way to live which would bring freedom from all bondage and give the deepest satisfaction. For the remainder of his life he went throughout India teaching men how to gain release from their bondage to selfish worldly pleasures and to attain the state of true enlightenment.

The Buddha was thirty-five years old at the time of his enlightenment. For the next forty-five years he organized communities of monks, converted people from all walks of life, and trained his disciples to continue his ministry after his death—or, as the Buddhists put it, after he passed into *nirvana*.

During the years of his ministry, the Buddha was extremely successful in gaining converts. The secret of his success is not apparent in the life he led, which was not especially spectacular or remarkable. Ordinarily he would get up before dawn, wash and dress himself, and then meditate in solitude until it was time for him to start out with his alms bowl in search of a meal. This was around noon because he usually ate only one meal a day. Often he ate in a home in a neighboring town or village—sometimes as the only guest, sometimes with disciples. After lunch he would discourse on the *Dharma* (Buddhist doctrine or teachings) for the benefit of his hosts, adapting his presentation to the capacity and background of his listeners. Then he would return to his lodgings and wait on the veranda for his disciples to return from their meal. After suggesting to them a subject for meditation, he would retire to his room for a short rest. In the latter part of the afternoon he would meet with larger groups of people, perhaps in a lecture hall, again adapting his presentation to their capacities for understanding. In the evening, he would expound his doctrines to his disciples, and then have another period of meditation before going to bed. When the weather permitted, he would walk from town to town, sometimes covering as much as ten or twenty miles in a day. During the three months of the rainy season, however, he usually stayed in one place, often lodgings offered by some wealthy man.

Undoubtedly, it was partly the versatility and flexibility of the Buddha's method of presentation which made his message so appealing. When talking to intellectuals, he would discuss his theories of the nature of suffering, the doctrine of non-ego, and the nature of nirvana, speaking formally and with cold logic. But when speaking to the common man, he dealt with moral precepts and illustrated his conversations and sermons with parables, fables, proverbs, anecdotes, and popular sayings. He gave no "commandments," but urged his followers to refrain from taking life, stealing, committing adultery, being deceitful, cursing, lying, boasting, coveting, insulting, flattering, and becoming angry or vengeful.

Possibly even more important than the Buddha's words, in accounting for the tremendous success of his ministry, was his personality. He was a kindly, compassionate man who would not knowingly harm any living thing; and, despite his repeated insistence that he was not a god, his charisma was unmistakable. This, then, was the man called by his followers the Master or the Revered One.[6]

## Teachings of the Buddha

In the world of today there are hundreds of Buddhist sects, each with a system of beliefs about what the Buddha taught or what he would have meant for modern society. Furthermore, none of the thousands of Buddhist scriptures was written during Gautama Buddha's lifetime, so just exactly what he taught is not known. However, there are certain principles and concepts which are accepted by all Buddhists, and these are generally believed to constitute the essence of what was revealed to the Buddha in the enlightenment which came to him as he was sitting under the bodhi tree. These teachings are found in the so-called *Pali Canon*, a series of texts written in one of the early Indian languages called Pali.[7]

The most basic of the messages conveyed by Sakyamuni Buddha were those concerned with the Four Noble Truths, the Noble Eightfold Path, the doctrine of impermanence, the non-ego doctrine, and the relation of *karma* (law of moral causation) to rebirth and nirvana. However, because these Buddhist doctrines were based on a theory of Dependent Origination or Chain of Causality, the latter should be considered a part of the teaching or Dharma. The theory is graphically portrayed in the form of a circle, often referred to as the "Wheel of Life," divided into twelve segments. Although no circle has a beginning, the Buddhist arbitrarily selects as a starting point that stage labelled *primordial ignorance*, meaning ignorance of the true nature of the self and of the phenomenal world. Any individual who has not attained enlightenment before he dies is reborn in a state of ignorance. And, as the result of the life he led in his previous incarnation, he will be born with certain *predispositions* for action in his next incarnation. So ignorance and predispositions represent his past.

Ignorance and predispositions from the past give rise to *consciousness*, which to the Buddhist is a principle activated at conception and representative of a reincarnation. Because of the principle of consciousness, *corporeality* (*mentality* and *body*) emerges, which is the third stage. Because of corporeality, the *six sense minds and organs* appear. Because of the six sense minds and organs, *sensations* and *perceptions* arise. Because of sensations and perceptions, *feelings* and *discriminations* come to be. Because of feelings and discriminations, *thirst* and *craving* arise. Because of thirst and craving, *grasping* and *clinging* appear. Because of grasping and clinging, the process of *existence* or *becoming* develops. Because of becoming, *birth* (rebirth) takes place. Because of rebirth, *growth, sickness, old age, decay*, and *death* take place. Because of these, *sorrow, lamentation, pain, grief*, and *despair* arise. Thus arises the whole of human suffering.

The concept of the chain expresses the doctrine that all physical and psychical phenomena are conditioned by antecedent physical or psychical factors, and that the whole of existence can be shown to be an uninterrupted flux of phenomena.[8]

*The Four Noble Truths.* Most basic of the tenets of Buddhism are the Four Noble Truths:

1. *The Noble Truth concerning the Universality of Suffering* states that all life is dominated by suffering. Birth is suffering; disease and decrepitude are suffering; death is suffering; sorrow, lamentation, pain, grief, and despair are suffering; not to get what one desires is suffering. In short, the five aggregates of existence—bodily form, feeling, perception, predispositions, and consciousness—are suffering

2. *The Noble Truth concerning the Origin of Suffering* says that suffering has its source in sensory desire or craving, and clinging to life

3. *The Noble Truth concerning the Extinction of Suffering* says that suffering can be eliminated by excluding all forms of craving, including the craving for existence

4. *The Noble Truth concerning the Path that Leads to the Extinction of Suffering* says that negating life may be accomplished by accumulating good deeds and by meditation, so that at death or before, one may enter a state of nirvana or enlightenment. More specifically, extinction of suffering comes by following the Noble Eightfold Path or *middle* path.

*The Noble Eightfold Path.* The eightfold path involves right views, right aspirations, right speech, right conduct, right livelihood, right effort, right attentiveness, and right concentration.

1. *Right views* or *right ideas* refer to the Buddhist theory of development in terms of the twelve stages or *nirdanas*, the Four Noble Truths, and certain views about the nature of the self and its destiny in the nirvana state

2. *Right aspirations, right mindedness,* or *right resolution* means a determination to renounce the life of pleasure and to nurture a spirit which is without malice and will not harm any creature. It means the development of unselfish motives, with a willingness to sacrifice personal convenience and comfort in order to benefit others

3. *Right speech* means abstaining from all falsehood, slander, harsh words, or foolish chatter

4. *Right conduct* or *right behavior* covers the whole range of moral living, but special stress is placed on abstaining from taking life, from stealing or coveting, from lying, from adultery, and from partaking of alcohol or drugs

5. *Right livelihood* or *right vocation* means entering only those vocations which will bring no harm or danger to any living thing. The Buddhist is expected to have nothing to do with war, gambling, or prostitution. His life is expected to be one of service rather than one of profit and indulgence

6. *Right effort* means the resolute suppression of all evil states of mind. It means cherishing a spirit of unselfish charity and good will that will prompt the individual to contribute to the relief of need and suffering of others and to be faithful in keeping the precepts; developing humility and patience so that one can bear the acts of others without anger or complaint; maintaining zeal and perseverance to keep one from becoming indolent and careless; fostering tranquillity in order to practice one-pointedness of mind

7. *Right mindfulness* or *right attentiveness* means keeping the mind and body under strict, disciplined control[9]

8. *Right concentration* or *right rapture* is called, in Sanskrit, *dhyana,* which is translated "concentration"; in Pali it is *jhyana* or "rapture." Having tranquillized the mind in the seventh stage, one sits quietly with an empty mind, although attentive and concentrating on the mind's pure essence. This leads eventually to the highest perfect wisdom, a greatly compassionate heart, and blissful peace (see chapter 8).

*Three Attributes of Existence.* Buddhist philosophy is based on the belief that three attributes characterize all phenomenal existence: (1) impermanence (*anicca*); (2) suffering or ill (*dukkha* or *duhkha*); and (3) egolessness or soullessness (*anatman* or *anatta*).[10]

1. The doctrine of impermanence is implicit in the chain of causation. According to this concept, not only are physical phenomena in a state of constant flux, but so is mind or consciousness, which arises and ceases from moment to moment, always changing. Continuity of mental processes, then, would be seen as illusory.

2. The term usually translated as "suffering" may also be translated as "ill," "evil," or "unsatisfactoriness." Actually the term covers all of these meanings, and affirmation of this characteristic of human existence constitutes the first of the Four Noble Truths.

3. One of the most confusing, but also most important doctrines of the Buddha was his anatta (Pali) or anatman (Sanskrit) doctrine, meaning the doctrine of no-self or no ego. This is tied with the doctrine of impermanence.

Ordinarily a person thinks of his "self" in terms of his physical characteristics, plus his thoughts, feelings, motivations, abilities, and ways of relating to people. And yet, the Buddha pointed out, if this is the "self," then there can be no permanent self, for all of these characteristics of the individual are constantly changing, and when the individual dies, they cease to be. Since in the Atman doctrine of the brahmins, the "self" or soul was seen as something which enters the body at birth and leaves it at death, but remains the same through various incarnations, the Buddha's view amounted to saying that there is no self or soul.

If there is no self, what is there? In each lifetime there are the five aggregates of body, sensation, perception, predisposition, and consciousness, which change in the course of a lifetime, and when the individual dies they fall apart and cease to constitute an individual being. If there is no soul, is there *anything* which survives death? Yes, the Buddha says—there is karma. What is karma and what determines its nature? Karma is the law of moral causation which operates to assemble another five aggregates that constitute another new individual being, and determine the consciousness of that being. This new being, while not identical with the old, is nevertheless conditioned by the old: karma carries over the characteristics, especially the moral qualities, of the old to the new. The nature of karma and the nature of the new being will be determined by the quality of life in the old existence. If the individual has led a good life, his next one will be on a higher plane—perhaps as a person or perhaps as a god in one of the

Buddhist heavens postulated by certain sects. If he has led an evil life, his next life will be on a lower level—perhaps as an animal. Thus, the concept of no-self or the impermanence of self is tied in with the Buddhist concept of karma and the theory of *rebirth*.

The theory of rebirth is also tied in with the concept of nirvana. According to the Buddha, the cycle of birth and death is repeated until the individual becomes "enlightened" and realizes that this life of the "five aggregates," or this empirical ego, is only a quasi-self. When this happens, the cycle of birth and rebirth ceases and the individual may enter nirvana.

*Nirvana.* Nirvana (in Pali, *nibbana*) means, in general, the state which the enlightened one attains in this life. *Parinirvana* (completion of nirvana) is the state beyond the enlightened one's death. In other words, when Siddhartha was enlightened at age thirty-five, he experienced nirvana. When, at age eighty, he said to his disciples, "I shall be passing into nirvana," he was speaking of what is now called parinirvana.

The primary meaning of the word nirvana is emptiness, or the void. One who has attained the nirvana state has emptied himself of all that makes up the life of the quasi-self, and feels assured that he will never again be born into this world. One experiences release from all that makes up his desires, the things that enslave him but can never satisfy. Nirvana is also spoken of in such positive terms as freedom, joy, happiness, the deathless and the changeless, and above all as a state of peace where desires have ceased.

It should be noted that different Buddhist sects have developed different ideas about the nature of enlightenment and the type of enlightenment necessary before one may finally be assured of the cessation of the cycle of rebirths. For example, the Theravadins as well as Zen Buddhists see enlightenment as having different degrees of depth, with most who attain enlightenment requiring several life spans before they can hope to attain parinirvana and Buddhahood. The True Pure Land Buddhists describe faith as a prerequisite for rebirth in a "pure land," where continued spiritual growth takes place, leading ultimately to nirvana.

But what happens when the fully enlightened one dies and attains parinirvana? Does he continue to exist as a personal being, a higher self, and what is the nature of that existence? The Buddha was reluctant to express himself on this, but before his death he implied that his own immortality would be in the form of the living on of the truth of his words. One thing which is certain is that the Buddha never regarded himself as a god; he considered himself as an enlightened being, and as a wise teacher, but always as a man. It probably never occurred to him that Buddhism would become a religion in which some of his followers would worship him as if he were a god.

## The Buddhist Way of Life

Just as the behavior of many who profess to be Christians could scarcely be designated as exemplifying the "Christian way of life," one must differentiate the way of life of individual Buddhists from the "Buddhist way of life."

In his first sermon, Gautama Buddha proclaimed the way to nirvana as the Middle Way. He condemned the extreme of sensual indulgence as vulgar, degrading, unspiritual, and unproductive; and he condemned self-mortification as painful, ignoble, and useless. The Middle Way, he said, was the way of the Noble Eightfold Path.

Christmas Humphreys sees the concept of the Middle Way as opening for examination and right reaction the whole field of duality,[11] and this has been the subject of many metaphysical discussions. But for the average Buddhist layman, the Middle Way is seen in terms of ethics and a style of life, uncomplicated by concerns with epistemology and metaphysics.

The man who seeks to follow the teachings of Gautama Buddha has modest needs as far as the material things of life are concerned, but is glad for the well-being of others. He is kind, benevolent, and charitable toward his fellowman. He seeks to love all creatures, leaving no room for malice, hatred, or jealousy. He is calm, gentle, and at peace with himself, but neither passive nor inactive. He radiates happiness. He is modest, but at the same time self-reliant, since the Buddha emphasized that man need not be dependent on anyone other than himself. He has a respect for his body, which he cares for by healthful living, avoiding excesses in food or drink.

Buddhism has no dogma, no commandments—only guides to living. Every Buddhist knows that not even the words of the Revered One are sacrosanct—that one is free to criticize them or to reinterpret them. At the same time, one is tolerant and appreciative of other faiths and points of view.

The Buddhist is grateful for the gifts of nature and does not waste or use them wantonly. For some Buddhists, commitment to the preservation of life is translated into vegetarianism, but there are many who consider meat necessary for bodily strength. Unnecessary killing of animals would be generally frowned upon.

Buddhism is a religion of peace. Buddhists do frequently serve in armies and fight well. However, as pointed out by Walters, "no man can be a genuine Buddhist and at the same time justify aggressive war and the violence of the bully."[12]

The Buddhist may or may not pay visits to a Buddhist temple. If he does, he may bow or kneel before an image of a Buddha or bodhisattva, or before a mandala of some kind. In doing so, he is not praying to the image, but is paying homage to the ideal or idea which the image represents.

Although Buddhism is not a religion of creeds and dogmas, in all sects Buddhist laymen accept the five precepts of abstaining from killing, stealing, adultery, lying, and drinking intoxicating liquors.[13] Furthermore, Buddhists usually sustain their faith and love by repeating the words of the Threefold Refuge:

I take my refuge in the Buddha.
I take my refuge in the Dharma.
I take my refuge in the Sangha.

The Buddha, the Dharma, and the Sangha are referred to as the "Three Jewels" or "Triple Gem" of Buddhism. Of these, the Sangha or community of monks remains to be discussed.

## THE SANGHA AND THE BUDDHIST LAYMAN
*The Sangha*

In the Buddha's forty-five-year ministry his followers numbered many thousands, in addition to the huge congregations of lay men and women who tried to understand his doctrines and lead the kind of life advocated by him. Those thousands whom he designated as his disciples were persons who tried to lead the same kind of life he led. They had given up their homes, families, and material possessions. They wandered from place to place, begging for food, depending upon the charity of others for shelter when they needed it, and dressing in rags discarded by others. The rest of their time was spent in preaching and meditation.

The Buddha viewed these disciples as the ones who would spread the Dharma after his death, and also as those who, because of their lack of worldly responsibilities, would have a chance to attain enlightenment and enter nirvana. However, he recognized that in order to have a group of disciples who could be effective as missionaries in teaching the Dharma to mankind, and who could experience the best possible conditions for individual development, it would be necessary to have organization and discipline in the group. So, within a few weeks of his enlightenment he organized them as a monastic order called the Sangha, and during his lifetime he was head of the Order. When he died there was no one to succeed him, and to this day there is neither a Buddhist pope nor a special body of men to define Buddhism. Each denomination and sect of Buddhism, and later each monastery within each sect, elected its own head, but this person was never more than first among equals. In some of the Japanese Buddhist sects there is an elaborate hierarchy, including "archbishops," "bishops," "chief priests," "priests," and so on. Actually, however, none of these are really priests, and many are not even monks. Some agree to obey the rules of poverty and chastity, but there is no vow of obedience, and the Buddhist monk does not take on such priestly duties as absolution of sins.

During the Buddha's lifetime, most monks were itinerant mendicants, with no home base. Today, in southeast Asia many Buddhist monks operate this way, modeling themselves after the life of the Buddha. However, in countries such as China, Korea, and Japan, the tendency is for the monks to live in monasteries. The food they eat is mostly what they raise themselves, or what is given to the monastery, rather than food which is obtained by begging.

How does one become a Buddhist monk? First, after a probationary period, the individual becomes a novice or postulant. For this, he usually must be at least fifteen years old. (The age varies somewhat in different sects and different monasteries.) Ordinarily, the novice has his head shaved to symbolize his renunciation of lay life; he also receives a new name and a new robe. Usually he takes the Threefold Refuge in the Buddha, the Dharma, and the Sangha, and accepts the ten precepts. The first five precepts are taken by Buddhists on all religious occasions:

> I undertake the rule of training to refrain from injury to living things.
> I undertake the rule of training to refrain from taking that which is not given.
> I undertake the rule of training to refrain from sexual immorality.
> I undertake the rule of training to refrain from falsehood.
> I undertake the rule of training to refrain from liquors which engender slothfulness.

The other five precepts, for the Theravadin monk, are concerned with eating at forbidden times, attending stage performances, using scents and garlands or a luxurious bed, and handling money. The Mahayana monk (and layman) agrees to refrain from speaking ill of others, boasting, giving spiritual or material aid grudgingly, expressing anger, and blaspheming the Three Treasures.

When the novice has thoroughly learned the Dharma and the Rules of the Order, if he is over twenty (again, the age varies from one sect to another), in good health, of good character, and solvent, he may apply for full ordination as a monk. When accepted, he obtains another new robe and name, but he takes no vows and he is free to leave the Order at any time, either temporarily or permanently, although, in a sense, his acceptance of the rules of the Order constitutes a set of "vows."

We may note that, in living a life of poverty, the Buddhist monk does not actually have to give up his property. He simply arranges his affairs so that the income from his property goes to someone else while he is a monk. If he decides to return to life as a layman, he may reclaim his property. If he dies while he is still a monk, his estate goes to whoever is taking care of him at the time of his death. If he is living in a monastery at the time, his estate will go to the Sangha.

Every Buddhist monk in the Orient is required twice a month to attend an assembly at which are recited the Rules of the Order. These rules represent a code of discipline for the monk. The number varies from 227 for the monks of the Theravada school to 250 or more for some of the Mahayana sects. Sometimes the recitation of the rules is accompanied by confessions. Violation of some of the rules results in expulsion from the Order. In the case of others, confession is all that is necessary.

There is some variation in the functions of the monks in Theravada and Mahayana Buddhism. In the Southern school of Buddhism (Theravada), such as that in Ceylon, Burma, Cambodia, and Thailand, the monks spend their time in study, meditation, and teaching. The monk does not belong to an apostolic succession, he has no power to save or condemn, to forgive sins or to administer sacraments. He has no parish for which he is responsible. He teaches the young and such adults as come to the temple on festival days, but there his responsibility to the lay public ends.

In the Northern school, as exemplified by some of the Mahayana sects of Japan, a fully ordained "priest" sometimes resembles the parish priest of the Anglican or Eastern Orthodox communion in two ways not characterizing the monks of the Southern school. He may marry, and he may be responsible for a parish of long-time supporters of the temple. He usually dresses more elaborately than the monk of the Southern group, although not necessarily. (It should be noted that clergy who are householders are sometimes inaccurately referred to as "monks.")

In Chinese and Japanese temples there are usually services twice a day, at which incense is burned and sutras are chanted, but lay people seldom attend except on special festival days; in most Mahayana sects in the Orient there is little or no preaching. In the past, in both China and Japan, the monks did some teaching of children in the villages. However, teaching is no longer a function of monks and priests in these countries, except to teach the Dharma to novices.

Although in the Northern school, the monk or priest in charge of a temple bears some resemblance to a Christian priest, this resemblance is only superficial. The Chinese and Japanese Buddhists have no sacraments, nor do Buddhist priests in these countries usually officiate at wedding.[14] They do not pray to a God, nor intercede with any power. Although they may dress more elaborately than the Theravadin monks, they are individually poor. In many instances, but not in all sects, they are vegetarians who drink no liquor,[15] and they submit to the strict discipline of the monastery in which they live. Mahayana monks may do some begging in the neighborhood of the monastery but for the most part they live on the fruits of their labor, supplemented by food bought with money supplied by parishioners. Most of the monks work in the fields, and those on duty in the monastery do all the cleaning, mending, cooking, and so on without regard to seniority. "He who does not work does not eat" is the policy.

In the beginning, the Buddha was against the idea of ordaining women or having nuns, but several disciples induced him to change his mind, and now, especially in the Northern group, there are many nuns. Some of them live in separate convent-temples; others share the same monastic settlement with the men. Some women have even become head priests in temples in the Orient. One such was an American-born woman, Ruth Fuller Sasaki, who in 1958 was ordained as head priest for the Zen Buddhist temple of Daitokuji Ryosen-An in Kyoto, Japan. She assumed the Buddhist name of Jyokei and accepted a richly brocaded red and gold silk scarf which signifies the Zen priesthood.[16]

The procedures for ordaining nuns are quite similar to those for ordaining monks, and the life styles of each are quite similar. In most monasteries in the Orient, nuns as well as monks shave their heads, and both are expected to be celibate. In Japan, however, it is possible for some ordained men to marry, although celibacy is usually required for ordained women. The number of the Rules of the Order to be observed is generally greater for nuns than for monks.

In modern Buddhism, there are differences in the life of members of the Sangha, not only on the basis of whether they belong to the Theravada or Mahayana school, but also from one sect to another and even in different monasteries sponsored by the same sect. This was evident in the report of a pilgrimage to India, Thailand and Japan, made by a group of American Buddhists from the Zen Center of Rochester, New York. The group visited temples and monasteries sponsored by various Buddhist groups and found considerable variation among them. Virtually all monasteries began their day before dawn, starting with a chanting of the sutras, and repeated this later in the day. However, they differed in the amount and kind of work performed by the monks, the length and frequency of periods of silence, the nature of diet permitted, the number of meals per day consumed, the frequency and significance of begging activities, hours spent in meditation, and relation between the Sangha and the lay community.

A dozen or more monastic communities have been established in the United States, representing Tibetan, Chinese, Korean, Thai, Ceylonese, and Japanese sects. The most numerous of these are Zen monasteries, the oldest being Zen Mountain Center at Tassajara Hot Springs, California (see chapter 4). For the most part, the American monasteries have been modeled after their Asian counterparts, with monks and students studying, working, chanting, eating, and meditating together. They differ from the Asian monasteries in their physical layout, with monks, students, and guests frequently staying in cabins. More frequently than in Asia, also, monks and nuns live in the same monastery. Meals are mostly vegetarian, and partaking of alcoholic beverages is usually forbidden. It is not always required that monks shave their heads, but most do, as do many male students. In some monastic communities in America, men shave their heads but women do not. However, in some monasteries nuns as well as monks are tonsured. In the American Buddhist monastery, unlike that of the Orient, there are few individuals who remain at the monastery as permanent residents. The majority are persons who have jobs or professions which they pursue for most of the year, but come to the monastery for spiritual renewal for a period of a few weeks or several months.[17]

*Buddhist Laymen in Relation to the Sangha*

In premodern times, Buddhism was a movement of monastic ascetics. However, a laity is essential to the success of a monastic community, because the monastery or temple is dependent on laymen for financial support and the medicant monks are dependent on laymen for food and shelter.

In Buddhism's early days, for the layman, much of the Buddha's message dealt with the practical problems of the moral life. It was the achievement of an ethical life that was the important thing. The Buddhist layman was expected to observe the five precepts already described: each particular station in life had its particular prescribed duties. Thus, parents were expected to guide and protect their children, and children were expected to honor their parents as well as to carry on family traditions. Teachers were expected to instruct their students, and in turn, would receive due respect from their students. Husbands were to be courteous, faithful, and respectful to wives, while wives were to show fidelity to their husbands and to be diligent in carrying out their household duties. Friends were to be courteous, generous, and benevolent to one another, observing the "golden rule" and keeping the faith. For the majority of lay adherents in the Buddhist world, this would still be considered the essence of Buddhism.

It was the Buddha's opinion that it would be impossible for the lay person to attain nirvana, because the layman would have so many worldly responsibilites that he wouldn't be able to meditate with sufficient concentration to experience enlightenment. If by some accident this happened, he would have to be ordained immediately. If the layman could not hope for nirvana, what was his reward for leading the good life? It was rebirth at a higher level of human existence, or rebirth as a deity in one of the Buddhist heavens.

For the Buddhist layman, one of the most important ways to gain merit is by supporting the Sangha. This may take the form of giving food and clothing to the monks, or it may take the form of providing financial support for the monastery and/or temple. Frequently, also, the Buddhist layman may spend a period of time in the monastery, studying and meditating.

In modern times, a closer relationship between the laity and the Sangha has developed within the Buddhist community. In most Buddhist sects, a layman or laywoman may formally become a Buddhist and a "disciple" of some member of the Sangha who is his precepter or preceptress. The ceremony for becoming a disciple is not always the same, but involves the individual's "taking the Refuge," accepting the precepts (five or ten), and making several general vows. In some sects there is also "lay ordination," with a senior disciple carrying out certain priestly functions such as leading services, and/or assisting the monks or teachers in various ways. The disciple also has a Buddhist name and a robe, but need not shave his head. Most disciples do not live in the temple or monastery, although some do and are treated as members of the Sangha. (Ordained laymen are always considered to be Sangha members.)

In the United States, many groups of Buddhists do not have a close relationship with any monastery, although most Buddhist temples or churches in the United States do have an affiliation with some temple and monastery in the Orient. However, most Buddhist monasteries in the United States have a close relationship with some temple or center, which supplies its leadership and participates in its financial support. Those with membership in the temple or center often spend periods ranging from a few days to a few months as students at the monastery. Examples of such relationships are that of the Zen Center at San Francisco with the monastery at Tassajara, and that of Cimarron Zen Center of Los Angeles with the monastery at Mount Baldy, California. Other groups frequently arrange for retreats of several days or weeks, in which their members lead a monastic life in the mountains or in a rural setting, away from the disturbances of urban life. In general, American Buddhists are expected to lead their lives within the lay community rather than in a monastic setting, but are also encouraged to have at least a taste of the monastic life for spiritual enrichment.

## THERAVADA AND MAHAYANA BUDDHISM

During Sakyamuni's lifetime his words were not committed to writing. Transmission of the Dharma after his death, therefore, depended upon his disciples' memory of what their Master had said and their understanding of what he meant. It is reported that, shortly after the Buddha's death, a council of five hundred *arhats* (saints) was held to review and rehearse the teachings of the Revered One as remembered by Ananda, the Buddha's closest and most beloved disciple. However, even at this time there were some who remembered the Buddha's message as quite different from the version reported by Ananda. It was four centuries before there was any systematic compilation of scriptures in written form.[18]

With monks living in widely scattered groups both during the Buddha's lifetime and after his death, and no written Canon to serve as a unifying force, it was inevitable that schisms would develop within the Sangha. As various disciples expounded their views of the Dharma, some of them doubtless became more influential than the Master whom they claimed to follow. At one time during the early period of Buddhism there were as many as eighteen schools of thought.[19] Most of these died out, and the only one which had any lasting influence was that which came to be known as the Theravada. One of the early schools which was opposed to the Theravada was a system called Mahasanghika. Like the others, it did not survive, but was responsible for the eventual development of Mahayana Buddhism.[20]

By the first century B.C., a group of scriptures was assembled, written in Pali. This collection, known as the *Pali Canon*, was later translated into Sanskrit, and was purported to be an accurate account of what the Buddha actually taught. It is this collection which forms the basis for Theravada beliefs and practices today.

Like Theravada thinking, Mahayana Buddhism developed gradually, and both views flourished together in India from the second to the fourth century A.D., before the Mahayana school became predominant in the years from 300 to 500 A.D.[21] After 500 A.D., Buddhism in India began to wane and eventually came to be absorbed by Hinduism in the country of its origin.[22] However, starting in King Asoka's reign (beginning in 236 B.C.), Buddhism had spread abroad. The Theravada tradition first became entrenched in Ceylon and Southeast Asia, and Mahayana Buddhism later became the accepted view in China, Korea, Japan, Mongolia, and Tibet.

## Hinayana (Theravada) Buddhism

Since the second century A.D., there have been two main streams of Buddhist thought, usually referred to as Hinayana ("Lesser vehicle" or "Small vehicle") and Mahayana ("Greater vehicle"). The Tantric Buddhism of Tibet, sometimes known as Lamaism, is considered by some to be a third stream of thought, but actually represents a variant of Mahayana called Vajrayana (see Chapter 5).

The name, Hinayana, was originated by the Mahayanists. It is generally not used by adherents to this school of Buddhist thought, who prefer "Theravada" ("doctrine of the Elders") as a designation for their view. Conze has referred to it as the "Old Wisdom" school.[23]

Beatrice Lane Suzuki explains that use of the term Hinayana to designate the Theravadin view implies that it is a way of salvation for only a few, whereas Mahayana is the "greater" vehicle because it makes provision for salvation of all men.[24] She notes, further, the claim of Mahayanists that whereas Hinayana may provide the letter of the Buddha's teaching, it remains for Mahayana to attempt to catch the true spirit of it.[25] Although there is not in this interpretation necessarily any implication of inferiority in the Hinayana view, it is not uncommon for Mahayanists to regard it as primitive and unsophisticated, and therefore of lesser value than the Mahayana.

Hinayana or Theravada Buddhism, based on the *Pali Canon*, has several basic characteristics: (1) it regards the Buddha as a human teacher and ethical guide—not as a divine or mystical being, (2) its goal is the development of the "arhat" or saint—not the improvement of the quality of life for all people, (3) it emphasizes that enlightenment can be obtained only by a rigid self-discipline involving abstention from all pleasures, meditation, concentration, and withdrawal from the world, and that, therefore, (4) escape from endless reincarnation into the world of suffering and entrance into nirvana is possible only for a select few.[26]

Common to Theravada and Mahayana teaching are the following points:

1. The object of Buddhism is to get rid of delusion, obtain enlightenment, and enter the world of the Infinite and Absolute

2. The world has no beginning and no end. All is explained by causation, but there is no first cause

3. All things change, all is impermanent, all is transient; this is true not only of men but of all life, even that which seems most enduring

4. There is no substantial entity known as the ego. As all is impermanent and transient, so there is no self or ego such as is popularly regarded as persisting behind consciousness

5. The law of causation is universally valid in the moral world as well as in the physical world. Every cause has an effect

6. Transmigration explains causation, and is due to karma, and karma is produced by the deeds in the life of birth and death. Transmigration leads to suffering, as the Four Noble Truths set out

7. Delusion is the cause of suffering, which is universal

8. Moral practices, such as the Noble Eightfold Path,... are prescribed in order to remove delusion.[27]

## Mahayana Buddhism

Mahayana Buddhists contend that the Buddha gave his message at many different levels, and that the message revealed in the *Pali Canon* was for the ignorant, dull, and unsophisticated—for those too primitive to understand the real spirit of Buddhism in its highest manifestations. Accordingly, although they accept the *Pali Canon*, they tend to place more emphasis on guidance provided by one or more of the thousands of sutras and commentaries written at a later date.

Mahayana Buddhism differs from the Theravada in five important ways:

1. Whereas the Theravada concept of the Buddha refers to the historical Buddha, Mahayana Buddhists give considerable prominence to Buddhas other than Sakyamuni. In fact, Mahayana Buddhists often indicate that there have been many Buddhas and that there is no particular reason to regard Gautama as being uniquely important. Some of the Buddhas venerated by Mahayana Buddhists are symbolic representatives of the spirit of Buddhism and not individuals who have ever had any human existence. Among the Buddhas frequently mentioned are the Buddha of Eternal Light and Infinite Life (Amitabha or Amida) and the cosmic Buddha (Vairocana or Daini-chi). In a sense, then, for the Mahayana Buddhist, Buddha is an eternal spirit or principle—not just a superior human being. The Buddha is seen as transcendental, eternal, and absolute, and therefore as saving all beings with his Three Bodies (*trikaya*).[28]

The first of the three bodies of the Buddha is the Body of Essence, or Body of the Law, which refers to some permanent essence or truth which exists outside the human body and which unites and connects all the Buddhas of the past, present, and future. Thus, whereas the physical body of a Buddha dies, the Body of Essence remains as the only real and permanent body of the Buddha. This body is serene and eternal, existing everywhere. When the Body of Essence is called upon to preach to the Bodhisattvas, it appears in an illusory form as the Body of Bliss or Communal Enjoyment, a marvelous symphony of light and sound. The third body, also an illusion, is the Body of Transformation. This refers to a fictitious phantom of the Eternal Buddha which he creates in his own image. This body takes on the characteristics of a human and appears on earth to save mankind. Sakyamuni is one example of such a manifestation. This notion of a Buddhist trinity has sometimes been compared to the concept of the unity of body, mind, and soul, and has also been said to have some similarity to the Christian Trinity of Father, Son, and Holy Spirit, with the Body of Essence representing the godhead. Yet, the concept is not really like either of these.[29]

Mahayana Buddhism, like the Theravada school, does not recognize a personal God, or God as ultimate reality.[30] However, with the Buddha being regarded as the manifestation of universal truth and light, he becomes something more than a human being. And when we look at the beliefs of some of the Amidists (the Jodo Shin sect, for example), the insistence on the efficacy of faith in Amida Buddha as the *sine qua non* for salvation sounds suspiciously like the deification of the Eternal Buddha.

2. Whereas Theravada Buddhism emphasizes the arhat ideal, Mahayana Buddhism gives great prominence to the bodhisattva or "being of enlightenment."

A bodhisattva is one who is qualified to enter nirvana and become a Buddha, but who voluntarily renounces this privilege to be reincarnated in the world and work for the salvation of unenlightened humans. The bodhisattva is a being of infinite compassion, love, and altruism. In China, one of the most popular of the bodhisattvas is *Kwan-yin*, or the Goddess of Mercy. This bodhisattva is popular in Japan, also, where it is called *Kwannon*. In Japan, however, the Kwannon is often depicted as a male rather than a female.

3. The Mahayana Buddhist takes the view that all sentient beings possess the Buddha-nature and are therefore capable of being enlightened.[31] Some sects (notably, the Jodo Shin sect) stress the belief that all who have faith in Amida Buddha will enter a Pure Land of Bliss after death—even though they may not have entered the state of nirvana—and that nirvana is not a reward reserved for the saint or arhat, but is a possible attainment for all men.

4. For most Mahayana Buddhists, enlightenment is perceived as attainable by living a life of faith and devotion to the Buddha, as well as showing love and compassion for all fellowmen, rather than calling for the strenuous discipline advocated by the Theravadins.[32] The importance of meditation is a central concept for the Zen group among the Mahayanists, but most Mahayana Buddhists do not stress meditation. The Zen Buddhists see meditation as a means of helping an individual to function better in his relationships with people.

5. Mahayana Buddhism differs from the Theravadin view in its concern with metaphysics, and some quite complex theories of knowledge have developed within the various denominations and sects in the Mahayana school.

In addition to the above basic differences between Theravadin and Mahayana views, it should be noted that Mahayana thinking tends to be experiential and intuitive rather than analytical and scholastic,[33] and differs somewhat from Theravadin thinking in its concept of nirvana and non-ego doctrine.[34] (See subsequent chapters for details.) Another difference seems to lie in the Theravadin view that the individual must work out his own salvation in contrast to the emphasis by most Mahayana sects on faith in an outside Power.[35]

## Vajrayana Buddhism

Vajrayana Buddhism or Tantrism is a branch of Mahayana, but is discussed separately here because of its unique features. Like the other Mahayana systems of thought, it subscribes to concepts of no "God" in the sense of a divine personage to be adored, absence of "self," impermanence of everything in the phenomenal world, suffering as a characteristic of all life, reincarnation, karma, causality, and the concept of nirvana as realization of the Buddha-nature which is present in all sentient beings.[36] Its uniqueness lies principally in its symbolism and in the methods which it employs.

The three methods of attaining enlightenment for the Tantric Buddhist are: (1) the repetition of *mantras* or mystic syllables, (2) the performance of certain symbolic gestures known as *mudras,* and (3) identification with deities on the basis of a special kind of meditation employing visualization.[37] These ritual practices, or *tantra,* must be carried out under the guidance of a master or *guru,* and are communicated by the master only to those who are initiated into the esoteric teachings.[38] There are two types of initiation ceremonies, called Right-hand Tantric and Left-hand Tantric.

Right-hand Tantrism is concerned generally with incantations of the sacred syllables, the ritual performance of certain body movements, and ceremonies and meditation in connection with the *mandala* or sacred circle. This circle is considered to be the gathering place for the various Buddhas and bodhisattvas, with the central position within the circle being occupied by the Vairocana Buddha, considered by Tantric Buddhists to be the highest being or the Absolute Buddha.[39]

Left-hand Tantrism, much misunderstood and maligned by its critics, incorporates into its rituals certain sexo-yogic practices. These practices represent a union of the ancient Indian cultic practice of worshipping the female element and Mahayana theology. In Mahayana Buddhism, enlightenment is seen as the union of wisdom and compassion. Wisdom (*prajna*) is interpreted as realization of the nonexistence of everything which appears to be in the phenomenal world, and compassion is the urge to carry out altruistic activities to save others. The Left-hand tantras accept these terms, but interpret wisdom to be female and compassion to be male. Consequently, one finds in the Tantric iconography Buddhas and bodhisattvas locked in passionate embraces with their consorts, symbolizing the inseparability of wisdom and compassion, or the absolute and the phenomenal.[40]

Vajrayana Buddhism is usually associated with the Tantrism of Mongolia and Tibet. However, like the mainstream of Mahayana thought, it originated in India, and traces of Tantrism are found in certain Mahayana sects in Japan, most notably the Shingon sect which embraces many esoteric practices.

## Theravada and Mahayana Buddhism in the West

The relative freedom from abstruse metaphysical theories characterizing the Theravadin thought, plus its appeal to analytical and logical thinking, until recently have generally made it more attractive to the Western mind than the more intuitive and/or esoteric Mahayana views. At present, however, the challenge to understanding presented by the more difficult and logic-defying Mahayana philosophies (especially Zen) seems to be reversing the earlier preference for the intellectually more comprehensible Theravada thought.

# part 2

# Buddhism in America

# 2

# The History and Nature of Buddhism in America: an Overview

Adherents to the beliefs of Buddhism and participants in the rituals and other practices associated with Buddhism as a religion and way of life have existed in the United States since the first Asian immigrants landed on the west coast of the North American continent. Yet it was not until nearly the turn of the century that the first Buddhist-sponsored groups were established on the soil of the American mainland.

This chapter sketches briefly the influences which led to the establishment of Buddhism in the United States, and summarizes the principal developments in American Buddhism in the twentieth century.[1] It also takes an overall look at the current American Buddhist scene.

## HISTORY OF BUDDHISM IN AMERICA

*Early History*

Interest in Buddhism on the part of a substantial number of Americans was first stimulated by the organization of the Theosophical Society in New York in 1875. Through the publications and lectures sponsored by this society, many people became acquainted with concepts such as reincarnation, karma, and nirvana. The real beginning of Buddhism for non-Oriental Americans, however, did not come until 1893, with the convening of the World's Parliament of Religions in Chicago. Among the more impressive participants in the two-week congress were two Buddhists, Anagarika Dharmapala and Soyen Shaku. The former was influential in establishing Mahabodhi Societies in America,[2] and the latter promoted the growth of Zen in the United States.

In the decade following the Chicago congress, an unprecedented number of Buddhist missionaries found their way to America. Interest in Buddhism began to develop among intellectuals other than Orientalists and faddists. Also contributing to this interest were, first, the books and articles on Buddhism written by Paul Carus, and, second, the books and journals issued by the Open Court Publishing Company, of which Carus was one of the publishers. The most important of the Open Court publications were the writings of Daisetz T. Suzuki.

A prolific writer on many subjects, Carus was frequently criticized as displaying defective scholarship. However, his books were well received by lay readers. They were also praised by Suzuki as having successfully conveyed the spirit of Buddhism.

Carus's involvement with Buddhism came about as the result of his attendance at the Parliament of Religions, where he reacted favorably to the papers presented by the Zen Master, Soyen Shaku. Consequently, when he appointed a new writer and editor for the Open Court Publications in 1897, he chose one of Soyen's[3] disciples, a young Japanese Zen scholar named Suzuki. Not only as an employee, but as a house guest in the Carus home for eleven years, Suzuki lived and worked in LaSalle, Illinois, until his return to Japan in 1909.

Until the 1960s, most of what the English-speaking world knew of Zen came from Suzuki's pen. It was in the articles, translations, and reviews written during his years with Carus that his influence began to make itself felt in the West.

Following the World's Parliament of Religions, Japanese Buddhist priests found America to be a fertile field for missionary endeavors. The early missionary priests also became aware of the need for some provision to care for the spiritual needs of the burgeoning population of Japanese-Americans of the Jodo Shinshu (True Pure Land sect) faith.[4] This led to the formal establishment of a mission in California in 1899, which later became a separate organization known as the Buddhist Churches of America, with independent and branch churches located in different parts of the country. Following the arrival of the Shinshu mission in California, several other Japanese sects soon organized missions in the United States. These included two other Pure Land groups,[5] a Nichiren sect,[6] and the Shingon[7] (True Word) sect.

While Japanese sectarian Buddhism was being formally established in the United States, the temples of Chinatown were usually a syncretistic combination of Buddhism, Taoism, Confucianism, and folk religion. Unlike the churches established by the Japanese, the churches of Chinatown were not generally official missions of religious groups in the Orient, but were usually adjuncts of Chinatown secular "associations."

## Beginnings of American Zen

During the first two decades of the twentieth century, for the first time non-Oriental Americans became involved in the practice of Buddhist meditation. This resulted from the efforts of a number of Japanese Zen missionaries. In 1905, Soyen returned to America. He was followed the next year by one of his disciples, Sokatsu Shaku, who brought six of his own disciples, including a lay disciple, Shigetsu Sasaki. These men were active in organizing Zen groups where Occidentals were encouraged to practice.

## Between the Two World Wars

During the years between the two World Wars, the Jodo Shinshu churches enjoyed a slow but steady growth. In addition, every large city had a few swamis, lamas, Zen priests, or bhikhus,[8] each with a small following. These were lean years for Buddhism, however, with few non-Orientals showing much interest in it. Although the First Zen Institute of New York was formed in 1930, it attracted only a small group until after World War II.

## After World War II

After World War II, many American servicemen stationed in Japan developed an interest in Buddhism. Some of these married Japanese women with Buddhist backgrounds. As a result, in the late 1940s and early 1950s there was an upsurge of interest in Buddhism in the United States. This diminished in the middle fifties, and was succeeded by the "Beat Zen" fad of the late fifties. More significant than these developments, however, from the long-term point of view, was the influence of the lectures on Zen given by D. T. Suzuki at Columbia University in the years between 1950 and 1958. These, plus Suzuki's writings, reawakened an interest in Zen among intellectuals, and prompted several future leaders of American Zen to go to Japan to study and practice Zen meditation under the direction of Japanese Zen masters.

In the middle 1950s to the early 1960s, several Zen centers were established in scattered areas of the United States, including Chicago; Cambridge, Massachusetts; and Rochester, New York, among others.

One of the "modern" Nichiren sects in America was established in 1959 with the opening of the Los Angeles branch of Rissho Kosei-kai[9] (Society for the Establishment of Righteousness and Friendly Intercourse). This was followed in 1960 by the organization of Nichiren Shoshu of America[10] (Nichiren True Buddhism sect), which also had its beginnings in Southern California. Rissho Koseikai in the United States has shown little growth, and has remained a church primarily for those of Japanese ancestry. In contrast, Nichiren Shoshu has grown very rapidly, and since 1967 its converts have been mostly non-Orientals.

During the 1960s Theravada Buddhism of southeast Asia and Ceylon attained a gradual but healthy growth in America, and had a broad appeal. The Vajrayana Buddhism of Tibet and Mongolia also found itself welcome in America, with its adherents first consisting mostly of refugees from Asia, but later including increasing numbers of American students and scholars. Chinese Buddhism involving meditation came to enjoy some popularity among Occidentals.

## American Buddhism in the 1970s

In the 1970s, Zen seems to be enjoying something of a boom. It appears to have its chief appeal to hippies, intellectuals, students, and professional men and women, although housewives and businessmen also are found among those who have accepted the Zen way of life. More than three-fourths of those beginning practice with a Zen group drop out within a year.[11] Despite the high drop-out rate, however, increasing numbers are remaining, many being attracted to the monastic life in one of the half-dozen Zen monasteries in the United States. Zen meditation groups are being formed everywhere, with most being affiliated with some center under the leadership of a Japanese Zen master or a Japanese-trained priest. Most of these adhere rather strictly to the rituals and procedures characterizing the routine in Japanese temples, although increasing numbers are experimenting with modifications of rituals to make them more appropriate for Americans and are introducing the practice of repeating sutras and invocations in English. Protestant and Roman Catholic clergymen are joining Zen groups, and Zen masters are often invited to conduct training sessions in Zen meditation at Catholic monasteries. Zen workshops and seminars on university campuses are becoming quite common.

The influence of Tibetan Buddhism is increasing rapidly in the United States in the seventies, in some areas growing more rapidly than Zen.

Nichiren Shoshu is currently emphasizing the discussion group, and in 1972 it was concentrating on the recruitment of students. A large part of its membership, however, comes from lower-class and lower middle-class young people, with a fairly large representation of minority groups.

Theravada Buddhism continues to grow, with non-Orientals being included in the membership at two of every three principal centers. Theravada monks frequently give instruction on meditation at colleges and universities.

Chinese Buddhism in its meditational and monastic aspects seems to have an appeal for non-Orientals as well as Chinese and Chinese-Americans, although the syncretistic types of Taoist-Buddhist temples are disappearing. Membership in the Shinshu churches continues to consist mostly of persons of Japanese ancestry, and membership figures remain quite stable.

Along with these most visible institutions representing the Buddhist faith in the United States, there continue to be smaller groups of Buddhists of different persuasions, as well as a few interdenominational Buddhist churches.

In the 1970s Buddhism appears to offer a viable alternative to Christianity and Judaism in America. What trends future decades will reveal remains to be seen.

## THE NATURE OF BUDDHISM IN AMERICA

Attempting to describe the nature of Buddhism in America is something like trying to answer the question, "What is the nature of America?" For neither America nor the Buddhist church in America is a monolithic entity, and neither is a melting pot. Yet the analogy does not quite hold, for Buddhism in America in the 1970s is not "American Buddhism." It is not even "Western" Buddhism in the sense that Christianity in the Western world is perceived as a Western religion. For the native-born American, whose language and intellectual traditions have encouraged abstract thinking and logical approaches to life problems, the Buddhist rejection of abstraction and logic is difficult to grasp and accept—it is foreign to his way of looking at things. Nor is it American to ask questions such as, "What is the sound of one hand clapping?" and to be unwilling to accept the common-sense answer. On the behavioral level, hours of immobility while engaging in meditation would certainly go against the action-oriented trends in American society.

Although Buddhism in America is not American and is not Western, neither is it completely "Eastern." As one looks over the Buddhist scene in America, he may find a *zendo* (Zen meditation hall) with straw *tatami*[12] mats on the floor, and observe robed, shaven-headed monks chanting sutras in Japanese. On the other hand, he may enter another zendo where sutras are read in English and meditation is engaged in by long-haired lads clad in jeans, sitting on straight-backed chairs. He may find services conducted in Korean, or he may visit a Buddhist Sunday School and wonder for a few minutes if he has wandered into the Presbyterian Church by mistake.

Buddhism in America is characterized by great diversity, with both conservative and liberal trends within the same sect and denomination. Of course, differences in furnishings and hair styles are superficial, and are either tangential or irrelevant to the Buddhist system of beliefs and basic way of life. But fundamental and widespread changes in American Buddhism are occurring. Its priests and adherents are recognizing that Buddhism must be shown to have relevant approaches to the solution of the problems which plague American society—problems such as crime, mental illness, racism, drug addiction, pollution, and war. Accordingly, sermons and lectures delivered by the clergy are making less use of illustrations recounted by ancient Buddhist saints and are becoming more applicable to everyday living in modern American society. In most Buddhist centers in America, discussion groups are dealing with the question of "What is the Buddhist way, here and now, in our society?"

# 3

# Amida's Pure Land and the Buddhist Churches of America

Before the gilt and teakwood altar, a thin thread of incense-bearing smoke curled from a jar-shaped burner. Between two tall candles were symbolic offerings of rice and apples. Worshippers sat quietly on benches and chairs. A priest in embroidered robes, with a string of ojuzu beads in one hand and a padded stick in the other, struck a bowl-like gong. A sonorous bass note echoed against yellow plaster walls.[1]

The scene was the shrine of the New York Buddhist Church, on June 1, 1947. For three days, two hundred young Japanese-Americans and a smattering of Caucasians had met in a conference to discuss the postwar condition of the Jodo Shinshu churches in America. They talked of such matters as building new churches in the east and midwest, recruiting of bilingual priests, and the need for Buddhist theological seminaries in America. In 1947, the fifteen thousand acknowledged members of the "Shin" faith were being served by sixty-five clergymen, all Japanese-trained.

Twenty-five years later, in 1972, the altar of the New York Buddhist Church looked much as it had in 1947, although the church had been moved to a new location adjoining the property occupied by the American Buddhist Academy. Reverend Hozen Seki, minister of the church since 1938, as well as founder and current president of the academy, looked much as he had in 1947 except for the discarding of the brocaded vestments for a plain black robe. Now, also, he had as assistants two young Caucasian lay ministers, both graduates of the academy which he heads.

The years from 1947 to 1972 saw the number of clergy in the Buddhist Churches of America increased to eighty and the number of members raised to an estimated forty thousand. It found a number of congregations enjoying new church buildings. It also witnessed a renewed concern over how the Shinshu groups in America could make their message more relevant to the needs of modern American society.[2]

The Buddhist Churches of America constitute an incorporated organization of Buddhist Churches of Jodo Shinshu (True Pure Land sect) faith, located on the mainland of the United States. Although it is an autonomous organization, it has spiritual ties with the Hompa Hongwanji (Western Hongwan Temple) of Kyoto and with the Japanese founder of the Shinshu faith, Shinran Shonin (1173–1262).

It is with the Buddhist Churches of America and their Pure Land heritage that this chapter is concerned.

## AMIDISM AND THE PURE LAND SECT

### The Nature of Shin Buddhism

The Jodo Shinshu or Shin sect of Buddhism is one of several sects which may be designated as *Amitabha* or *Amida* (Japanese equivalent of Amitabha) sects. These sects advocate salvation by *tariki* (other power), rather than by *jiriki* (self-power). They argue that the teachings of the sutras are too difficult for most people to understand; that few can hope to attain enlightenment by meditation; and that man's past incarnations have resulted in the accumulation of so much bad karma that only a saint, through his own efforts, could possibly accumulate enough merit in a lifetime to be able to attain nirvana. However, they say, if one has faith in Amida Buddha and repeats the *nembutsu* or invocation, *"Namu Amida Butsu"* (Hail to the Buddha of Eternal Light and Infinite Life), he will be saved by the grace of Amida Buddha. After he dies he will be reborn in a "Pure Land" or "Western Paradise" presided over by Amida Buddha, and there he will finally attain nirvana.[3] It is believed that one who has arrived in the Western Paradise may return to the world and labor for the salvation of others, but such a returning does not mean a reentry into the cycle of birth and rebirth.[4]

Amidism does not deny the importance of good works, and some sects regard them as a means of gaining merit. Shin Buddhism, however, looks upon good works as an expression of gratitude for the love and compassion of Amida Buddha, rather than as a means of earning merit and making progress toward enlightenment in this life. The Shin Buddhist also believes that if one has faith, right conduct will arise out of that faith.

Adherents of the Pure Land sects of Buddhism often regard Amida Buddha as a historical person, but Bunce has suggested that Amida is an abstraction whose principal attribute is infinite benevolence.[5]

The teachings of Jodo Shinshu are based on the three Amitabha sutras of the Chinese Canon, plus T'an-luan's commentary on Vasubandhu's *Treatise on the Pure Land*. These texts teach that the bodhisattva, Hozo, long before the birth of Siddhartha Gautama, renounced a throne to bring light to the ignorant and love to the hopeless. He made a vow to be an eternal savior, saying that he would not accept Buddhahood until he had accumulated enough merit to save from their bad karma all who called on him in humility and faith. Through numerous rebirths Hozo accumulated much merit, turning over the karma for his good deeds to the emancipation of others. Finally, through his perfect compassion, he became the Buddha Amida, that is, the Buddha of Eternal Light and Infinite Life.[6]

Shugaku Yamabe points out that the concept of Amida as the savior of mankind resembles to some extent the God of Christianity.[7] However, whereas the Christian God is a god of love and justice as well as the creator of the universe, Amida is not the creator and shows only mercy.

In contrast to other forms of Buddhism, Shinshu is regarded by its adherents as being the "easy" way to salvation. The Shin Buddhist is not expected to live a life of great sacrifice. He is not expected to understand an abstruse philosophy. He is not expected to spend hours in meditation. He is not even expected to be completely without sin. (The Shinshu way has been described as the way of faith and morality, but morality is considered to be a duty to the social order rather than the path of salvation.) All that is really required of the Shin Buddhist is that he repeat, reverently and with sincere faith, "Namu Amida Butsu." If he can do this, salvation after death is guaranteed.

With Shinshu representing the easy way, it is not surprising that it is the most popular traditional Buddhist sect in Japan today. But its appeal is not only to the ignorant and uneducated. Actually, the philosophy of its Japanese founder has been the subject of study of Japan's most outstanding thinkers, and presents a real challenge to the dialectician.

## History of Shin Buddhism

*Amidism in India and China.* The cult of Amitabha Buddha is believed to have originated in northwestern India about 100 A.D.[8] In its original form, however, calling on the name of Amitabha Buddha was used as an adjunct to meditation, and faith without works was not considered sufficient for rebirth in Buddha's Pure Land.

By the second century the practice of calling on the name of Amitabha was followed in China. The first Chinese Pure Land master, T'an-luan (476-542), developed important innovations which had a profound effect on later Shinshu thought and practice in Japan and the West. Being convinced of the primacy of "other-power" rather than "self-power," he advocated repetition of Amitabha's name with faith, rather than stressing meditation. He also claimed that even sinners could go to the Pure Land, because all living beings possess the Buddha nature.

*Jodo Shu and Jodo Shinshu in Japan.* Long before the Pure Land theory was molded into a Japanese sect, it was part of the teaching and practice of other Japanese schools of Buddhism, most notably Tendai[9] and Shingon. However, the presence of Amida in these sects was as an esoteric divinity. Like other esoteric gods, Amida was an object of meditation, with the goal being to possess the virtues of Amida through meditation. "Nembutsu" was used as a support for the meditative process, but was not considered sufficient in and of itself to assure the attainment of salvation. Moreover, although Amida was considered to be quite suitable as an object of meditation, concentration on any esoteric Buddha was believed to be a way of attaining paradise.[10]

In the seventh to ninth centuries, it was fairly common practice in Japan to invoke the name of Amida Buddha when concentrating on an image of Amida, but this practice was confined mostly to scholarly and monastic circles.[11] It remained for Honen (1133-1212) and his disciple, Shinran (1173-1262), to take the Pure Land ideology of China and develop it into a type of sectarian Buddhism for the common people of Japan.

Honen was a monk of the Tendai sect, which advocated multiple practices for the attainment of salvation. Dissatisfied with the syncretism of Tendai thinking, he began to explore other ideas. He finally found what he sought in the writings of Shan-t'ao and a Tendai monk named Genshin, who favored the nembutsu way of salvation because it was open to all. It was 1175 when he made his discovery and began to preach it to others. This date is traditionally accepted as the founding date for the Jodo (Pure Land) sect in Japan. Honen's views, with their hope of salvation for all, became tremendously popular with the common people. However, in 1207 jealous priests had Honen exiled to a remote area of Japan, where he remained for five years.[12]

Shinran, another Tendai monk, was with Honen in exile. A number of years earlier, Shinran had reported a dream in which Kwannon had instructed him to marry. This he had done, with Honen's approval, establishing the pattern of a married Buddhist clergy in Japan. After his release from exile in 1212, Shinran started on an eighteen-year missionary journey from Kyoto to northeastern Japan, expounding on Honen's ideas and adding some interpretations of his own. In 1224, he published his teachings in a work regarded as the basic Shinshu text, *Doctrine, Practice, Faith, and Realization*. This consists of 143 selected passages from twenty-three sutras, with commentary.[13]

Shinran regarded himself as an interpreter of Honen's ideas, rather than as the founder of a new sect. In fact, it was not until 1265, after his death, that his followers organized the sect, calling it Jodo Shinshu (True Pure Land sect).

Both Jodo and Shin Buddhism should be called schools rather than sects, since both have many subsects. Shinshu has two principal branches, known as Hompa Hongwanji or Nishi Hongwanji (Western Hongwanji) and Otani or Higashi Hongwanji (Eastern Hongwanji) sects, respectively.[14]

*Shinran's concept of tariki-eko.*[15] As Honen's teaching spread throughout Japan, Buddhist scholars criticized it on several counts, most notably: (1) central to Mahayana thinking is the crucial importance of *bodhicitta* (aspiration for enlightenment) in the Way of the Buddha—Honen seemed to be neglecting the importance of bodhicitta, replacing it with nembutsu; (2) the concreteness of the concept of the Pure Land seemed out of keeping with Mahayana philosophy of *sunyata* (emptiness, the void); (3) with other sects emphasizing nondependency, the tariki concept of the Amidists seemed in conflict with this.

While concerning himself with converting the common people to what he believed to be Honen's view of the correct path to salvation, Shinran felt that he must also come forth with a scholarly defense of Pure Land ideology which would satisfy his master's critics. In the treatise which he wrote for this purpose, he drew heavily on the works of T'an-luan. Shinran's indebtedness to T'an-luan is discussed in detail by Bando.[16]

Although the descriptions of the Pure Land included in the sutras are in very concrete terms, T'an-luan considered the Pure Land or Happy Land to be simply one of many positive expressions used to convey something of the transcendental and indescribable experience of enlightenment. In other words, Pure Land is a positive concrete expression of nirvana. Furthermore, he did not look upon "birth" in the Pure Land as involving a matter of geography or physical movement, but as being a spiritual birth or conversion, which he expressed as "birth of non-birth." Following T'an-luan's lead, the final realization Shinran attained was that "the essence of Pure Land is nirvana itself. Pure Land is not a static or physical place but a dynamic reality or a ceaseless function of *satori*.[17] It is not only a place all men are expected to reach, it is something to be realized amidst the actual human existence beset with all forms of predicament and suffering."[18]

For the average Shinshu believer tariki stands for "external help" or "other-power," and faith in Amida Buddha implies a dependency on Amida's benevolence. Viewed in this light, "faith" would not lead to enlightenment, involving true independence from all external things. However, T'an-luan added a transcendental meaning to the term tariki to make it a religious term. In this context, tariki-power is the power of Amida's original vow. Both T'an-luan and Shinran believed that only the tariki faith in the truly religious sense can make man really autonomous and set him free.[19]

The interaction of Amida and man through Amida's vow power and man's faith was referred to as *eko* by T'an-luan. This was a term commonly used in India to mean either "transformation" or "the transferring of merit accumulated by someone for the benefit of others." Until the time of Honen, eko always meant *man's* act of transferring merit to others, and Honen looked upon the nembutsu as man's eko, but for Shinran it was Amida's eko. He used the term, *tariki-eko*, meaning that it is the Original Vow of Amida which realizes itself in man's faith, thus truly establishing his subjectivity.[20]

## Shin Buddhist Temples and Forms of Worship

In the temples of the Pure Land and True Pure Land sects, the chief object of worship is usually a statue of the Buddha Amida. Frequently it is accompanied on either side by the bodhisattva of Compassion and bodhisattva of Wisdom.

In Japan it is not customary to have corporate worship in a Jodo

Shu or Jodo Shinshu temple, except on special occasions such as festivals and memorial services for the dead. Priests will read sutras and engage in rituals several times a day, but if a layman enters the temple he will usually either kneel or bow before the figure of Amida Buddha, repeat the nembutsu several times, and leave.

## THE BUDDHIST CHURCHES OF AMERICA

Although the Jodo Shu and the Otani sect of Shinshu are represented by missions in America, and each of these groups has jurisdiction over several churches in the continental United States as well as Hawaii and Canada, the Pure Land tradition in the western hemisphere is most visibly manifested in the work of the Buddhist Churches of America (BCA).

### Origins and Growth of the Buddhist Churches of America

The "father and midwife" of BCA was a Japanese immigrant named Nisaburo Hirano, whose unrelenting efforts resulted in the establishment of an official Shinshu mission in San Francisco in 1899.[21]

Before the 1890s, the number of Japanese in America was still small and there were no Buddhist churches on the North American continent. As the pace of immigration stepped up, however, so did the evangelizing efforts of American missionaries, who sought to convert the new arrivals to Christianity. Responding to this situation, devout Buddhists of Shinshu faith felt it imperative that the message of Amida's saving mercy not be lost. It was as the representative of these immigrant Buddhists that Hirano went to the sect headquarters in Japan to plead their cause.[22]

In the early 1900s, Shin Buddhism in the continental United States was confined to the West Coast, and it is still largely a West Coast phenomenon. However, as Japanese-Americans have relocated in the East and Midwest, Shin Buddhism has reached those areas. Today there are Shinshu churches in ten midwestern and eastern states, and the District of Columbia, in addition to those on the western seaboard.

The administrative head of BCA is Rev. Kenryu T. Tsuji, who is referred to as the "bishop." Actually, this title is a misnomer, since there is no episcopacy involved in the Buddhist priesthood, and the Japanese title, *Sosho*, meaning "head of an organization," is a more accurate designation of the nature of the position.

### Relation to Hompa Hongwanji

Although BCA is now an autonomous organization and no longer a mission, it is also considered to be a "district" of Hompa Hongwanji.

The BCA receives no support from Japan, but is obligated to contribute financially to the home temple and to follow the guidelines set out by Hompa Hongwanji. Until after World War II, the bishops for the United States were all chosen in Japan. Since the war, however, although the bishop is still appointed by the Lord Abbot of Hompa Hongwanji, he is nominated and elected by the clergy and laymen of the American church, so that his official appointment is little other than a formality.

The BCA headquarters hopes, eventually, to be able to provide adequate ministerial training in the United States. However, in the early seventies it was still necessary for ministerial candidates to go to Japan to complete their theological training. This means that the Shinshu ministry has been open only to those who were fluent in Japanese.

## National, Regional, and Local Organizations

The business of BCA is carried out by national and regional organizations in which clergy, administrative personnel, and lay members are represented. Some members of these bodies are appointed and others are elected. These organizations function variously as policy-making, legislative, and governing bodies.[23]

Each church sponsors various organizations to meet the spiritual, social, and educational needs of all age groups in its membership. Some of these also work on fund-raising programs. Of these, the Buddhist Women's Association (*Fujinkai*) and the Young Men's Buddhist Association are usually especially active. Most churches also have a "culture department" for propagating and preserving Japanese culture through language classes and instruction in Japanese folk arts. Many administer athletic and scouting programs and some have meditational groups.

## Educational Centers

The BCA sponsors two educational centers in the United States. The Institute of Buddhist Studies in Berkeley, California, has a program of Buddhist studies leading to a Master of Arts degree. It is planned that, eventually, those completing the course of study at this institution may be ordained as Buddhist ministers without having to go to Japan for further study. The American Buddhist Academy in New York offers pre-ministerial training, sponsors seminars and workshops of various sorts, and handles the educational aspects of the program of the New York Buddhist Church. As theological seminaries, these institutions are not yet having much impact on the Buddhist church. When this writer made inquiries in early 1972, there were six preministerial students enrolled in the Institute of Buddhist Studies and three in the American Buddhist Academy.

## The Churches—What They Look Like

As one travels about the United States, one encounters considerable variety in the external appearance of the Jodo Shinshu churches. Many of the newer churches on the West Coast bear a close resemblance to Buddhist temples in Japan, and frequently include a Japanese garden on the temple grounds. The older churches and most of the churches farther east resemble school houses, residences, post offices, telephone companies, or Christian churches. The San Jose Buddhist Church Betsuin (branch temple) is a faithful replica of a Japanese temple. Seabrook Buddhist Church in New Jersey is a white-washed, cinderblock structure with a wooden porch between the second-floor front door and the flight of cement steps leading from the ground to the second-floor porch. It has the appearance of a house of worship, but there is nothing Oriental about it, and nothing distinctively Buddhist. Since 1937, the San Francisco Buddhist Church has occupied a building which looks like an elementary school, except for the stupa on top of the building enshrining the holy relics of the Buddha. In Cleveland, the Buddhist temple is a brown and buff brick building with a flat roof and blue stained-glass windows. It is identified as a Buddhist temple by the Buddhist wheel at the left, in the front, and on the right by the words "Cleveland Buddhist Temple."

In contrast to the varied exteriors, the American Buddhist churches are remarkably uniform on the inside. The main hall of the temple (*hondo*) is similar to a Christian church in terms of its division into nave and chancel, with the chancel area sometimes being separated into choir and sanctuary. In the nave are pews or chairs, occupied by the congregation (some churches provide kneeling pads). At the front of the nave, on one side of the altar, there is usually a piano or an electronic organ; on the other side is a pulpit. Sometimes there is, in addition, a lectern, usually on the same side as the piano or organ. In the center front area there is likely to be a large incense burner on a stand, used by the congregation in presenting incense.

A visitor wandering into a BCA church in Los Angeles, New York, or Chicago might feel that he was entering a Christian church rather than a Buddhist temple, until he noticed the altar, which is unmistakably Buddhist and Japanese. Some of the altars are extremely elaborate, others quite simple. Generally speaking, older members seem to favor an elaborate altar, younger members favor simplicity.

The central position on the altar is occupied by the gold figure of Amida Buddha. (In some churches there may be substituted a painting of Amida or a scroll bearing the Japanese characters "Namu Amida Butsu.") The Buddha is seen standing, with his right hand held up in a gesture of reassurance and his left hand lowered in a gesture of conferring blessings on all.

On the right of Amida, as one faces the altar, there is commonly a scroll bearing the image of Saint Shinran, and on the left a scroll bearing the picture of one of the chief abbots descended from Shinran. There may be other scrolls or figures on the altar, commemorating various leaders in the history of Jodo Shinshu. Of the images or scrolls in the altar area, however, only Amida Buddha is an object of worship. Other figures are placed on the altar, not to be worshipped but as a gesture of respect and thanksgiving for the contributions they may have made to the teachings.

As on other Buddhist altars, candles symbolize enlightenment, flowers express impermanence, and the burning of incense symbolizes the act of purification before worship, or before going out into the world after worship. Food is placed on the altar in symbolic praise and thanksgiving for Amida's eternal guidance. In front of the altar there are usually placed copies of the sutras and there is a kneeling pad for the use of the minister. On each side of the altar are percussion instruments—gongs, bells, *mokugyo* (wooden fish), and drums—used to designate parts of the service and to punctuate chants. There are also chairs for the priests or ministers. Of the above, only the chairs would not be found in a Japanese temple and in Japan the chancel and nave would be covered with tatami mats. In America, both are usually carpeted.

In designating the figure of Amida Buddha as the object of worship, it should be noted that when worshippers bow in reverence before the statue, they are not praying to Amida, but are revering the wisdom and compassion of Amida, which the statue symbolizes.[24]

All BCA churches have offices, Sunday School rooms, rest rooms, and space analogous to the parish hall in a Christian church. There is usually a kitchen and in the larger churches there may be extra chapels, meeting rooms for different groups, and rooms for special projects.

*Sunday Services and Rituals*

In the Buddhist calendar every day is a holy day. In America, however, Shin Buddhists and a number of other Buddhist groups usually follow the Christian custom of having weekly worship services on Sunday. (Branch churches and others without a full-time minister may have services on days other than Sunday, or services less frequently than once a week.) In churches where there are weekly services on Sunday, there is almost always an adult service in Japanese, attended by Japanese-born members (*issei*) and many second-generation Americans of Japanese ancestry (*nisei*). In the larger churches there is also a service in English. The latter may be a family service attended by nisei and their children (*sansei*), as well as by a few non-Orientals. It may be an adult service attended by members who are more at home in English than in Japanese, or it may be a service for young people. In addition to these services, on Sunday there are also Sunday School classes for children, which are always in English.

An American of Christian background who attends services in a BCA church will find much that is familiar, and some that is strange. He will note that the minister—known in Japan as a priest—wears a plain black robe over a business suit, and has a very simple Buddhist stole. (On festival days the minister may wear more elaborate vestments, but on ordinary Sundays he looks very much like his Methodist or Presbyterian counterpart.)

As members of the congregation enter the church, most will be carrying rosaries (*ojuzu* beads).[25] Before seating themselves, they will bow toward the altar, hands together in the traditional gesture of respect and reverence (*gassho*), holding the rosary between thumbs and forefingers, encircling both hands.

The BCA publishes service books in English and Japanese. These books contain the order of worship, rituals, sutras for chanting, and hymns (called *gathas*). Some churches follow these service books quite faithfully, some modify the rituals, and others make up their own rituals. However, the pattern for most services is quite similar, and the visitor will be surprised to find in the order of worship such non-Buddhist terms as "invocation," "aspiration," "creed," "offertory," and "benediction." He will be further surprised when he hears an organ prelude and postlude and when the congregation sings hymns with tunes suggestive of some of the worst of western church music.

In most BCA churches there is a lay leader, called the chairman, who announces the different parts of the service and reads certain portions of the ritual. The minister ordinarily delivers the sermon, and sometimes he reads sentences in Sanskrit, with the congregation responding in English or Japanese. In both the English-language and

Japanese-language services, the sutras are usually chanted in Japanese, with the chanting being quite monotonous.

Following is a typical order of worship found in these churches:

1. Organ prelude
2. Temple bell (minister)
3. Offering incense (chairman)
4. Meditation (congregation)
5. Aspiration (chairman)
6. Gatha (congregation)
7. Homage, Threefold Refuge (minister and congregation)
8. Invocation (chairman)
9. Creed (congregation) :

> We rely upon Tathagata Amitabha with our whole heart for the Enlightenment in the world to come, abstaining from all sundry practices and teachings, and giving up the trust in our powerless self.
>
> We believe that the assurance of our rebirth through his salvation comes at the very moment we put our faith in Him, and we call the name, Namu Amida Butsu, in happiness and thankfulness for his mercy.
>
> We also acknowledge gratefully the benign benevolence of our founder and the succeeding Masters who have led us to believe in this profound teaching, and we do now endeavor to follow throughout our lives the Way laid down for us.

10. Chanting of the sutra (congregation)
11. Responsive reading (chairman and congregation)
12. Sermon (minister)
13. Offertory
14. Meditation (congregation)
15. Benediction and nembutsu (all)
16. Postlude

There is considerable variation in the manner of presenting incense. In some churches the chairman presents it for the entire congregation; in some, one representative for each organization in the church presents it; and in some churches, all in the congregation are given an opportunity to do so during the postlude. In the presentation, the individual bows toward the Buddha with palms together in front of his chest, places a pinch of incense on the glowing embers, and then bows again with hands in gassho and holding his ojuzu beads.

*Sunday School*

The BCA Sunday School, sometimes referred to as the Dharma School, is modeled after the church schools of the Protestant churches. Although the Buddhist Education Committee in each church has the privilege of accepting, revising, or rejecting the course of study prepared by the Sunday School department in national headquarters, most churches make some use of the materials supplied by headquarters. These include teachers' guides, lesson plans, pamphlets and books for children and adolescents, materials related to interest-centered teaching methods, films, and slides.

Representative of materials available to Sunday School teachers is Nekoda's pamphlet, *A Guide to Creative Teaching in the Sunday School*, published by BCA's Sunday School department.[26]

Nekoda's booklet includes a brief outline of the Sunday School course of study, a page dealing with the Buddhist way of life and the Buddhist family, the aims and objectives of Buddhist education in the Sunday School, specific objectives for each grade level, instructions on how to prepare lesson plans, an article on meeting the needs of children, criteria for selecting and using activities, 101 projects, and a bibliography of reference books. The course of study outlined in this work is usually described by Buddhist clergy as a combination of "basic Buddhism" with the "life and teachings of Saint Shinran." The general aims and objectives are listed as follows:

> The purpose of the Buddhist Sunday School of America is to educate the children to be good Buddhists who believe in Amida Buddha, learn the teachings of Buddha, and live according to these teachings.
>
> Ultimate Objectives
> 1. To help children discover their true selves.
> 2. To help children realize that they live in Amida's wisdom and compassion.
> 3. To guide children to live intimately with Amida Buddha in his wisdom and compassion.
> 4. To teach children rebirth in Amida's Pure Land as the final objective.

Immediate Objectives
5. To teach children the Mahayana spirit.
6. To develop children's character along the Buddhistic spirit of love, compassion and wisdom.
7. To teach children to lead a life of gratitude.
8. To apply the best teaching methods to make Buddhism meaningful to children.
9. To develop the children's sense of appreciation for their Buddhist heritage.
10. To work in harmony with the home and the school to help children become well-rounded, wholesome individuals.[27]

## Special Services and Observances

In addition to Sunday Services for children and adults, and, in some churches, special meditational sessions, services which BCA clergy conduct include weddings, funerals, memorial services for the dead, and special festival observances.

In the Orient, weddings are considered to be secular affairs, and to suggest that a Buddhist couple be married in a Buddhist temple would be interpreted as analogous to a suggestion that they be married in a mortuary. However, in the United States, Buddhist clergy are licensed to perform marriages, and do so. Lacking an established liturgy for this purpose, most BCA ministers make up their own. These weddings include some portions of the civil marriage service, usually the acceptance of the Buddhist precepts by the couple being married, and often the sharing of cups of *sake* included in the traditional Japanese wedding ceremony.

Of the special holidays and festivals observed, some are observed in all Buddhist churches, and some are observed only in Pure Land churches. Two are western and secular in origin.

## Church Administration and Membership

Each BCA church has an elected Board, which runs the church, freeing the minister to devote his major efforts to religious education. The minister is a member of the Board and plays a major role in determining its budget as well as the agenda of its meetings. Most Board members are nisei. The minister of a church is appointed on the basis of a joint decision involving the local Board, the candidate, and national headquarters.

Although the total membership is assessed at forty thousand, BCA indicates that there are one hundred thousand Buddhists of Shinshu faith in the continental United States.[28] In the twelve churches visited by this writer, the estimated membership figures for the individual churches ranged from one hundred to one thousand families, with most ministers having no idea how many individuals might be involved. Membership figures reported were usually in terms of those making regular financial contributions, rather than indicating the number of confirmed or committed Buddhists.

As the issei population diminishes in relation to nisei and sansei, the membership of BCA churches is becoming predominantly American-born individuals of Japanese ancestry. Most ministers report that about seventy percent of their members are in this category. In none of the BCA churches visited was there a large membership of persons of non-Japanese background. In some congregations there were no Caucasians or blacks; in others there was a handful of non-Orientals, comprising one to five percent of the membership.

Those ministers discussing the Caucasian membership indicated that it consisted principally of two groups—Caucasian men with Japanese wives, and Americans with an interest in Oriental religions. Reverend Masao Kodani of Senshin Temple, Los Angeles, commented that the Caucasian members of his church were for the most part "very healthy individuals with a good understanding of Buddhism—not persons who need counseling or are looking for the esoteric."

In visiting Jodo Shinshu churches, my impression was that most Americans coming from a Judaeo-Christian background, and disillusioned with what Judaism and Christianity have to offer, would not be attracted to Amidism of the type expressed through the forms and rituals of BCA—that they would probably perceive in the Pure Land tradition more of what they were rejecting in the Judaeo-Christian way.

## Projects, Trends, and Problems

The BCA celebrated its seventy-fifth anniversary in August, 1974. In anticipation of this milestone in the history of Buddhism in America, the year 1972 found various projects in different stages of progress or completion: the modern headquarters complex on Octavia Street in San Francisco was completed in 1971; plans for a fully operating Jodo Shinshu Church in Washington, D.C., were under consideration; a written history of Jodo Shinshu in America was in preparation; translation of sutras into both English and modern Japanese poetic style was in process; and more involvement in social welfare programs, such as work with Buddhists in local and state prisons, had been started.

It is difficult to say what the trends are in BCA churches at present. The nisei members, currently in the majority and dominating the governing Boards of the churches, want everything to be as "American" as possible. For most of them, there is a satisfaction with the Western accretions which came to Buddhism on the mainland of the United States as the result of the influence of Christian missionaries in Hawaii —the pews, organs, and pulpits in the American Buddhist churches; the Sunday School programs which are so similar to those in American Christian churches; and the order of worship and rituals with which many Protestants might feel quite comfortable. Many of these nisei, originally from Buddhist families, were sent to Christian Sunday Schools when they were growing up because this seemed to be advantageous for members of a minority group. With this background, the westernized forms of worship seem natural to them.

In contrast to the attitude of the lay Board members, some of the clergy—both younger and older ones—are working toward a reversal of the trend to "Christianize" and "Westernize" Buddhism in America and are seeking to eliminate Western accretions and syncretisms as well as to emphasize the basics of Buddhism and Jodo Shinshu faith. To this end, some of the churches are now being referred to as temples, and some ministers are being designated as priests, although teacher would perhaps be a more accurate designation of their function. Several churches have done away with the lay chairman in Buddhist services, as well as having eliminated what seem to be Christian accretions in the service. More time and attention are being devoted to meditation, with Zen masters being invited to come in and give instructions. In one church the prescribed Sunday School curriculum has been abandoned and the children are started out with ghost stories to prepare them for a later understanding of symbolism. A headquarters staff member, working with Buddhist prison inmates, has them sit on the floor for services, instead of on chairs, and finds that they like the change.

The situation with reference to the role of the Jodo Shinshu churches in the perpetuation and preservation of the Japanese cultural heritage is somewhat confused. Some churches have discontinued the Japanese language school because the young people are not interested, and have also curtailed other Japanese-oriented cultural programs. Others report increased interest in Japanese folk dances and music, as well as No drama, tea ceremonies, and flower arrangement. The developments in these areas seem to depend not only on the age composition of the membership and ethnic composition of the community in which the church is located, but on the interests, enthusiasms, and personality characteristics of the leaders. One would anticipate, however, that as third-generation and fourth-generation Americans become more numerous in the membership, these culturally-related activities will tend to become less prominent in the church program.

In discussing the changes taking place in BCA churches, a headquarters staff member mentioned three: (1) because members now have other social outlets, the church is becoming less of a community center or social activity center; (2) the church is becoming more ecumenical; and (3) rituals are becoming simplified.

The literature published by BCA depicts the Pure Land as being attainable after death, and places considerable emphasis on other-power (tariki) as opposed to self-power (jiriki). In contrast to this position, a number of clergy interviewed would agree with Suzuki that the Pure Land is on this earth waiting to be realized, and that tariki is really not opposed to jiriki—that "Namu Amida Butsu" symbolizes the unification of self-power and other-power.[29] The gap between these two positions would seem to create confusion in the minds of non-Japanese inquirers looking into the Jodo Shinshu faith.

Clergy and lay members of BCA churches give several reasons for the problems of the churches. First, it is extremely difficult to keep the interest of the young people. They tend to drift away after graduation from junior high school or high school, although some do return after college or marriage. Second, with the issei dying off, and the bulk of the membership consisting of nisei and sansei, there is a declining interest in perpetuating the Japanese culture, as well as in a church which seems to have an ethnocentric orientation despite its emphasis on universal brotherhood. Third, decreasing numbers of members are fluent in Japanese, and there is an acute shortage of clergy who are fluent in English. Finally, few sutras or Buddhist theological texts have been translated into English, so that it is impossible to give adequate training to ministerial candidates who are not literate in Japanese.

As is true among the clergy of other religions, the clergy of BCA churches differ among themselves on various issues. Some tend to be "fundamentalist," interpreting the Pure Land and other-power quite literally. Others are more liberal, regarding the Pure Land as an attitude, and other-power as identified with self-power. Further, some favor chanting the sutras in English; others feel that they should be kept in their present Sanskrit-Chinese-Japanese form. Some of those arguing for keeping them as they are point out that it is impossible to find terms in either modern Japanese or English which would convey the same meaning. Others contend that chanting is a form of meditation, and that understanding the meaning of the sutras would cause people to think about the meaning, thus interfering with the effectiveness of meditation. Additionally, although some are pushing for theological training in the United States, others believe that it should be in Japan, where Buddhism is a "living tradition."

*Jodo Shinshu for Americans*

Jodo Shinshu is probably the second largest Buddhist group in the United States, and possibly the one with the largest stable membership. However, in America it has a membership consisting almost entirely of individuals whose ancestors have been Jodo Shinshu adherents in Japan. Its total membership has increased significantly since World War II, but it now appears to be leveling off, and in some areas is declining. Also, although it is becoming a church dominated by nisei and sansei rather than by issei, it has not yet made any significant impact on white or black Americans.

With Buddhism being a nontheistic religion, it has potential appeal for many American intellectuals. But in its present form, Judo Shimshu is not likely to gain converts outside of the Japanese-American group, except for a few who have studied Buddhism and understand the Jodo Shinshu philosophy. We have already mentioned the Protestant accretions which make the Jodo Shinshu service in the United States seem superficially to be like that of a Christian church, and the concept of "salvation by grace" which has already been rejected by most former Christians looking for something else. Also, there is nothing to indicate that potential American converts to Buddhism are looking for an easy way. Zen and Tibetan Buddhism, now booming in the United States, place great emphasis on self-power, and require a tremendous amount of self-discipline. For young Americans rebelling against society, a religion which seems to them to be based on dependency would have little appeal unless, like Nichiren Shoshu, it is associated with peer group support and continuous reinforcement (see chapter 5).

Some of the younger BCA clergy predict that the Shin Buddhism of the future, in America, will involve fewer members but will have greater depth. If the Jodo Shinshu Church in the United States becomes less of a Japanese community center and abandons its non-Buddhist liturgies as well as clarifying its basic philosophy, then the nature of its membership may change. Current concern on the part of BCA clergy and lay leaders with how the Buddhist ideals of universal brotherhood and world peace can best be promoted on American soil may eventuate in an increase in the non-Oriental membership. However, in my opinion, although in the East and Midwest there may be some increase in the non-Oriental membership in BCA churches within the next few years, the membership in the West Coast churches will be drawn almost entirely from the Japanese community for many years to come.

# 4

# Zeal for Zen

Occupying a 240-year-old former mill on a wooded hill near Easton, Pennsylvania, six to twelve devotees of Zen Buddhism live and work and meditate. On weekends, they are joined by others. Under the direction of a British-born priest, who also is an artist, male nurse, and former merchant-seaman, young American adults seek relief from suffering. Theirs is a simple life, but a disciplined one. Beginning their day at 4:00 A.M., the residents of Hui-neng Zen Temple engage in at least three periods of meditation a day, with chanting of sutras in Korean, and individual guidance by their priest-teacher. Between meditation sessions, they work at maintaining and improving the thirty-five-acre temple property. Like most other Zen Buddhists living in a monastic setting, they do not partake of alcoholic beverages, and are not permitted to experiment with LSD or other drugs. Like many other Buddhists, also, they are vegetarians.[1]

Originally a residential club for Jewish women, the three-storied square red brick building in a principally black neighborhood in San Francisco serves as a temple, meditation hall, and residence for seventy Zen students, together with their American Zen master. Countless others come in for meditation and instructions in Zen, although living elsewhere. Robed, shaven-headed Japanese and American monks go in and out. Some of the students, also, have shaved their heads as a symbol of is faith in his own Buddha-nature, and determination to persevere with zazen until and after he experiences satori.

## Origins and Development of Zen

Zen adherents claim that their school of Buddhism came from Sakyamuni Buddha, himself. The story they tell is this: Once, when the Buddha was sitting with his disciples, he was approached by a brahmin raja who gave him a golden flower and asked him to preach the Dharma. The Buddha accepted the flower, held it aloft, and gazed at it in silence. After a while the Venerable Mahakasyapa, one of the disciples, smiled. This was the beginning of Zen, and Mahakasyapa was designated the first Zen patriarch. It is said that Mahakasyapa's smile was handed down to twenty-eight successive patriarchs, the last being the Indian philosopher, Bodhidarma, who arrived in China in A.D. 520. Bodhidarma taught the principles and techniques of what at that time was called the *Dhyana* school, but which the Chinese later transliterated to *Ch'an,* and the Japanese to Zen.[6]

The story of the origin of Zen is probably legendary, and it is not certain that Bodhidarma ever arrived in China. Suzuki indicates that Zen originated in China in the middle of the T'ang dynasty, and that it was a combination of Chinese psychology with Indian philosophy.[7] Certainly it has traces in it of Taoist influence. However, wherever it originated, it flourished in China for over five hundred years, with its greatest exponent being the sixth and last of the Chinese patriarchs, Hui-neng. From China its power was transferred to Japan, where it became a significant force in the twelfth century.

In Japan three Zen sects developed—the first in the latter part of the twelfth century, the second early in the thirteenth century, and the third in the seventeenth century. The earliest Zen sect to be established in Japan was the *Rinzai* sect, which was founded in 1191 by a Tendai monk named Eisai, who had been converted when studying in China. Shortly afterwards, another monk, Dogen, established the *Soto* sect. In the seventeenth century, a Chinese priest named Ingen founded the *Obaku* sect.[8] The Obaku sect is very small, and has had virtually no influence in the West, but both the Soto and Rinzai sects have prospered in Japan and have spread to Europe and the United States.

## Soto and Rinzai Zen

Soto and Rinzai Zen are alike in basic philosophy, and both use zazen as a means of attaining satori or enlightenment, but their techniques and aims are slightly different. Basically, Soto Zen considers enlightenment as a state which is attained gradually, and its technique is that of *shikantaza,* or sitting quietly; Rinzai Zen regards satori as a sudden illumination, attained by hard and concentrated work on koans, or riddles which are insoluble by the processes of reason.[9] In addition, Soto Zen places more emphasis on study and intellectual understanding than does Rinzai.

### Korean Zen (Chogye Sect)

Next to the Japanese Zen sects, Korean Zen has been most influential in America, although its impact has been minor in comparison with that of the Japanese groups.

Buddhism was introduced into Korea from China in 372 A.D. and flourished there after 668. Over the years there was a proliferation of sects, with nine Zen sects and twelve *Chiao* sects. (The Zen sects emphasized meditation, whereas the Chiao sects, of which the Pure Land was one, emphasized sutra study.) After a unification of the nine Zen sects to form the *Sonjong* sect, and a unification of the twelve Chiao sects to form the *Kyojong* sect, there was a final unification of these two sects in 1935, to form the *Chogye* sect.

The Chogye sect emphasizes the practice of Buddhism through both Zen and Chiao. It provides for three kinds of study: Zen practice in Zen monasteries; scriptural study in monasteries and Buddhist schools; and translation of scriptures from Chinese into Korean. In Korea, Zen and Chiao are sometimes studied at the same temple, and sometimes at different temples. As far as Korean Zen practice is concerned, it has features of both Rinzai and Soto.[10]

### Zen Practice

*Zazen.* In the Zen training center, temple, or monastery, priests, monks, disciples, and uncommitted students participate in rituals in which chanting of sutras,[11] repetition of vows, offering of incense, and bowing assume a prominent place in the devotional services that take place several times a day. These rituals, however, are engaged in principally to help the Zen practitioner to attain a frame of mind which will enable him to gain the most from the activity which is most central to Zen practice—zazen.

Zazen, or Zen meditation, is technically sitting meditation, although meditation may be engaged in while walking or performing some type of physical labor. In doing zazen, the individual is usually seated cross-legged on a thick round cushion which is placed on a larger and thinner square cushion or pad on the floor or a low platform. The preferred position is the full-lotus or half-lotus position, but other positions are considered acceptable, especially for beginners.[12] In some Zen centers in the United States, it is even permissible to do zazen while seated on a chair. Regardless of the position of the legs and feet, the back is straight and the eyes are directed toward the floor a short distance ahead of the body. Attention is centered in the area just below the navel.[13] In the Soto meditation hall, those engaging in zazen are facing the wall, whereas in Rinzai centers it is customary to have participants in zazen in rows facing one another.

In both Rinzai and Soto sects, as well as in Korean Zen, the *kyosaku* is used (in the Rinzai sect it is called *keisaku*). This is a wooden stick somewhat resembling a narrow paddle. The kyosaku is wielded by a monitor who cracks it across the shoulders of anyone who shows signs of slumping or letting his mind wander.[14]

The novice at zazen is frequently advised to spend his first few sessions counting inhalations or exhalations—counting from one to ten and then repeating it innumerable times. After he has become accustomed to the sitting, the procedure changes. If he is under the guidance of a Zen-master of the Soto sect, his zazen is likely to consist of engaging in *shikan-taza*, or sitting quietly, thinking of nothing. In this type of meditation, as thoughts intrude themselves into the mind of the sitter he permits them to float through his consciousness, neither clinging to them nor trying to forcibly eject them.

In the Rinzai sect the Zen practitioner works on koans, such as, "What was your original face before your parents were born?" In solving a koan the Zen student must reject logical reasoning and find a solution through the awakening of a "deeper level of the mind beyond the discursive intellect."[15] The solution of the koan constitutes satori or *kensho* (enlightenment) and results in a new way of seeing the world, in which the perceiver is one with the universe and has an ineffable sense of happiness. The same result is said to eventuate from shikan-taza, but by less strenuous means and more gradually.

Although the awakening of awareness of the essence of being is the most basic and specific goal of Zen practice, zazen is said also to improve mental and physical health, to promote improved concentration, and to generally enrich the personality. Most important, it is believed to result in "actualization of the Supreme Way in our daily lives."[16]

It should be noted that, although the attainment of satori is the goal of zazen, it is not the signal for discontinuing the practice. There are different degrees of depth of the kensho experience and continued practice results in a deepening and enrichment of that experience.

*Sanzen and sesshin.* The Zen adherent may engage in zazen with a group at a temple or Zen center, as well as at home by himself or with his family. Some Zen Buddhists seldom go to the temple, but do engage in zazen at home. This is permissible, but is not considered to be desirable, especially for the beginner. Serious students of Zen usually do attend services at a Zen center with some regularity, and for them an important aspect of their Zen practice is sanzen—the regular personal contacts which they have with a Zen master *(roshi)* or teacher. These personal contacts may be of three types: general lectures on Zen practice and principles *(teisho)*, scheduled private sessions with the roshi or teacher to give guidance and discuss progress in zazen, and special sessions when circumstances warrant them.[17]

Most regular participants in zazen will at intervals want to attend a *sesshin.* This is an extended period of zazen, lasting from a few days to a week or more. During the sesshin there are several periods of zazen a day, interspersed with walking meditation *(kinhin)*, interviews with the roshi *(dokusan[18])*, and chanting of sutras. Frequently, participants in a sesshin will hope to attain satori during this concentrated and extended experience with zazen.

## Satori

For one who has not experienced "enlightenment" to attempt a description of satori would indeed be presumptuous. Yet, because satori is the "heart of Zen," and, in fact, the very *raison d'être* for Buddhism itself, it cannot be ignored.[19]

Christmas Humphreys, after stating that one cannot define satori since it lies beyond the intellect, says that "it is the condition of consciousness wherein the pendulum of Opposites has come to rest, where both sides of the coin are equally valued and immediately seen."[20] He says, further, that it is "seeing into one's own nature, and that Nature is not one's own. . . . It is a foretaste of the Absolute Moment, of Cosmic Consciousness, of the condition in which I and my Father are one."[21]

Suzuki defines satori as "an intuitive looking into the nature of things in contradistinction to the analytical or logical understanding of it." It is an experience in which all the opposites and contradictions of the world "are united and harmonized into a consistent organic whole."[22]

More revealing than attempts at definition are descriptions of satori as it has been experienced. Several such experiences have been recounted in Philip Kapleau's book, *The Three Pillars of Zen.* Useful also is Suzuki's list of the chief characteristics of satori, which includes the following:

1. *Irrationality.* By this is meant that satori is not a type of insight that can be reached by reasoning, or that can be rationally explained and communicated.

2. *Intuitive insight.* Although satori is irrational and intuitive, at the same time it has a noetic quality; that is, it involves "seeing" or "perceiving" the nature of reality.

3. *Authoritativeness.* The knowledge realized by satori is recognized as final, and no amount of logical argument can refute it.

4. *Affirmative.* Satori involves a positive attitude toward life—toward all things that exist.

5. *Sense of the beyond.* In satori a person breaks through the shell of his individuality and attains a sense of oneness with that which is beyond the self.

6. *Impersonal tone.* Satori is impersonal and intellectual, in contrast with the Christian mystical experience which entails love, closeness, romance, and belongingness.

7. *Feeling of exaltation.* Although satori has an impersonal tone, at the same time the breaking up of the restrictions imposed on one as an individual being separate from the rest of the universe gives a feeling of expansiveness and exaltation.

8. *Momentariness.* According to Suzuki, satori comes upon one abruptly and is a momentary experience. If it is not abrupt and sudden, it is not satori.[23]

Suzuki was an adherent of the Rinzai sect, and his insistence on suddenness and momentariness as requisites of satori would perhaps deny that designation to the more gradual enlightenment which is the aim of the Soto sect. Actually, with the exception of this one characteristic, Suzuki's list would be accepted by the Soto group, although the Soto Zen adherent looks for something less specific as the result of zazen.

## Koans and Mondos

As a means of breaking through the barriers of the ego and forcing the individual into a nonrational, nonlogical pattern of thought in order to transcend the subject-object duality and attain satori, two devices used extensively by the Rinzai sect are the *mondo* and the *koan*.

The mondo is a form of rapid question-answer between two persons, often master and pupil, which aims at speeding the process of thought so that it is suddenly transcended.[24] It is short, abrupt, and not serial. Frequently the answer given is simply a repetition of the question, or is another question. Sometimes it is a statement which makes sense only when one goes beyond concerns with time, space, and causal sequences, to grasp the root of the question. Examples of mondos are the following:

> A monk asked, "What is my mind?" The master answered, "Who is asking?"[25]
>
> Chosui Shiye once asked a Zen master called Roya Hyoro, "The Originally Pure—how can the mountains and the rivers and the great earth come out of it?" The master answered, "The Originally Pure—how can the mountains and the rivers and the great earth come out of it?" [26]

A koan is a word or phrase which is insoluble to the intellect. Frequently it is a compressed mondo. Perhaps the most famous koan is that called *mu*. It goes like this: "Is there Buddha-nature in a dog?" asked a monk. "Mu," said the master.[27] (Mu means "no" or "not," and the master's answer is a contradiction of the Buddhist belief that all sentient beings have the Buddha-nature.) The Zen student is given mu as his koan to solve during zazen.

Other koans are: "If all things are reducible to One, to what is the One reduced?" "How to remove a live goose from a bottle without hurting the goose or breaking the bottle?" "What is the sound of one hand clapping?"[28]

## Dhyana and Prajna

Satori can be attained anywhere—not just while doing zazen or conferring with a Zen master. It is through zazen, however, that the student seeks for a state of no-mind or emptiness of mind, which opens the way for satori.

Most Zen Buddhists will chant daily the Sutra of the Heart of Perfect Wisdom or Transcendental Wisdom (Prajna Paramita), which expresses some important Mahayana concepts. In this sutra the Buddha is speaking to one of his disciples about the achievement of Avalokita, who became the Bodhisattva of Compassion through his discovery that the human personality is made up of five aggregates (*skandhas*) and that they are empty of enduring substance.[29] As freely translated into English, this sutra says:

> The Bodhisattva of Compassion,
> moving in deep perfect wisdom,
> saw the emptiness of the five skandhas.

O Sariputra, he said,
Here form is emptiness and emptiness is form;
emptiness does not differ from form,
form does not differ from emptiness;
what form is, that is emptiness;
what emptiness is, that is form.
Like this are feelings, perceptions,
     impulses, and consciousness.
Here all elements of existence
     are marked with emptiness;
they do not begin, nor do they end;
they are not pure, and not impure,
     not deficient and not complete.
Therefore, Sariputra,
in emptiness there is no form, no feeling,
no perception, no impressions, and no consciousness;
no eye, ear, nose, tongue, body, mind;
no form, sound, smell, taste, touch,
     objects, and no act of sensing.
There is no ignorance, no end of
     ignorance,
no aging and death, no extinction of it;
there is no suffering, no cause or end
     of it, no path;
no knowing, no attainment,
     and no non-attainment.
So, Sariputra,
a bodhisattva, dwelling in perfect wisdom
     is freed of all delusion.
With no delusion he is free
     from fear,
is certain of Nirvana.
All those who appear as Buddhas
in the three periods of time
awake fully to the highest perfect enlightenment
     by relying on the perfection of wisdom.
Therefore one should know the perfect wisdom
     as the great mantra,
     the highest mantra, peerless mantra,
allayer of all suffering.
This is the truth of the prajnaparamita—

GATE, GATE, PARAGATE,
PARA SAMGATE,
BODHI, SVAHA!
[Gone, gone, gone beyond
gone altogether beyond,
O what an awakening, all hail!][30]

Prior to the time of Hui-neng, the popular view of Mahayana Buddhists committed to the use of meditation was that the Buddha-nature with which all beings are endowed is pure and undefiled, and that the self-realization sought by the Yogin was the bringing out of his self-nature or Buddha-nature in all its purity. The term used for meditation at that time was *k'an-chien,* meaning, in Chinese, "to keep an eye on purity," and this carried with it the idea that there is a viewer as well as something to see, that is, a subject-object duality.[31] This purpose is contrary to the purpose of Zen meditation as it was understood by Hui-neng.

Hui-neng criticized his predecessors on the basis of his insistence that purity has neither form nor shape, and that when one sets as a goal for meditation the realization of a form known as "purity," he is obstructing his own self-nature. Hui-neng rejected the concept of *dhyana* or meditation as "k'an-chien," and substituted the term *chien-hsing,* meaning "to look into the nature (of the Mind)." The verb "chien," in contrast to "k'an," refers to the pure act of seeing in which seer and the object seen are brought together as the Mind becomes conscious of its own working.[32]

For Hui-neng, meditation must involve an identification of dhyana with prajna, with prajna being the power to intuitively penetrate into the nature of one's being, as well as the truth itself thus intuited.[33] The wisdom of prajna goes beyond the duality of subject and object, or action and object toward which the action is directed. When seeing is no-seeing there is real seeing into one's self-nature; when hearing is no-hearing there is real hearing. This is the intuition of the Prajna Paramita.[34]

When the Zen Buddhist says that seeing is no-seeing, he is not denying the reality of that which exists in the phenomenal world (*samsara*) and impinges on the senses. Rather, he states that there are two kinds of truth or reality—relative or conditional truth which constitutes "practical" reality and transcendental or absolute truth, which is prajna.[35]

Watts indicates that the doctrine of the "void" is a doctrine of relativity.[36] According to this doctrine, nothing in the phenomenal world has reality because things have existence only in relation to other things. Life is defined by death, stillness by motion, pleasure by pain, waking by sleeping, and so on. In saying that the highest truth is "void" or "emptiness," there is no implication that it is nothingness in a nihilistic sense. Rather, "emptiness" means that thought is empty of all relative terms and descriptions.[37]

Prajna is to be seen also as *tathata*, which may be translated as "suchness," "thusness," or "thatness." To see something in its "thus-ness" or "suchness" means to see it in its concrete reality apart from concepts, symbols, abstractions, and discriminations.[38] According to Mrs. Suzuki, this means going back to the state of mind before the division of knowing and the known takes place. Suchness, she warns, is not in the world of the senses, for that which we experience via the senses we divide, classify, discriminate, and think about. Rather, it is some-thing "unthinkable, unrepresentable, unnameable, indescribable."[39]

Related to the concepts of emptiness and suchness is also that of "no-Mind," "no-thought," or the Unconsciousness. The Unconscious-ness, in Zen, is equated with emptiness and suchness, and enlighten-ment comes at the point when the Unconscious breaks into conscious-ness.[40] (The Unconscious, in Zen, has no relation to the Freudian concept of the unconscious, although it may have some features in common with Jung's concept of the collective unconscious.)

## ZEN IN AMERICA

### *History of Zen in America*

Of all the Buddhist schools of thought, Zen has the longest his-tory of continuous propagation in North America. This history is de-scribed in some detail in two issues of *Wind Bell*, a quarterly publica-tion of Zen Center of San Francisco.[41]

Anyone may receive instruction in Zen philosophy and the tech-nique of zazen. However, the propagation of Zen as a way of life in its fullest sense is dependent on the close and devoted relationship be-tween the Zen master and his disciples. The message of the master, then, is passed on by his disciples to new generations of followers. The relation between master and disciple is such a close and meaningful one that in some ways it is closer than a blood relationship. In fact, Zen adherents use genealogical terms to describe the relationship be-tween a master and his followers. Several generations of teachers are referred to as a "lineage" and disciples of a teacher who studied under a particular master are designated as "descendants" of that master.

Terms such as "Dharma heir" and "Dharma brother" also are used.[42]

Since the development of Zen is so closely tied to the personalities of individual Zen masters and their relationships with their students, it seems appropriate to trace the history of Zen in America in terms of the influence of the men who have served as the principal guides for each of the approaches to Zen found in the United States.

Until recently, most Zen students in America were the "descendants" of one or more of three Japanese teachers: Rinzai master Imakita Kosen of Engaku Temple who, through his successors and the teachers whom they invited from other lineages, may be considered the founder of most American Zen until 1959; Sogaku Harada of Hosshin Temple, who taught a synthesis of Rinzai and Soto Zen; and Soto Zen master Shinryu Suzuki of Eihei Temple and Zen Center of California. In the late 1960s there was added to these a significant figure in the history of American Zen, the Korean Zen master, Dr. Kyung Beo Seo.

*Descendants of Imakita Kosen and other Rinzai masters.* Zen in America had its beginnings in 1893, when Rinzai master Soyen Shaku (1859–1919), the Dharma heir of Imakita Kosen, went to Chicago to attend the World's Parliament of Religions. At the time of his visit, no formal Zen groups were formed in America. However, considerable interest was aroused among those attending the Congress, as well as among those who were already interested in theosophy. Known by his Buddhist name of Soyen, this man's appeal to Americans may be attributed in part to his thorough understanding of western culture and modern society.

Among those who were attracted to Soyen were Mr. and Mrs. Alexander Russell of San Francisco, who in 1905 appeared at the roshi's home temple in Japan, requesting instruction in Zen. Soyen returned to the United States with the Russells the following summer. During the nine months of his second stay in this country he visited many American cities and became convinced that America was ready for Zen. Subsequently selected by him for the task of promoting Zen in America were three of his disciples: Sokatsu Shaku, Nyogen Senzaki, and Daisetz T. Suzuki.

Sokatsu Shaku (1869–1954) had studied under Imakita Kosen as well as Soyen. He came to California in 1906, bringing six disciples with him, and had two sojourns in America, from 1906 to 1908, and again in 1909 and 1910. After brief periods in Berkeley and Hayward, he and his group opened a Zen center in San Francisco, where about fifty Japanese students were joined by a few Caucasian Americans.

When Sokatsu left the United States for the last time he took five of his disciples with him, leaving behind a lay disciple, Shigetsu Sasaki (1882–1946).

Sasaki, an artist and writer who practiced Zen on the side, wandered around the country, finally arriving in New York in 1918. In 1919 he returned to Japan to complete his Zen studies, and over the next several years made several trips between New York and Japan. Finally, in 1928, he was made a roshi by Sokatsu, and was told that his mission was to teach Zen in America. So once more he returned to New York, this time on a permanent basis. As the result of his efforts, the Buddhist Society of America came into being in 1930 and was incorporated the following year. Renamed the First Zen Institute of America in 1945, the group has had a continuous existence since 1931.

Although still a layman when he began his work in New York, Sasaki was later ordained, and became known as Sokei-An. In 1944 he married an American widow, Mrs. Ruth Fuller, who had been a disciple and supporter of the institute since 1938.

After Sokei-An's death in 1945, the First Zen Institute had a difficult time. For a time Isshu Miura made periodic visits there, and now Joshu Sasaki-roshi comes for visits several times a year. But with or without a teacher, its faithful members continue their practice.

Another Soyen disciple, Nyogen Senzaki (1876–1958), came to California in 1905, but did not establish his own zendo in San Francisco until 1928. In 1929 he started another in Los Angeles. Except for the war years, when he was interned, he served continuously as Zen master in Los Angeles from 1929 until his death in 1958. His influence lives on in the California Basatsukai of Los Angeles and in the work of one of his disciples, Robert Aitken, who established the Diamond Sangha in Honolulu.

Although neither a priest nor a Zen master, the one person who had the greatest influence on the propagation of Zen in America was Dr. Daisetz Teitaro Suzuki (1870–1966). He also was Soyen's disciple, and it was Soyen who persuaded him to go to LaSalle, Illinois, in 1897 to become an editor for the Open Court Publishing Company. On his return to Japan in 1909, he became a professor of English at Otani University, and in 1911 he married an American, Beatrice Lane, who for nineteen years shared with him the editing of the *Eastern Buddhist,* an English-language journal published in Japan. In the 1920s and 1930s he wrote many books on Buddhism, in English, but did not return to the United States until 1936. He spent the war years and his last years in Japan, but from 1950 to 1958 he was in America, where he lectured at several universities. The upsurge of intellectual interest in

Zen in the middle and late fifties was the direct result of a series of lectures which he gave at Columbia University. He served as president of the Cambridge Buddhist Association, and the Zen Studies Society of New York was organized to support his work. However, it is principally through his books that most Americans interested in Zen have known him.

Continuing the Rinzai tradition in the United States is another Japanese Zen master, Joshu Sasaki. Coming from a position as Abbot of Shojuan Zen Temple in Japan, Sasaki-roshi arrived in California in 1962 to continue the work started by Senzaki. At first he used a garage in Gardena as his zendo, and later a dentist's office. In 1966 he founded Cimarron Zen Center in Los Angeles, a residential center which also serves a group of nonresident students. In 1971 Mount Baldy Zen Center of Rinzai-ji came into being as a monastery affiliated with Cimarron. Joshu Sasaki-roshi works also with other affiliated groups on the West Coast, as well as lecturing and conducting sesshins in other parts of the United States and Canada. Although trained in the old Japanese Rinzai tradition and continuing the practice of chanting sutras in Japanese, Sasaki believes that Chinese koans are not suitable for use with Westerners, so he composes koans and mondos based on Western concepts, for use with American students.

Other Rinzai teachers who have been influential on the American scene include Soen Nakagawa-roshi and Eido Tai Shimano. The latter is now with the Zen Studies Society of New York.

*Harada, Yasutani, Kapleau, and Maezumi.* The combined Rinzai and Soto teachings of Sogaku Harada of Hosshin Temple are known to American Zen adherents through the teachings of his Dharma heirs, Hakuun Yasutani, Philip Kapleau, and Taizan Maezumi.

Yasutani, who died in 1973 at the age of 88, spent many years as an elementary school teacher and principal in Japan and did not become a full-time temple priest and Zen master until quite late in life. In the early 1960s he began making regular trips to the United States to conduct sesshins in different cities. Among American groups for which he has served as Zen master are the Diamond Sangha in Honolulu, the California Bosatsukai, and the Zen Studies Society.

Of Yasutani-roshi's disciples, the best known in America is Philip Kapleau, Spiritual Director of the Zen Center of Rochester, New York.

A former court reporter and ex-businessman, Philip Kapleau began attending Suzuki's lectures at Columbia in 1951. Being dissatisfied with a purely intellectual approach to Zen and plagued by an ulcer, in 1953 he decided to go to Japan in search of enlightenment. For thirteen years he led a monastic life, studying first with Kakagawa-roshi at Ryutaku Temple, then with Harada-roshi at Hosshin Temple, and finally with Yasutani-roshi. Eventually he was ordained as a Zen priest, and in 1966 Yasutani-roshi sanctioned him as a teacher of Zen. In the winter of 1971–1972, his students decided that it was high time for him to be recognized as roshi.

In 1966 Kapleau founded the Zen Meditation Center of Rochester (now called Zen Center), and since then has also conducted many seminars and workshops on Zen at various universities throughout the country. The Zen Center now has many affiliated groups throughout the United States and Canada.

Kapleau-roshi is one of the few who have tried to initiate a genuinely "American" Zen. In this attempt he has modified traditional rituals, introduced the practice of chanting in English, and made other changes so that Americans would be more comfortable with Zen.

Not as well-known as Kapleau but with an ever-increasing following is Taizan Maezumi-roshi, spiritual leader of the Zen Center of Los Angeles. Born in 1930, Maezumi-roshi comes from a prominent Soto family. Originally trained in Soto practices at Eihei Temple, he also received training in Rinzai Zen under Koryu Osaka-roshi as well as in Yasutani's system under that master. Hence, Maezumi represents a continuation of the Harada-Yasutani line, using both koan and shikan-taza, depending on the individual.

Maezumi-roshi first came to Los Angeles in 1956. At the Zen Center he supervises the training of several monks as well as fifty to sixty lay students. He describes himself as "American but traditional." Like Kapleau, he has introduced some chanting in English. However, with respect to structure and discipline, he is the traditional Zen master, being quite directive in his instructions to students about their responsibilities.

*Shunryu Suzuki and the Soto masters.* Born in 1905, Shunryu Suzuki was the son of a Zen master. While still a boy, he began an apprenticeship under Gyokujun Soon-Daiosho, one of the leading Soto masters of the time, although he later studied with other masters. He was quite young when he was acknowledged as a roshi, and his responsibilities in Japan included several temples and a monastery.

In 1958, at the age of fifty-three, Suzuki came to the United States to lead the Japanese congregation at the Zen temple in San Francisco. Shortly after his arrival, Americans from outside the Japanese community began seeking him out for instruction in zazen, and joined him in his daily 5:45 A.M. sitting. Within a year a group of zazen students had evolved a daily program of sitting, and Suzuki-roshi was lecturing regularly in English. The first students sat in pews and then in a small zendo which they built upstairs in the temple. In 1961 the group incorporated as Zen Center, with offices across the street from the temple, on Bush Street. The zendo was enlarged, and students began moving into communal apartments near the temple.

By 1967 Zen Center was strong enough to realize one of Suzuki-roshi's dreams—that of establishing a mountain monastery. That summer Zen Mountain Center opened at Tassajara Hot Springs, with seventy students training there for periods ranging from a few days to six months. Some stayed on beyond the summer, and in 1972 a few had been there for more than four years.

In 1969 Zen Center of San Francisco took another important step, when it purchased a building on Page Street. This building houses all the facilities for a temple, meditation center, and place of residence. For some of the residents this is a monastic setting in which the student is immersed for twenty-four hours a day. Some who live here have jobs outside, and some who live and work outside come to the center for zazen and services. Zen Center now has a number of affiliates in northern California, all started under the spiritual leadership of Suzuki-roshi.

After twelve fruitful years in the United States, Shunryu Suzuki died in December, 1971, leaving Zen Center and its affiliates in the able hands of his Dharma heir, Richard Baker-roshi.

Richard Baker, a true follower of his master, is nevertheless very much attuned to modern society and its needs, and is determined to make the Zen Way a way which will show America how to live. For example, he has implemented a farm operation for the center, and conceives of this as an operation which is consistent with conservation of nature's resources.

Associated with Shunryu Suzuki for a while, but now with his own center in Monterey is Dainin Katagiri-roshi. Trained in the Soto tradition at Taizoin and Eihei temples, he came to the United States in 1965 to work with the Japanese congregation at the Zen Temple in Los Angeles. After five months he moved to San Francisco, where he was appointed priest at both the Zen Temple and Zen Center. He continued there until after Suzuki's death.

Most responsible for the modest development of Zen in the midwest is another Soto master, Soyu Matsuoka-roshi. Matsuoka began his career with two assignments in Japan. In the United States, he has served as Zen priest in Los Angeles, San Francisco, Compton, and Long

Beach, California, as well as in Chicago. For several years he taught at the University of Colorado. He established the Zen Temple of Chicago in the middle fifties, and is still its spiritual leader, although since 1970 he has devoted his major efforts to promoting Zen in California. Originally the Chicago temple served principally the Japanese congregation, but Matsuoka's present disciples in Chicago are mostly non-Orientals. The present head of the Chicago Buddhist Temple is one of the Matsuoka's disciples, Richard Langlois, who in 1974 became a roshi. The temple now has an affiliate group in Milwaukee.

More recently arrived on the American scene is Jiyu Kennett-roshi, a British woman who was the founder of the Zen Mission Society and its northern California monastery, Shasta Abbey. Kennett-roshi was trained in Japan, where she was the disciple of Koho Zenji at Soji Temple. At Shasta Abbey, where she is Abbess, western customs are prevalent; knives and forks rather than chopsticks are used for eating, students sleep on beds, and western type work clothing is worn. In 1975 Shasta Abbey had affiliate groups in Canada and England, as well as in the United States.

*Korean, Vietnamese, and Chinese Zen in America.* Although Japanese-trained teachers have been most responsible for determining the shape of Zen in America, several people from other Asian countries have been making their influence felt since the late sixties. Of these, recognition should be given to Dr. Thich Thien-An, director of the International Buddhist Meditation Center in Los Angeles and president of the College of Oriental Studies; Hsuan Hua, Chinese Ch'an Master of the Sino-American Buddhist Association in San Francisco; and Korean Master Dr. Kyung-Bo Seo, at present back in Korea. Dr. Seo is represented in America by a group of ordained Dharma heirs, a number of whom have their own followers.

## Beat Zen

Outside the mainstream of American Zen but nevertheless helping to shape its development in the sixties and seventies was the "Beat Zen" of the late 1950s.

A half-century of missionary work by Zen priests in America's metropolitan centers, the enthusiasm for Zen brought back from Japan by returning occupation troops, and lectures on Zen by articulate scholars like D. T. Suzuki and Alan W. Watts combined to produce an upsurge in Zen from 1955 to 1960. During these years, two factions—referred to by Alan Watts as Beat Zen and Square Zen—developed within the Zen movement in this country.[43]

Square Zen was the Zen of serious students of philosophy and those seeking answers to the problems of the world, while at the same time remaining responsibly *in* the world. Beat Zen was the Zen of artists and poets. For the most part, it sought escape from the ills of society and a shying away from the dictates of social conscience. It was used by the "Beat" generation to justify its libertine ways.

Beat novelist Jack Kerouac depicts the Zen adherent of the Beat generation as one who was happily free to run around naked in a drunken orgy.[44] Stephen Mahoney describes it as "goofball," making kicks possible for hung-up, inhibited people.[45] Despite such descriptions as these, however, some artists and writers identified as belonging to the Beat generation have been serious students of Zen and responsible citizens, as well as talented, creative persons. In fact, Mahoney stated: "For people who find the hothouse atmosphere of Western culture stifling, . . . Zen is a cool, clean early-morning breeze."[46] Also, even though beatniks eventually gave way to hippies, the richness of natural detail and the buoyancy of expression of the Beat novelist, poet, and painter have left a legacy which future generations will value.

## Zen, Psychology, and Psychiatry

One sizable group among serious students of Zen in the late fifties and early sixties consisted of psychologists and psychiatrists who attended Zen lectures, avidly read Suzuki's books, and joined zazen groups. Many of these were clinicians interested in the therapeutic potentialiteis of Zen, and/or were looking for analogies between certain Zen concepts and psychoanalytic concepts. *Psychologia,* a journal of international psychology published in Japan, ran many articles on various aspects of psychology in relation to Zen, with some of them being written by American psychologists. American psychology journals also published articles on Zen. Indeed, the prestigious Erich Fromm collaborated with D. T. Suzuki in planning and conducting a workshop on psychoanalysis and Zen (see chapter 11 for details).[47]

## Current Developments

Although interest in Zen lagged somewhat in the early sixties, it is presently showing a significant growth in America, with new groups and affiliates appearing throughout the country, zendos expanding, and numbers of Zen practitioners increasing. Some of the new Zen inquirers are college students who have become disillusioned by the failure of the traditional Western religions to come to grips with the problems of society and their failure to meet a felt need for a "mystical" dimension in religion. Doubtless some of these will remain with Zen, but others will go on to sample other Oriental religions or go back to working "within the system." Some of the new faces in the zendo are those of former drug users looking for a more permanent kind of psychedelic experience. Perhaps a small percentage of these will stick, but most will doubtless give up Zen and/or return to the drug scene. But many of the new Zen Buddhists are intellectuals and idealists in their twenties and thirties, who are willing to work hard to form the core of American Zen Buddhists in the next decade.

Aside from the increase in the number of Zen adherents in the seventies, there appear to be several other significant ongoing developments.

*American Zen monasticism.* An expanding interest in the monastic life on the part of American Zen Buddhists is reflected in the increasing numbers who are spending extended periods of time in one of the several Zen monasteries which have been established since 1966. This is a highly structured and disciplined life, suggesting a felt need on the part of young Americans for structure and discipline of their own choosing.

*Interest in communal living.* A number of Zen Centers are residential and semimonastic in nature, with some students living at the center but having jobs outside. Settings of this type are found at Cimarron Zen Center, Zen Center of Los Angeles, Zen Center of Rochester, and Zen Center of San Francisco. In this sort of situation, frequently members not living at the center rent rooms or apartments in the neighborhood, sometimes in a communal living arrangement, so that the members come to form a Zen "community." Those who live in or near the center report that this enhances their practice.

*Zen on the university campus.* Newsletters of Zen centers are full of reports of lectures given or workshops conducted by Zen priests on university campuses. Frequently these lead to the formation of zazen groups on the campuses, or to some students' moving to where they can have access to a Zen master.

*Zen and Catholicism.* In the early 1960s a frequent visitor to the zazen group of the Cambridge Buddhist Society was Dom Aelred Graham, a Benedictine scholar and for many years prior of the Portsmouth Priory at Portsmouth, Rhode Island. In 1963 he published a book, *Zen Catholicism,* which aroused much interest among Roman Catholics.[48] His interest in Zen continued, and in 1967 the Cambridge Buddhist Society arranged for him to visit Buddhist temples and teachers in

Japan. This trip resulted in another book, published in 1968: *Conversations: Christian and Buddhist*.[49]

Another Roman Catholic monk with a profound interest in Zen was the mystic, Father Thomas Merton. Father Merton was a close friend of Dr. Suzuki and found many similarities between Western mysticism and Zen. The author of *Zen and the Birds of Appetite* and *Mystics and Zen Masters*, he was about to undertake a trip to Japan planned by the Cambridge Buddhist Society, when he died in Bangkok in 1968.[50]

Following the lead of Dom Aelred Graham and Father Merton, many Roman Catholic monasteries have been issuing invitations to Zen teachers to conduct instructional sessions in zazen for the benefit of the monks. It is of interest, also, that among the regular participants in zazen sessions at most Zen centers are several Catholic priests as well as a few Protestant clergymen.

*American Zen priests.* It has been said that there cannot be a truly American Zen until there are American Zen masters. As far as this writer knows, there are at present not more than five or six recognized non-Oriental American roshis. However, each year American Zen priests are being ordained, and quite a few of these have been approved as teachers. Also, American lay Zen Buddhists are conducting and assisting in services.

*Zen and American society.* Zen in America is principally a Japanese transplant and has grown up more or less isolated from American society. The increasing trend toward monastic living, if anything, is increasing its isolation from that society. Americans and Japanese alike, however, recognize that if Zen is to have any significant and lasting impact in the United States, it must be a uniquely American Zen—not a carbon copy of Japanese Zen. Most Zen centers in the United States have made modifications in established procedures so that they are more in keeping with the American Way. Virtually all Zen centers are discussing the need for further changes.

### The Zen Way, and Its Setting, in America

*The Zen center.* The physical plant of a Zen center depends upon space available and the purposes which the center is intended to serve. The Soto Zen temple in Los Angeles (Zenshuji) is constructed to resemble a Japanese temple on the outside. On the inside it has a main hall equipped with pews, pulpit, and so forth, so that—except for the altar which includes a Buddha image, the usual percussion instruments and other Buddhist ornaments—the interior resembles a Christian church, as is true of the Jodo Shinshu churches. The Soto temple in San Francisco (Sokoji) has a similar interior, but its exterior is dingy and nondescript—not readily identifiable as a house of worship—and there are two semi-gothic towers on top of the building At both temples, there are weekly congregational services similar in format to those at the Jodo Shinshu churches, as well as Sunday School classes for children. There is also provision for weekly zazen for interested persons, so that a zendo forms a part of the temple. However, the temple is principally a community center for Japanese and Japanese-Americans of Zen background, and its physical plant is adapted to this function.

In the Zen center not identified specifically as a temple, the principal function usually is the practice of zazen, and training in its techniques. In this sort of center, the only essential is a zendo, which may in some instances also serve as a Buddha hall or sutra hall. The zendo may be a converted garage, a room in an apartment, a doctor's waiting room, a warehouse, or any room large enough so that those practicing will not distract one another. The room, which may or may not have some sort of floor covering, is free of furniture. Usually, there is an altar at one end of the room, with a Buddha and the usual symbols and appurtenances (candles, incense burner, flowers, percussion instruments). It is not required that the zendo have an altar, but there is usually at least a simple one. When the zendo is used also as a sutra hall, the altar may be larger and more elaborate, although seldom as elaborate as those usually found in Jodo Shinshu churches.

If the zendo is of a center belonging to the Rinzai sect, there may be a low platform extending the length of the room on both sides, and possibly also in the center, on which meditators will sit facing each other. If it is a Soto center, there usually is not such a platform. Whether meditators sit on the floor or on a platform, cushions for sitting are provided—usually a large, square, thin cushion or pad and small, thick, round cushions.

In the Zen center there may or may not be a separate Buddha hall where the sutras are chanted. Where there is such a hall, it is a large room with an altar but no furniture, where cushions for sitting on the floor are available. In most Zen centers there will be also a small room used by the roshi for private interviews.

If the center is used for training monks, it will normally have a library and/or a room for study, as well as an office. If it is a residential center, there will be a kitchen, refectory, and sleeping rooms. Usually, residents sleep on mattresses placed on the floor or have beds with wood placed over the springs.

*Zen Practice.* For the Zen Buddhist who has committed himself to the Zen Way, every activity in which he engages is a part of his Zen "practice." His commitment involves his relating to both the animate and inanimate world with complete "mindfulness," so that whether he is chopping wood, peeling potatoes, spreading jam on a piece of bread, sweeping the porch, pounding a typewriter, or playing bridge, the experience is deeper, richer, and more meaningful because of his Zen attitude. (Of course, this concept of the Zen Way represents an ideal which probably is not even approached by most who strive to be good Zen Buddhists. And it is particularly difficult in the technological age and among the pressures of modern society.)

Although Zen practice is considered by Zen devotees to be a "Way of Life," the heart of Zen practice is zazen, which in most Zen centers will be combined with sutra chanting. In some Zen centers members will get together perhaps one evening a week or two evenings a week for chanting and zazen. This is a common procedure for groups without a regular Zen master, or with a Zen teacher who has secular employment during the day. When a roshi is avilable on an occasional basis, there may be a change in procedure, with provision for individual interviews with the roshi or perhaps a lecture by the roshi when he meets with the group. In residential centers where there is a roshi available on a regular basis and where there is provision for the training of monks and nuns, there will usually be two or three periods of zazen a day, with more scheduled during sesshins or intensive training periods. The first period usually begins between 3:00 and 5:00 A.M.

There is some variation in procedure from one center to another. However, typically, when chanting is followed by zazen, the procedure is something like the following: After a priest or disciple has lit the candles on the altar and presented incense, the service begins with three or nine prostrations before the Buddha (by a priest or by everyone, or both). This is followed by the chanting of sutras and dharanis, which may continue for fifteen to forty-five minutes. Chanting may be in Japanese, Korean, Vietnamese, Chinese, or English; or there may be some chanting in English and some in an Oriental language. The chanting will always include the "Heart of Perfect Wisdom" sutra, and may or may not include others. At the conclusion of the chanting, which is punctuated by percussion instruments, there are further prostrations, which may be toward the Buddha or toward the person standing opposite each individual. After the chanting there will be a short break before zazen. Where the Buddha hall and zendo are separate, the break is used in moving from one room to another.

Zazen may be done facing the wall or facing the center of the zendo, depending on the sect and the preference of the Zen master or teacher. In either case, a monitor strikes wooden clappers together as a signal for everyone to prepare for zazen. Then he will ring a small hand bell three times, with an interval between each two signals. After the sounding of the clappers and before the third ringing of the bell, each individual will bow and then arrange himself in the zazen position. For most persons this will be the full-lotus or half-lotus cross-legged sitting position, with the back of the left hand in the palm of the right, thumbs touching, and hands in front of the abdomen. The back and head will be held erect, and eyes directed downward at about a forty-five degree angle. Some who cannot handle full-lotus or half-lotus sitting may kneel in Japanese sitting style, but either straddling a round cushion or with a cushion between buttocks and heels. Others may be kneeling with legs under a low, slanted bench which supports the hips. Occasionally, there will be someone sitting on a chair. Before zazen, the lights are turned off in the zendo, so that the only light is that provided by candles on the altar.

Signaling the termination of zazen is the sound of the wooden clappers, followed by the bell, which is rung three times. The session ends with the chanting of the Four Great Vows, in English or some other language, followed by bowing. The vows are repeated three times.

Zazen is usually done in two or more sessions, separated by walking meditation (*kinhin*). Kinhin may be a slow circumambulation of the zendo, with or without chanting; or it may be a fast, brisk walk outside of the zendo. With this arrangement, the sitting may be for twenty minutes to an hour at a stretch, with a total session of zazen and kinhin consuming an hour and a half to two hours, and the Four Vows repeated only at the end of the last sitting.

When there is a roshi present, dokusan may follow zazen, or individuals may leave the zendo for their session with the roshi some time during zazen. Dokusan may be several times a day, or it may be scheduled no more often than two or three times a week. When the Zen student reports for his session with the roshi, he prostrates himself at the door, and again in front of the roshi, who is seated on a cushion. The student sits in the Japanese kneeling position before the master, as he reports on the progress which he is making with his koan or other aspects of his practice, and waits for the roshi's reactions and instructions. When the roshi is finished with a given student, he rings a bell in dismissal. This bell is also a signal for the next person to enter. No two Zen masters will use exactly the same technique, but the roshi's responses are designed to give the kind of feedback that will be helpful to the student who is seeking enlightenment.

In a residential Zen center or one where meals are served, Zen practice involves meal chants and certain mealtime rituals. These vary from one center to another. Usually there will be chants before and after breakfast and lunch. In the monastic setting there may or may not be chants in connection with the evening meal. (When these are omitted, it is because the evening meal is considered to be "medicinal," in keeping with the ancient rule which prohibits eating after noon for members of the Sangha.)

Examples of mealtime chants are the following:

*Before the Midday Meal*
 (At the midday meal, after the food is served, bowl and plate are raised) :
>  The meal has three virtues and six
>   tastes
>  Offered to the Buddha and the
>   Sangha;
>  Let all sentient beings in the Dharmadatu
>   share alike the suffering.

(Plates are set down.)

*Verse of the Three Morsels of Food*
>  The first morsel is to
>   destroy all evils
>  The second to practice
>   all good deeds,
>  The third to save all sentient beings—
>  May I attain the Path to Buddhahood.[51]

In the monastic setting, meals are usually eaten in silence, occasionally in zazen position in the zendo. When the meal is served, it is with much exchanging of bows by served and server and gassho (raised palms together) by the one being served. Permanent residents usually have their own dishes which they wrap in a large square cloth, with the parcel containing also a small white wiping cloth. After the meal is finished, an attendant pours hot water into one of each person's bowls. This is used for washing the dishes with fingers and utensils. The dirty water is then poured into a receptacle which is passed to each person, and the white cloth is used for drying the dishes. (Sometimes tea is used for washing the dishes, with the tea then being consumed.) Each person wraps his dishes in the large square cloth, ready to be used for the next meal. In the several Zen centers where this writer has eaten, meals have always been vegetarian and frequently eaten with chopsticks. In some centers, however, meat is served.

*Special holidays and ordination services.* In the Zen center there are special celebrations of such Buddhist holidays as Buddha's birthday, Enlightenment Day, the anniversary of Buddha's death, and O-Bon (Festival of the Dead), as well as special services of significance only for the particular center, such as celebration of the roshi's birthday or birthday of the founder.

Many persons practicing zazen do not formally become Buddhists. When a person does become a Zen Buddhist, however, he goes through a special ceremony called *jukai,* in which he accepts the Three Treasures and ten precepts, agrees to avoid evil and practice good, and vows to strive for the salvation of all sentient beings. In doing so, the fledgling Buddhist also becomes the disciple of his Zen teacher. There are other special ceremonies for becoming a Zen teacher, and for becoming a Dharma heir. These ceremonies are similar to analogous affairs in the Orient, but an individual roshi may make modifications in the ceremonies.

*Life, death, marriage.* Like other Buddhist priests in America, Zen priests perform marriages. Each makes up his own ceremony, which is usually partly Western, partly Oriental, partly religious, partly secular. American Zen Buddhists often ask the roshi to bless a new born baby before anointing him with holy water. Funerals and memorial services in Zen centers are modeled after those of the Orient.

Recently Kapleau has pointed out the importance of adequately preparing the Zen Buddhist for approaching death. He has written specific instructions for giving spiritual guidance to the dying. These are included in several issues of *Zen Bow,*[52] and in Kapleau's book, *Wheel of Death.*[53] The procedures include giving reassurance, having the dying person take the Threefold Refuge and ten precepts, and repeating the Heart of Wisdom sutra.

## The Practitioners

Who are the Americans whom one sees in the zendo in New York, Illinois, or California? There are a few blacks, an occasional Oriental, and a few middle-aged or elderly persons. Most adherents, however, are young, middle-class, well-educated Caucasians—many hippie types, many from Jewish or Roman Catholic families, and many with poorly defined personal problems (see Part 3).

## Is There an American Zen?

The Judaeo-Christian ethic of service to one's fellowman is an essential part of the fabric of the American way. Peter Fingeston sees the aim of Zen Buddhism as being opposed to this tradition.[54] Of the religions and philosophies of the Orient, he says, "They teach non-action in a world of action, non-suffering in a world of suffering, and declare that neither exists, finding in this delusion a convenient way of evading the problem of helping the masses of Asia."[55] However, such an indictment of Zen seems unfair. As a form of Mahayana Buddhism, Zen also promotes the way of the bodhisattva, seeing enlightenment as an experience which transforms the *total life* of the individual so that he is better able to respond to the needs of others.

Perhaps a more important question than whether or not Zen is the polar opposite of Christianity is whether or not Zen *in America* is such as to promote the bodhisattva ideal. For some it undeniably is; but with the increasing tendency on the part of Zen Buddhists to become isolated in enclaves, for many it would seem *not* to be consonant with the Judaeo-Christian goal of involvement of man with man.

Zen in America at this time is certainly far from being "American." In most Zen services the chanting is in Japanese. In the Zen meditation hall, shoes are removed and sitting is done cross-legged on cushions placed on the floor or a platform. Japanese terminology is used to designate the various aspects of the Zen experience. In some zendos students wear kimonos and/or the pleated skirts called *hakamas*. To be sure, some modifications have been made, so that Zen will be more palatable to Americans. As examples: In American zendos the stick is used only when the student requests it. Frequently it is permissible for beginners to practice meditation seated on chairs. Sesshins are often shorter than those in Japan, to meet the needs of persons who cannot spare more than a day or two. In some centers sutras and other parts of the ritual are repeated in English.

## Zen and American Thought

Over a period of ten years, and at some length, Christmas Humphreys has been pleading for a *Western* approach to Zen. In a talk to the Buddhist Society in London in 1970, he pointed out once again that Zen training in Japan involves long days and years of deep meditation, and that this requires a monastic life and almost unlimited time—time which hundreds of Westerners interested in Zen do not have.[56] He goes on to say that these Westerners must find an alternative to the traditional training of Japan, and supports this statement with four arguments: (1) that it is unreasonable to expect Westerners in the 1970s to adopt a system of spiritual training formulated for the Chinese in 700 A.D.; (2) that if it were right for the West, it would require a large body of Japanese teachers expert in many languages, or Westerners with facility in the Japanese language as well as time and money to make it possible for them to spend years in Japan; (3) that, since Westerners are oriented primarily toward use of the intellect, in the West the intellect must be developed and used to the fullest before the bounds of intellect can be broken through to prajna-intuition; and (4) that since most Westerners are householders, while including meditation as a part of our daily lives "we must find an approach to Zen awareness which uses the day's adventure to that end."[57]

Humphreys's method of zazen includes four stages. It begins with an examination of the nature of thought and its relation to past conditioning. The individual next learns to control thought and stop it when necessary. Then he goes on to using great thought to raise consciousness to the threshold of intuition. In the final stage he goes beyond thought.[58]

Humphreys's books have had a wide sale in the United States. However, American Zen adherents so far seem to be more attracted to the less analytical and more intuitive approach of the Japanese.

In speaking of a Western approach to Zen, Humphreys is speaking about the *methods* and *techniques* by which prajna-intuition is attained, rather than of the *goal* of zazen. Rather than concerning ourselves with the appropriateness of the methods for Americans, it might be better to ask if the Zen way of looking at the world is consistent with American thought. Certainly it has attracted the interest and attention of American intellectuals for more than three-quarters of a century, and it would be taking a superficial view to attribute its continuing appeal to its nontheistic approach which is not in conflict with the findings of science. Nor is the answer to be found in the appeal of mysticism, or the way in which Zen speaks to the artist and poet.

Van Meter Ames convincingly argues that Zen, almost more than any other foreign influence, has affinity with the most American thinking.[59] He points out that Americans believe in the pursuit of happiness, as well as in the bodhisattva way, and that the naturalistic outlook of Zen is something with which Americans feel comfortable. More significantly, however, he sees Zen masters as having voiced concepts later developed by the Chicago philosopher, George Herbert Mead (1863–1931), "who disposed of dualism by accounting for the human self and mind without any transcendent or supernatural principles."[60] He notes, also, that the tone of the Zen masters is close to that of Mead's predecessors in America: Jefferson, Emerson, Thoreau, Whitman, and William James.[61] In discussing the way in which the Zen masters anticipated Mead, he says:

> Their sayings confirm his finding that experience is continuous, taking the most enduring landmarks into the passing moment, bringing the mountains to the man, having eternity here. The perspectives of science come back to this mystic insight. The oneness of all in Buddha, Emerson's "unquestionable Present," Dewey's aesthetic experience, are scientifically stated in Mead's account of the self, as it grows from taking the roles of others to joining them in a generalized other, to commune with in the "inner forum." There the social and the alone come together in the social self, its civilized "me" guiding the aboriginal "I" into the unpredictable. So, in Mead, the scientific west arrives at something like the fusion of the Confucian cultivation of virtue through the bonds of family and community, Taoist *laissez faire* and yearning for Nature, and Buddhist compassion for man's need of Nirvana.[62]

# 5

# From Tibetan Peaks to Berkeley Hills—Tantrism in America

An earnest young man stands before a homemade altar, above which hangs a Tibetan *thanka* (temple banner) depicting Sakyamuni Buddha surrounded by other buddhas and bodhisattvas. Flowers and symbolic offerings have been placed on the shrine. Incense is burning. A red and yellow cushion on the rug before the shrine will later be used for meditation, but now the young man is performing prostrations. Raising his hands, he holds them palm to palm, with palms not quite touching. Between them he is holding symbolically a precious jewel for offering to the Buddha, the Dharma, and the Sangha. With his hands at the level of the top of his head, he salutes the Buddha; as he moves them to the level of his throat, he gives a salutation to the Dharma; and as his hands are lowered to a position in front of his heart, he gives a salutation to the Sangha. Then he goes down so that his body touches the floor in five places—the two knees, the palms of the hands, and the forehead. With each gesture, he repeats a formula in Tibetan and engages in a complex visualization, always mindful that with each prostration he is taking refuge in the Buddha, the Dharma, and the Sangha. He does this with complete involvement of body, speech, and mind, aware that he is doing it for every sentient being.

A middle-aged woman from North Carolina is finishing a solitary ten-day retreat in a hut in the Rocky Mountain foothills of Colorado. She is beginning to feel "stir-crazy," and considers whether or not she can stick it out for the two more days she has to go. She's been spending about eight hours a day meditating on the Three Refuges. Of course she has interrupted her meditation to eat from the supply of canned goods she brought with her, and Rinpoche said it was all right to spend some time in reading and study, but there's no electricity in this hut and she has run out of kerosene for the lamp, so the nights seem pretty long. But day after tomorrow she goes back to civilization again—and back to people.

A tourist in San Francisco, driving past a beach, notices some people in checkered robes who seem to be cavorting around a fire on the beach. At the same time about thirty or forty Japanese seated in the pews of a Los Angeles temple are raising their hands in gassho and chanting, *"Namu Shakya Muni Butsu, Namu Daishi Henjo Kongo"*— "I put my faith in Sakyamuni Buddha, I put my faith in Kobo Daishi."

All of this is Tantric Buddhism, as practiced in America.

The Tantric tradition in America is expressed in three modes of practice—that of Tibetan and Mongolian Buddhism (sometimes called "Lamaism"), the practice of the Japanese Shingon sect, and the mountain practice of the Shugendo of Japan. Of these, the Tantrism of Tibet is the only one which has had any substantial impact in America. Therefore, the present chapter will deal principally with Tibetan Tantrism, with Shingon and Shugendo being touched on only briefly.

## TIBETAN BUDDHISM

### Nature of Tibetan Buddhism

Tibetan Buddhism is a combination of the ancient cult of "Bon," the teachings of the *Pali Canon* accepted by the Theravada group, the later popular Mahayana teachings, and the Tantrism taught in the Vajrayana canon.

*Pre-Buddhist religion.* The pre-Buddhist religion of Tibet, called Bon, was a form of shamanism about which little is known, since Tibet had no written language before the advent of Buddhism, and Chinese reports on Bon were subject to the distortions of an alien point of view.[1] According to these reports, it involved nature worship as well as demon worship, magic, and rites of both human and animal sacrifice. Its central figure was the shaman, a sorcerer who performed various rituals to placate both good and bad gods, as well as to produce the right weather and take care of the other needs of an agricultural population.[2] Frequently the shaman fell into a trance in order to communicate with these spirits.[3] Bon still exists in Tibet today, and has its monasteries, temples, and priests oriented toward the performance of magical rites to the extent that these are permitted by the Chinese Communists; but modern Bon has lost most of its sinister elements and is a minority religion.[4] Its most visible manifestations today are in the deities and rituals which have been incorporated into Tibetan Buddhist Tantric practices.[5]

*The Mahayana setting.* As a type of Mahayana Buddhism, Tibetan Buddhism accepts the basic Theravada and Mahayana teachings. These include concepts such as the Four Noble Truths, the Noble Eightfold Path, no God, no Self, impermanence, incarnation, nirvana, and karma, as well as belief in multiple Buddhas, and stress on bodhisattvas.[6]

*The Vajrayana and Tantric Buddhism.* The esoteric Vajrayana or Adamantine Vehicle is a special additional section of the Mahayana sutras found only in the Tibetan canon and describing the Tantric practices which represent the uniqueness of Tibetan Buddhism. Although the Tantric adept studies the scriptures, the essence of Tantric Buddhism is not conveyed to him through the printed word, but in his relationship with a teacher or *guru*, who guides him individually along his spiritual path. In this directed practice, he will learn the use of *mantras* (powerful mystical syllables or invocations), *mudras* (sacred gestures), and *sadhanas* (visualizations), involving unification of body, speech, and mind.[7]

*Tibetan religious practice and Tantric meditation.* Religion was central in the life of the Buddhist in pre-Communist Tibet and Mongolia. Usually he had a personal shrine in his home. This shrine ordinarily included an image of a Buddha, a famous teacher, or a Buddhist deity serving as his special guardian. It included also other Buddhist articles. Before this shrine he performed his daily devotions, which included the repetition of the Threefold Refuge. In addition, they included the repetition of the syllables *Om mani padme Hum*— an invocation to the Bodhisattva Avalokitesvara, believed to be incarnate in the Dalai Lama. This invocation was uttered once for each of the 108 beads of the Buddhist's rosary. If he had time, the worshipper might use the sacred images and paintings on the shrine as focal points for meditation on the attributes of moral perfection, compassion, and wisdom. In any event, as he went about his daily tasks he would accumulate karmic merit by repeating the syllables, "Om mani padme Hum," which he would also see painted on the sides of buildings and on numerous prayer wheels and flags, keeping the sacred thoughts always at least on the periphery of consciousness.

For the average Tibetan or Mongolian peasant, there would have been no guru available, so that the Tibetan form of meditation would not have played a major role in his life. For the monk, priest, or lay yogin, however, meditation would have been of central importance, as it still may be in Tibet, and certainly is among those who have left Tibet or Mongolia to take refuge in south Asia or the West. It is this aspect of Tantric Buddhism, also, which has appealed to many European and American followers of the Tibetan and Mongolian gurus who have established communities and meditation centers in the West. Something of what can be gained through such meditation has been described by the Tibetan teacher, Chogyam Trungpa.[8] Its techniques have been detailed by John Blofeld.[9]

The student or disciple of a guru giving guidance in Tantric meditation will be instructed individually, with the sadhanas or specific visualization-rites which characterize Tibetan meditation being prescribed to suit the disciple's personal characteristics. However, each session will begin with some preliminary rites and meditation involving worship, offerings, breathing exercises, generating *bodhicitta* (enlightened mind), and various discursive meditations. Like the main body of the meditation, these preliminaries involve the use of mudras, mantras, and *bija-mantras* (the seed-syllables from which the visualizations spring), and whirling *dharanis* (revolving strings of syllables).[10]

The sadhana itself, like the preliminaries, involves the interplay of body, speech, and mind. As described by Blofeld,

> The *body* takes part through prostrations, offerings and mudras. Offerings are made by holding or touching with the fingers symbolical objects such as flowers, incense, lights, water and grain while mentally creating what they symbolize. Mudras are symbolical gestures made with hands and fingers. . . . They must be conjoined with their mental equivalents. . . . Their chief function is to help the achievement of higher states of consciousness.
>
> *Speech* in this connection means mantric sound. Mantras help to call into being the mental creations and to bring about their transformation. . . .
>
> Besides reciting mantras or combining recitation with yogic breathing exercises, it is usual to visualize their component syllables in color. For use in this way there are bija-mantras

and dharanis. A bija or seed syllable is visualized springing from a void . . . and magically transforming itself into a lotus. This unfolds to disclose a second bija-syllable which instantly assumes the form of a deity. In the deity's heart shines still another bija and within the tiny circle at its top . . . is one so small that only the mind can perceive it. This is the essence that connects the manifestation with the void.

Dharanis or written mantras are often visualized in the form of a circle. At times, one of them is seen whirling round in the deity's heart; or, if adept and deity have merged, in the heart of both of them. Their whirling produces the perfect, limitless stillness of the void. Like bijas, dharanis glow with color. . . .[11]

Although Blofeld seems to emphasize the centrality of visualizations in Tantric practice, in actuality the Buddhism of Tibet offers choice among a variety of practices for those seeking liberation from the sufferings of human existence. Among the practices available, the use of mantra is said to be a particularly effective means of "dispelling the ignorance on which our anxious lives are founded and leads the practitioner to a realization of the nature of mind."[12] In Tibet, the mantra is considered of such importance that Tibetan Buddhism has often been referred to as Mantrayana.

The mantras of Tibetan Buddhism are not words with concrete meanings;[13] neither are they magical incantations.[14] For the sophisticated modern practitioner, mantra is considered to be "a scientific method of bringing the mind into harmony with high levels of awareness and of reopening avenues of communication which otherwise remain closed."[15]

For the neophyte in Tantric meditation, the repetition of and attention to the sound of sonorous syllables such as OM-ΛH-HUM aids in concentration and frequently promotes tranquility and relaxation. However, as warned by Lama Govinda, "the power and effect of a mantra depend on the spiritual attitude, the knowledge and responsiveness of the individual. . . . The sound of the mantra is not a physical sound . . . but a spiritual one."[16] Thus, the full power of a mantra could be experienced only by one who had been initiated into the mysteries of esoteric practice under the guidance of a competent guru.

The complexity, depth, and richness of mantrayana are illustrated by Govinda's explication of the great mantra, "Om mani padme Hum."[17] These characteristics are illustrated also in translations which Tarthang Tulku's students have made of commentaries by Tulku Karma Lingpa on the Vajra Guru Mantra, which goes, "Om Ah Hum Vajra Guru Padma Siddhi Hum."[18]

Of the power of the Vajra Guru Mantra it is said,

If, sitting quietly, one concentrates one's complete attention on one's own voice slowly chanting the mantra, the worry and distress which continually enturbulate the mind will gradually subside and one will gradually be suffused with a deep calm. With practice skill will be acquired to extend the period of peaceful concentration, thus creating a respite from fears, doubts and other painful mental distractions. As this serenity is developed and expanded, the mind will gradually attain the placidity of the surface of a still pond. From this calmness awareness will arise and the self-nature of the mind will be realized.[19]

The commentaries on the Vajra Guru Mantra include a number of interpretations on the meaning of the syllables, among which are the following:

As for *Om, Ah* and *Hum,* they are the supreme essence of the Body, Speech, and Mind. *Vajra* is the supreme essence of the *Vajra* family. *Guru* is the supreme essence of the Jewel Family. *Padma* is the supreme essence of the Lotus Family. *Siddhi* is the supreme essence of the *Karma* Family. As for *Hum,* it is the supreme essence of the Tathagata Family.[20]

By *Om, Ah* and *Hum,* All obscurations which derive from the Three Poisons will be purified. By *Vajra* all obscurations which derive from pride will be purified. By *Guru* all obscurations which derive from envy will be purified. By *Hum* all obscurations which derive from the defilements (*klesas*) will be purified.[21]

By *Om, Ah* and *Hum* one will attain the Six Perfections. By *Vajra* one will realize all the magical rites which are peaceful. By *Guru* one will realize all the magical rites which increase prosperity. By *Padma* one will realize all the magical rites of overpowering enchantment. By *Siddhi* one will realize all of the magical rites of worldly success. By *Hum* one will realize all the magical rites which are terrifying.[22]

What is the purpose of Tantric meditation? Like all Buddhist practices, its ultimate goal is enlightenment. But there are other rewards to be attained along the path to enlightenment—rewards such as "increasing control over body, speech and mind, the progressive negation of the ego, and the development of ever higher states of consciousness—all of them accompanied by an increasing influx of intuitive wisdom."[23]

*Sects of Tibetan Buddhism.* Tibetan Buddhism has two principal schools, known popularly as "Red Hat" and "Yellow Hat" lamaism, with the former comprising three sects.

Of the Red Hat sects, the *Nyingmapa* is the oldest and most faithful to the ancient traditions, tracing its lineage to 747 A.D. The Nyingmapas are expert Tantrists, schooled in the practices of all Buddhist meditational systems. Although they wear a special habit, most of the Nyingmapa lamas are married clergy, rather than celibate monks, and they believe that spiritual growth is best promoted by living *in* the world rather than being isolated from it. [24]

The Kargyupa or *Kargyutpa* sect, which developed in the eleventh century, emphasizes austerity in living, strict adherence to Buddhist discipline, and a type of meditation which is quite similar to that of Zen, except for its use of visualization. Many of its members spend years meditating alone in caves where they see or hear no other human beings as they are perfecting their meditational techniques.[25] This sect is sometimes referred to as "semi-reformed."[26]

The third of the Red Hat group, the *Sakyapa* sect, also had its origins in the eleventh century. Like the Kargyupa, considered a semi-reformed group, in its practices this sect is almost indistinguishable from the Yellow Hats.[27]

The *Gelugpas* or Yellow Hats are designated as the "reformed" sect and constitute the "established church" in Tibet. In Mongolia almost all Buddhists are affiliated with this sect. The Yellow Hats originated in the fifteenth century. This sect emphasizes monastic discipline and learning, postponing the tantras until the end of a long course of study. After 1640 the leader of the Gelugpas, the Dalai Lama, was king as well as pontiff of Tibet and is still recognized in both roles by many Tibetans, despite his exiled status.[28]

## Tulkus or Incarnate Lamas

A unique feature of Tibetan and Mongolian Buddhism is the doctrine of *tulkus* or incarnate lamas. According to this doctrine, certain outstanding lamas before death may give clues as to the birthplace and identity of their incarnation. These clues are not definitive, and frequently the incarnation is not located until after much research, consultation of oracles, and analysis of visions. When the child is finally located, he is tested for recognition of objects belonging to the deceased. The system of selecting and training tulkus is described by Chogyam Trungpa and Marco Pallis.[29]

Among the tulkus of Tibet, the best known is the Dalai Lama, who is believed to be the reincarnation of the Bodhisattva of Compassion, Avalokitesvara (Tibetan: Chen-re-zi).

## Tantric Mythology and the Tibetan Pantheon

Like other Mahayanists, the Tibetan Buddhist uses the term Buddha to embrace three aspects, referred to collectively as the Tri-kaya or "Triple Body." The first aspect is the Dharma-Body or Buddhist Principle (Body of Essence, Body of Law). The second is the Body of Transformation; the third is the Body of Bliss.[30]

The concepts of the Dharma-Body and the Body of Transformation are not significantly different in Tibetan Buddhism from their conceptualization by other Mahayanists (see chapter 1). In the Vajrayana, however, the Body of Bliss is elaborated in the idea of the Five Jinas, each of whom embodies one aspect of Divine Wisdom.[31] *Jina* means "victor" or "conqueror," and is used as a designation for the Buddha to indicate his conquest over passion.[32] The Five Jinas appeared in Tibet about 750 A.D., and included *Vairocana*, the "Il-luminator" or the "Brilliant"; *Akshobhya*, the "Imperturbable"; *Ratna Sambhava*, the "Jewel-born"; *Amitabha*, the "Infinite Light and Life"; and *Amoghasiddhi*, the "Unfailing Success." Unlike previous Buddhas, who were assumed to have once been animals or humans and to have worked their way to Buddhahood in previous incarnations, the Five Jinas were assumed to have always been Buddhas.[33]

The Five Jinas were believed to constitute the body of the universe. In addition, a system was worked out in which each Buddha corresponded to certain constituents of the universe, with a given Jina representing a sense organ, a direction, a color, a sound, and so on. Further, each celestial Buddha was believed to be reflected in a human Buddha and a celestial Buddha, and to be united with a feminine force, *Shakti*, as well as having jurisdiction over various accessory or subsidiary deities.[34]

As the doctrine of the Five Jinas developed, it was gradually elaborated to include the idea that each of the Jinas was an emanation from one first, primeval Buddha called the *Adi-Buddha*, who was believed to be the one eternal Buddha also called the *Adi-Buddha*, who in turn was believed to be the one eternal living principle of the entire universe.[35]

The various deities of the Tantric pantheon figure prominently in the mandalas used in the rites of worship, and in the visualization which is so central to the Tibetan form of meditation.

## History of Tibetan Buddhism

Buddhism first entered Tibet from India and China during the seventh century.[36] However, it did not have much influence until a century later, when active sponsorship by the king resulted in the ordination of monks and construction of many temples. At this time the support of Buddhism by the royal family was opposed by the nobles, who allied themselves with the Bon priests against the "foreign" religion. When a pestilence broke out in Tibet in 1840, it was interpreted as representing the displeasure of the Bon spirits. The king then invited a famous Indian Tantric master to Tibet to subdue these spirits. The master was Padmasambhava, regarded as the founder of Tibetan Buddhism.

In 749 Padmasambhava established the Samye monastery in Llasa. At this monastery was founded the first Tibetan monastic order, the Nyingmapa.

After the early part of the ninth century, Buddhism in Tibet declined, and discipline in the monasteries became lax. The eleventh century, however, saw the establishment of the Kadampa, Kagyupa, and Sakya orders as part of a reform movement to restore monastic discipline. It saw also the increase of power and wealth of the larger monasteries.

Tibetan Buddhism survived the Mongol invasion of the thirteenth century, but by the fourteenth century religious discipline had again broken down. Once more a reform movement was initiated, this time in the founding of the Gelugpa or Yellow Hat sect. This sect soon became politically quite powerful. In 1578 the third Grand Lama of the Yellow Hat Sect went to Mongolia to negotiate an alliance and to propagate Buddhism among the Mongolians. This led to the adoption of Tantric Buddhism by the Mongolians, but also to the conferring on the Grand Lama of the title of Dalai Lama (*dalai* being the Mongolian term for great ocean).

In the seventeenth century the Dalai Lama became the temporal ruler as well as the spiritual leader of Tibet. The status of the Dalai Lama remained unchanged until 1959, when he was forced by the Chinese Communists to flee from Tibet.

Since the late 1950s, thousands of Tibetans have left their country to settle in India, Nepal, Bhutan, Sikkim, Switzerland, France, Great Britain, and the United States. In all of these areas monastic communities have been set up by Tibetan lamas, and Tantric practices have been introduced to nationals of the host countries. The teachings of the founders and early gurus of the different sects also have been propagated. Consequently, the names and lives of fourteenth-century monks such as Marpa, Naropa, and Milarepa are familiar to most Tantric Buddhists in the West as well as in Asia.

## TIBETAN BUDDHISM IN AMERICA

Before the Communist takeover of Tibet, a few Tibetan lamas were found on American university campuses, teaching the Tibetan language as well as courses on Tibetan culture and Buddhism. Until the late 1960s, however, the Tibetan presence in the United States was scarcely visible. Since 1965 all that has changed, and Tibetan Buddhism is making itself known in America in three ways: through the establishment of monasteries and refugee communities in America; through an increase in the number of Tibetans serving on the faculties of American universities; and through the establishment of meditation centers for Americans. Of these three, the meditation centers have had the greatest impact on Americans, although a few Americans have entered lamaseries and a small number have interested themselves in Tibetan studies at universities employing Tibetan teachers. The meditation centers will be discussed here.

All of the major sects of Tibetan Buddhism have established meditation centers in the United States. Several of these are under the direction of tulkus who were abbots of large and influential monasteries in Tibet. Now most of these men are married and have families, and are no longer living a monastic existence. Usually they are called *Rinpoche* (pronounced Rim-po-shay), a title meaning "precious master"—the Tibetan equivalent of "roshi." The Tibetan meditation centers are still relatively few in number and some are quite small. However, they are multiplying quite rapidly and are gaining new disciples every day.

Among the best-known and most influential of the Tibetan masters are Chogyam Trungpa Tulku and Tarthang Tulku. On the basis of the contributions of men such as these, Needleman has expressed the opinion that "Tibetan Buddhism will be for the West in the coming decade what Zen Buddhism has been in the last decade and . . . will enrich our understanding of religion no less than Zen Buddhism has."[37]

As is the case with Zen, the nature of Tibetan Buddhism in America is determined by the masters and gurus who are guiding the spiritual development of their disciples. Therefore, discussion here of Tibetan Buddhism in America will be largely in terms of the men who are determining its destiny.

### Chogyam Trungpa and the Kagyupa School

Chogyam Trungpa, Rinpoche. Chogyam Trungpa, the eleventh Trungpa Tulku, was born in northeastern Tibet in 1939. His family was a very poor one, but when he was a year old he was "discovered" as the reincarnation of the tenth Trungpa Tulku. His mother was permitted to be with him while he was growing up, but the rigorous monastic training which comprised his life was taken over by monks of the Kagyupa school, and his entire childhood and adolescence were spent in monasteries. The story of his first twenty years, including his flight to India in 1959, is told in his aforementioned autobiography, *Born in Tibet.*

Following his escape to India, the young Tulku proceeded to England, where he attended Oxford University. After Oxford he went on in 1967 to establish the Samye-Ling Meditation Center in Scotland. At Samye-Ling he developed an orientation which he called "meditation in action," and Samye-Ling became the training ground for "the living of daily life with the simplicity of meditation."[38]

Despite his success in Scotland, Trungpa Tulku came increasingly to feel that the role of guru and holy man was a false role for him, and that he could function more effectively and sincerely as a layman. This feeling became even stronger during a retreat in India in 1969, but he was still unable to make the decision to renounce his exalted status. Then, on his return to England, he was in an automobile accident which left him paralyzed on one side. He said, "This led to my taking off the robe. The purpose of this was to gain for me personally the strength to continue teaching by unmasking, and also to do away with the 'exotic' externals which were too fascinating to students in the West."[39]

Shortly after removing the robe, Trungpa married an English teen-ager. The changes in his status and way of life were upsetting to the "guru-lovers" among his disciples and caused chaos in the Samye-Ling community. This resulted in Trungpa's leaving Scotland to join a group of his students in the United States.

In March, 1970, Chogyam Trungpa, Rinpoche, founded the Tail of the Tiger community near Barnet, Vermont. Organized initially as a summer retreat, it now has facilities for year-round residence and practice. In November of the same year, Rinpoche moved to Boulder,

Colorado, where he now lives with his family. In March, 1971, the Karma Dzong Meditation Center was organized in Boulder.

Since his arrival in North America in early 1970, Trungpa Rinpoche's fame and influence have increased tremendously. The program which he supervises now has many facets and involves centers scattered over the United States. With Rinpoche being almost constantly on the move, his students sometimes complain that they do not see him enough; yet, they are grateful for the time which he does give them, and it is a part of his philosophy that people must find their security within themselves rather than becoming dependent on a guru.

What sort of person is Chogyam Trungpa? Even those who are closest to him do not really know who or what he is. His students admire his intellect and wisdom, revere him as their teacher and spiritual leader, and feel close to him on the basis of his humanity and compassion. They glow with pleasure when he gives them encouragement, and dread his disapproval. They are critical of him because of his tendency at times to disregard schedules, and because of his fondness for beer and for using somewhat pungent four-letter words on occasion. At the same time, they are fiercely protective if outsiders presume to criticize any aspect of his behavior.

Every individual reacts to Chogyam Trungpa in a different way. His initial impression on this writer was expressed in journal entries after he was seen on two successive days in Boulder, Colorado. The first occasion was at a lecture given by Rinpoche to a class at the University of Colorado. The second occasion was during an interview for which an appointment had been made. The notes read as follows:

Tuesday evening

I arrived at the classroom fifteen minutes before the class was scheduled to begin, in order to be sure of getting a good seat and to give myself time to set up the tape recorder. The classroom had about 200 seats, and more than half of them were occupied when I arrived at 7:15, but I was able to get a seat in the front row. As 7:30 approached the remaining seats were filled, and for the next half hour people continued to come in, some sitting on window sills and others leaning against the wall. About half of those present were university students and the remainder were members of the Boulder community or of Karma Dzong. Someone placed a chair and small table on the platform at the front of the room, and a man tinkered with a large tape recorder to the left of the dais.

Still Rinpoche did not arrive, although it was now eight o'clock. Everyone chatted easily and nobody seemed especially disturbed about the teacher's nonarrival. Not a single person left the room, and I couldn't help but wonder how many of *my* students would still be waiting if I were that late to class! Finally, at 9 o'clock, a short, stocky Oriental with longish hair, wearing a business suit, appeared at the door. Immediately the talking ceased as Rinpoche slowly walked across the floor, limping slightly, mounted the dais, and took his seat. Notebooks and pens appeared, and all eyes were riveted on the teacher.

While everyone waited for Rinpoche to start his lecture, the Tibetan sat in silence, an enigmatic look on his face. Suddenly he smiled, and chuckled. His audience tittered nervously. There was another period of silence as Rinpoche lit a cigarette, and then he laughed again. (Good heavens! Could this be the charismatic figure I'd heard so much about?) Finally he started to speak, slowly and hesitantly, with many pauses between words and phrases as well as fillers of the "ah-um-er-uh" variety. (How could this man be in such demand as a lecturer?) Then, after his first few sentences, I became so interested and involved in what he was saying that I no longer paid any attention to his delivery. His half-hour talk was on the subject of *prajna*, which he explained clearly and precisely, with well-chosen words spoken in a well-modulated voice with a slight British accent. When he finished I realized that, despite his pauses, I had just listened to the most comprehensible explanation of prajna I had ever heard. It was then that I wondered if all the hesitation had been intentional. After all, prajna is not a simple concept and the pauses were needed by the listeners, not only for notetaking but to digest what was said.

With the formal presentation finished, there was time for questions and answers. Rinpoche listened to each question carefully, considered it seriously, and answered it clearly and articulately, with no signs of the hesitation which characterized his lecture. Some of the questions were poor ones, but the Rinpoche always managed to phrase his answers so that the questions appeared to be intelligent ones. Thus no student was allowed to appear as a fool before his peers.

I left the lecture hall with very mixed feelings about this

Tibetan teacher. I did not find his personality very prepossessing and I was annoyed at having had to wait so long. At the same time, I admired him as a clear and incisive thinker, and envied him his rapport with even the dullest students.

Wednesday afternoon Rinpoche had given me an appointment for two o'clock at his office in the Karma Dzong Meditation Center. I arrived early, left my shoes in the hall in compliance with instructions on the posted sign, and seated myself on the bench which extended around the walls of the large anteroom adjoining the office area. A barefooted, long-haired, male student was stretched out on the floor, sleeping, and two others were working in an outer office. The Rinpoche had not arrived, but was expected.

As I sat waiting for the Venerable Chogyam Trungpa, I thought about how surprising it was that I'd been given this appointment at all and told myself that Rinpoche probably would not have time to see me. After all, he had just returned from the East the day before, would be leaving again the following day, and had about a hundred students in Boulder who wanted to see him. In addition, his wife had just returned from a trip to England that very day. I really had a nerve to expect him to visit with me!

During my wait for Rinpoche I had time to talk with several students who came to wait for him also, and I took a look at the large meditation hall which opened off of the anteroom on the side opposite the offices. Finally the great man arrived and entered his office without looking at or speaking to any of the people who were waiting. One of the students rose and followed him.

At ten minutes past three a girl in shorts told me that Rinpoche was ready to see me. She led me to the inner office and closed the door behind me. It was a small room containing a desk, a chair, and a mattress on the floor along one wall. Rinpoche was seated in the chair. He greeted me with a smile and extended his hand. Since there were no chairs other than the one which he was occupying, I sat on the mattress.

I had nearly an hour with Rinpoche. During that time he related to me in a warm, friendly way. He answered my questions with an air of considering them of great significance, expressed interest in my research, and at no time gave the slightest hint of being annoyed at having his precious time taken up in this way. The ideas he expressed, also, were ones which, as a psychologist, I found sound and appealing. As I left, I understood something of why this man's followers found him so wonderful, and he had added one more admirer to his "fan club." I told myself that, no matter how long he kept me waiting, what he had to say would always be worth waiting for.

Since my initial contact with Chogyam Trungpa, I have attended several more of his lectures and have participated in a weekend seminar on "Meditation in Action." I have come to understand the tremendous demands that are made on Rinpoche's time and energy. I have also become comfortable with waiting and have learned to use it as a spiritual exercise. More importantly, I have come to appreciate Rinpoche as a deeply religious person dedicated to the application of Buddhist insights for the relief of human suffering.

*Tail of the Tiger.* Tail of the Tiger, located in the Green Mountains of Vermont, in 1972 was in its third year as a community, meditation center, and spiritual training ground. The central core of residents numbered twenty-three people. Some of these had remained in the community for more than a year; others had come for long weekends and vacation periods. While here they lived in a central building, but spent retreats in huts or tents (depending on the season). They spent hours a day in study and meditation, and also in work. Work included such varied activities as building cabins, installing a water system, engaging in various crafts, and growing vegetables. Rinpoche's schedule for 1972 showed ninety-six days spent at Tail of the Tiger.[40]

*Karma Dzong meditation center.* Karma Dzong, with its headquarters in Boulder, Colorado, consisted of two groups in 1972—an "urban" living-work-meditation community in Boulder, and the Fort Collins community (the Rocky Mountain Dharma Center) located on a 345-acre site in the mountains about 50 miles northwest of Fort Collins.

When Karma Dzong was first organized, in Boulder, it was not with the idea of establishing a "community," and it has never been a "commune," in any sense. It was planned that members of the center would live where they chose and work at jobs of their own choosing, but with a regular schedule of meditation twice a day in the headquarters on Pearl Street, longer periods of meditation on weekends at the center or in the mountains, and both individual and group sessions with Rinpoche. From the beginning, however, the members of Karma Dzong felt themselves to be a community, psychologically speaking, even though they were not living in close proximity to one another. Indeed, in some, the urge to live together was strong. Consequently, in June, 1972, a portion of the Karma Dzong community moved into a fourteen-bedroom house on Broadway.

The Rocky Mountain Dharma Center came into being in September, 1971. Here members of Karma Dzong wanting to leave the urban setting constructed A-frames, domes, cabins, huts, and a meditation hall. Most of these initially were temporary structures, but permanent buildings either have been built or are under construction. Water and electricity were brought in, sanitation provided for, and roads cut.

At both the urban and the Fort Collins community, crafts and leatherwork cooperatives were formed. In 1972, further projects were under way. In the journal published by the center, these projects and the way of life at Karma Dzong were described as follows:

> At any time there are at least several people in retreat somewhere in the mountains. People are studying Sanskrit and Tibetan, and Rinpoche is working with one of his students on a new translation of the Tibetan Book of the Dead. He is also, assisted by others of his students, preparing his lectures for publication in book form and teaching courses at the University of Colorado and at the Denver Free University.
>
> But in spite of the diversity of activities, projects and lifestyles with which people involve themselves, certain common themes persist: a willingness on the part of the individual to "work on himself"; a recognition that meditation is the tool by which this work can be accomplished, and the application of this tool within the context of the individual's relationship with Rinpoche, the Karma Dzong community, and the world in general. By living and meditating, alone and together, we grow closer as a community.[41]

In the spring of 1972, there were about 120 committed members participating fully in the Karma Dzong Meditation Center, with several hundred other persons taking part in its activities in various ways. There were about forty living in the Fort Collins community. These were mostly young, well-educated Caucasians, although there were some blacks, and some older persons in the group. Quite a few were married and had children. (Rinpoche works with the children who are over eight years of age.) A number of couples who were not married were living together. Many students were former drug addicts and many had tried psychotherapy or some religious solutions to their problems. They were generally "antiestablishment" but willing to work at anything, e.g., a sociologist with a master's degree worked as a janitor and his psychology-major wife did housework. The members of the community often described themselves as "hippie types," but they were devoted to Chogyam Trungpa and completely committed to the way of life which they had chosen (see Part 3 for details). Rinpoche's schedule for 1972 showed 121 days at Karma Dzong.

*Affiliated groups.* The various small groups affiliated with Karma Dzong or Tail of the Tiger have different types of relationships with Chogyam Trungpa. Usually Rinpoche gives them careful instructions on the design and construction of a shrine and meditation hall, and inspects the results. He also gives them initial instructions on meditation, and may return to meet with them once or twice a year. In most instances one or more "senior" students will work more closely with the group. In addition, tapes of talks by Rinpoche are made available to play at group meetings.

I visited one of these small groups, the Dharmadatu Meditation Center in San Francisco.

The San Francisco Dharmadatu, which in the spring of 1972 had been in existence for about a year, had ten members who paid their dues regularly, but nonmembers sometimes visited, so there might be anywhere from two or three to twenty at meetings. The members were young Caucasian adults, most of them artists. Meetings were scheduled for three times a week. On Monday evening there was an hour of meditation, followed by playing of a tape of one of Chogyam Trungpa's talks, and discussion of the tape. On Thursday evening there was an hour of meditation followed by tea and informal talk. On alternate Sundays there was day-long meditation from 9:00 A.M. to 10:00 P.M., interspersed with eating and work periods; on the other Sundays there was an hour of meditation in the evening, and then a business meeting. I had the opportunity to participate in a meditation session on a Thursday evening.

Meetings were held in a warehouse which the meditation center shared with a group of artists. (I understand that the center has since moved to other quarters.) The outside door opened into a hallway, to the left of which was a small shrine room which served also as a meditation hall. Behind the entrance hall and shrine room were a restroom and a large carpeted room without furniture, which served as a meeting room. Beyond the meeting room was a kitchen.

The shrine room contained a two-level altar. At the back of the altar, against the wall, was a painted thanka on a red silk background, flanked by two representations of the "knot of eternity," in red on a yellow background. (The knot of eternity stands for the indestructable quality of meditation and its discovery of sunyata or "emptiness.") On the upper stage of the altar, next to the wall, the central position was occupied by a crystal ball. On each side of the crystal ball was a vase of flowers and in front of it was a bell surrounded by four small piles of rice. This portion of the altar was green; the lower portion of the altar was red. On it were flowers, candles, incense, a vase, and seven glasses of water. The round cushions, used for meditation before the shrine, were red and yellow. (Red and yellow are colors associated with Tibetan Buddhism—the cushions at Karma Dzong also were red and yellow.)

In the meditation session one member of the group sat at center front, before the shrine, while all members sat on cushions facing the altar. Most were seated cross-legged, but not necessarily in full-lotus or half-lotus position. The hands of some were folded, but others placed their hands on their thighs. The meditation session began when the leader struck a metal percussion instrument shaped something like a bottle. Then, after all had repeated the Threefold Refuge in Sanskrit, everyone chanted three times:

> Namo:
> Earth, water, fire, and all the elements,
> The animate and the inanimate, the trees and the
>     greenery and so on,
> All partake of the nature of self-existing
>     equanimity,
>     Which is quite simply what the Great Wrathful
>     One is.[42]
> I take refuge with body, speech and mind.
> In order to free those who have suffered at the
>     hands of the Three Lords of Materialism
> And have become afraid of external phenomena,
>     which are their own projections,
> I take this vow in meditation.

After an hour of meditation the leader again struck the metal drum and all chanted, three times, the well-known dharani, "Gate, gate, para gate, para samgate, Bodhi svaha!"

*New developments.* Since 1972 the programs sponsored by Chogyam Trungpa and his followers have increased in number and diversity. Basically, there are two organizations, Vajradhatu and Nalanda, each having several branches.[43]

Vajradhatu is described as an association of Buddhist churches having as its purpose "to further the study and practice of Hinayana, Mahayana and Vajrayana Buddhism."[44] The branches of Vajradhatu in 1974 included Karma Dzong Meditation Center, the Rocky Mountain Dharma Center, Tail of the Tiger, a retreat center on Greenhorn Mountain in Huerfano County, Colorado, and several urban study centers (Dharmadatus) located in major cities.[45] The latter have increased in number in the past three years.

Nalanda is a "non-sectarian non-profit educational and social service institution."[46] In early 1974 it included Naropa Institute, a degree-granting educational institution in Boulder, Colorado, which began operation in the summer of 1974; the Maitri Therapeutic Community, a center for mentally disturbed young adults located on a farm in Elizabethtown, New York; the Green Mountain Community School in Maine for alienated teen-agers, which uses farming and sailing as media for independence training and self-growth; and Padma Jong, a community of artists, craftsmen, and musicians on 275 acres in Mendocino County, California. The school and arts community opened in the fall of 1974.[47]

*Meditation, as taught by Chogyam Trungpa.* In explaining Buddhist meditation, Chogyam Trungpa states first that it differs from the meditation of Christianity and that in some other Oriental religions in not involving a concept of some "higher Being" with which one tries to communicate.[48] Rather, since there is no belief in a higher outside power in Buddhism, there is no seeking for something higher, but rather seeking to see what *is*. All of the techniques, according to Trungpa, are techniques for "opening oneself."[49]

Trungpa states that in Buddhist meditation practice, "the concept of *nowness* plays an important part. Whatever one does...is not aimed at achieving a higher state or at following some theory or ideal, but simply...trying to see what is here and now."[50] One means of becoming aware of the present moment is to concentrate on breathing.

The basic pattern of the kind of meditation advocated by Trungpa is based on three fundamental factors: "firstly, not centralizing inwards; secondly, not having any longing to become higher; and thirdly, becoming completely identified with here and now."[51]

None of the above gives any picture of Tibetan meditation as radically different from that of Zen, or perhaps that of the Theravada school. Where are the mantras, mudras, and visualizations?

In talking with some of Trungpa's students and with Rinpoche, himself, this writer learned that although all of the students attend his lectures and seminars, as far as *practice* is concerned the techniques suggested are based on individual needs and the student's level of spiritual development. For most, meditation is on a simple level, with little if any use of mantras and mudras. For the more advanced students, more use is made of the traditional Tibetan meditational techniques, but even these are at a relatively simple level. As Rinpoche said, "They can't start at the Ph.D. level when they are just ready for kindergarten."

Not only with respect to meditation, but in other aspects of practice, Rinpoche individualizes his students. Some he encourages to read and study, others he advises *not* to do so, in terms of what they need at any particular time.

*Guru, therapist, or friend?* How does Chogyam Trungpa see his role in relation to his students? He is quite emphatic that he wants to be a friend, and not a guru. He believes that it is wrong for the teacher to impose his ego on the student, and it is partly for this reason that he does not favor uniformity in practice.

Trungpa does not view himself as a psychotherapist; yet he states that his approach is psychological, geared toward helping his students to develop "basic sanity." Much of his time is spent in counseling individual students. Apropos of this, he says, "I act as a mirror, I encourage and suggest, but I do not *tell* them what to do." However, his students are well aware that Rinpoche does not want them to abdicate from their responsibilities to society.

*Esoteric Buddhism and American society.* In an interview with Chogyam Trungpa, I asked, "As you see it, is Buddhism as practiced in Asia suitable for the United States? If not, what modifications need to be made in order for it to be most meaningful to Americans, and relevant to American society?"

In answering this question, Rinpoche pointed out that, in Asia, while the individual is growing up, Buddhism is a part of his life so that he has a natural understanding of it. Consequently, when he enters a monastery he is ready for advanced practice. In the United States, on the other hand, there is a gap between religious discipline and everyday life. When Americans begin Buddhist practice they must begin with the simple, original style developed in the seventh century. At the same time, they must develop the "Buddhist outlook." Their expectations of "perfect bliss" must be broken down, and they must, instead, look for basic sanity.

Rinpoche's ideas about this are expressed in his article, "Cutting Through."[52] He warns that when Americans who become dissatisfied with the basic teachings of Christianity become fascinated with the colorful robes and rituals of Oriental religions, and try clumsily to become Tibetans or Japanese or Burmese, they are being fascinated by externals and therefore are involving themselves in materialism. He sees this fascination with externals as a neurotic pattern—a substitute for or escape from the necessity of taking an honest look at themselves. He states also that the answer to one's disillusionment with the hypocrisy of society is not to run away from that society, but "to learn to dance with the situation, to work with it."[53] While working within society, however, Trungpa says, one must work honestly with the pattern of ego through meditation:

> The nowness of meditation is a precise way of sudden penetration into the heart of the matter. What must be penetrated? It is the heart of the past, the idea of the future and the conception of achievement in either of these that you need to cut through. You have to forget all these ambitions and hopes, and just open, look directly and thoroughly into the situation of the nowness. It will leave you completely bland, purposeless, open and speechless, because there is nothing to secure. Everything is direct, sharp and precise. This experience is described as the sword of Manjushri, the Bodhisattva of Wisdom. There is a sudden penetration of cutting, one slash of a sword which may take a fraction of a second, but with each stroke the past and future networks are severed completely. It is a very sharp sword.
>
> This is what meditation is. It cuts through the fascination of attaching ourselves to a particular colorful scene, and cuts through the expectation of a final, ideal and comfortable way of life, which has confused us. Perhaps we have thought of a spiritual life as a life of being dressed up in some particular fashion and striving to reach some level of perception or another. I have heard people say that English is the language of barbarians and that is why we have to learn Tibetan or

Sanskrit. If both languages convey what is, I see no reason to distinguish between them. In fact, what is more inspiring is that we transcend the racial and cultural divisions: as we are, we can penetrate directly into the heart of it. This is the penetration of wisdom cutting through the fascination. Once we are on the spiritual path, there can still be the demons of particular attitudes involved with further fascination. The sword of Manjushri cuts directly through that.[54]

When asked to comment about the proliferation of Buddhist monasteries in America, and the increasing number of young Americans entering monasteries, both here and abroad, Rinpoche expressed the opinion that American young people need to develop an understanding of the principle of spirituality before thinking about entering monasteries. He feels that many who enter monasteries do so on the basis of romantic notions; that if they first develop an understanding of spirituality, it will make for a more solid monastic life. He is of the opinion that, at this time, the emphasis should be on developing American yogis rather than monks.

Rinpoche was asked if he saw any patterns in the sorts of people who became interested in practicing Tibetan Buddhism, and whether or not these patterns made for problems. He said that many had already been on spiritual "trips" such as Yoga or Rama, and had read books on Buddhism. Most, he found, were reacting against established society, and one problem was to get them to return to the world. When asked specifically about drugs, he conceded that many were on drugs when they began practicing at the center. He does not specifically forbid this, but most drop the drug habit after a few months.

When I asked whether esoteric Buddhism was appropriate for Americans, Rinpoche answered, "It's a matter of timing. After they mature in their practice—in another ten or fifteen years—it would be perfect."

When asked what he saw as the future of Buddhism in this country, Trungpa said, "It is scientific and practical, so is ideal for the Western mind. If it becomes a Church it will be a failure; if it is spiritual practice it will have strong influence in all areas—art, music, psychology."

## Tarthang Tulku and Nyingma Meditation

*Tarthang Tulku, Rinpoche.* Tarthang Tulku was born to the royal family of Gellek, in east Tibet. His father was a reincarnate lama who had renounced political rule to lead a religious life. At an early age the present Rinpoche of California was recognized as one of thirty reincarnate lamas of Tarthang Monastery. At the age of seven he began his religious training under the guidance of a guru. When he was fourteen he commenced a thirteen-year period of more intensive meditation and scholastic practice under lamas representing all of the sects of Tibetan Buddhism. When the Communists entered Tibet, Tarthang Tulku was abbot of a large Nyingmapa monastery. In 1959 he fled to Sikkim, taking with him a number of valuable Sanskrit manuscripts. Being proficient in the Tibetan, Sanskrit, Pali, Hindi, and English languages, in 1962 Tarthang Tulku was sent by the Dalai Lama to teach at Sanskrit University at Benares, India. It was there that he began what was to become his life work—the task of publishing the larger part of the remaining Tibetan literary tradition. For seven years he lectured at Sanskrit University on Buddhist philosophy and practice. During this time he published several books of his own as well as limited editions of the tantras which he had brought with him from Tibet.

In 1968 Tarthang Rinpoche arrived in the United States, and in the spring of 1969 established the Tibetan Nyingmapa Meditation Center in Berkeley, California. This was the first Tibetan meditation center organized specifically for Americans. By the summer of 1971 he had sixty students and was ready to expand his operation.[55]

Tarthang Tulku is described by Jacob Needleman as a "husky, cat-like man" who, when he speaks, does so in words which "explode like fireworks or penetrate one's chest like high-velocity missiles."[56]

My initial impressions of Tarthang Tulku are recorded in my journal:

> Wednesday
>
> I saw Tarthang Tulku after waiting for an hour and a half in a small, crowded office where a pleasant young lady held forth as secretary. From time to time she got up to answer the tinkling of Rinpoche's bell or to let someone in the front door. Wednesday afternoons Tarthang Tulku devotes to interviews with prospective students and others interested in learning about the center, and a steady stream of people—young and middleaged, but all neatly dressed—went in and out of the large living room where the Tibetan guru sat on a sofa.
>
> Finally my turn came. As I entered the rather dim room where Rinpoche was sitting, wearing a simple, maroon robe, he rose to greet me, smiled, and motioned me to another sofa

across the room. He looks younger than his years (around forty), wears his hair cut short but not shaved, and has sparkling black eyes. He speaks incisively, with an air of authority, and in telegraphic style. His answers to my questions were always to the point. As I was about to leave, he questioned me about my background. When I told him that I was a psychologist, he detained me to tell me about his plans for a school of Buddhist Psychology, and to ask for suggestions.

*Tibetan Nyingmapa Meditation Center.* When the Tibetan Nyingmapa Meditation Center was established in 1969, Tarthang Tulku rented a small house on Webster Street in Berkeley. For two and one-half years this served as the residence for Tarthang Tulku and his family, as well as the location for all of the center's functions. As the activities of the center expanded and the number of Tarthang's students increased, these quarters became inadequate. Consequently, the center obtained an option to purchase a thirty-seven-room fraternity house in the Berkeley Hills, and moved its base of operations to the new location. This provided a semi-monastic situation for twenty-five of Rinpoche's practicing students, rooms for meditation and study, an office, a library, print shop, and arts studio.[57] Located on roomy grounds, the ivy-covered building, guarded by a statue of a bear standing on a blue pedestal, has a gaily painted trim in red and yellow, with numerous prayer flags waving in the breeze. Unlike the Karma Dzong Center, where the door is open to the inquirer, the door to Nyingmapa Meditation Center is opened to those who push the doorbell and announce themselves.

Under the direction of Tarthang Rinpoche, a wide variety of activities at the center have developed, including meditation classes, rituals, Tibetan language classes, and study of Mahayana philosophical texts, as well as Tibetan Buddhist art studies, publication of texts and prints, and support for Tibetan refugees in India.[58]

Tarthang Tulku interviews all of those wishing to study at the center to determine whether or not they are "ready." He looks especially carefully at those who are heavily involved with drugs, since students at this center are forbidden to have anything to do with drugs.

As far as actual practice is concerned, although Americans have to start at a simple level, no adaptation of the practices developed in Tibet has been made. As stated by one of Tarthang Tulku's students,

"We believe the success and longevity of the Teachings to depend on their being presented in the purity of their original form."[59]

As he advances in his practice, the student goes through three general stages, described by one student as follows: " (1) outer, for we cannot immediately achieve realization—practices help overcome the hindrances due to karma, (2) inner, since as karmic blocks weaken, practices support the meditation (and the meditation supports the practices) ; through our actions clarity develops, and (3) secret, involving liberation from all obscurations."[60]

Students who are accepted by Tarthang Tulku begin their training with *bhum Inga*, "which has been part of both lay training and monastic training of Lamas since the inception of Nyingmapa in the 8th century A.D. . . . The new student also begins silent meditation and reads selections from an extensive reading list."[61]

The bhum Inga, which represents the student's introduction to Tibetan Buddhism, consists of five exercises, performed 100,000 times each (bhum means 100,000 in Tibetan). "Briefly, it comprises: (1) Refuge in the Buddha, Dharma, and Sangha—through prostrations, chanting mantra, and visualization; (2) Bodhisattva Vows—promising not to enter Nirvana until all sentient beings are liberated; (3) merit offering to all Buddhas and Bodhisattvas; (4) esoteric visualization of the Dhyana Buddhas; and (5) preparation for initiation through meditation on Guru Rinpoche (Padmasambhava) ."[62] All of these bhumi involve physical actions; repetition of mantras, prayers, and other formulas in Tibetan; and complex visualizations. And it all requires physical stamina as well as infinite patience.

After the student completes the five bhumi, he is ready for initiation into the esoteric Vajrayana teachings to bring him to the third stage of development—the ultimate realization state. To attain this he enters solitary meditation for about three years.[36] (In 1973 Tarthang Tulku indicated that he felt American students were not yet ready for this experience.)

In addition to the numerous classes to instruct students in the practice of Tibetan Buddhism and in the rich culture and art of Tibet, Tarthang Tulku maintains a close master-disciple relationship with each of his students. At the center, there are also many special rituals and celebrations in which all participate.

On the tenth and twenty-fifth day of the Tibetan month, a *puja* or offering mandala is performed. This is a complex ritual in which chanting, meditation, prostrations, and formalized eating and drinking are involved.[64] Traditionally, the students bring an offering, such as food, flowers, candles, and incense. Dressed in meditation robes, they chant a liturgy consisting of Prayers to Guru Padmasambhava[65] and the Nyingmapa lineage, followed by recitation of the Refuge, Bodhisattva Vow, meditation on the Guru, invocation of Vajrasattva (one of the Five Jinas), offering, prayer for the blessing, and dedication of merit to all sentient beings. The ceremony is usually punctuated by drums, cymbals, and horns, and may be accompanied by various mudras. At the close of the ceremony each participant is served a portion of each offering which is believed to have been transformed into the "elixir of life."[66]

On the full moon and new moon days of each month, from 6:00 to 10:00 P.M. there is a sutra reading ceremony. In this ceremony the Padmasambhava prayer, Refuge, and Bodhisattva Vows are recited in Tibetan. After the recitation there is mantra chanting and silent meditation.[67]

Nyung Nay is the annual traditional observance of vows by nonmonks. For a forty-eight-hour period, vows are observed strictly. During the day those observing this period of intensive practice and purification assemble at the center for performance of rituals. These consist of taking the vows, chanting mantras, and doing many prostrations. In the evening all distraction and entertainment are avoided, and at home there are rituals and meditation.[68]

Other occasions for special observances at the center are a weeklong celebration of parinirvana of Long Chen Pa (the greatest of Nyingmapa lamas); a three-day celebration of the parinirvana of the Buddha; and special puja ceremonies commemorating Rinpoche's "root" guru.[69]

Tarthang Rinpoche describes the Tibetan Nyingmapa Meditation Center as a center for religious training and practice, rather than as a center for the clinical treatment of neurotics and others with personal problems. However, he does recognize the potential value of meditation as a clinical tool and in 1973 developed a training program in Buddhist psychology with a clinical orientation.

Tarthang Tulku's students come from all over the United States, and, he says, include all kinds. Some he describes as "classical Americans," by which he means scholars and professional men and women. About one-third, he indicated, are college graduates, and some are university students. (A more recent survey states that all are college graduates.) They range in age from twenty to sixty-five, with most being in their thirties. Rinpoche believes that it is important for people to assume responsibilities in society and insists that his students work. Consequently, most have jobs.

*The Nyingma Institute.* Since the beginning of his stay in Berkeley, Tarthang Tulku has conducted seminars and lectured extensively on various aspects of Buddhist philosophy and practice, not only for the benefit of his students but also for the edification of the interested public. This program led to the establishment of the Nyingma Institute, now a degree-granting institution housed in another former fraternity house, about a mile from the meditation center in Berkeley. The institute is described as a center for the preservation and dissemination of the secular teachings of Nyingma Buddhism, and it is stressed that this is not a religious center. Some of the courses and seminars are taught by Tarthang Tulku, but others are taught by Western scholars and advanced students. The offerings include courses in philosophy, art, language, and meditational theory and practice.

The first program offered at the institute was an eight-week summer course for psychologists and others in the helping professions. Offered first in 1973, this dealt with the Nyingma approach to the promotion of personal growth. Enrolled in the program were nearly sixty professional workers in the mental health field, including this writer.

The program was under Tarthang Tulku's personal direction, and consisted of lectures, discussion, yoga exercises, and instruction in a variety of approaches to meditation, ranging from attention to breathing and listening to heart beats to complex combinations of mantra, postures, and visualizations. Although most of the participants in the program were at the institute primarily to learn techniques which could be applied in their clinical practice, the emphasis was on the fruitfulness of the participants' own practice. Most of the students, whether or not they were Buddhists, reported beneficial changes in themselves (see cases reported in chapter 11).

In the psychology program, Rinpoche consulted with each student individually, in addition to leading discussions and meditation sessions. Although never stepping down from his role as guru, and at times generating hostility in students who felt that the program should be conducted differently, the overall impression he created was of a warm, sensitive, wise, intuitive human being who is also a magnificent teacher and a skilled therapist.

Even though the Nyingma Institute is not a religious center, for those who lived there during the eight-week summer session the way of life was completely unlike that in the usual American college dormitory. All who lived in the building had housekeeping chores, ranging from cleaning the living room to helping in the kitchen. No shoes were worn in the building and people spoke in whispers or low tones so that the noise of clacking shoes or loud voices would not disturb meditators. Each meal was preceded by the mantra OM-AH-HUM, repeated three times, and meals were eaten in silence. (For some, meditation continued throughout the meal.) Since many of the participants in the program were vegetarians, no meat was served, although Nyingma Buddhists are allowed to eat meat except at certain times during the year. There was some visiting and chatting during breaks for tea, but many spent their rest periods with eyes closed, meditating. In the combination classroom-lecture hall-meditation room in the basement, students sat cross-legged on square cushions on the floor, facing Rinpoche. The lama sat in a similar position on a raised dais, his legs covered by a striped, quilted, satin lap-robe. On the walls of the classroom at the front were small pictures of various Buddhas and bodhisattvas, and usually a stick of incense burned in a container on a small table beside Rinpoche.

*The Phoenix Center.* A recent development is the establishment of the Tibetan Nyingma Institute of Phoenix. Organized under the guidance of Tarthang Tulku, it provides a meditation center for thirty practitioners, and sponsors a shop for the sale of Buddhist and metaphysical books. Tarthang Tulku conducts monthly seminars and gives scheduled talks. He also gives talks to other groups in various parts of the country.

*The country center.* In 1975, the Tibetan Nyingma Meditation Center acquired 900 wooded acres in Northern California's Sonoma County. This is the site for the projected Odiyan Tibetan Nyingma Culture Center. The new country center will be a temple-educational-residential complex. It will serve not only as a retreat and country center for the lama's American students, but also as a dwelling place and means of livelihood for Tibetan refugees. Various crafts will be practiced here, with the products marketed, and there will be farming on a small scale.

*Tarthang's Views on Buddhism for Americans.* Whereas Chogyam Trungpa rejects the role of guru and sees himself as a wise friend, Tarthang Tulku perceives himself as a spiritual guide and teacher, and as one whose mission it is to bring to the West the literature, art, religion, and philosophy of Tibet.

Tarthang Tulku views Buddhism in general, and Nyingma Buddhism in particular, as good for America. From the standpoint of the social good, he sees the Buddhist ideals of humanity, peace, harmony, and love as being what America needs. He also sees meditation as being good for Americans. Among the Buddhist sects, he believes Nyingmapa to be especially appropriate for the West, because of its looseness and flexibility.

In discussing the differences between Buddhist practices in Tibet and those in the United States, the Rinpoche said, "In Tibet, monastery is away from world. Here is more social interest. Buddhism in America is for teachers, for families—to make happy families."

In commenting about Americans interested in Buddhism, Tarthang Tulku noted that they tend to be impatient. Although some of them have read many books on Buddhism, this has served to create confusion rather than an understanding of Eastern philosophy. For these reasons, Americans have to start at a simple level. However, he conceded, they are very intelligent, and reach high intellectually. Many professors and others will study and practice hard, and perhaps will attain wisdom. However, it is difficult for Americans to break through concepts to avoid confusing delusions with reality.

## Trungpa and Tarthang—a Comparison

The Tibetan Nyingmapa Meditation Center and its affiliates, and the various centers with which Chogyam Trungpa is associated, have been chosen as examples of Tibetan Buddhism because while they represent different approaches, they do have features in common.

Both Rinpoches recognize that Americans who are accustomed to intellectualization, and have not grown up in an Asian culture, will have to start their practice at an elementary level. Both believe, also, that Tibetan Buddhism in America will be Buddhism which will become a way of life in the family, in American society, in the context of discharging one's responsibilities to society, rather than something which develops in the context of a monastery. Both are concerned, also, with encouraging academic study as a means of enhancing knowledge and appreciation of the literary, religious, and artistic heritage of Tibet. However, whereas Tarhtang Tulku attempts to develop a practice which is similar to that in a Tibetan monastery, and views his role as that of the guru, Trungpa Tulku dislikes the guru role. Trungpa also believes that encouraging Americans to try to behave like Tibetans is a hindrance to their spiritual development because it encourages them to remain attached to externals. Also, whereas

Trungpa Rinpoche believes that most Americans are not yet ready for esoteric Buddhism, Tarthang Rinpoche does not hesitate to introduce them to both exoteric and esoteric Buddhism. The meditation centers mentioned above are two of many. Others are the Ewam Choden Tibetan Buddhist Center of the Sakyapa sect under the direction of Lama Kunga and located in Kensington, California; the Retreat House of the Yellow Hat sect under Reverend Geshe Wangjal, in Washington, New Jersey; and the monastery of the Kargyupa sect in Freewood Acres, New Jersey. These by no means exhaust the list of centers, and a number of lamas are working with small groups in various cities.

## SHINGON

### Shingon Buddhism

Shingon ("true word") is the Japanese form of a Vajrayana system introduced into China about 720 A.D., and was established in Japan in 816. Its Japanese founder was Kukai, usually known by his posthumous name, Kobo Daishi (774–835). It is a branch of so-called Right-handed Tantrism, with practices which include not only mantras, but initiations, ritual gestures, mandalas, and contemplations.[70] Meditational practices, however, are engaged in only by priests, monks, and nuns.

The Shingon sect is based mainly on the Mahavairocana Sutra (Great Sun Sutra) and the Vajrashekarayoga Sutra (Diamond Sutra). These texts describe a pantheon heavily influenced by Hinduism, containing numerous divinities not purely Buddhist.[71] Bunce describes Shingon as "a pantheistic mysticism—a mixture of realism and idealism."[72]

To clarify the Buddhist pantheon, Shingon employs two mandalas, one depicting the "ideal" and the other the dynamic aspect of the cosmos.[73] In the Shingon rituals, these mandalas are placed on the ceremonial dais, and the mysterious powers attributed to the figures and symbols are evoked by the worshiper by means of the appropriate body posture, hand gestures, and mystical formulas.[74]

The cosmic Buddha Vairocana is presumably the object of worship in Shingon Buddhism. However, a figure of Kukai is also usually enshrined on the altar and is an object of worship. A part of the ritual involves recitation of the formula, "Namu Daishi Henjo Kongo," which means, "Hail to the Great Master who is shining upon us like a diamond."[75]

*Koyasan in America*

Shingon came to America in 1912, with the establishment of the Koyasan Buddhist Temple and mission in Los Angeles. (It is named for Mt. Koya, the place of its founding in Japan.) The sect now has five churches in the United States, with four of these being on the West Coast. With the exception of the large headquarters temple, all of the churches are very small, and most are located in one-room apartments. The total Shingon membership in this country is probably about fifteen hundred families, practically all of Japanese ancestry.

The Los Angeles temple with its elaborate, ornate altar is located in the heart of the "Little Tokyo" area. It serves as a community center for the Japanese population of the area and organizes and administers many types of activity programs.

Koyasan follows the pattern of most BCA churches in having Sunday School in English, a Sunday church service in English for young people, and a service for adults in Japanese. It also has a family service on an evening during the week. Worshipers sit in pews. Although its worship service has perhaps fewer Protestant accretions than that of BCA, its general format is quite similar, with sermon, gatha, presentation of incense, and chanting of sutras. It does not, of course, include "Namu Amida Butsu," since Amida is not a central figure in the Shingon pantheon. Instead, the Shingon Buddhist repeats three times, in Japanese, "Hail to the Universal Buddha, Great Sun, Jewel of Lotus! Adoration to the Universal Buddha of the Great Seal! Turn the Wheels of Eternal Compassion!" One also repeats, three times, "I put my faith in Sakyamuni Buddha. I put my faith in Kobo Daishi."[76]

The lay worshiper of Shingon faith in America does not make use of many mantras or mudras, and he does not engage in meditation. Occasionally, however, there are special services which are more elaborate and make use of fire symbolism.

Shingon has the potentiality for the same kind of appeal which Tibetan Buddhism has in the United States. However, unless the monastic, meditational, and esoteric aspects become available to lay adherents, its chances for making any significant impact on American society seem very slight.

## SHUGENDO

*The Nature of Shugendo*

A second example of Japanese tantrism is *Shugendo*, meaning "Way of Spiritual Power."[77] This is a system of beliefs combined with magic-ascetic practices which take place principally in the setting of sacred mountains. Its adherents are referred to as *Yamabushi*, that is, "ones who lie down or sleep in the mountains."[78]

Practitioners of Shugendo trace their origins to the eighth century and designate as their founder a semi-legendary figure named En on Obasoku (Ozunu). In actuality, however, the practices of the Yamabushi had their origins in Japanese prehistory when various religious beliefs combined to form an indigenous body of "mountain beliefs" or "mountain creeds," known as *sengaku shinko*. In its broadest sense, sengaku shinko includes not only mountain worship but also "mythology, folk beliefs, festivals, rituals, asceticism, shrine and temple buildings, all of whose religious import is related to the mountain as a religious site."[79]

Although the origins of Shugendo are indigenous, beliefs and practices of Taoism and Buddhism came to be incorporated into it. As it became organized on a doctrinal and ritual basis, it drew heavily on two streams of Japanese esoteric Buddhism, Tendai and Shingon.[80]

As in Shingon, the principal object of veneration in Shugendo is the Sun Buddha Vairocana. Shugendo has also taken from Shingon the idea of "becoming a Buddha in this very body." For the Yamabushi, the ascetic retreat in sacred mountains and the performing of rituals in the mountains are considered means of attaining this goal.[81]

Outdoor fire practices are prominent in Shugendo.[82] However, most important are the ascetic practices during mountain retreat. These practices are representations of the ten stages of movement from hell to the perfection of Buddha. These stages are based on the traditional Buddhist concept of different stages of existence.[83] In Shugendo these have been translated into specific practices connected with the mountains.[84]

## Yamabushi in America—Kailas Shugendo

The Yamabushi tradition is carried out in America in the practices of the Kailas Shugendo. This is a group of Vajrayana students in San Francisco, under the spiritual leadership of Lama Anagarika Govinda. The group was organized by Dr. Neville Warwick, who is called *Ajari*, a title conferred upon those who have completed certain studies as well as ascetic practices.[85] Dr. Warwick serves as teacher of the group.

Warwick designates the practice of his group as *Obas'kudo*, or the way of Obasoku.[86]

> The Obas'kudo practices Buddhism in the light of the wisdom of equality; recognizing that all beings are the Bud-

dha, he does not adhere to the conventional ideas of the priest versus the layman, to the isolationism of the monastic life, or to the ideas concerning monkhood and sexuality. Rather, the Obas'kudo utilizes the Tantric means, encompassing all the elements of life, and weaving them into a meaningful foundation for spiritual practice. Basic to the practice of this tantracism is the development of the relationship between men and women, where in the context of sexuality is sought a means to the enlightenment experience itself.

Shugendo encourages community life in order that people may work more creatively and efficiently toward their ideals, as well as to effect an economic liberation, a basic necessity to all creative individuals....

The Yamabushi ... follow a very rich ritual life cycle, which involves living alternately in both the working atmosphere of the cities, and in the mountains. Daily ritual activity includes morning and evening GOMA (fire offering), cold water practices, chanting, music, and MANTRA practice throughout the day.

Each week the Yamabushi move their center of operation to one of the holy mountains within reach of the Bay area.... During their mountain confinement they practice *Shugyo* (ritual circumambulation of the mountain), *hiwatari* (fire walking), and many other practices designed to tone the body into a healthful state ... and to give the practitioners the spiritual strength and clarity of mind to deal with the problems of the people and our different times.[87]

Warwick designates the mandala as the key to the understanding of maleness/femaleness in the universe. He sees everyone as containing both male and female elements as the result of past incarnations, and suggests that one should see the compassion/womb mandala in everyone. He states that sexuality has a deeply religious and spiritual function, saying, "It is a rite and set to liturgy. The partners must respect each other as the two mandalas, the vajradhatu (diamond) and the Garbhadhatu (womb), the union of which produces the ecstasy of infinite love, which extends to all living in countless universes."[88]

Members of the Shugendo of San Francisco are mostly Caucasians. On ceremonial occasions they wear the blue and white checkered robes favored by the sect. Their most colorful rite, the fire walk, is performed not just on mountains, but also in other open places, such as beaches.

As yet, Shugendo in America is a small group. It would seem, also, that it would be limited in its growth since there must be appropriate mountains available and the austerities of mountain practice demand a considerable physical stamina. Yet, the stress on esoteric practices, the lack of differentiation between priests and lay members, and the rigorous effort and discipline demanded will continue to appeal to some Americans.

Looking at the three varieties of Tantric Buddhism found in America, some generalizations can be made: (1) the sect (Shingon) which distinguishes between practices for priests and laymen, and which utilizes congregational worship of a type similar to that found in BCA, has little appeal for non-Orientals; (2) sects stressing meditation, the master-disciple relation, and strenuous self-discipline—with or without emphasis on esoteric practices—have a considerable appeal for Americans of all ages and are increasing in their influence; and (3) of the three modes of trantric Buddhism, the Tibetan variety is increasing its membership most rapidly in the 1970s. However, since the first Tibetan meditation center organized specifically for Americans was founded as recently as 1969, it is not yet possible to predict the future of Tibetan Buddhism in America.

# 6

# Nichiren Shoshu of America: A Religion of Peace through Happiness

Most of the young men and women have a fresh and wholesome look. Their clothes are clean but casual, and their hair is neatly groomed. A few are Orientals and a few are blacks, but most are Caucasians. All have removed their shoes before entering the carpeted living room converted to worship hall. The room is in a frame dwelling on the northwest side of Chicago. One by one the worshipers have taken their places, kneeling before the altar which comprises the only furnishing in the room. It is ten o'clock on a Saturday night, at the midwest headquarters of Nichiren Shoshu of America, where Mr. Paul Liebmann, headquarters chief, meets with a group each night to lead them in the service of chanting, and to answer any questions which group members may wish to ask.

The altar which serves as the focus of attention is black and gold, with the place of honor being occupied by the *gohonzon* (mandala), a slab of wood with Chinese characters lettered on it in black on a buff background. This is the object of worship, with the principal characters on the gohonzon saying, in Japanese, *"Namu myoho renge kyo,"* or, in English, "Hail to the Lotus Sutra of the Mystical Law." There are lighted candles on the altar, with incense burning. To one side is the large hammered metal bowl called a *kei*, which is struck to make a gong-like sound. In the center before the altar are a kneeling pad and a microphone on a low pedestal.

The young people visit informally while waiting for their leader. Then, a dark-haired, grey-eyed man of about forty enters, kneels before the gohonzon, and strikes the kei with a padded stick. With all eyes turned toward the altar and prayer beads between hands pressed palm to palm, the members of the group chant the *daimoku* or invocation—"*Nam' myoho renge kyo, nam' myoho renge kyo, nam' myoho renge kyo, nam' myoho renge kyo.*" Finally with the sounding of the gong, there is a pause in the chanting. This is followed by a very rapid chanting of the Lotus Sutra, in Japanese, and thirty minutes of chanting of the daimoku, before the question period. The chanting of each part of the sutra ends with the sounding of the gong, followed by a slow chanting of the daimoku. However, in the final continuous chanting of daimoku, the tempo picks up and the formula becomes abbreviated so that at the end the group is chanting, "*Myoho renge, myoho renge, myoho renge.*" With the leader chanting into the microphone, which also picks up the group chanting, the room reverberates with sound.

Shifting the scene to Texas, a similar performance can be observed at a chapter meeting before the gohonzon on a homemade altar in the recreation room of a ranch-style house. Here, after the chanting there is group singing. The tunes are familiar—"I've been Working on the Railroad," "I'm a Yankee Doodle Dandy," and "When You're Smiling"—but the words are changed to make them into Nichiren Shoshu "commercials." For example, "When You're Smiling," becomes "When You're Chanting." Pretty girls lead the singing with hips snapping and arms flashing, as everyone claps in time to the music. After each song there is a vigorous shouting of, "*Eh, eh, oh! Eh, eh, oh! Eh, eh, oh!*"—the Japanese equivalent of "Hip, hip, hooray!" The chapter leader makes some announcements, and asks if there are any guests present. There are four guests, who are introduced and welcomed. Then comes what is perhaps the most important part of the meeting—the giving of testimonials as each person rises to tell how the gohonzon has helped him. A teen-aged girl speaks of having lost the hate with which she used to be filled; an older man tells of having been cured of his arthritis; a college boy talks of improved study habits; a ranch hand says that he got a raise. All of these changes are believed to be the result of chanting and faith in the gohonzon.

In a university dormitory in Florida, four young men are discussing the state of the world, the Arab-Israeli conflict, the energy crisis, pollution, Watergate, religion, philosophy, inflation, the cost of higher education, the unfairness of professors, and the job market. Names mentioned include Jesus Christ, Gautama Buddha, Immanuel Kant, David Hume, John Locke, George Herbert Mead, Richard Nixon, Gerald Ford, Henry Kissinger, Karl Marx, and Nichiren Daishonin. One earnest young man, a Latin-American, commands the attention of the others. "I don't ask you to take my word for it," he says. "All I ask is that you *try* it and see if you're not happier than you've ever been in your whole life. And if you can conceive of war in a world where everyone is happy—in a world dominated by *humanistic* values based on *science*—then you don't really understand what Nichiren Daishonin[1] is trying to say."

Standing in a crowded New York subway train, a middle-aged Jewish secretary is riding to work. She clutches an overhead strap with her left hand as she concentrates on the magazine held tightly in her right hand. It is the latest issue of the *NSA Quarterly*, which she is studying in preparation for Nichiren Shoshu Study Department examinations. Until recently, she hasn't even considered the possibility of taking the exams. But the headquarters chief has encouraged her to study, saying that people of her intelligence are needed as discussion leaders. So she'll do the best she can. Besides, after saying daimoku and studying the philosophy of Nichiren Daishonin, the course in theories of education which she's taking at New York University is making so much more sense to her. She's found that she is able to get along much better with her boss and coworkers, too. Everyone has noticed how she glows with happiness all the time.

These four scenes represent some of the many facets of Nichiren Shoshu (the True Sect of Nichiren), a fast-growing American version of Japan's Soka Gakkai, or "Value Creation Society." In the United States, this group has grown from a membership of 30,000 in 1965 to over 200,000 in 1974.

This chapter deals with the nature, development, and goals of Soka Gakkai and its sister organization, Nichiren Shoshu Academy.

## SOKA GAKKAI IN JAPAN

Soka Gakkai is a Japanese organization of lay believers in Nichiren Orthodox Sect Buddhism or "True" Buddhism (Nichiren Shoshu), who are committed to the principle of using *shakubuku* (forceful persuasion) for *kosen-rufu* (world conversion).[2]

Saint Nichiren (1222–82), considered the founder of Nichiren Buddhism, was a nationalistic Tendai monk from southeastern Japan.

He became disturbed at the proliferation of Buddhist sects in Japan, and the failure of any to make much impact on Japan's rulers. He also was distressed about the syncretistic nature of Tendai and was convinced that its teachings had been corrupted by practices such as invoking the name of Amida Buddha to gain salvation. He saw such practices as completely ineffective in changing men's lives or solving the problems of government. He urged his followers to stop chanting the nembutsu, and to say, "Namu Myoho Renge Kyo"—"Hail to the Lotus Sutra of the Mystical Law." He did this on the basis of his contention that the Lotus Sutra set forth the most universal laws of nature.

The Lotus Sutra teaches that the path of salvation is the way of the bodhisattva, and that the eternal Buddha is absolute mercy and eventually will save all men. It promises rewards for those who receive it in faith, and punishment for those who reject it. The so-called "Mystical Law" is the law of simultaneous cause and effect, uniting past, present and future.

Nichiren applied the teachings of the Lotus Sutra when he predicted an invasion of Japan by the Mongols, and other impending perils. He was a fearless preacher, attacking the greatest religious and political leaders of his time. Because of his criticism of current Tendai practices, he was forced to leave the sect; and because of his criticism of government leaders, he was twice exiled to relatively remote and isolated areas of Japan.

Nichiren regarded himself as a prophet and as the reincarnation of Jogyo Bosatsu, one of the four chiefs of the bodhisattvas mentioned in the Lotus Sutra. Orthodox Nichiren Buddhism goes even further, claiming that Jogyo is a reincarnation of the eternal Buddha and that Nichiren and the eternal Buddha actually are one.

Nichiren's principal teachings were threefold. First, Japan has met with disasters because she has gone down the bypaths of Amidism, Shingon, Risshu,[3] Zen, and other heresies. Therefore, only by returning to the Lotus Sutra can the two calamities of foreign invasion and rebellion be avoided. Second, all possess the Buddha-nature and can achieve Buddhahood in their present condition without a change of nature. Third, the aim of the true religion is the happiness and prosperity of the people, a stable government, and a peaceful nation.[4]

After Nichiren's death, several of his disciples perpetuated his ideas and established various Nichiren sects in Japan. Most of them soon lost interest in politics, tending to become more mystical in orientation. A small minority, however, did continue in Nichiren's pattern, characterized by nationalism, militance, fanaticism, and intolerance. One such group became the Nichiren Sho sect (Nichiren Shoshu), which was a very small group until it became linked with Soka Gakkai.

## Origins and History of Soka Gakkai

The precursor of Soka Gakkai was a publishing organization called *Soka Kyoiku Gakkai* (Value Creation Education Society), organized informally in 1930 by a former elementary school principal, Tsunesaburo Makiguchi, and Makiguchi's protégé, Josei Toda. Both men converted to Nichiren Shoshu in 1928.

The formal founding of Soka Kyoiku Gakkai occurred in 1937, with Makiguchi as president and Toda chairman of the board of directors. At this time there were sixty members. The basic contention of the organization was that happiness is the principal goal of education and that the role of educators is to give guidance in the ways to achieve "benefit, good and beauty for the individual and society."[5]

As the Pacific war approached, Soka Kyoiku Gakkai came increasingly into conflict with the use of state Shinto as an instrument of government, and the organization came under surveillance. In order to escape complete proscription, the word *kyoiku* (education) was dropped from the name of the organization and greater emphasis was placed on its affiliation with Nichiren Buddhism. In July, 1943, however, Makiguchi, Toda, and twenty-one others were imprisoned, and Makiguchi died in prison in 1944.

When government harrassment began, the membership of Soka Gakkai was about 3,000. However, with the imprisonment of Makiguchi and Toda, the members dispersed and the organization became inactive. When Toda was released from prison in July, 1945, he began the task of reorganizing the society, reassembling the members, and training new leaders. In May, 1951, he was installed as second president. At this time the membership consisted of 5,000 families. By the end of 1957, there were more than 750,000 families in the group.[6]

Toda died in 1958, and was succeeded by a young disciple named Daisaku Ikeda, who became president in 1960 at the age of thirty-two. Under his leadership Soka Gakkai has continued to grow, and has made a significant showing in the field of politics.

## Soka Gakkai Membership Statistics

It is impossible to obtain accurate statistics concerning the membership of Soka Gakkai. In 1970, however, the membership figure most frequently mentioned in Soka Gakkai literature was over eight million households or sixteen million individual members in Japan. Since 1970 there has been a deemphasis of the importance of gaining new members in Japan, so it is doubtful if there has been any very substantial change since that time.

## Goals of Soka Gakkai

The stated goal of Soka Gakkai is kosen-rufu—the conversion of the world to Nichiren Shoshu, with Japan being the religious center of the world.[7] In stating his plan for world conversion, Ikeda initially indicated that Japan was to be converted first, then the rest of the Orient (starting with India), and finally the western world.[8] This plan seems to have been modified on the basis of the fact that Americans have been more receptive to Nichiren Shoshu evangelism than have Asians outside of Japan. At one time, 1979 was mentioned as the date for Nichiren Shoshu to be established as Japan's national religion.[9] More recently, Ikeda has suggested that by 1979 Soka Gakkai should have converted one-third of the Japanese people, with another one-third being sympathetic. Under these circumstances, he says, Soka Gakkai will have enough political power to implement its programs in social reconstruction and reform.[10]

For the individual member of Soka Gakkai, the purposes pertain to his own health, wealth, and happiness. The philosophical basis for these goals is found in Makiguchi's essay entitled *Kachiron* (The Theory of Value). This essay consists of a critical examination of the three Greek values of truth, goodness, and beauty. Makiguchi states that beauty and goodness are rightly designated as values, because value is relative, changeable, and related to man's happiness. On the other hand, he suggests that truth should not be called a value because truth is absolute and may make for either happiness or unhappiness. As a substitute for truth as a basic value, Makiguchi proposes "benefit" or "personal advantage."

Toda took Makiguchi's theory of value and developed it into a theory of enlightenment and human revolution, leading to world peace. He saw enlightenment (*jobutsu*) as the ultimate stage of the value-creation process. Unlike the Zen theory of satori as a breaking away from the wheel of karma into a state of nonbeing, Toda regarded enlightenment as a state of absolute happiness to be attained in this life and enjoyed in future lives. The winning of jobutsu, or the realization of personal bliss through religious faith in the gohonzon, he designated as "human revolution."[11]

Interpreting Toda's concept of human revolution and applying it in a social context, Ikeda has pointed out that a believer's personal happiness is incomplete by itself—that the goal of Soka Gakkai is not a selfish happiness to be enjoyed in solitude by the faithful, unmindful of the miseries of the rest of mankind. Rather, no man's happiness will be complete until all men are happy. Every Soka Gakkai member, therefore, for the realization of his own happiness, will devote his energies to converting others, so that eventually the attainment of kosen-rufu will usher in a millenium.[12]

Ikeda's goal for society is described in terms of "humanistic socialism," which is the unification of social and individual welfare. The humanistic socialist economy, as Ikeda sees it, will involve a redistribution of values and materials so as to maximize the value position of each member of society. This goes farther than the mere redistribution of material wealth. Although it provides for the correction of injustice and gross inequalities, at the same time it recognizes individual differences in what is regarded as necessary for human happiness.[13]

## Religious Aspects of Soka Gakkai

Nichiren Shoshu is one of nine sects within the Nichiren tradition. All members of Soka Gakkai are considered to be members of the Nichiren Sho sect, but not all Nichiren Shoshu adherents are members of Soka Gakkai.[14]

The principal temple for Nichiren Shoshu Buddhism, and the "mecca" for all Soka Gakkai members, is *Taisekiji* near Mount Fuji, where Soka Gakkai has constructed a huge ferro-concrete reception hall, dormitories, and other buildings used by the organization. An immense marble shrine on the site was completed in 1972. Some eight thousand to twenty thousand pilgrims a day are said to visit at Taisekiji, to view the relic which is purported to be a tooth of Nichiren with living flesh attached, to pay their respects at Toda's tomb, and to worship before the revered *Dai-gohonzon*. The Dai-gohonzon (Great Mandala) is a tablet of camphor wood on which is printed the daimoku. It is reported to have been inscribed by Nichiren, himself, but the authenticity of this work is denied by many Japanese scholars. Each member of the sect has a replica of this gohonzon in his home.

In the Nichiren tradition, Soka Gakkai is intolerant of other religious groups, with its members regarding Nichiren Shoshu as the only true vehicle of Buddhism. For believers, faith is presumed to aid in healing the sick, to strengthen the moral fiber of the weak, to cause one's business to prosper, and to generally promote one's success, well-being, and happiness.[15] In the act of group worship, there are endless repetitions of the daimoku, followed by reading from the Lotus Sutra, all of this accompanied by beating of drums, interspersed with the sounding of gongs. Frequently there also are testimonials, and the atmosphere is one of heightened emotion. Worship services are supplemented by discussion groups and other meetings.

### Characteristics of the Soka Gakkai Membership

Soka Gakkai has made its appeal especially to the rootless and lonely and to those in the lower class and lower middle class, who have little in the way of material security or social status and are groping for something to give them a feeling of satisfaction in life. Included in the membership are coal miners, unskilled laborers, waitresses, bar hostesses, housemaids, clerks, taxi drivers, policemen, and employers of medium and small enterprises.[16] However, although these sorts of persons comprise the bulk of the membership, in recent years the organization has made inroads into the middle-class and upper middle-class group.

### Organization of Soka Gakkai

Soka Gakkai has a hierarchical, cellular structure. The president and vice presidents are at the top, and under them are the general director, general administrators, and board of directors. The general administrators include the heads of various committees and bureaus. In 1970 the organizational structure showed regional divisions, general chapters, chapters, districts, groups, and units. In addition, responsible to the general director were directors of the youth division, women's division, student division, theory department, study department, financial department, pilgrimage department, culture bureau, and various minor departments. (Since 1970 there have been only minor changes in this structure.)

Although the members of Soka Gakkai claim to be pacifistic, the organizational structure has a quasi-military character and when Soka Gakkai mobilizes its members it is with bands, marching, singing, and waving of flags.

### Recruitment and Initiation

Playing a major role in recruiting members for Soka Gakkai has been the technique known as *shakubuku*, which was developed by Toda and taught to all Soka Gakkai initiates. As Toda taught it, shakubuku consisted of an aggressive means of propagating the Nichiren Shoshu faith by attacking all competing faiths, propounding the values of Nichiren Shoshu as the one true faith, calling attention to the calamities which might befall one who was not converted, and exerting pressure to persuade people to worship the gohonzon at Taisekiji.[17] The individual practicing shakubuku did not take "no" for an answer, and occasionally might use physical force if words would not do the job.

In recruiting campaigns of Toda's day, overenthusiastic Soka Gakkai youths surrounded the homes of potential members, shouted slogans or banged on drums, and refused to leave until at least one representative of the household had signed up as a member. They were satisfied with only one member from each household, because it was the duty of each recruit to convince other members of the family to join the organization. Recruits were constantly urged to deliver the entire household, and to attend all of the meetings called by the block leader.[18]

Since 1964, Ikeda has advocated a less aggressive type of propagation technique than that promoted by Toda. White has described this as "soft-sell shakubuku."[19] As the style of propagation has shifted from hard-sell to soft-sell, there has been less confrontation in the streets or the target person's home, with most attempts at conversion taking place at discussion meetings to which the prospect has been invited as a guest.

The dedication of the new temple at Taisekiji in 1972 marked the end of the "propagational phase" in the history of Soka Gakkai in Japan, and the beginning of the "ceremonial phase." In the ceremonial phase there is less emphasis on shakubuku and recruitment of new members, with more emphasis on the quality of religious practice.

Although shakubuku is less aggressive now than it was a few years ago and is being deemphasized as Soka Gakkai moves into the ceremonial phase, discipline within the organization is quite tight. Once an individual agrees to become a member, he is assigned to a block unit, the leaders of which keep him under surveillance and discourage any deviation from the expected behavior. The recruit undergoes an initiation at the local temple, and receives his own gohonzon. Then he must participate in daily chanting of daimoku and parts of the Lotus Sutra, practice shakubuku, and study Nichiren Shoshu doctrine. He is expected to attend block discussion meetings once a week, go to indoctrination lectures, subscribe to the Soka Gakkai publications, and make a pilgrimage to Taisekiji.[20]

## Soka Gakkai in Politics

Although classed as a religious organization, Soka Gakkai has been politically active in Japan since 1955, when it got fifty-two of fifty-three candidates elected in local elections. At first all of its candidates ran as members of the "Fair Politics League." In 1962, this became the "Fair and Brightness Association." Each of these organizations served as the political arm of Soka Gakkai. However, in response to complaints about the unconstitutionality of the religious exercise of political authority, in 1964 Soka Gakkai organized a political party, called *Komeito* (Clean Government Party). It was described as being independent of Soka Gakkai, but actually consisted of Gakkai members and was organized to further the goals of the parent organization.

Until recently, the record of Komeito in politics was impressive, and it came to rank third in terms of number of seats held in the Diet (Parliament).[21] In the 1972 general elections, however, its performance was relatively poor, with a number of its seats in the Diet being lost to Socialist candidates. Its poor showing in this election has been attributed to the fact that, in 1970, Ikeda forced the resignation from Soka Gakkai of all Komeito leaders and candidates. This was done to make unequivocal the separation of the political and religious organizations. With this separation, there no longer is the pressure for the Soka Gakkai membership to vote for Komeito candidates. Also, the Komeito platform is not sufficiently unique to make it clear to Soka Gakkai members that they would benefit by electing these candidates.

## NICHIREN SHOSHU IN AMERICA

### History of Nichiren Shoshu in America

Nichiren Shoshu Soka Gakkai first appeared in America in 1960, when President Ikeda established chapters in California and South America. Its members in the United States at first consisted mostly of persons of Japanese ancestry, plus a few Caucasian and black ex-G.I.'s who had married Japanese women while on military duty in Japan. The membership in the early days, also, was drawn principally from the families of small businessmen. The organization in North America grew quite rapidly, and in 1963 the American office was a general chapter which comprised ten chapters. By 1965 the membership was increasing at the rate of about one thousand per month. By 1967, however, it appeared that the rate of growth of Soka Gakkai in America would begin to decline, if recruiting efforts continued to be centered on the Japanese-American population.

Starting in 1967, new shakubuku drives were aimed at non-Orientals. Since then, ninety-five percent of the new converts have been persons of non-Oriental background, and the membership has increased nearly eightfold. The North American general chapter of Nichiren Shoshu Soka Gakkai became the North American joint headquarters, with a joint headquarters chief responsible to the Soka Gakkai board of directors in Japan. Next, Nichiren Shoshu of America came into being as a separate organization, with its own general director. Finally, the name was changed to Nichiren Shoshu Academy, embracing groups in North America, Central America, South America, and the Caribbean. Symbolizing the identity of NSA as an American organization, the former joint headquarters chief, Mr. Masayasu Sadanaga, arranged for a legal change of name and became General Director George M. Williams. In contrast to the 10 chapters existing in 1963, by 1974 there were 258 chapters in the Nichiren Shoshu Academy with members in every state of the United States as well as in twenty other American and Caribbean countries.

Playing an important role in keeping the membership interested and involved are two NSA publications, the *World Tribune* and the *NSA Quarterly.*

Started in 1964 as a bi-monthly tabloid-sized paper, by 1974 the *World Tribune* was a full-sized newspaper published three times a week, with sixty thousand subscribers.

The *NSA Quarterly*, started in 1973, is a journal devoted primarily to the Nichiren Shoshu philosophy, as interpreted by Ikeda.

One notable development in the growth of Nichiren Shoshu in America has been the considerable increase in interest on the part of university students, especially since 1967. In 1974 there were student groups of Nichiren Shoshu members on over sixty American campuses. The student membership in NSA has stemmed largely from a program of seminars offered on college and university campuses, and from the organizing of discussion groups for college students.

Although Nichiren Shoshu in America was initially a branch of Soka Gakkai, from almost the beginning it was usually referred to as "Nichiren Shoshu" rather than as "Soka Gakkai." One reason for this was the fact that Soka Gakkai in Japan has been tied in with Japanese nationalism and politics, whereas it was desired that all overseas branches be completely nonpolitical. Another reason was the fact that the establishment of overseas branches was for the dual purpose of making progress toward the conversion of the world to the Nichiren

Shoshu faith and obtaining support of overseas members for the construction of the new temple at Taisekiji, which was to be a symbol of that world faith and its goal of world peace.

The choice of "Nichiren Shoshu of America" as the name initially selected for the autonomous American group made for confusion in the thinking of some members. Like Soka Gakkai, NSA is an organization of *laymen*. When the first chapters were established in North America, there were no Nichiren Shoshu temples in the West, so there was a tendency on the part of some members to think of their organization as a church. However, in 1967, Myohoji Temple in Etiwanda, California, and Honseiji Temple in Honolulu were opened. In 1972 a third temple, Myosenji, in Washington, D.C., was established. A Japanese priest is assigned to each of these temples. He not only conducts ceremonies in the temple, but "rides the circuit" for weddings and funerals and administers the conversion ceremony. The establishment of these temples and use of priests to conduct religious ceremonies has made it possible to establish a relationship between the lay organization and the Nichiren Sho sect which is more like that existing in Japan, and has helped to clear up some of the confusion of Americans who thought of NSA as a church. (Changing the name to Nichiren Shoshu *Academy* also helped.)

## Nichiren Shoshu Academy and President Ikeda

Although NSA and Soka Gakkai are described as separate entities and sister organizations, they have a "human link" in the person of Daisaku Ikeda. Both organizations are responsible to the head temple at Taisekiji, and Soka Gakkai President Ikeda has been designated as the official lay representative to the head temple. Hence, although organizational charts do not show NSA as being responsible to Soka Gakkai, President Ikeda's dual position means that the same person is spiritual leader for both organizations. In fact, it is Ikeda who determines policies and programs for both NSA and Soka Gakkai.

In addition to the perquisites of power and influence associated with his position as lay representative of Taisekiji, Ikeda influences the development of NSA in another way—through the traditional Buddhist relationship of master and disciple. Ikeda, himself, is the disciple and Dharma heir of Toda. He, in turn, is the master of his disciple, George Williams. Williams, as editor of the *World Tribune* and *NSA Quarterly*, as well as general director of the "little sister" organization, passes on to the NSA membership information concerning the policies, wishes, plans, decisions, and thoughts of President Ikeda.

*Administrative Structure and its Functional Significance*

The administrative structure of NSA is very similar to that of Soka Gakkai in Japan, involving a vertical line or socializing hierarchy, a peer group structure, and various front organizations.

At the top of the hierarchy is the general headquarters of NSA, located at Santa Monica, California. The general director of NSA is assisted by three executive directors, each responsible for a "territory" (Eastern, Western, Pacific). Within the territories are "area" headquarters offices, each with its director. In 1974 there were sixteen areas within the United States. Every area is divided into four or five "communities," each of which, in turn, is divided into "chapters." A chapter includes five to ten "districts," and each district consists of five to ten "groups" (*han*). At every level there is a chief or supervisor. (The organizational structure of NSA is shown in Fig. 1.)

In addition to the formal vertical administrative structure, any member who brings in a convert becomes the teacher or spiritual guide of that person. When he has brought in several converts these form an informal "unit," of which he is the recognized leader. Thus, each follower, if he does his duty in converting others, also becomes a teacher or leader, and at the same time is under the socializing influence of the one who converted him as well as of all those above him in the vertical line.

At every level in the hierarchy there are meetings. At the higher levels these may be largely administrative, but at the lower levels they are for indoctrination of the membership, as well as for the maintenance of enthusiasm and morale. In case there are leaders who are tempted to neglect their preparation for meetings, there is a system of inspection in which area chiefs visit meetings outside of their areas and write reports to be submitted to higher authorities.

After the individual has received the gohonzon and is a member of a group, he is expected to chant the daimoku and recite portions of the Lotus Sutra (do *gongyo*) in his private daily devotions at home. He is encouraged to spend as much time on this as possible and at the same time to work toward whatever he believes is necessary to bring him happiness. In addition, he is expected to attend discussion meetings, lectures, and worship services. At these meetings there will be much chanting of daimoku, reciting of sutras, singing of Nichiren Shoshu songs, listening to explanations of the philosophy of Saint Nichiren and instructions from President Ikeda, and participation in testimonial sessions. Members are urged to bring guests to meetings,

**Fig. 1. Organizational Structure of Nichiren Shoshu Academy (1974)**

NSA
General Director
Board of Directors

Territory    Territory Executive Director

Area    Area Director
Women's Division Area Supervisor
Young Men's Division Area Supervisor
Young Women's Division Area Supervisor

| | Men's Division | Women's Division | Young Men's Division | Young Women's Division |
|---|---|---|---|---|
| Community ... | Community Supervisor | Supervisor | Division Chief | Division Chief |
| Chapter ... | Chapter Chief | Chapter Chief | Subdivision Chief | Subdivision Chief |
| District ... | District Chief | | | |
| Senior Group ... | Senior Group Chief | Senior Group Chief | Senior Group Chief | Senior Group Chief |
| Group ... | Group Chief | Group Chief | Group Chief | Group Chief |
| Junior Group ... | Junior Group Chief | Junior Group Chief | Junior Group Chief | Junior Group Chief |

with each guest being regarded as a potential convert. Every member is very close to those whom he has converted. If the convert becomes discouraged or disinterested and shows signs of discontinuing his chanting, his mentor urges him to keep it up and encourages him to have faith that all good things will come if he chants with diligence.

Once an individual joins Nichiren Shoshu and becomes a member of a han, he also automatically becomes a member of a peer group. As noted by White, "Whereas the vertical line arrangement addresses itself primarily to members' individual social and psychological needs, the peer groups deal mainly in the intercommunication and mobilization of the membership."[22] The latter include four branches—the men's division, the women's division, the young men's division, and the young women's division.

The peer groups parallel the vertical structure, with supervisors or chiefs at the group, chapter, community, and area levels. They sponsor meetings of various kinds, as well as activity organizations such as the Drum and Fife Corps, the Brass Band, and the "Junior Pioneers." Although in the United States the peer groups are most often activity-oriented, they also provide further opportunities for indoctrination through group worship, lectures, exhortations, and encouragement to give testimonials. The peer groups are often used in a competitive context, also, to see which division will have the greatest number attending the national convention, which will have the greatest number making pilgrimages to Japan, which will have the greatest number of subscriptions to the *World Tribune*, and so on.

As indicated above, both the vertical line and the peer group are multipurpose in nature. Having more specific purposes in socialization, however, are the study department and the "front" organizations.

Once a person has joined Nichiren Shoshu, he is encouraged to begin preparing for the Study Department examinations. These examinations are available beginning at the junior high level. In 1970, some three thousand persons in America took the tests, which were given at sixty-five examination centers. In preparing for these examinations, candidates study relevant articles in the *World Tribune* and *NSA Quarterly*, looking for answers to the questions which the Study Department has made available to them through their leaders. They will also attend discussion and coaching sessions to help prepare themselves for the examinations.

If the applicant passes the initial test, he may now begin to prepare himself for a series of more difficult examinations. Passing these may lead to a bachelor's degree or master's degree in Buddhism. Before being awarded the degree, the student must also submit a dissertation which demonstrates his understanding of Nichiren philosophy and its applicability to modern life. The Study Department examinations and the lectures and study plans sponsored by NSA are chiefly for the purpose of indoctrinating the membership as a whole and to provide intensive doctrinal training for the future leaders of the organization. One activity of the academy, however, also fulfills an important recruitment function. This is the program of Nichiren Shoshu seminars being held on university and college campuses.

The seminar program is planned and conducted by Mr. Williams, who, in addition to being general director of NSA and editor of the *NSA Quarterly* and *World Tribune*, is also Professor of Buddhism. Over a six year period, from 1968 through 1973, he held seminars on eighty different campuses. At the seminars, Professor Williams makes the following points:

1. The meaning of True Buddhism is true humanism.

2. Nichiren Shoshu follows the stream of the Buddhist tradition, which began in India 3,000 years ago.

3. Our daily life is governed by the Law of Cause and Effect.

4. In True Buddhism of today, practice is more important than theory.

5. Human revolution is the essential ingredient missing in our society.

6. Through our individual human revolution, we can effect change in the entire world.

7. Let's work together to create a society truly "of the people, by the people, for the people."[23]

The "front" groups perhaps play a less significant role in Nichiren Shoshu Academy than they do in Soka Gakkai. Of these, the most important are the musical (*min-on*) groups, the members of which are not all members of Nichiren Shoshu. The fact that these are not secular groups but are tied in with Nichiren Shoshu's indoctrination program is reflected in the practice schedules for bands and orchestras, which include time set aside for daimoku, gongyo, and testimonials.

As in Japan, the pilgrimage program is active in the United States. Each summer a sizable group representing NSA makes the trip to Taisekiji and comes home with a new enthusiasm for propagating the faith.

## Membership

At the end of 1970, Nichiren Shoshu of America issued a membership figure of approximately 200,000.[24] This figure represented the total number in America who had committed themselves to Nichiren Shoshu, from which had been subtracted an estimate of the probable number who had dropped out or become inactive. At that time, with shakubuku campaigns producing almost unbelievably fantastic results in terms of new members reported each month, Ikeda and the NSA leadership made the decision to deemphasize the importance of increasing the membership so rapidly, and to place more emphasis on the quality of practice. It was hoped that the result of this would be a reduction in the dropout rate. Despite this decision at the policy-making level, however, it seemed that the chapters in 1974 were still placing a great deal of emphasis on the importance of gaining new members, and that the members were very much involved in shakubuku. At that time the total membership for NSA was said to be 230,000, but no separate figures were given for the United States.[25]

Nichiren Shoshu is the only Buddhist group in the United States to have published detailed demographic data. (These are presented in Part 3.) The participant-observer attending NSA meetings in Chicago, New York, and Los Angeles will note that, in the East and Midwest, there are many more non-Orientals than persons of Japanese ancestry at the meetings, but that on the West Coast those of Japanese ancestry are frequently as numerous as non-Orientals; that there are many more Orientals attending these meetings than are found in Zen groups; that other minority groups—Latin-Americans and blacks—are more heavily represented than in most Buddhist sects in America, but are less numerous than "Anglos"; that members come from all socioeconomic classes, but that there are more housewives and more in the unskilled and semi-skilled categories than is true of those affiliated with Zen groups; that the many college students attending meetings are as enthusiastic and sincere as those with less education.

*Nichiren Shoshu in America versus Soka Gakkai in Japan*

*Philosophy and programs.* In both Japan and the United States, the goals and programs of Nichiren Shoshu are based on the philosophies of Nichiren and Toda, as interpreted by Ikeda. In both countries, the works of Makiguchi are now largely ignored, with the only remnant of Makiguchi's theory of value still retained being his concept of the importance of happiness as a human value.

*The humanistic revolution and world peace.* Again, in both Japan and the United States, considerable emphasis has been placed on the importance of a humanistic revolution for the attainment of world peace, with humanism to be attained through the worldwide propagation of the "True Buddhism" of Nichiren Daishonin. More specifically, the prospective convert is told that, through faith in the gohonzon, accompanied by regular chanting of daimoku and recitation of the Lotus Sutra, he will receive whatever is needed to make him happy. As he attains happiness, his happiness will be communicated to others and he will be better able to meet their needs. When he shares the secret of his happiness with others, they, too, will begin chanting to the gohonzon and will become happy. In a world populated by happy people—people whose needs have been met, people whose faith in the gohonzon has made it possible for them to raise the level of their spiritual lives—war and conflict are impossible.

*Propagation and shakabuku.* Ikeda has stated that world peace will come when at least one third of mankind has adopted "True Buddhism"[26] and a humanistic society has been established. This is to take place in two stages, which he calls the propagation phase and the ceremonial phase. The propagation phase, when shakubuku is most important, involves building a base in society by the conversion of masses of people. The ceremonial phase refers to the creation of a new culture by the mass of the people who, as their own happiness increases and deepens, contribute to the prosperity and welfare of society and so create a new, humanistic culture.

Ikeda considers that the propagation phase has ended in Japan, and the ceremonial phase has begun. This does not mean that attempts at conversion will cease, but it does mean that there will be no vigorous shakubuku campaigns in Japan. The emphasis in Japan will now be on building a "Nichiren Shoshu trusted by and endeared to society"—in other words, to build a favorable image by contributions to the welfare of society.

Ikeda plans that in the United States and elsewhere outside of Japan the propagation phase is to continue. With the new temple at Taisekiji to be a symbol of world conversion, it is important that there be mass support from abroad. Hence, efforts at increasing the non-Japanese membership must continue. However, Ikeda has suggested that the Nichiren Shoshu organization of each country should develop its own method of propagation. The university seminars in the United States are cited as an example of this.

Techniques of shakubuku considered appropriate for America in the propagation phase of development are used also in Japan as Soka Gakkai is moving into its ceremonial phase. These are considerably less vigorous and aggressive than those used in Japan in the fifties and early sixties.

Propagation activities in NSA are on four levels: (1) the rendering of community services on the part of Nichiren Shoshu members, with these happy, service-oriented people serving as examples of what True Buddhism can do for the America people and American society; (2) lectures and seminars at universities, where students are encouraged to take a scientific approach and seek proof of the benefits of chanting by trying it for themselves; (3) the extensive use of testimonials at meetings to which guests are invited, with the guests being encouraged to join in the chanting as well as to ask questions; and (4) attempts at conversion by individual members.

Individual attempts at converting others are quite varied. Sometimes a member will notice a stranger who looks discouraged and down on his luck and will stop him on the street to invite him to a Buddhist meeting, perhaps also telling him about the benefits of chanting. This has happened quite frequently in areas of San Francisco frequented by hippies. All members are expected to tell their friends and coworkers about Nichhiren Shoshu with the stress on how True Buddhism has helped them, and are expected to invite their acquaintances to meetings. After a guest has attended a meeting, his sponsor does a follow-up, telling him how much he could be helped by chanting. In doing so, he focuses his arguments on the specific needs of the particular individual. Once the friend or acquaintance has begun chanting, his mentor makes appropriate interpretations of the good or poor fortune which ensues. For example, if he gets the job he is seeking, it is interpreted as due to the effects of chanting the daimoku. If he does not get the job, he will be given encouraging words and urged to chant all the harder.

At times shakubuku takes a Nichiren Shoshu member into the home of his prospect. Under these circumstances he is careful to be a pleasant and considerate guest.

Nichiren Shoshu in America, like its Japanese counterpart but unlike other Buddhist groups, is hostile toward other religions and sects, which it regards as "heretical." In a country with a dominant Judaeo-Christian tradition, conversion to Buddhism frequently is vigorously opposed by the families of prospective converts. For this reason, opposition to Judaism and Christianity is played down in dealing with the families of American converts, and emphasis is placed on the positive values of chanting.

In the past there have been problems with keeping members whose families have been unsympathetic, as well as members who have taken the gohonzon without really knowing much about Nichiren Shoshu. For this reason, in the early 1970s it became official policy of Nichiren Shoshu in America to accept a convert as a member of the organization only after he had attended at least three discussion meetings, his family had agreed to his joining, and he had been interviewed by a senior leader.[27] (It seems in the middle seventies that there is not strict adherence to this policy.)

*Politics, nationalism, and patriotism.* The founder of Nichiren Buddhism was, above all, a political man, devoting much time and attention to criticism of the Japanese government. Soka Gakkai in Japan, also, has been very much involved in politics. In contrast, the official policy has always been that Nichiren Shoshu outside of Japan will not be involved in politics. This policy is carried out very meticulously, even to the point of Mr. Williams's refusal to endorse any candidate running for public office. Furthermore, in Japan as well as other countries, the concept of a *world* religion, rather than a religion in which non-Japanese submit to the tutelage of the more enlightened Japanese, is now encouraged.

In Japan until recently Soka Gakkai's program was geared mostly to what was good for Japan and would contribute to its glory. In contrast, members of Nichiren Shoshu in America have always been encouraged to think of their religion in terms of what it could contribute to the realization of American values. For example, in 1969, the national convention in Washington had as its theme, "The Spirit of 1776," and in 1975–76, the American Bicentennial is being stressed. General Director Williams, speaking as an American, said, "Only Nichiren Shoshu can actualize our forefathers' dream of a perfect democracy."[28] Conforming with this policy of making NSA a patriotic organization is the fact that the American flag flies over all Nichiren Shoshu buildings in this country, with the flags flying over the Denver and Seattle headquarters being certified as having flown over the Capitol in Washington, D.C.

*Use of the Japanese language.* Whether one is a Nichiren Shoshu member in Detroit, Mexico City, Paris, or Bonn, the convert to True Buddhism will repeat the daimoku, using the words, "*Namu myoho renge kyo.*" He will also "do *gongyo,*" repeating the words of the Lotus Sutra in the Japanese pronunciation of the Chinese transliteration of the original Sanskrit version. In addition, he will memorize what he has been told are Buddhist terms—words such as *daishonin* (great saint), *gohonzon* (mandala symbolizing the eternal Buddha), *kosen-rufu* (conversion of the world to Nichiren Shoshu), *mappo* (Latter Day of the Law, that is, the present, degenerate era), *ichinen-sanzen* (three thousand worlds in a single moment), and *shakubuku* ("break and flatten"—propagation of Nichiren Shoshu). Although all of these terms have special meanings in the context of Nichiren Shoshu, they are Japanese terms, and have an alien sound in connection with the spirit of 1776 or "actualizing the dream of our forefathers."

A senior leader from Dayton, Ohio had this to say about why the daimoku must be repeated in Japanese: "When you strike a 'C' tuning fork, another 'C' tuning fork will vibrate, but an 'A' will not." The implication is that the formula repeated in English would not strike a responsive chord in whatever is the force that makes the daimoku so effective.

### Psychological Aspects

Why has Nichiren Shoshu become so popular, even in the United States, where Nichiren's Japanese nationalism is dissonant with the concept of American superiority and where the sect's intolerance of all other religious views as heretical is in sharp contrast with the Judaeo-Christian tradition? General Director Williams explains that the reason so many Americans are chanting *"Nam' myoho renge kyo"* is because it *works*. They chant, he says, because they see their own lives changing and the lives of others transformed. He concedes that the basis for the success of the formula may be understood by studying the Lotus Sutra and Nichiren's theories. However, it is not scriptures and theories which cause people to continue chanting, but the alleviation of their suffering and the increased meaningfulness in their lives.[29]

Perhaps the nonbeliever can find a partial answer concerning the reasons for the success of Nichiren Shoshu in the United States through a psychological analysis of some of its concepts and the techniques of socialization which it employs.

*Reinforcement and behavior modification.* Most modern learning theories accept reinforcement as a central concept in the forming of new associations and acquisition of new habits. Reinforcement theory is an elaboration and refinement of older theories related to reward and punishment as essential to learning. According to these theories, behavior associated with pleasurable concomitants or consequences will tend to be repeated, and that associated with unpleasant concomitants or consequences will tend to drop out of the picture.

Coupled with the concepts and procedures involving reinforcement is what Skinner has called "shaping."[30] This is illustrated in the animal learning laboratory by rewarding the animal when he makes a movement in the direction of the desired behavior, but requiring him to come closer to the goal on each successive trial, before the reward is given.

Reinforcement techniques form the basis of a modern psychotherapeutic approach called "behavior therapy" or "behavior modification therapy," in which undesirable behavior is eliminated by associating it with unpleasant concomitants or consequences and "shaping" is used to enable the individual to learn new patterns of behavior. The behavior modification therapist believes that if an individual's behavior is altered, his personality also will change, since personality *is* behavior.

The Nichiren Shoshu convert is frequently an individual who has been lonely, discouraged, and disillusioned. What Nichiren Shoshu seeks is for him to (1) accept the gohonzon; (2) come to believe that chanting daimoku and doing gongyo are the means of obtaining what he wants and values; (3) attain what he believes will make him happy, even if it is something on a crass, material level; (4) gradually learn to chant for less selfish and less material values; (5) attain supreme happiness in his own life through human revolution; and (6) assume responsibility for helping others to have faith and in other ways to meet their needs.

When the inquirer goes to his first Nichiren Shoshu meeting, he is encouraged to try chanting for whatever he wants. Perhaps he needs an apartment. He starts chanting, and his Nichiren Shoshu friend praises him for his diligence in chanting, at the same time urging him to chant harder and also to look harder for the apartment. Perhaps at first he is unsuccessful, but he continues to receive praise for his chanting, his apartment-hunting activities, and his fortitude in not giving up. Perhaps his Nichiren Shoshu friends, mindful of his need, tell him of apartments they know about, or speak in his behalf to possible landlords. Eventually, he finds the apartment, so now his chanting as well as his persistence are reinforced, not only by praise and approval, but also by the reward of having found the apartment.

As time goes on, the new convert begins to bring in converts of his own. This activity also is praised, and he has the additional reinforcement of an increase in status in the hierarchy of the organization. As his feeling of self-worth increases, so does the effectiveness of his functioning, and the material needs which seemed so important before are now either met or else perceived as not *really* important. He attends discussion meetings and takes Study Department examinations, finding his reward not only in becoming a "teacher," but in the fact that learning itself is satisfying and fulfilling. As the convert progresses in his socialization, he experiences many kinds of reinforcement—praise, group acceptance, material rewards, heightened status, and others. And, as he experiences increased self-actualization, the "human revolution" becomes its own reward.

*Emphasis on the worth of the individual.* Among the characteristics of the neurotic individual frequently mentioned is a basic feeling of a lack of self-worth. The psychotherapist, on the other hand, although wanting to change his patient, regards this individual as an eminently worthwhile person, and his treatment conveys to the patient his respect for him as a person.

For the member of Nichiren Shoshu, each individual is of unconditional worth. When General Director Williams makes his opening speech in a university seminar, his first words are, "You are a Buddha." When the drug user is approached by a member of Nichiren Shoshu, there is no mention of his reprehensible habit—only of showing him the road to happiness. There is no talk of "sin" or "evil"—rather, there is talk of the individual's right to receive whatever will make him happy. One convert reported that he chanted for a "handful of drugs." He received the drugs, and also praise for his faith and diligence in chanting! It is not that drugs are approved by the organization. It is, rather, that members of Nichiren Shoshu believe firmly that if selfish needs are met, the individual will outgrow these needs and eventually will realize his Buddha nature.

The apparent permissiveness of Nichiren Shoshu with respect to personal habits is not to be construed as implying that the group looks with favor on habits that are physically damaging to the individual or harmful to society. Rather, it is the contention of NSA leaders that if the dignity and worth of the individual are respected, the person will grow in such ways as to merit that respect and will change his own values so that they will correspond to what is best for him and best for society. This is much like the contention of the therapist who says that, if the patient is respected by his therapist, he will learn that decent human relationships are possible. Learning this, he will change his concept of self, his outlook on life, and his behavior patterns.

*Auto-suggestion or self-hypnosis.* In a sense, some of the techniques used by Nichiren Shoshu may be regarded as analogous to auto-suggestion or self-hypnosis. The hypnotist, in attempting to get his subject into a receptive state, commonly speaks in a soothing monotone which has a somewhat soporific effect. There is something hypnotic, also, about the sound of *Nam' myoho renge kyo,* repeated again and again. While repeating this, the individual is also telling himself that he *will* get that job, or that apartment, or that raise. He is also focusing on the gohonzon. When he has finished chanting he is convinced that he will receive these benefits for which he has chanted. In his confidence, he approaches his task with an attitude which produces a favorable response. In essence, the success of all "positive thinking" approaches to life's problems may reflect the results of auto-suggestion.

*Self-actualization and social actualization.* Among personality theorists who have concerned themselves with the question of what are the basic needs, one of the most influential has been Abraham Maslow. Maslow's theory of motivation is in terms of a hierarchy of needs. According to this theory, the most basic of all needs is that for *homeostasis*, which must be satisfied at least reasonably well for the individual to survive. If this need is fairly well satisfied, the individual seeks satisfaction of the need for *safety*; if this is satisfied, he will seek to meet the need for *affection and belongingness*, and then the need for *esteem*. These four needs are seen as related to *deficiency* motivation, that is, they operate as motives only when the needs have not been met. If these needs *are* met, the individual then seeks *self-actualization*, together with *aesthetic* experience as well as *knowledge and understanding*. Self-actualization and the other higher-level needs differ from the lower-level needs in that they operate as *growth* motivation rather than as *deficiency* motivation. For example, the more the individual actualizes his potentialities, the more he tends to continue to actualize them. Maslow, also, viewed self-actualization as a prerequisite to the attainment of social actualization.[31]

Nichiren Shoshu's concept of the "human revolution" is very similar to Maslow's concept of self-actualization, and is perceived as being attained after the lower-level needs have been met.

When one talks with Nichiren Shoshu converts and their families, the fact that a personality change has taken place is inescapable. For most who have experienced this change, it does not appear to have been the result of a "mystical" experience, like the change which occurs in the Zen practitioner who has experienced satori. However, the descriptions of the experience of changed perceptions and feelings after satori, the descriptions of the personal bliss of jobutsu characterizing the "human revolution," and Maslow's description of the self-actualizing person are almost identical.

As noted in chapter 4, for the Zen Buddhist self-actualization is attained through zazen combined with other practices having as their purpose helping the individual toward complete "mindfulness." Among these practices is chanting. Also, in Zen, even if a person does not become enlightened, he may during zazen attain the state called *samadhi*. Some Zen masters have expressed the opinion that the Nichiren Shoshu devotee who becomes completely absorbed in his chanting may be in a state of samadhi. For the most part, they would reject the equating of jobutsu with satori but would concede the possibility that the repeated chanting of daimoku could be one path to satori and the attainment of nirvana.

For an individual of limited intelligence or a lack of interest in the more abstruse aspects of philosophy and theology, the simplicity of the magical formula, *"Nam' myoho renge kyo,"* has a strong appeal, and not much will be expected of him other than to be faithful in his chanting and to tell others of its benefits. However, for the college student and the intellectual, Nichiren's philosophy presents a challenge for serious analysis and study. It might be said, then, that Nichiren Shoshu has something in it for everyone, from the most naive to the most sophisticated.

# 7

# Chinese Buddhism for Americans

It is a cold, winter afternoon in New York's Chinatown. Crowded between souvenir shops on Mott Street is the Eastern States Buddhist Temple. At the back of the ground-floor house of worship are three pews. These serve as a convenient refuge for the somewhat ragged, elderly Chinese men who have come in for warmth and companionship. Some are reading Chinese newspapers, but most are exchanging the neighborhood gossip. Extending down the center of the room is a narrow table with chairs on either side. On the table are service books in Chinese, and black-robed Chinese women of all ages are seating themselves in preparation for the chanting which will be starting shortly. A brisk business in the sale of incense sticks is taking place at a counter in the rear, to the right. On the left, Caucasian tourists are depositing coins in a box and receiving their fortunes printed in English on tiny rolled-up scrolls. At the front is an elaborate altar on which is enthroned a large gilded image of a many-armed *Kuan-yin* (Goddess of Mercy) and a number of smaller images of various Buddhas and bodhisattvas, all against a red silk backdrop. On the altar are flowers, incense, fruit, bottles of water, and various ornaments. Paintings depicting the life of Sakyamuni Buddha line the walls of the hall.

A number of Chinese women come to kneel before the altar, presenting incense and praying silently. Then several Chinese priests enter

**Plate I. Main Hall and Annex of San Jose Buddhist Church Betsuin. Stone lanterns in front are characteristic of Japanese temples. Between the two buildings is a Japanese garden. (Photo by P. M. Itatani)**

**Plate II. Exterior of the
Cleveland Buddhist Temple.**
(Courtesy Cleveland Buddhist Temple)

**Plate III. Altar and part of
Nave, Cleveland Buddhist Temple.**
(Courtesy Cleveland Buddhist Temple)

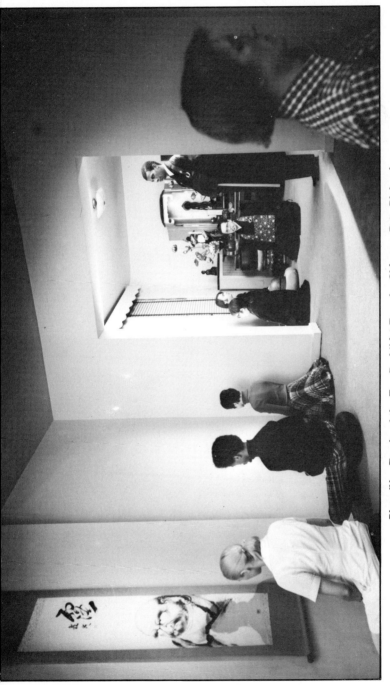

Plate IV.  Zendo of the Zen Buddhist Temple, Chicago. Rev. Richard Langlois, roshi, sits before the altar. Monitor, standing to the right, holds the kyosaku. Individual seated near the roshi is responsible for percussion instruments. Picture on the wall is of Bodhidarma, said to be the first Zen patriarch. Zazen is done facing the wall, in Soto style.

(Courtesy Zen Buddhist Temple, Chicago)

Plate V.  A Colorful Mosaic Image
of the Buddha Created by
Margaret Bruton of Carmel, California,
for Buddha's Universal Church.
(Courtesy Buddha's Universal Church)

**Plate VI.** Dedication of the Mahayana Temple, South Cairo, New York. Normally a large incense burner stands where the lectern was at the time of the dedication. (Courtesy Mrs. James Ying)

**Plate VII.   Three Buddhas in the
Great Hall, Mahayana Temple.**
(Courtesy Mrs. James Ying)

**Plate VIII.   Kuan-yin Bodhisattva,
Mahayana Temple.**
(Courtesy Mrs. James Ying)

Plate IX.  Ti-shen Temple, Mahayana Temple Complex. The Ti-shen Bodhisattva is said to be the protector of children.
(Courtesy Mrs. James Ying)

Plate X.  Kuan-yin Temple, Mahayana Temple Complex.
(Courtesy Mrs. James Ying)

and take their places next to the altar. Their heads are shaved, and each has two rows of tiny scars on his head. They are wearing brown robes, each with a black over-robe covering the left shoulder but not the right. When the talking has ceased, the priests lead the women in the chanting of a sutra, accompanied by the beat of the wooden fish.

In the Great Hall of the Temple Mahayana in the Catskills, near South Cairo, New York, a brown-and-yellow robed Chinese abbot leads a motley crowd of worshipers in the liturgy for the celebration of the Feast of Avalokitesvara Bodhisattva. As twenty to thirty persons participate in the ceremonies of prostration, circumambulation, bowing, and falsetto chanting in Chinese before the three great Buddhas, several hundred others either observe from positions on the benches extending the length of the hall or engage in other activities in the temple or its grounds. Most are Orientals, but a few are Caucasians.

In the meditation hall of the Temple of Enlightenment in the Bronx, a dozen non-Oriental Americans and several third-generation Chinese-Americans sit in cross-legged meditation. They are seated on cushions placed on the carpeted floor, facing each other across the hall as candles flicker before the Kuan-yin on the altar.

It is the Chinese New Year season in San Francisco. In the main hall of the four-story Buddha's Universal Church, the Chinese young people of the church are presenting a new chapter of the *Amitabha* Play. This is their closing night, and even after nineteen performances they are still good. The choir, too, is doing unusually well tonight. The audience is mostly well-dressed, prosperous Orientals, with a few Caucasians, and one black.

In another part of San Francisco is the Gold Mountain Temple, a monastery converted from a warehouse, where robed monks, nuns, and disciples are joined by more informally-clad inquirers, all circumambulating the Buddha Hall while chanting, *"Kuan-yin P'u-sa, Kuan-yin P'u-sa"* (Avalokitesvara Bodhisattva). Soon they will seat themselves on the benches extending down either side of the hall, to listen to the lecture given by a Dharma master seated on the dais in front of three large Buddhas. The lecturer is dressed in a yellow robe with red outer garment over one shoulder. Monks, nuns, and novices are dressed in gray with brown over-robes or brown with black. Both monks and nuns have shaven heads, with the small scars characteristic of Chinese who have been initiated into the Sangha. The lecturer, a young Caucasian, will deliver his lecture first in Mandarin, and then in English. Among the faces in his audience, two are Oriental; the remainder Caucasian.

Such is Chinese Buddhism in America. This chapter deals with the history and nature of Buddhism in China, and the forms which Chinese Buddhism takes in the United States.

## BUDDHISM IN CHINA

Like Buddhism in Tibet and Japan, the Buddhism which developed in China was influenced by indigenous religions existing before the arrival of Buddhism. As in Japan, also, the Buddhism which developed in China was a Buddhism of a number of different sects; in fact, most of the sects which thrived in Japan came there from China. However, in China the tendency toward both ecumenism and syncretism in religion has been much stronger than in Japan. In China the principal division has not been on a sectarian basis, but on the basis of *ecumenical* Buddhism versus *syncretism* of different religions. Buddhist monks and intellectuals have tended to accept the teachings of a number of different Buddhist "schools" or sects, and the working people have had a religion representing a combination of Buddhism, religious Taoism, Confucianism, folk religion, and superstition.

### History of Buddhism in China

Buddhism came to China from India and Central Asia during the Han dynasty (205 B.C.–A.D. 220), probably some time during the first century A.D.[1] After a slow start, it went through periods of alternating growth and government suppression, reaching its zenith during the great T'ang dynasty (619–907).

Under the friendly patronage of the T'ang emperors, Buddhism served all classes of society. State temples were established, Buddhist festivals became a way of life, and the temples became involved in numerous charitable as well as industrial enterprises. As a result of the latter, the temples and monasteries became the repositories of immense wealth and art. The profitable secular activities of the Buddhists prompted jealous Taoist priests to put pressure on the emperor to take strong repressive measures against Buddhism. This resulted in the suppression of the year 845, the most widespread of its kind in China. In response to an imperial edict, more than 4,600 monasteries and 40,000 temples and shrines were destroyed, over 260,000 monks and nuns were returned to the laity, all temple lands were confiscated, and images made of precious metals and stones were turned over to the government. This event marked both the apogee and the beginning of decline of Buddhism in China.

After the ninth century, Buddhism in China had periods of upsurge and decline. However, except for a few monasteries and the contributions of a small number of scholars, the Buddhism of China for the most part was a Buddho-Taoist operation mixed with superstition and folk practices, with an uneducated clergy.[2]

## Buddhism in the Chinese Republics

After the downfall of the Chinese empire and formation of the Republic in 1911, China's intellectuals began to see that Confucianism was not appropriate for modern Chinese society. Concurrently, there was an interest in science as an approach to modernization. To some intellectuals it seemed that Buddhism might be more consistent with the results of scientific research than either Confucianism or Taoism, and both Buddhist monks and intelligent laymen were eager to "purify" Buddhism.

In the early days of the Republic of China, the lay Buddhists organized themselves in a variety of efforts to revitalize and update Buddhism for modern China.[3] They sponsored study groups and devotional groups, started Buddhist publishing houses, and sponsored new seminaries for the training of Buddhist clergy. Various local and regional Buddhist Associations were formed, as well as a National Buddhist Association, organized to defend and promote Buddhist interests. However, as noted by Wright, "All the new activities were confined for the most part to the educated class, and Buddhism remained socially stratified; for the literate there were refurbished Buddhist ideas and a scattering of modern institutions; the peasantry were left with their old Sinicized cults and a corrupt and illiterate Buddho-Taoist clergy."[4]

When the Communists took over the Chinese mainland in 1949, the Republic of China moved its governmental offices to Taiwan. In 1952 the Buddhist Association of the Republic of China was reorganized in Taiwan, where, by 1966, it had 33,357 individual and 843 "organizational" members.[5] The association operates colleges and lecture groups, sponsors the study of Chinese priests in other Buddhist countries, publishes books and journals, raises money for the needy, and is responsible for coordinating contacts between Taiwan Buddhists and the world Buddhist community.[6] Other organizations also sponsor various Buddhist activities in Taiwan.

On the Chinese mainland, the government of the People's Republic of China has simultaneouly claimed to support freedom of religion and deprecated all religions. Buddhist temples which exist are supported by the government, but the number of temples as well as the number of Buddhist adherents has decreased quite markedly since the establishment of the People's Republic. In 1953 a new Chinese Buddhist Association was established on the mainland, having as its principal purpose the development of a "cadre to carry out the policy of educating Buddhists to socialism."[7] Buddhist ideology was revamped to make it consistent with Marxism and the goals of the People's Republic. Since the "cultural revolution" of 1966, most temples have been closed or put to other uses; many priests have been defrocked; and there is little visiting of temples on the part of lay worshipers. At this time, the future of Buddhism in China is quite uncertain.[8]

## Buddhist Sectarianism in China

Whereas the Japanese monk, nun, or lay disciple usually will indicate that he practices Zen, Shingon, Jodo Shinshu, or some other type of Buddhism, and almost all Buddhist temples and monasteries in Japan have a sectarian designation, this is not the case in China. Holmes Welch, in his study of Buddhist monasteries as they existed in China from 1900 to 1950, found it quite common for a Chinese monk to belong to one sect on the basis of tonsure, to another on the basis of training, and to a third on the basis of doctrinal belief and practice.[9] He found, also, that sectarian labels of temples often bore little relation to the doctrine taught, and that many monasteries carried on the joint practice of Ch'an and Pure Land.[10] Chinese Buddhism, then, tends to be ecumenical and flexible rather than sectarian, although definable sects do exist.

By the eighth century, more than ten Buddhist schools of thought had developed in China.[11] Two or three were Theravada systems; the remainder Mahayana. Some of these dropped out of the picture, so that by the twentieth century Chinese Buddhism included five schools of thought of interest to lay adherents, and another of concern only to monks and nuns.

According to Welch, the Chinese Buddhists commonly divide their schools and sects into three main categories: "teaching" or "doctrinal" schools; "lineal" schools, and the Vinaya (morality) school.[12] Of the teaching schools, the principal one found at present in Taiwan and Hong Kong, and among overseas Chinese, is the T'ien-t'ai school. The lineal schools include the several Ch'an (Zen) sects. The Vinaya school is concerned with the teaching of rules, prohibitions, and courtesies involved in monastic discipline. The Pure Land school is considered over and beyond such categories, as is the esoteric or "true word" school.

*T'ien-t'ai.* One of the most uniquely Chinese schools of Buddhism, because it embodies the Chinese genius for compromise and synthesis, is the T'ien-t'ai school.

The lineage of the T'ien-t'ai school begins with Hui-ssu (515–76), who arrived at the insight that the highest level of truth was to be found in the Lotus Sutra, and who eventually settled in a monastery on Mount T'ien-t'ai. Among his disciples at the monastery was a monk named Chih-i (558–97), who systematized the doctrines of the T'ien-t'ai school and is considered to be its founder.[13]

By Chih-i's time, many different sutras had been translated into Chinese. The diversity and contradictions in the various teachings attributed to the Buddha were troubling to Chinese Buddhists. Chih-i attempted to resolve the contradictions by classifying the sutras into five periods of teaching.

According to the "five periods" theory the Buddha, immediately after his enlightenment, preached the *Avatansaka Sutra* (Garland Sutra), but found that this was too profound for the people to whom he was preaching. Therefore, after three weeks, he started on a second period which lasted for twelve years, during which he preached the Hinayana doctrines. In the third phase, which lasted for eight years, he pointed out that the Hinayana scriptures did not contain the complete truth, and preached the more elementary of the Mahayana doctrines, explaining the bodhisattva ideal of concern for others. The fourth phase consisted of twenty-two years spent in teaching the Wisdom Sutras. Finally, in the last eight years of his life, he taught that all the vehicles or paths leading to salvation are included in the one path or vehicle taught in the Lotus Sutra.[14] By this theory, Chih-i established a unifying principle bringing together the divergent forms of Buddhism, with the Buddha depicted as having unfolded the truth as his disciples became more advanced spiritually and intellectually.[15]

In the realm of doctrine, T'ien't'ai resolves the contradictions in the formulation of the three-fold truth of emptiness, temporariness, and the middle. The truth of *emptiness* states that things have no independent existence. The truth of *temporariness* states that, although a thing is empty, it has a temporary existence as a phenomenon in the world of change. The fact that a thing is empty and temporary at the same time is called the *middle* truth. This doctrine of the three-fold truth expresses the identification of the phenomenal world with the absolute.[16]

In terms of practice, T'ien-t'ai Buddhism recognizes that there are multiple roads to enlightenment, and that not all persons will discover the truth in the same way. It teaches meditation as a means to the attainment of nirvana, but also advocates study of the sutras, repeating the name of Amitabha Buddha, and living a disciplined life.

*Ch'an.* The history and nature of Ch'an Buddhism in China, or the Chinese Dhyana school, have been discussed in the chapter on Zen. In a publication dealing with Buddhism in Taiwan, the following statement is found: "The school of contemplative and intuitive enlightenment, Ch'an views Absolute Truth as incapable of being described in words or depicted in images. Thus, it turns away from external aids, sermons, rituals, books, and even Bodhisattvas and Buddhas, to search for truth in the inner light of the individual heart."[17] Yet, in the Ch'an temple and monastery we do find images of Buddhas and bodhisattvas, and monks engage in the chanting of sutras as well as other liturgies.

The approaches to Zen meditation used in Japan had their origins in China, These include the Soto approach (Chinese: *Ts'ao tung*) and the Rinzai approach (Chinese: *Lin Chi*), as well as three other less common sects. As in Japanese Zen, Ch'an Buddhism makes use of the koan (Chinese: *Kung an*).[18] On the basis of conversations with two Ch'an masters, however, it was my impression that the Chinese approach to meditation may be more flexible than that of most Japanese Zen masters.

*Pure Land (Ching T'u).* The majority of Buddhists in Taiwan and Hong Kong are adherents of the Pure Land (Ching T'u) sect. The origins and history of this sect have been described in chapter 3. As in the case of the Japanese Jodo and Jodo Shin sects, the Ching T'u sect advocates salvation by faith. It promises believers that they may escape from the sufferings of this world after death, and enter the Western Paradise of eternal blessings. The chief instrument for attaining this Pure Land is recital of the formula, *"Namo Amit'o-fo"* ("Hail to Amitabha Buddha"), whenever the mind is free to think. "By concentrating on the Buddha the believer frees his mind from carnal desire and prepares himself for the Buddha's saving grace which will deliver the faithful from karma and transmigration."[19] In contrast to the Jodo Shin sect of Japan, which says that a single repetition of the formula is sufficient if it is said with faith, the Chinese Pure Land sect teaches that continuous repetition of the invocation carries with it greater purification than more occasional repetition of the words.[20]

*Vinaya school.* The Vinaya or Morality school involves principally the study of the 250 rules (348 for women) and 58 prohibitions that constitute the so-called vows of the *bhikshu* (monk) or *bhikshuni* (nun) and the bodhisattva vows which are taken by the individual being ordained as a monk or nun. It involves also the study of the rules and customs of the particular temple or monastery in which the aspirant to monastic orders is studying. Any temple classed as an "ordination temple" would be of the Vinaya school, and other temples training persons for the monastic life would be classed as transmitting the Vinaya teachings.

*Esoteric* or *"true word" school (Chen Yen).* The Chen Yen or "true word" school is the Chinese variety of esoteric Buddhism, sometimes called the "secret" school. In China, the members of this sect believe especially that the words of the Buddha have magical powers when repeated by the believer, but they also have made extensive use of mantras, mudras, and dharanis as well.[21] The Chen Yen school is the Chinese ancestor of Japanese Shingon, and derived from the Tantric Buddhism brought to Tibet from India (see chapter 5). In modern times, monks affiliated with this sect have frequently studied under Tibetan lamas or Japanese Shingon priests. There is a close resemblance between Chen Yen Buddhism and Shingon.

## Syncretism

Over the years, both in China and in Chinese overseas communities, Buddhism and Taoism remained institutionally separate although influencing one another. Both also were influenced by Confucianism. Taoist temples incorporated the local folk deities and sometimes some of the Buddhas and bodhisattvas. Frequently found in Taoist temples were (and still are) images of Kuan-yin. In Buddhist temples images of folk heroes and kitchen gods have commonly been installed as devas, door gods, or temple guardians, and occasionally there have been Taoist images in a Buddhist temple. However, these non-Buddhist images are not found on the main altar, and are not involved in the liturgies engaged in by Buddhist monks.

In existence since ancient times have been the temples of the popular, "classical" folk religions. It is these in which syncretism is most pronounced, with folk deities, Taoist figures, and Buddhist icons all having a place. During the Ching dynasty (1644–1911) these were proscribed, but most of them existed under the cloak of secret societies, trade guilds, or other organizations not specifically identified as religious. With the beginning of the Republican period in 1912, however, these groups not only existed more openly, but increased in number. Some of these heterodox temples had their own ordination rites for priests but frequently they operated without any formally ordained priest. How extensive the operations of these syncretistic groups are today in mainland China is uncertain, but Western observers report that they are no longer allowed to operate openly. In Taiwan, Hong Kong, and overseas Chinatowns, however, syncretism is still quite common and dominates home worship practice.

In a pamphlet describing Buddhism in Taiwan, it is stated that in almost every farmhouse in Taiwan, on the wall of the room in which ancestors are venerated, there are pictures of Buddhist, Taoist, and folk deities. In a prominent position is Kuan-yin, with servants and attendants. Below Kuan-yin is the goddess *Ma-tsu* (Holy Mother), also flanked by attendants. Known in Hong Kong as *T'ien-hou* or Queen of Heaven, she is the Taoist equivalent of Kuan-yin. Below and to the left of Ma-tsu's picture is usually a portrait of *Tu Ti Kung*, the Duke of Earth. A tax official of early imperial times, known for his kindness and leniency, he was deified after his death. Farmers believe he will protect their crops and merchants believe he will cause their businesses to prosper. To the left of the Duke may be *Tsao-chun*, the Kitchen God. The third son of the Jade Emperor, Tsao-chun is said to have been sent down from heaven to watch the kitchen because of his fondness for female company. This variety of supernatural beings indicates the tolerance and sycretism in the Chinese religious outlook, which provides the means for several faiths to live peacefully side by side.[22]

## CHINESE BUDDHISM IN AMERICA

### Chinese Buddhism and the "Associations" of Chinatown

Most (but not all) Chinese temples are located in the Chinatowns of large cities, or in towns where large numbers of Chinese settled during the nineteenth century. These temples—Buddhist, Taoist, Buddhist-Taoist mixed, and heterodox—are frequently difficult for non-Oriental Americans to locate. In fact, even the residents of Chinatown do not always know of temples other than their own.

One of the problems in locating Chinatown temples lies in the fact that many of them have no affiliation with any institutionalized church. Another lies in the fact that many of them do not have listed telephone numbers. Even if they are listed in the classified section of the telephone directory or city directory, most will not be listed as churches but as associations. Sometimes the name of the association will be such as to make it readily identifiable as a religious group, for example, Buddhist Association of the United States, Eastern States Buddhist Association, Buddhist Association of America, Quong Ming Buddhism and Taoism Society. However, most Chinese temples are sponsored by associations organized principally for secular purposes, with no religious designation in the name of the association.

A temple affiliated with an association usually occupies a room in the association headquarters, with nothing on the outside of the building to indicate that there is a temple within. Often the headquarters building itself is locked most of the time, with no personnel on hand to answer doorbells or phone calls. The personnel are also likely to be unfamiliar with English and so usually do not answer inquiries written in English.

In studying the nature and impact of Chinese Buddhism in America I was able to participate in services and arrange interviews at five Chinese Buddhist temples, go through several others, and receive some instruction in T'ien-t'ai meditation. I also had access to publications of several Chinese Buddhist groups in the United States. However, for information on the syncretistic groups with some Buddhist elements, particularly those connected with secret societies or secular associations, it was necessary to rely on the verbal reports of others who had visited these groups, supplementing their reports with information found in Mariann Wells' thesis on *Chinese Temples in California*.[23]

Where the associations are Buddhist in identity, their functions are similar to those of the Buddhist associations in China in the first half of the twentieth century, and in Taiwan today. For example, the Sino-American Buddhist Association of San Francisco has under its aegis the Gold Mountain Dhyana Monastery, the Buddhist Text Translation Society, and Vajra Bodhi Sea Publication Society. It also sponsors sessions of sutra study and meditation for laymen, as well as lecture tours by its Dharma masters.

## Joss Houses and the Chinatown Temples

The first Chinese to settle in the United States arrived in the late 1840s, most of them responding to the news of gold in California. The first news of the discovery of gold was made in January, 1848, and by 1851 several thousand Chinese had arrived, most of them from Canton.[24] Although many of the Chinese coming to America in the late 1840s and early 1850s worked in the gold fields, others settled in towns en route to the gold fields and started businesses such as stores and laundries. These groups of small businesses eventually became the China-towns which later dotted the state of California.

Despite discrimination against the Chinese and various forms of harassment during the gold rush, the immigrants remained and made significant contributions in the construction of railroads after the Civil War. When the railroads were completed, the racial problem rose again and discrimination against Orientals, supported by rigid immigration laws, remained a shameful part of the American scene until after World War II. Nevertheless, the Chinese were in America to stay, and they brought their religions with them.

The Chinese who migrated to America during the gold rush for the most part were poorly educated, working-class people. In most instances, the religion which they brought with them was the syncretistic religion which they had embraced in China, with its folk deities in some cases supplemented by worship of Taoist gods and the Buddhist Kuan-yin. At first worship was confined to the home, with small home shrines being used as they had been in China.

The first Chinese temple constructed on American soil was the *Kong Chow* temple of San Francisco, believed to have been built in 1853. This temple was constructed by the Kong Chow Association, an organization which had as its purpose to promote and protect the welfare of immigrants coming from certain parts of Kwangtung province. The organization was concerned with the needs of the poor and the aged, and also was concerned with the education of children. In establishing a temple, the association was providing not only a place of worship, but also a place to keep the bones of the dead which were to be shipped back to China for burial. The principal deity in this temple was *Kuan Kung*, a national hero who had been deified as the "god of war." Images of other folk deities were placed in the temple, as well as one of the Taoist goddess, T'ien-hou.[25]

Another temple built in California in the early 1850s was the *T'ien-hou* temple of San Francisco, believed to have been under the auspices of the Sue Hing Benevolent Association. As indicated by its name, this temple had T'ien-hou as its main deity. In the temple however, there were also images of many folk deities.[26]

The Kong Chow and T'ien-hou temples served as the prototypes for the many other temples constructed in California and Chinatowns of other American cities, in the late nineteenth century and early years of the twentieth century. Most of these had Kuan Kung as the principal deity, although T'ien-hou was also popular. In these temples for the working class Chinese, Buddhist influence was very minor. Frequently an image of Kuan-yin was placed in the temple for the convenience of Buddhist members of the association, but no systematic attempt was made to promote Buddhism in America.

Most of the temples of the type described above had no ordained priest in charge. A layman was usually appointed to serve as custodian, to sell incense and fortunes, and to assist worshipers.[27] Caucasians have frequently referred to these Chinatown temples as "joss houses," with joss probably referring to the slivers of sandalwood sold to worshipers and burned like incense before an image.[28]

Even today, most of the Chinatown temples are identified more with popular folk religion than with either Buddhism or Taoism. However, there are some temples which are principally Taoist, some which are principally Buddhist, and a fair number which are a combination of Buddhism and Taoism. The membership of these syncretistic groups is almost entirely Chinese. Also, with the appeal of these groups being to the poorly educated, the membership tends to be mostly elderly Chinese who do not speak English. As these older people die, the membership of the temples dwindles, and many have closed their doors.

## Growth of Chinese Buddhism in America

In contrast to the decline of the syncretistic Chinese temples, since 1950 there has been a slow but steady growth in the nonsyncretistic forms of Chinese Buddhism in America. For the most part this is T'ient'ai Buddhism, nonsectarian Buddhism, or an ecumenical type of Buddhism. Some of the Buddhist groups have been organized under Chinese lay leadership in Chinatown. Others represent missionary enterprises, with priests being sent from Taiwan or Hong Kong. Whereas the syncretistic groups have a membership which includes almost no non-Orientals, the truly Buddhist groups have attracted a good many Caucasians. As yet, these Chinese Buddhist groups have not even begun to rival the Japanese Zen groups in popularity among non-Orientals, and have not enjoyed a mushroom growth comparable to that of the Tibetan groups. However, Americans are displaying an interest in Ch'an and T'ien-t'ai meditation as well as in the highly disciplined life of the Chinese Buddhist monk or nun.

Two groups from the West Coast and two from the East have been selected as examples of Chinese-style Buddhism in America: Buddha's Universal Church of San Francisco; Gold Mountain Dhyana Monastery of San Francisco; Temple Mahayana of South Cairo, New York; and Temple of Enlightenment Monastery in the Bronx.

## Buddha's Universal Church

Quite unique in the history of Buddhism is Buddha's Universal Church, located at the edge of San Francisco's Chinatown. This handsome, modern, four-story building of concrete, steel terrazzo, marble, gold leaf, and shining woods was built by members and friends of the church who donated their time and labor over a period of more than eleven years. People from all walks of life, representing many different creeds and ethnic groups, participated in the construction of the church. Since its dedication in 1963, this church has not only been the recipient of donations from Buddhist groups all over the world, but is the pride of the Chinatown community.

Until his death in late 1971, the principal leader of Buddha's Universal Church was Dr. Paul Fung, assisted by Drs. George Fung and Frederick Hong. Now Fung and Hong carry on the work. Dr. Paul Fung was a physician who also had a Ph.D.; Dr. George Fung also is a physician, and Dr. Hong a dentist, both with Ph.D.'s in addition to their professional degrees. All three men were trained as Buddhist scholars, and Dr. Paul Fung was vice-president of the World Buddhist Fellowship at the time of his death. These men have preached and taught in the church and are called "Doctors of the Dharma."

Unlike most Chinese Buddhist temples, the main hall of Buddha's Universal Church is furnished with pews, like a church. The hall is golden-colored, reflecting Buddha's aura; the altar is shaped like a ship and is flanked by teak panels representing sails. This symbolizes the "Ship of Dharma," on which one crosses the ocean of life. On the altar is a large mosaic figure of Sakyamuni Buddha.

In addition to the main hall, the church has several smaller chapels, each with a figure of Sakyamuni Buddha at a different stage of his life. In each case, the decor of the chapel reflects the environment of the Buddha at the stage of life depicted. For example, the Bamboo Chapel on the mezzanine seeks to reproduce the Monastery of the Bamboo Grove, where twenty-five hundred years ago the Buddha delivered some of his sermons. Also included in the building are a library, research and translation rooms, an assembly room containing another mosaic Buddha-figure, and an audiovisual room. The well-equipped audiovisual department experiments with moving pictures, closed circuit television, and special sound effects. The roof garden has a lotus pool and a small grove of trees which contains a bodhi tree grown from a cutting taken from the tree under which the Buddha sat.

The school of thought of this church is designated as the "Pristine Orthodox Dharma." The emphasis is on the development of moral virtues based on truth, or in the application of Buddhism in people's daily lives. It is not considered necessary to retreat into the mountains—discipline is best tested in society in relationships with others. Dr. Hong explains it this way: "The Chinese say that peace in the country requires peace in the province; peace in the province requires peace in the village; peace in the village requires peace in the family; peace in the family requires peace in the heart and mind. For world peace, then, the individual must first work on himself. The Buddhist concept of spontaneity is that, through study and self-discipline, one becomes spontaneously virtuous to others, and the individual discovers that this is his *true* nature."[29]

In this church there is sutra study, but very little chanting, with the study being geared to a consideration of practical applications of the Buddha's teachings. As far as meditation is concerned, members are advised to meditate at midday or at the end of the day, or both. This is not the Ch'an or Zen type of meditation, but a retrospection on mistakes made, with a resolution not to repeat them.

No incense is burned in Buddha's Universal Church. Research has revealed that the burning of incense was not originally associated with Buddhism,[30] and the attitude at this church is that the only fragrance needed is that of pure thoughts of heart and mind, stemming from pure motivations.

There are about three hundred members who contribute regularly to the church, most of these being Chinese-Americans from the San Francisco Bay area, with some Caucasians. Two Sunday afternoons each month there is a lecture in Chinese and one in English, followed by tours of the church. Those attending the English-language lectures are mostly Caucasians. On Saturdays there are frequently special lectures for university and church groups, and often these are quite large.

A featured activity at the church is the *Amitabha Play,* given during the Chinese New Year season, with a new chapter being presented each year. Most of the regular activities for members take place during the week, generally in the evening. For study, the membership is divided into seven classes, most meeting every week but some only once a month. The children are divided according to age, and adults according to progress in the Dharma. In the beginning class there is emphasis on the ten moral virtues: filial devotion, brotherhood, loyalty, trustworthiness, graciousness, generosity, frugality, humility, determination, and moral foundation. The aim of the study is to give a deeper understanding of these virtues. "For example," said Dr. Hong, "frugality means spending less on oneself in order to have more to help others. Humility means acknowledging one's errors so that he may progress."

There is a research council in the church, engaged in translating the sutras into English. *The Sutra of the Sixth Patriarch* has been published.[31] Among other organizations are a Mother's Club, a Youth Education Fund, and a large music department. There are seventy-five persons in the choir, which is open only to those who pass a test. The choir gives special concerts and also sings whenever public lectures are given. The music is Chinese with either English or Chinese words, but is accompanied by piano and violin rather than Chinese instruments.

The Doctors of the Dharma do a good bit of personal counseling and also perform marriage and funeral ceremonies. In the marriage service the first two pages relate to the marriage contract and the last ten pages to practicing the Dharma in life.

Other Buddhist groups in the San Francisco Bay area tend to derogate the work of Buddha's Universal Church, labeling it a "tourist attraction," "not really Buddhist," and "concerned mostly with filial piety." Certainly it is a tourist attraction, but the members feel that the short, easily-understood lectures followed by the conducted tours provide one means of spreading the Dharma. As for its being "non-Buddhist," one might say that the Buddhist message taught here is one which fits in with the Confucian background of the middle-class and upper middle-class Chinese-Americans who comprise the bulk of the membership. But it is Buddhism, of a type which sees self-discipline as a means to the way of the bodhisattva, and there is no question of the dedication and commitment of the people who made this church a possibility.

*Gold Mountain Dhyana Monastery*

The Gold Mountain Dhyana Monastery, on Fifteenth Street in San Francisco, was dedicated in May, 1972. Its parent organization, the Sino-American Buddhist Association, has been in existence since 1959, when a Chinese Buddhist laywoman persuaded Tripitaka Master Hsuan Hua to come to San Francisco from Hong Kong, to take over spiritual leadership of the group and serve as Ch'an master. When it was organized, the association's headquarters and temple were located in the Buddhist Lecture Hall on the fourth floor of a dingy building on Waverly Place. As the number of Hsuan Hua's disciples grew, this space became increasingly inadequate and necessitated the purchase of a new building to serve as a monastery as well as the center for all of the association's activities.

When the Sino-American Buddhist Association was first organized, its members were mostly Buddhists of Chinese ancestry. However, beginning in about 1967, Master Hsuan Hua's reputation began to spread outside the Chinese community, and Caucasian Americans joined his group of disciples in considerable numbers. By 1971, more than two-thirds of his disciples were Caucasians. In 1969, five disciples went to Taiwan to receive the "complete precepts" for ordination as bhikshus and bhikshunis and four more went in 1971. In 1972 at the Gold Mountain Monastery there were ten fully-ordained monks and nuns—all but one of them Caucasian—and several novices preparing for final ordination. Several hundred Americans had "taken the refuge" and become disciples, over a hundred had taken the five precepts accepted by all Buddhists, and about forty had taken various ones of the bodhisattva vows, indicating a deeper commitment.

The building which houses the Sino-American Buddhist Association and Gold Mountain Dhyana Monastery is a large, square, red brick building with a wooden trim painted yellow and red. The entrance opens onto an office area, which adjoins the Great Hall or Buddha Hall, said to be large enough to accommodate eight hundred people at a lecture or meeting.

The arrangement in the Buddha Hall is similar to that found in small Chinese monasteries, where the same hall may have to serve for chanting, sutra study, lectures, and meditation. There are tables about the room on which are placed copies of the liturgies. Cushions for kneeling and meditation are on the floor, facing the altar. These may be moved to the side for meditation. Enthroned on the altar are three, large, seated Buddhas. In the center is Sakyamuni Buddha, and he is flanked on the right and left respectively by Amitabha Buddha and Bhaishajyaguru Buddha (the Healing Buddha). Extending the length of the hall on each side is a bench, where devotees sit during lectures and for meditation. On the walls are pictures depicting the life of Sakyamuni Buddha. In addition to the Buddha Hall, there are in the building kitchen, refectory, guesthall, living quarters, areas for study and translation, and editorial offices for the association's monthly publication, *Vajra Bodhi Sea*. (It is possible that some of these have been moved to other quarters since 1972.)

In this temple bhikshus and bhikshunis dress in the brown-over-black robes of Chinese Buddhist monks and nuns, and their shaved heads show the small scars of the Chinese Buddhist monks who have been through the *moxa* ceremony involving the burning of small piles of incense on the head as a part of the initiation. Novices, also with heads shaved, wear grey and brown. Lay disciples wear what they wish while working, but on ceremonial occasions some wear black robes. They do not shave their heads.

Fully ordained monks and nuns as well as novices and lay disciples at Gold Mountain Monastery have Chinese Buddhist names. Welch explains that those becoming monks and nuns receive as their surname *Shih* which is the first character of the Chinese rendition of Sakyamuni. The "personal" tonsure name, given to the individual by the master under whom he has taken his vows as a novice, usually consists of two characters. The first is taken from a Gatha or religious poem that has been used, character by character, to name monks, generation by generation, so that all members of one generation with the same tonsure master have the same character embodied in their respective names. The second character in their personal name is a "style" name, which may be different for each person. Those who take the Three Refuges and become lay disciples are also given special names, but here there is more flexibility with respect to method for choosing the name.[32]

All of the bhikshus, bhikshunis and novices who have received their novice vows from Master Hsuan Hua have tonsure names which include the syllable "Heng," for example, Heng Ching, Heng Ch'ien, Heng Shou, Heng Ch'ih. All *Upasakas* or *Upasikas* who have become his lay disciples have "Kuo" in their names. Ordinarily, bhikshus and bhikshunis stop using their family names, since they have left home. However, lay disciples continue to use the family surname and frequently continue to use the given name as well. Thus, Edward Smith, who has the Dharma name of "Kuo T'ien," might be known either as "Kuo T'ein Smith" or "Edward Smith."

Bhikshus and some male lay disciples live at Gold Mountain Monastery, but women—whether nuns or lay persons—live elsewhere, because of monastic vows and monastery regulations which forbid housing men and women together.

The first step in becoming a Buddhist at Gold Mountain Temple is to take the Three Refuges from Tripitaka Master Hsuan Hua. Most will accept the five lay precepts also. Others go on to accept eight lay precepts, and then the ten heavy and forty-eight light bodhisattva precepts. In the past, those accepted as novice monks and nuns received the novice precepts from Master Hsuan Hua, but went to Taiwan to receive the complete precepts for the bhikshu (250 precepts) or bhikshuni (348 precepts). In the summer of 1972, for the first time, the complete precepts were transmitted in San Francisco at Gold Mountain Monastery.

Most of those at this monastery who have accepted the precepts of the bhikshu or bhikshuni have made additional personal vows and adopted various ascetic practices such as eating only once a day and never lying down to sleep. (Frequently these practices are adopted by lay Buddhists also.)

The majority of those who cultivate the Buddhist Way at Gold Mountain Temple are between twenty and thirty years of age, with a little over half being women. They come from all walks of life but most have had some college work and a number have graduate or professional degrees. The young monk serving as guest master said, "They are motivated by an awareness of existence and suffering and are looking for an alternative. Some have experimented with drugs and are looking for something permanent."

The rules by which this temple operates are those originated at the Gold Mountain Monastery on the Chinese mainland. There is great emphasis here on keeping the precepts, which are adhered to very strictly. About ninety percent of those who begin to practice here drop out, but those who remain are very dedicated people, who really want to be Buddhists. Those who live here are vegetarians who do not eat after noon, and both monks and nuns are required to be celibate.

Gold Mountain Temple emphasizes dual practice—sutra study and meditation. Sutra study involves language study, translation of sutras, and writing of commentaries, as well as giving and listening to lectures on sutras and chanting them. Sutra study and meditation are equally emphasized, and study is believed to help with meditation.

In the summer there is a period of twelve weeks of intensive study, with five to seven hours of meditation a day, as well as lectures and sutra study. The day lasts from 4:00 A.M. to 10:30 P.M. In fall and spring the day is the same length and includes meditation, sutra study, language study, lectures, and temple work. However, this is not as intensive as the summer program, and monks have five to six hours a day to spend on whatever work appeals to them. In the winter there are extended meditation sessions, with the shortest being a week and the longest fourteen weeks. During this time the day lasts from 3:00 A.M. to midnight. There is meditation for twenty hours a day, with a short break in the morning and evening for tea. Some sit for twenty-four hours.

Some of the lay disciples living in the monastery have jobs outside, and some monks and nuns as well as laymen are taking work in universities. These participate in as much of the temple program as is possible, but all are highly disciplined.

Every evening and on Sunday afternoon (except during the intensive meditation periods) there are lectures and liturgies which are open to the public. The liturgy is chanted in Chinese, accompanied by percussion instruments. The lecture is given first in Chinese, and then is translated into English. The liturgy involves prostrations, bowing, sutra recitation, and circumambulation while repeating mantras. While attending one of these sessions, I noted that, in contrast to the monotonous, sonorous chanting in the Japanese temples, the chanting here was tonal and quite musical in effect. Also, in contrast to the somewhat nasal, strident chanting of Chinese monks, the voices of the Americans had a rather sweet, gentle quality.

The Sino-American Buddhist Association states that it teaches the "Orthodox Buddhadharma," and that it teaches the five basic schools: (1) Dhyana meditation school (Ch'an), (2) Vinaya (morality) school, (3) the Teachings school; (4) The secret school (Tantrism); and (5) the Pure Land school.

Meditation sessions at the Gold Mountain Monastery involve several different approaches. They may be similar to Zen, or may involve alternation of recitation of a name (like Kuan-yin) or mantra (such as *"Om Mani Padme Hum"* or *"Namo Amit'o-fo"*) and meditation on the name or mantra.

Consultation with the Ch'an master takes many forms and involves different timing. Sometimes it is on a group basis and sometimes on an individual basis. The Ch'an master determines if and when an individual is ready. If he can be "mindful" all day, then he is ready for consultation.

Master Hsuan Hua still remains the teacher and spiritual leader of this group, and this temple has close ties with Buddhism in Taiwan and Hong Kong. However, the management of the affairs of the temple is in the hands of Caucasian Americans, and the Sino-American Buddhist Association has become an organization of Buddhist practice and cultivation for Americans, modeled after the forms and interpretations of Buddhism which were adopted or developed in China before and during the T'ang dynasty.

Of the more than a dozen monastic or semi-monastic Buddhist groups in the United States which I visited, this one seemed to involve the strictest discipline. Yet, the percentage of students and inquirers who drop out is no greater than for other groups with less rigid discipline.

When the Gold Mountain Monastery was visited in the spring of 1972, all activities of the Sino-American Buddhist Association were centered at the temple on Fifteenth Street. In 1973, however, a new branch of the association was established and housed in a large building at 3936 Washington Street in San Francisco. This is the International Institute for the Translation of Buddhist Texts. The new institute is dedicated to translation and the training of translators. In addition to having translation and research facilities, as well as living accomodations for serious students and translators, the building houses a Buddha Hall to insure that cultivators of the Buddhist Way will have the opportunity to put the fruits of their research into practice. At the time of the institute's establishment, it was announced that an image of the Thousand Handed Thousand Eyed Avelokitesvara Bodhisattva would be installed to preside over the Hall. The translation institute plans to unite Buddhists of all nationalities and sects, working for the cause of enlightenment and peace by translating Buddhist texts into all of the world's languages.[33]

## Temple Mahayana

Temple Mahayana, located in a wooded area in the Catskills, is a temple complex and monastery which serves as a retreat for the Eastern States Buddhist Association of New York City. The Eastern States Buddhist Temple, located in Chinatown, is a T'ien-t'ai temple where the membership is mostly Chinese and Chinese-Americans. For this membership, Temple Mahayana with its spacious grounds provides a place for family outings and picnics, where worship can be combined with enjoyment of nature away from the noise and dirt of the city. On special feast days chartered buses bring members from New York, and on such occasions there may be several hundred on hand.

Temple Mahayana has several monks in residence. The abbot is Dharma Master Bhikshu Hsi Ch'en, a man who left China following the Communist takeover. He went to Burma and for over twenty years lived at the Chung Hua Monastery in Rangoon. In 1971 he took over his duties at the newly constructed Temple Mahayana. Among the monks in residence when it was visited in the summer of 1972 were two Caucasian-Americans, at least one of whom was there temporarily from the Sino-American Buddhist Association. The size of the Sangha here fluctuates considerably, since visiting bhikshus come and go. Also, lay inquirers and students come for varying periods of time, to study, worship, and meditate. These include a fair number of Caucasians. Especially popular with non-Orientals are the regular classes in meditation offered at the temple.

The temple itself, in its layout and furnishings, resembles quite closely many village temples in China. For this reason, it is described in some detail.

The entrance to the temple grounds is marked by a tall rectangular gateway, with the name of the temple in English and Chinese on the front. On the back is printed in Chinese characters and romanization, *"Namo Amit'o Fo."* The road approaching the temple winds through the trees and past one of the three small lakes designated as the Lakes of Mercifulness. (Buddhists release fish into the lakes to symbolize their compassion for all living beings.) Beyond the lake, in front of the main temple, is a large parking lot. The temple itself is on a large grassy hill and some attempt has been made at landscaping, but not with the meticulous care characteristic of the landscaping at Japanese temples. Facing the temple, on the opposite side of the parking lot, is a small shrine containing a gold image of the Buddha of the Soil.

On the approach to the temple building, about midway up the incline is a large incense burner. From here it is possible to see the statue of the Maitreya Buddha facing the door.

The temple itself is white and red, with a green corrugated tin roof. Although a temple in China would have a tiled roof, the shape of the temple (including its roof) is in conformity to Chinese-style temple architecture. The entrance to the temple goes into an entryway where the Maitreya Buddha is. On either side, there are doors leading into the Great Hall. In the Great Hall, facing the worshipers, is the main altar. This is a three-stage altar in red and gold, on which are three large gold Buddhas. (These are similar to the Buddhas at the Gold Mountain Temple.) In front of the three large Buddhas is a small image of a Buddha or bodhisattva. On the lower stages of the altar are the usual candles, flowers, fruit, water, incense sticks, and other offerings. A large drum, wooden fish, and other percussion instruments are in evidence. Before the altar are leather-covered, padded kneelers. At the rear, across from the Buddhas, is a fierce-looking image wielding a sword. This is one of the guardians of the temple. On each side of the main hall are benches used for meditation and for lecture audiences.

Behind the main altar is a second altar, on which is an image of

Kuan-yin, its back to the Buddhas. Visitors to the temple almost always *k'ou-t'ou* or kneel before this image, and present offerings.

At festival times, in the area occupied by the Kuan-yin altar, a member of the temple staff will be on hand to sell incense sticks which are lighted and placed before the Kuan-yin. He also sells "fortunes." The method of telling fortunes here and at many Chinese temples is for the petitioner to be given a large cylinder containing numbered bamboo sticks. Kneeling before the altar, he shakes the sticks, then tips the cylinder until one of the sticks falls out. Noting the number on this stick, he matches it to a number on one of many paper slips fastened on the wall, which tells him his fortune. Actually, these fortunes are usually quotations from the sutras, which are not too intelligible unless interpreted by a priest. On the festival day when the temple was visited, quite a large number of persons were making offerings to Kuan-yin, presenting sticks of incense, and purchasing fortunes.

In the temple, other rooms include a refectory, kitchen, library, offices, and sleeping rooms. Donation boxes are placed in inconspicuous locations.

Since the construction of Temple Mahayana, two smaller branch temples or chapels have been constructed on the temple property, near the main temple building. The smaller temples are dedicated to Kuanyin and Ti-shen bodhisattvas, respectively. (Ti-shen is designated as the protector of children.) Each of these small temples contains an image of the appropriate bodhisattva. The entire temple complex was developed largely through the efforts and inspiration of Mrs. James Ying of New York. A gift shop owner and devout Buddhist, Mrs. Ying has worked tirelessly to help meet the spiritual needs of the Chinese Buddhists of New York. The establishment of Temple Mahayana and its satellite temples represents the culmination of a program begun in 1963 with the opening of the Eastern States Buddhist Temple as the first New York City Chinese temple with a priest in attendance.

As at Gold Mountain Temple, worship services at Temple Mahayana are in Chinese. However, on the liturgy sheets the texts of anthems, hymns, and invocations are given in Chinese characters with romanized transliteration above the characters and tentative English translation below. Incantations are usually not translated into English because these are mantras which do not readily lend themselves to translation. Following is an example of the type of anthem used in general worship, following three genuflections[34] and preceding an invocation to Sakyamuni Buddha and recitation of the Heart sutra.

### Incense Anthem

Incense, true to precepts and equanimity,
    Burns to reach heavens above.
We the disciples devoutly
    Offer it on an exquisite censer.
In a few moments, copiously,
    It permeates over all quarters,
As in the past it led Yasodhara
    To avoid distress and avert calamities,
We pay homage to Bodhisattvas, Mahasattvas,
    Under canopy of incense clouds.
We pay homage to Bodhisattvas, Mahasattvas,
    Under canopy of incense clouds.
We pay homage to Bodhisattvas, Mahasattvas,
    Under canopy of incense clouds.

Since Mahayana Temple is new, its leader still relatively unknown, and its location away from an urban center, its future is still uncertain as far as its appeal to non-Orientals is concerned. However, there does seem to be the possibility that there could be a development here similar to what has taken place at Gold Mountain Temple.

## Temple of Enlightenment

The Temple of Enlightenment, which is simultaneously a T'ient'ai monastery, church, meditation center, and headquarters of the Buddhist Association of the United States, is located on Albany Crescent in the Bronx. In 1972 there were four Chinese monks in residence, with the Very Reverend Dharma Master Lok-to as abbot and also president of the association.

The temple is a brick building with a circular entrance ("moon gate") closed by an iron gate kept locked at night. Over this entrance is the name of the temple in Chinese characters. Inside the gate is an entryway where one rings the bell for admission to the temple proper. The front door opens into a hallway, from which one enters the Buddha Hall, on the altar of which are the usual three Buddhas, somewhat smaller than those in San Francisco and South Cairo, but of exquisite workmanship. There are percussion instruments and other appurtenances in the temple area, with kneelers before the altar.

Adjoining the Buddha Hall is a room with a long table, which appears to be used as a guest hall. Next to this, through another moon door, is the meditation hall. This room is carpeted, and there are leather-covered cushions around the edges. At the front of this hall is an image of Kuan-yin. Other rooms, as found in any monastery, are for living, study, worship, and administration.

The monks at this monastery live a life of meditation, participation in liturgies, study, teaching, and temple work. They are celibate, and vegetarians.

On Sundays the temple becomes a "church," with the customary liturgy of prostrations, invocations, sutra recital, and incantations as well as sermons or lectures. Most attending these services are Chinese, but there are also some Caucasians. Even more Caucasians are disciples of Master Lok-to, receiving guidance in T'ien-t'ai meditation.

## Ch'an and T'ien-t'ai Meditation

As mentioned in the chapter on Zen, the techniques used in Zen practice were brought to Japan from China, where they were called Ch'an. The various Zen sects were exported to Japan from China and the koan originated in China, where it was called *kung an.* Ch'an is generally considered to be the same as Zen and to use the same methods. However, Ch'an masters believe that it is not possible to practice Ch'an until one has first learned to control the wandering mind and strip it of all thoughts. A technique devised in ancient China to help prevent thoughts from arising in the mind is called the *hua-t'ou* device.[35] This technique is still being used by Ch'an masters in the Orient and in the West.

Hua-t'ou means the mind before it hears, sees, feels, or is stirred by thought.[36] When the individual asks himself, "WHO is sitting?" "WHO is eating?" "WHO is walking?" he is talking about hua-t'ou, which is "self-Mind." By concentrating on this, he is able to get rid of thoughts and prepares himself for work on kung ans. Hua-t'ou is not to be confused with "just sitting." It is an active technique, but a gentle one and a preparatory one.[37]

Of the various approaches to self-cultivation by meditation, the T'ien-t'ai teaching is said to be the most comprehensive. This teaching has been summarized by Lu K'uan Yu (Charles Luk), who quotes from instructions given in treatises by T'ien-t'ai patriarchs.[38]

Preliminary to getting into the heart of T'ien-t'ai meditation are procedures for regulation of the body, breath, and mind.

Regulation of the body means, first of all, going into meditation with the body clean and comfortable, being neither too hot nor too cold, wearing loose and unrestrained clothing, and maintaining a posture that is erect and stable without being either tense or slack. A half-lotus or full-lotus position is preferred, but other positions are permissible. Meditation is usually done with the eyes closed.

Regulation of the breath means avoiding "coarse," deep, audible breathing and cultivating breathing which is continuous, quiet, "fine," and barely perceptible.

Regulating the mind at the start of meditation is accomplished partly by regulating body and breath, since physical discomfort or strain, drowsiness, or noisy breathing can have a distracting effect. It also involves control of aspects of the physical environment which can disturb concentration. The latter means meditating in a calm, tranquil environment where the temperature is cool but not uncomfortable. It involves avoiding exciting or disturbing situations before meditation and choosing a time for meditation when these are least likely to have occurred, for example, early in the morning. However, even when one is comfortable, relaxed but alert, breathing quietly, in a tranquil environment, and undisturbed, wandering thoughts are still likely to come to mind. A method suggested for controlling these thoughts is to fix one's mind on some point such as the tip of the nose or the navel; or to follow the breath in one's thoughts.

The main practice in T'ien-t'ai meditation is referred to as the *chih-kuan* method, which blends with and overlaps the preliminary techniques just described. When the mind of the cultivator is "unsettled," he uses *chih* ("stoppage") to settle it. There are three chih methods that are usually advocated: (1) "fixing the wandering mind to a post."[39] as described above;[34] (2) the restraining method; and (3) the method of embodying the real.

According to Chiang Wei Ch'iao, a Chinese T'ien-t'ai expert quoted by Charles Luk, the method of restraint consists of grasping at the mind itself. This means that "we should look into it to find out where a thought arises, thereby stopping it and preventing it from following externals."[40] Embodying the real means turning the attention inward and contemplating the thoughts that arise, understanding that all thoughts already belong to the past as soon as they arise, and are therefore unreal.[41]

When the individual uses the techniques of chih and the thinking process comes to an end, he usually becomes drowsy, and uses *kuan* (contemplation) techniques to waken the "sinking mind." There are three kinds of kuan in most common use: (1) contemplation of the void, (2) looking into the unreal, and (3) contemplation of the mean.[42]

Contemplation of the void means looking into all things in the universe and perceiving that "all of them change every instant and are thus non-existent and void."[43] Looking into the unreal involves looking into the mind from which thoughts arise and seeing that thoughts stem from objects, thus finding that "all phenomena owe their existence to a union of inner direct cause and outer concurring circumstances."[44] When the individual achieves contemplation of the void, he does not "cling" to the void; when he looks into the unreal, he does not "grasp" the unreal. When he succeeds in avoiding both extremes, he is engaging in contemplation of the mean.[45] Other techniques of chih and kuan have been suggested by different T'ien-t'ai masters, but will not be discussed here.

When the individual comes out of meditation, mind, breath, and body again are regulated. He releases his thoughts from the subjects of contemplation; opens his mouth and exhales while following his breath; moves his trunk and gently shakes his shoulders, arms, hands, head, and neck; moves his feet to relax them; with his hands rubs his body, knees, and legs; rubs his hands together and rubs his eyes before opening them. Then he permits his body to cool before rising.

Although kung an practice is not a T'ien-t'ai technique, and is generally considered by T'ien-t'ai masters as too difficult for laymen, monks of the T'ien-t'ai school have frequently used it as an advanced kuan technique.

To the beginner in T'ien-t'ai meditation, the master usually says, "Go slowly." The Chinese for this, "*man-man*," also carries the connotation of "take it easy," something which impatient Americans frequently find it difficult to do. In general, most beginners practicing daily meditation would be expected to spend about three months following the breath before they would be considered ready for more subtle methods of mind control.

### Trends and Speculations

Several trends with reference to Chinese Buddhism in America seem apparent.

The syncretistic temples of Chinatown, with only marginal relationships to Buddhism, seem to be dying operations—some fading more rapidly than others. In any event, their impact on American society—particularly its young, non-Oriental, well-educated segments—is minimal, and this will almost certainly continue to be the case. Also, it would appear that a type of Buddhism based almost exclusively on a "social gospel" type of message and having neither a monastic nor a meditational tradition (for example, Buddha's Universal Church) is not likely to attract great numbers of non-Orientals, who might be more comfortable with Zen or in some of the more liberal Christian denominations. (Some, however, who have rejected a theistic orientation in Judaism or Christianity, would be attracted to this sort of church.)

The Chinese Buddhist groups with a monastic tradition probably will continue to attract those who feel the need for this sort of life, but some seeking the monastic life will turn away from monasteries advocating the more ascetic practices, in favor of the less demanding and constraining Zen groups. The emphasis on language study and the use of Chinese in rituals and lectures also will limit the appeal of these groups, although the language study and translation activities will continue to attract intellectuals interested in Asian linguistics and philosophies.

On the basis of my limited contacts with Chinese Buddhism in America, it seems that most persons outside of the Chinese community who become involved in Chinese Buddhism come to it because they hope that Ch'an Buddhism or T'ien-t'ai meditation will relieve their suffering and make life more meaningful. If they stay with it, it is because they find a meditation master to whom they can relate, and because they get a glimpse of what Buddhist meditation can do for them. It is not unreasonable to anticipate that, in the future, its chief appeal will be on the basis of its approaches to meditation, and that Americans not interested in meditation will not be drawn to a religion which includes in its pantheon Oriental door-gods as well as a multiplicity of Buddhas and bodhisattvas, and makes frequent references to ghosts and demons.

# 8

# Satipatthana Comes West:
# The Old Wisdom School
# in America

It is a Sunday afternoon in the spring of 1972. A shaven-headed, brown-skinned, yellow-robed monk from Ceylon glances at his watch and jumps from his seat behind a desk at the Washington Buddhist Vihara. "Time for meditation," he says briskly, as he hurries from the room and heads for the stairs to the basement, where the meditation room is located. The half-dozen young Americans who have been chatting with the monk while consuming cookies and tea hastily place their cups on the desk and follow their teacher.

In the small meditation room presided over by a carved, wooden figure of Sakyamuni Buddha, the students select cushions from the pile stacked against one wall, and seat themselves facing each other on the floor. The monk turns out the light, and joins the meditators in the darkness. All is silent for an hour, except for the faint sound of breathing and an occasional cough. Then the silence is broken as the monk chants a few sentences in Pali, before turning on the light. "Well, how did it go?" he asks.

The scent of incense greets the visitor to the Denver apartment on Quebec Street, as she steps into what she identifies as the living room and is greeted by a slender, fresh-skinned, blue-eyed young man with neatly trimmed blond hair, wearing an orange smock. The young man and his middle-aged female visitor seat themselves on cushions placed at either end of a low, oval table, which constitutes the only piece of furniture in this carpeted room, which on other occasions serves as a meditation hall. A quiet young woman serves them tea as they talk. The serious, eager young man is a former Theravadin monk from Florida, in 1972 serving as resident teacher of the Buddhist Society of Denver, Colorado. His visitor is a psychology professor at a Methodist college in Iowa, and she finds herself nodding in agreement when the Buddhist teacher states that he has had contact with her in a previous incarnation.

On a corner lot in North Hollywood, California, two small, one-story, yellow frame buildings constitute the Wat Thai—the Theravada temple and monastery serving as the temporary spiritual home for the eight to nine thousand Thai Buddhists living in the Los Angeles area. On an afternoon in July, 1973, a thin young Oriental bows before the splendid gold figure of Sakyamuni, as the elderly abbot seated on a cushion before him helps him to exchange a white robe for the yellow robe of the Theravada monk. Seated on the carpet, watching the ordination ceremony, are several other Thai monks, as well as family and friends of the newly ordained novice.

In an Ohio college, a Burmese monk and meditation instructor, wearing a yellow sweater beneath his yellow robe, instructs a group of college students in the technique of "insight" meditation. The students are seated on cushions placed on the floor, facing their instructor, who also is seated on the floor in the traditional cross-legged position. Soon they will close their eyes and begin their meditation exercise of concentrating on the movement of the abdomen, rising and falling, as they inhale and exhale.

This is Buddhism of the Old Wisdom or Theravada School—the latest to take root in the United States in institutionalized form. It is with Theravada and its practice in America that this chapter is concerned.

## The Way of the Elders

Theravada Buddhism, or the "Way of the Elders," is the Buddhism of Ceylon, Burma, Thailand, Cambodia, and Laos. The oldest of the surviving schools of Buddhism, it is based on the *Pali Canon*, which was assembled several centuries before the Mahayana scriptures began to appear. Conze has termed it the "Old Wisdom School."[1] Various other labels have been placed on the system of beliefs and practices of this group. The Mahayanists have called it Hinayana, or "lesser vehicle," which name the Theravadins reject as having derogatory connotations. It has also been referred to as "primitive Buddhism."[2] In the West, its adherents, as well as non-Buddhists, have described it as Basic Buddhism.[3]

Aside from the question of the superiority or inferiority of the Theravadin and Mahayanan views, the followers of the Old Wisdom School point out that the designation of the Theravada as "Hinayana" is incorrect, since the Theravada School was scarcely known to the Mahayanists who coined the term. What they had in mind were certain other schools somewhat similar to the Theravada, especially the Sarvastivada.[4] These schools have died out, and when the term Hinayana is used today it is assumed to refer to the Theravada.

## THE PALI CANON

The doctrines and practices of Theravada Buddhism are based on the scriptures written in Pali, known as the *Tipitaka* (Sanskrit, *Tripitaka*) or "three baskets." The first basket or group of scriptures is the *Vinaya Pitaka*, which consists of the codified rules for the Sangha of monks and nuns. The second basket is the *Sutta Pitaka* (Sanskrit, *Sutra*), consisting of five collections of sutras or discourses. The third basket is the *Abhidamma Pitaka* (Sanskrit, *Abhidarma*), which consists of seven works in which the Buddha's teachings are presented systematically and analytically from the standpoint of logic, psychology, and metaphysics.[5]

Of the three baskets, the *Vinaya* with its rigid codes for the monastic orders even today is the accepted rule book for monks and nuns. Some modifications in these rules have been made since ancient times. However, even with these modifications, the demands made on Theravadin monks and nuns are such that it is extremely difficult for them to maintain their way of life in modern society. This may account for the fact that Theravada monasteries have developed much more slowly in the West than their more flexible Mahayana counterparts.

The *Sutta Pitaka* contains most of the sermons of Sakyamuni Buddha. Its style is interesting and simple, and it is replete with anecdotes, fables, and illustrative examples. The collections of the *Sutta Pitaka* contain most of what we know about the life of Sakyamuni Buddha, as well as his basic teachings, and serve as the guide for the Theravada Buddhist layman. Of the sutras in this group, the one of particular interest to American Theravada Buddhists is the *Mahasatipatthana Sutta*. This is a discourse said to have been given by the

Buddha to monks of Kammassadamma about the Four Noble Truths and about the basis of *Satipatthana* (Mindfulness), through which *nibbana* (Sanskrit, *nirvana*) was to be gained. Parts or all of this sutra are found in several of the collections of the second basket. The teachings found in this sutra form the basis for the Theravada system of meditation.[6]

The *Adhidamma Pitaka*, in contrast to the second basket, tends to be dry and abstruse. It is of interest to philosophers, psychologists, and Buddhist scholars, but is incomprehensible to the average Buddhist layman.

## THERAVADA, THE FOUR NOBLE TRUTHS AND THE EIGHTFOLD PATH

What is the Buddhist Way, according to the Theravada practitioner? Stated in practical terms, following the Theravada path means "doing good, avoiding evil, and purifying one's mind."[7] According to Farkas, the Buddha's Way is often thought of as being therapeutic.[8] The first of the Four Noble Truths diagnoses the aspirant's dis-ease as dukkha—suffering, agony, or disharmony. The second Noble Truth discovers the cause of this suffering as being craving or attachment. The third Noble Truth assures the sufferer that a cure exists—that with the abandonment of craving suffering will cease. The fourth Noble Truth describes the cure for suffering, with the cure consisting of following the Noble Eightfold Path.

For the Theravadin, the quest for relief from suffering starts and ends with "right understanding." With this as a beginning, the Eightfold Path falls into three divisions—*sila* (virtue or morality), *samadhi* (concentration), and *prajna* (intuitive wisdom)—representing the three stages of spiritual progress.[9]

Right speech, right action, and right livelihood comprise the stage of "virtue," and are considered the necessary prerequisites for the second and third stages, since purity of mind is promoted by purity of conduct.[10]

The "concentration" stage involves the paths of right effort, right mindfulness, and right concentration. Right effort is seen as preventing the arising of evil states of mind, overcoming those that have arisen, and promoting the development of good states of mind. Particularly, right effort is said to develop the seven elements of enlightenment—mindfulness, investigation, energy, rapture, tranquility, concentration, and equanimity.[11] Right mindfulness is developed by contemplation of the body, the sensations, the processes of consciousness, and mental contents.[12] Right mindfulness may lead to insight, or it may lead to stillness of mind and one-pointedness of concentration, which is the ability to focus one's mind steadily on one object to the exclusion of all else.[13] In the path of concentration, if it is adopted, various dhyanas (Pali, *jhanas*) or trance stages enter the picture.

For the average Buddhist layman in southeast Asia, the Buddhist Way involves only the stage of sila, since the stage of samadhi involves meditation, which traditionally is the way pursued by the monk and nun. The Buddhist layman may elect to spend a period of some weeks or months as a temporary monk, in which case he will have some experience with meditation, but will probably not make significant progress toward prajna. In recent years, however, meditation centers in Burma have instituted training programs in meditation for interested laymen, and these are becoming quite popular.

## THERAVADA BUDDHISM AND THE WEST

Despite the antiquity of Theravada Buddhism, and the fact that the Way of the Elders has been much more popular in England and Europe than have the Mahayana groups, this has been the latest of the Buddhist sects to attract a following in the United States. This, also, is despite the fact that it was an American who was largely responsible for the nineteenth century revival of Theravada Buddhism in Asia.

According to Conze, the Old Wisdom School has been dying slowly for the past fifteen hundred years.[14] During the years when southeast Asia was colonized, the decline of the Theravada was hastened by Christian missionary efforts. In the nineteenth century, however, two developments in the West served to slow down the pace of decline of the Way of the Elders in southeast Asia, as well as to stimulate interest among the British and Europeans. One development was the appearance of translations of Pali texts into Western languages; the other was the activity of Henry Olcott on behalf of Buddhism in Asia and the West.

### T. W. Rhys Davids and the Pali Text Society[15]

During the nineteenth century there developed in Europe and Britain a scholarly interest in studying the Buddhist texts of India and China. This interest at first was either philological or philosophical. The philological and philosophical studies became a part of a study known as "Indology" which in some areas then gave way to

"Buddhology." All of this inevitably involved the translation of Pali and Sanskrit texts into English and European languages.

The first efforts toward translation of Buddhist texts into Western languages were made by George Turnour, a British civil servant who was born and served in Ceylon. In 1826 he put out a romanized version and English translation of the first thirty-eight chapters of the *Mahavamsa*.[16] More significant than this, however, was the organization in 1881 of the Pali Text Society. The founder and first president of the Society was T. W. Rhys Davids. The second president was his wife, and the third and current president, Miss I. B. Horner. These dedicated scholars have been responsible for directing the work which has resulted in the publication in English of much of the *Pali Canon*. This has had two effects: (1) the initiation of a preference for the Theravada tradition in England, and, until recently, in Europe; (2) an increased appreciation of the Pali texts in India and southeast Asia. In the latter areas, the name of T. W. Rhys Davids is greatly revered.

The first British Buddhist monks to be ordained were trained in Burma and then returned as missionaries to their own land. There currently are several Theravada *viharas* (monastery-temples) in England. Since the early 1900s, the Theravada missionary effort in England has been present, although the Sangha in Britain consists principally of Asians.

Since 1900, a number of Buddhist societies have been formed in England, with those organized before 1920 being Theravadin in their outlook. The present Buddhist Society of London, organized in 1924 by Christmas Humphreys as the Buddhist Lodge of the Theosophical Society, is described by its founder and president as eclectic in its outlook.[17] However, although both Zen and Tibetan Buddhism have attracted a number of followers, the Theravadin approach seems to be preferred by most British Buddhists.

In Europe, as in Britain—and especially in Germany—most Buddhism was of the Old Wisdom School prior to World War II. Currently, the Theravada view is promoted in Europe by representatives of the Maha Bodhi Society. Since the war, however, Zen, Tibetan Buddhism, and Jodo Shinshu have begun to rival it in popularity.[18]

## Henry S. Olcott and Buddhism in Ceylon

Among southeast Asian Buddhist countries, Ceylon was one in which Theravada thought flourished from the middle of the third century B.C. through the fifth century A.D. From the sixth through the eleventh centuries, Buddhism in Ceylon declined. There was a temporary revival in the twelfth through the fourteenth centuries, but this was followed by a period leading to almost total eclipse of the religion. By the middle of the nineteenth century Ceylonese Buddhism had reached its nadir, due in large part to the activities of Christian missionaries sent to Ceylon by the colonial powers. In the latter half of the nineteenth century, however, the Buddhists of Ceylon launched an offensive against the Christian missionaries, and this resulted in a turning of the tide. Of importance in this counteroffensive were three men: Mohotiwatte Gunananda, Henry S. Olcott, and Anagarika Dharmapala.[19]

Mohotiwatte Gunananda was a gifted Ceylonese monk, who not only studied the Christian scriptures, but also rationalist writings of the West that were critical of Christianity. Armed with anti-Chrisian arguments, he went from village to village, preaching against the missionaries and advocating a return to Buddhism. Having a dynamic, energetic personality, he attracted large crowds wherever he went. Pleased with the response received, he then challenged the missionaries to a series of public debates on the relative merits of the two religions. His challenge was accepted, and debates were held in 1866, 1871, and 1873. The debates aroused much interest, and, in the eyes of the Buddhists, Gunananda had won them all.[20]

An American scholar named Peebles happened to be in Ceylon in 1873 at the time of the last of the series of debates between Gunananda and his Christian adversaries. He was so impressed with the proceedings that he published them in a book on his return to the United States. The book was read by another American, Henry S. Olcott, a former farmer and Civil War colonel. It was largely the influence of this book which led him, with Madame Blavatsky, to organize the Theosophical Society in 1875, and it was curiosity aroused by this report that led him to go to Ceylon with Madame Blavatsky, in 1880. On reaching Ceylon the two began their serious study of Buddhism, and embraced it in 1881.[21]

On his arrival in Ceylon in 1880, Colonel Olcott organized the Buddhist Theosophical Society, which adopted as its principal project the establishment of Buddhist schools in Ceylon. Olcott and his supporters went from village to village, appealing for funds to start and support such schools. At the time of his arrival, there were only three Ceylonese Buddhist schools receiving government grants. By 1879 the society had founded 46 schools in Ceylon, by 1903 the number had increased to 174, and by 1940 it had risen to 429.[22]

In addition to promoting Buddhist education, Colonel Olcott promoted the initiation of Buddhist publications. It was as a result of his efforts, also, that the Buddhists of Ceylon gained freedom to hold their Buddhist processions and that Buddha's birthday was declared a public holiday. His efforts resulted in the appointment of Buddhist registrars of marriages; the present Buddhist flag was his creation.[23]

It was largely through Colonel Olcott's efforts that Ceylon became the center for the Theravada missionary movement. He is known to Buddhists of the West chiefly through his "Buddhist Catechism"—an abbreviated statement of the beliefs involved in Basic Buddhism— although "Henry S. Olcott Day" is celebrated in Washington, D.C., as well as in Ceylon, as a holy day for Theravada Buddhists.

The third person of importance in the Ceylonese Buddhist revival was another monk whose name was linked with that of Olcott. This was Anagarika Dharmapala, who chose to live in the world rather than in a monastery. Inspired by the activities of Gunananda and Colonel Olcott, he served first as Olcott's interpreter, but later worked independently, making speeches and writing articles. His main thrust was one of supporting and developing pride in Buddhist culture. To the purpose of achieving this aim, he organized the Maha Bodhi Society in 1891. This organization now has branches all over the world, including several in Europe and the United States, and has done much to stimulate an interest in Theravada Buddhism in the West.[24]

## Theravada Meditation

Theravada meditation is of two basic types, called "insight" meditation (*vipassana*) and "calming down" (*samatha*).[25] Of these, insight meditation is easier and generally more popular than the other. In their initial stages both approaches are somewhat similar, since both begin with mindfulness. However, after the initial stages they differ in method, course, and object.

Insight meditation uses the attention and awareness of mindfulness for the attainment of the wisdom which is the comprehension of reality as it truly is. The more such wisdom develops, the clearer is the individual's intuition of emptiness. "Calming down" is the result of samadhi or concentration which is marked by one-pointedness of thought. Its method involves the development of trances in which the meditator approaches a condition of rapt attention to an objectless inwardness. According to the *Pali Canon,* it is the combination of objectless awareness and intuition of emptiness which leads to final emancipation in nibbana. However, from a practical standpoint, since trance does not increase wisdom and continued mindfulness does not produce trance states, it is generally conceded that in a given existence most people will be forced to specialize in one approach.[26]

Narasapo suggests that the method of meditation which is most appropriate may depend on the personality of the meditator,[27] while Nyanoponika Thera indicates that one method may precede the other.[28] Most agree that the vipassana approach is the most direct one to attaining nirvana. The relationship between mindfulness, concentration, wisdom, and nirvana are shown in figure 2, adapted from Conze.[29]

## Preparation

In the West it is common for those doing Theravada meditation to set aside a period of an hour or so each day for meditation at home, with perhaps arrangements for a consultation with a teacher once a week. Most authorities would agree, however, that a more desirable procedure is for the would-be meditator to arrange his affairs so that

**Fig. 2. Attainment of Nirvana through Vipassana and Samatha Meditation**

Mindfulness

Calming down meditation
(Samatha)

Insight meditation
(Vipassana)

One-pointed concentration

Practice of internal awareness

Trance states
(dhyanas)

Intuitive wisdom
(prajna)

Objectless
inwardness

Unsubstantial
emptiness

Nirvana

he can live in a meditation center or monastery for a period of time. During this period he will be doing meditation continuously. This means that, whether he is sitting, standing, walking, washing, eating, urinating, going to bed, getting up, or performing any other function, it will be with complete mindfulness. In Burma a course of meditation practice lasts for one to two months,[30] and in the Theravada monastery in California a course usually requires several weeks, with the program involving $18\frac{1}{2}$ hours of daily practice,[31] in which sitting meditation is alternated with walking meditation. Mahasi advises that the serious seeker arrange his life so that he can spend an indefinite period of life at a meditation center.[32]

Theravada monks and intelligent laymen are encouraged to study the *Pali Canon* in order to gain an intellectual understanding of Buddhism, as well as to engage in meditational practice. However, while actually involved in a course of intensive meditation practice, the individual is usually advised not to read or study. He is instructed also to dispose of potential distractions before beginning the course—distractions such as letter writing, shopping, family worries, and business and financial problems. He is expected to keep his life simple, avoiding unnecessary talk and gadding about. As much as possible, he gives up worldly thoughts and actions during training, accepts the eight precepts which the lay Buddhist of southeast Asia accepts during a course of meditation. These precepts involve abstention from: killing; stealing; sexual intercourse; lying; intoxicants; partaking of solids and certain liquids after noon; dressing for show, using cosmetics, attending or performing in entertainments, etc; and sleeping on luxurious beds.

The place selected for meditation should be quiet, although this is less important for insight meditation than for concentrative meditation.

As is the case for all types of Buddhist meditation, the preferred sitting position for Theravada meditation is the full-lotus or half-lotus position, with straight back. However, other cross-legged positions are acceptable, as well as the kneeling position sitting on the heels, or even sitting on a chair with feet flat on the floor. The hands are in the lap, usually with palms up and one hand resting lightly on the other. Emphasis is placed on finding a position which is natural and comfortable. The eyes are closed, at least in the initial stages of meditation.

Once the meditative pose has been assumed, the Theravada Buddhist usually begins his meditation with the repetition of the three-fold refuge. Mahasi suggests that the meditation begin with brief contemplations on the "Four Protections: the Buddha, loving-kindness, the loathesome aspects of the body, and death."[33] Gunaratana states that the meditator should "radiate universal loving-kindness," and gives instructions for this.[34] The meditator then chooses the primary object of meditation.

## Right Mindfulness

Whether one chooses the way of vipassana or of samatha, it begins with mindfulness or awareness. The term most frequently translated as "mindfulness" (*sati*) is usually interpreted as "bare attention" to, or "awareness" of, all that is going on within the psyche. This includes awareness of sense experiences having their source in external stimuli. It does not imply ability to take appropriate action in the phenomenal world or active reflective thoughts on things observed. This latter more active aspect of mindfulness is termed "clear comprehension" (*sampajanna*).[35]

Bare attention leads to knowing, shaping, and liberating the mind —it leads to *insight*. By insight is meant the direct and penetrative realization of the Three Characteristics of Existence, i.e., impermanence, suffering, and the non-existence of Self. This implies not just an intellectual understanding, but personal experience of what Buddhism regards as basic truth. The result of insight is said to be freedom from desire, aversion, and delusion, and the ability to see all things clearly as "bare phenomena."[36]

The task of "clear comprehension"—the second aspect of Right Mindfulness—is to make all activities "purposeful and efficient, accordant with actuality, with our ideals and with the highest level of our understanding. ... To the *clarity* of bare mindfulness is added the full *comprehension* of purpose and of actuality, internal and external, or, in other words: Clear Comprehension is right knowledge or wisdom, based on right attentiveness."[37] There are four kinds of clear comprehension—clear comprehension of purpose, suitability, the domain of meditation, and reality.[38]

Mindfulness in both of its aspects provides the key to the distinctive methods of Satipatthana—the methods of cultivating mindfulness.

## The Burmese Method of Insight Meditation

The most popular method of meditation among Theravadins is the approach to insight meditation developed and taught in Burma.[39] In this method, the primary object of meditation is the movement of the abdomen up and down as the individual inhales and exhales. (Other possibilities are concentrating on the point where the breath is felt to go in and out, or counting the inhalations and exhalations.) The meditator observes the rising and falling of the abdomen, wordlessly noting "rising" and "falling." As he is observing these movements, he may note a pain in his knee or an itching nose, in which case he will note "pain, pain," or "itching, itching," and then return to the observation of the movements of his breathing. As a thought comes to mind, he will note, "thinking, thinking," and then return to observing his breathing. When he must shift positions he observes "intending,

intending," and then "moving, moving." Then he will return to the primary object of attention. In this manner he will develop and display awareness of all that is going on within.

While walking, the meditator will observe what he is doing as he lifts his foot, moves it forward, and places it down. While eating he will note each movement as he spears the food, lifts it with his fork, places it in his mouth, chews it, and swallows it. He will note also the fleeting thoughts which go through his mind, silently labeling them. Sounds, sights, smells, tastes, and touch sensations he notes as "hearing, hearing," "seeing, seeing," "smelling, smelling," "tasting, tasting," "touching, touching." Desires are noted as "wanting, wanting," and emotions as "fear, fear," "anger, anger," "love, love," and so on. He does not cling to any of these sensations or feelings—simply observes them and notes them with detachment.

In the Burmese method, concentration on the action of breathing is used as an approach to the individual's developing complete awareness of all else that is going on, so that it is not necessary to shift the primary object of contemplation.

By the method described above, the meditator makes contact with nirvana as he destroys the three fetters of illusion of self, doubt about the path, and belief in rites and ceremonies. Afterwards the person is filled with great happiness. Having attained nirvana, the individual becomes an "aryan" (saint)—he sees the three characteristics of existence, attains mindfulness and insight, renounces things as objects, and takes nirvana as the object. Having attained nirvana, however, he renounces it and works back up, now cutting off lust and hate. Each time insight is vaster and deeper. The aryan lives in the present moment, with tranquility and clearness of mind. As the method of insight meditation is taught by Sujata, four courses are required for each attainment.

The Theravada Buddhist recognizes three levels of knowledge: (1) that acquired through the senses, such as in hearing a person speak; (2) reflective knowledge; and (3) insight knowledge. Insight knowledge, in turn, is of two kinds—mundane and super-mundane—with the meditator seeking the attainment of super-mundane knowledge.[40]

## Samatha Meditation

Samatha or samadhi meditation, having as its purpose the attainment of tranquility, may precede, follow, or be substituted for insight meditation.[41] Unlike vipassana, however, its method is to limit the contents of consciousness through one-pointedness of mind. Like insight meditation, it frequently starts with attention to breathing, with the meditator focusing on the point at which he can feel the touch of the breath being inhaled and exhaled. Frequently this point is the tip of the nose. The adept does not attend to the random thoughts which come to mind, but seeks to attend only to the breath being inhaled and exhaled.

Although starting with concentration on the breath, samadhi meditation usually involves concentration on other sense objects as a means of achieving various trance states or dhyanas. As described by Conze, the dhyanas are means for transcending the impact of sensory stimuli and normal reactions to them.[42] One begins by concentrating on a sense stimulus, usually with eyes partially open.

Conze says,

> The first stage of trance is achieved when one can suppress for the time being one's unwholesome tendencies—i.e., sense desire, ill-will, sloth and torpor, excitedness and perplexity. One learns to become detached from them and is able to direct all one's thoughts onto the chosen object. One ceases to be discursive and adopts a more unified, peaceful and assured attitude of confidence.... This attitude ... results in elation and rapturous delight. In a manner of speaking, this elation is still a blot and a pollution, and in its turn it has to be overcome. This task is achieved in the next two stages, so that in the fourth dhyana one ceases to be conscious of ease and disease, well-fare and ill-fare, elation and dejection, promotion or hindrance as applied to oneself.... What remains is a condition of limpid, translucent and alert receptiveness *in utter purity of mindfulness and evenmindedness.*[43]

Above this are four "formless" dhyanas, representing stages of overcoming the vestiges of the object until one attains the complete obliteration of the self which is necessary before one can attain nirvana.[44]

When one has attained right concentration, it is said, it is then possible for wisdom to enter the Great Emptiness. By wisdom, as the Theravadist views it, is meant the methodical contemplation of Dharmas. The formal definition of wisdom given by Buddhagosa, quoted by Conze, is, "Wisdom has the characteristic of penetrating into dharmas as they are themselves. It has the function of destroying delusion which covers the own-being of dharmas. It has the manifestation of not being deluded. Because of the statement: 'He who is concentrated knows, sees what really is,' concentration is its proximate cause."[45] Wisdom, as so defined, means the perception of reality. Highest understanding then occurs, as does the cessation of craving and attainment of nirvana.[46]

## THERAVADA BUDDHISM IN AMERICA

Although most United States residents from Burma, Thailand, Cambodia, Laos, and Ceylon are at least nominally Theravada Buddhists, few of them have any involvement with a Buddhist temple or engage in Buddhist practices with any degree of frequency. Among non-Asiatic Americans there is a growing intellectual acceptance of the teachings of Basic Buddhism, and a rapidly increasing interest in the practice of Theravada meditation. However, unlike the situation in Europe and Great Britain, relatively few non-Oriental Americans are as yet adherents of Theravada Buddhism, as compared with the greater popularity of Zen, Tibetan Buddhism, and Nichiren Shoshu.

Until the latter part of 1966 there was no formally organized American center devoted to presentation of the Theravada viewpoint and providing a setting for ceremonial observances and meditational practice in the Theravada context. Prior to that time there were some Theravadins teaching in American universities or working with small meditation groups, but most Americans who knew anything at all about Theravada Buddhism attained their knowledge either through reading about it or taking a university course.

Since 1966 several developments have occurred, which may well eventuate in an acceleration of interest in Theravada Buddhism, analogous to that which has occurred in the case of Zen and Tibetan Buddhism. These developments include (1) the establishment of the Washington Buddhist Vihara; (2) the organization of the Buddhist Society in Denver (now Stillpoint Institute of San Jose) ; (3) the establishment of the Wat Thai in North Hollywood; (4) the enrollment of increasing numbers of Americans in the Theravada meditation centers of Burma and Thailand; and (5) increasing numbers of invitations issued to Theravadin monks to give instruction in meditation on American college and university campuses, as well as to lecture to college audiences.

### Washington Buddhist Vihara

Founded in 1966, the Buddhist Vihara Society of Washington, D.C., was created "to provide a religious and educational center to present Buddhist thought, practice and culture, and more broadly, to aid cross-cultural communication and understanding—prerequisites for a peaceful world."[47]

The idea for the society in the District of Columbia originated in 1964, when the Most Venerable Madihe Pannaseeha, Maha Nayaka Thera of Ceylon was visiting in the United States and noted both the growing interest in Buddhism and the lack of an American center for presenting the Theravada view. Acting on the Maha Nayaka Thera's suggestion, the Sasana Sevaka Society of Maharagama, Ceylon, sent the Venerable Thera Bope Vinita of Colombo, Ceylon, to Washington in August, 1965. The Venerable Vinita founded the society on December 10, 1966, and served as its first president, being succeeded in 1967 by another Ceylonese monk, the Venerable Pandita Mahathera Dickwela Piyananda. In September, 1968, the Venerable Mahathera Henepola Gunaratana from Malaysia came as secretary.

On May 26, 1968, the society moved into its present home on Sixteenth Street, which became the Washington Buddhist Vihara—a combination of temple, monastery, and cultural center. This property was acquired with the help of the Sasana Sevaka Society, the government of Ceylon, and the government of Thailand. Since that time the staff has been augmented by the Venerable Punnaji. An additional member of the Sangha also is a Nichiren Shu Japanese monk, who conducts Japanese services for members of his sect.

The building housing the vihara is a large former residence. On the first floor, in the front, is the secretary's office, behind which is a large shrine room. In the latter are rows of folding chairs facing a twelve-foot square area in the front, which is carpeted in red. At the front of this area is a low carved table which holds a small Buddha, incense, flowers, and various artifacts. The sanctuary beyond it, where the altar is located, is also carpeted, and a medium-sized gilded Buddha image stands in front of a larger one about five feet in height. In the basement are a bookstore and meditation hall, and on the second floor are a library and monks' quarters. In the rear of the building is a garden focusing on an eight-foot bronze statue of the Venerable Ananda, beloved disciple of the Buddha.

The activities of the vihara are numerous. They include (1) celebration of the various Buddhist holidays, with special colorful ceremonies; (2) regular Sunday devotions with sermon; (3) individual and group instruction in meditation; (4) lectures and discussions on Buddhism, not only at the vihara, but at colleges and universities throughout the United States; (5) classes in Sinhalese and Sanskrit;

(6) maintenance of a library and bookstore with books on all aspects of Buddhism; (7) publication of a newsletter which includes articles on Buddhism and commentaries on the sutras, as well as news items; and (8) publication of the "Vihara Papers," the first of which was a pamphlet on Theravada meditation, written by the Venerable Gunaratana.[48]

I attended the Sunday activities in the vihara one afternoon in the winter of 1972. These consisted of the devotional service followed by a discussion during which tea and refreshments were served in the office, and then an hour of meditation. Of those attending the service, about two-thirds were Asian and the remainder Caucasian. Those participating in meditation were all Caucasian, mostly between the ages of thirty and fifty.

During the devotional service the barefooted monks, wearing yellow or orange robes with the right shoulder uncovered, were seated on the carpet in the sanctuary, facing the altar. Most of those in the congregation were seated on chairs, but a few sat cross-legged or knelt on the carpet in front of the rows of chairs. During the service, which began and ended with "Sadhu! Sadhu! Sadhu!" some parts of the liturgy were read by the monks, some by the congregation, and some by both. Parts were in Pali, parts in English, and parts were said in Pali by the monks, followed by the English equivalent said by the congregation. It included the Refuge, the precepts, the eightfold path, readings from the sutras, blessings, and a sermon. (The sermon which the writer heard was on "Meditation.") The monk delivering the sermon faced the congregation while seated cross-legged in front of the altar.

In the meditation which took place on Sunday afternoon, there was no chanting or bowing preceding the meditation, but the meditation master ended the session with a brief chant in Pali.

Since the establishment of the vihara a substantial number of Americans in the Washington area have taken the vows of the lay Buddhist, and many others have involved themselves in meditation for varying periods of time.

### Stillpoint Institutes

In various parts of the United States, former Theravada monks and laymen, trained in Asia, are living in a semi-monastic existence and teaching meditation techniques to groups of Americans. The majority of these teachers are Asian nationals, but some are native Americans. Notable among the latter is the Venerable Anagarika

Sujata, founder and resident teacher of the Stillpoint Institutes of San Jose, California.

Sujata is an American in his middle twenties, who became interested in Buddhism when he was a college student in Florida. He dropped out of college to study Buddhism in Asia under teachers from Ceylon, Burma, and England. He was ordained as a Buddhist monk but gave up the robe when it was apparent that he could not live and work in the United States, and at the same time keep all of the rules specified for the Theravada monk. In 1970 he returned to the United States and established a meditation center in Clearwater, Florida. In September, 1971, he moved the center to Denver, where he organized a Buddhist Society, and shortly thereafter went on a four-month retreat in Burma and Ceylon. In Denver, the center was located in a small apartment on Quebec Street, where at first three students supported the teacher and the society's activities.

In the summer of 1972 the society moved its headquarters to a larger building on Scranton Court, which became also the Sasana Yeiktha Monastery and Nunnery Meditation Center. In its larger quarters the center had complete meditation facilities for up to three-month retreats, and provided residence for the teacher and five full-time students. The facilities included private meditation rooms, indoor areas for walking meditation, meditation gardens, and a library with the *Pali Canon* and related material.[49] In 1973 the name of the center was changed to the Stillpoint Institutes, and Sujata announced that the group would soon be moving to California.

In 1974 the institutes moved to a building in a woodsy, tranquil setting in San Jose. There Sujata conducts intensive retreats of from ten to thirty days, in addition to weekend programs consisting of discussion of the theories behind vipassana meditation practice.

In addition to serving as a teacher of vipassana meditation and the *Pali Canon*, Sujata also keeps a busy lecture schedule from coast to coast, and has published a small book. A serious and dedicated young man, a gifted teacher, a competent scholar in his chosen specialty, and an articulate speaker, Sujata is a very able advocate of the Theravada way.

## The Wat Thai

The Thai government has supported the Washington Vihara from its founding, the Thai ambassador participates in its ceremonies, and it provides a spiritual home for the Thais living in the Washington area. However, the Buddhists of Thailand have been concerned with the problem of how to more adequately meet the needs of the thirty thousand Thais in the United States, with the majority of them living on the West coast.

Responding to the need for a West Coast vihara, after a short experiment with a meditation center in Sepulveda, California, in 1972, the Thai Buddhists established in North Hollywood a small temple and monastery. Here five Thai monks study and conduct services. They are also working toward raising money for constructing a larger, more elaborate temple which they hope to erect on the property. In the summer of 1973, those visiting the temple were principally persons of Thai ancestry, but pamphlets on Theravada Buddhism, printed in English, were being distributed to non-Asian visitors. The abbot of the monastery is an expert on meditation, and hopes that eventually he may work with meditation groups, but indicated that limited space would not make this possible until completion of the new temple.

Until more space is available, it is doubtful if the Thai temple will make much impression on the non-Asian community. However, as has happened at all Zen temples in the United States, Westerners probably will become interested in this temple as soon as it becomes a center for the practice of meditation.

*Vipassana on the American Campus*

A growing trend in private colleges of the United States is to invite a Theravada monk or teacher from England to visit the campus for the purpose of teaching insight meditation. (Sometimes a Zen master or Tibetan lama is invited.) This is usually combined with study of Buddhist literature. Although most of the students involved in these programs of meditation and study are not Buddhist and will discontinue their studies and meditation after the program is over, there are some students who become seriously interested in Buddhism and go to England or Asia to continue their studies in a monastic setting. Probably most of these will return to the United States and some of them will form the core of an American Sangha of Theravada monks.

*What of the future?*

The Theravada missionary movement in the United States is still in its infancy, and it is too early yet to predict what its future will be among non-Orientals. Because of the strictness of the rules for monks and nuns and the difficulty of living a Theravadin monastic life in a modern western society, it is doubtful if there will ever be a very large American Sangha. However, there are indications that the teachings of the *Pali Canon* have an appeal for American intellectuals and that Theravada meditation may have the potential for a significant growth in this country as an alternative to Zen, Tibetan Buddhist practices, and transcendental meditation for the layman. The relative simplicity of vipassana techniques, which produce results rather quickly, plus the existence of several good manuals of instruction, make this method attractive to those who wish to begin meditation without a teacher. Undoubtedly some of these "do-it-yourself" meditators will eventually find their way to meditation groups or centers with competent teachers.

# 9

# Buddhism and the Problems of American Society

What does Buddhism have to say about the problems of American society? Can it make any significant contribution toward the solution of these problems? It is with these questions that the present chapter is concerned.

## APPROACH TO THE PROBLEMS

Is Buddhism escapist? Many Westerners contend that it is—that the young Americans who are entering Buddhist monasteries or involving themselves in Buddhist "communities" are seeking to leave the real world with its multiple problems, and abdicate their responsibilities to society; that they are substituting a passive meditation for an active grappling with reality. Asia gurus and Zen masters, also, admit that the desire to escape from the world *is* a factor which often leads young Americans to the Buddhist temple or monastery; that persuading these young people to "return to the world" and cope with its problems is difficult. At the same time they argue that Buddhism is *not* escapist—that, on the contrary, it contains the answers to many of the problems that plague society. These include problems such as those of war, racial prejudice, poverty, pollution, and drug abuse.

## Buddhism and the Peace Movement

It was 1893 in Chicago when Soyen Shaku rose before the World's Congress of Religions to make an impassioned plea for negotiation and attempts at international understanding in place of war as a solution to world problems. On this occasion the Zen master said,

I am a Buddhist, but please do not be so narrow-minded as to refuse my opinion on account of its expression on the tongue of one who belongs to a different nation, different creed and different civilization.

Our Buddha, who taught that all people entering into Buddhism are entirely equal, ... preached this plan in ... India just three thousand years ago. Not only Buddha alone, but Jesus Christ, as well as Confucius, taught about universal love and fraternity. We also acknowledge the glory of universal brotherhood. Then let us ... unite ourselves for the sake of helping the helpless and living glorious lives of brotherhood under the control of truth....

International law has been very successful in protecting the nations from each other and has done a great deal toward arbitration instead of war. But can we not hope that this system shall be carried out on a more and more enlarged scale so that the world will be blessed with the everlasting bright sunshine of peace and love instead of the gloomy, cloudy weather of bloodshed, battles and wars?

We are not born to fight one against another. We are born to enlighten our wisdom and cultivate our virtues according to the guidance of truth. And happily, we see the movement toward the abolition of war and the establishment of a peace-making society. But how will our hope be realized? Simply by the help of the religion of truth....

We must not make any distinction between race and race, ... civilization and civilization, ... creed and creed, ... faith and faith.... We are all sisters and brothers; we are all sons and daughters of truth, and let us understand one another much better and be true sons and daughters of truth. Truth be praised![1]

Despite these words uttered by a Buddhist scholar from a country where a majority of the people are at least nominal Buddhists, since that date Japan has been involved in five major wars. Also, if one looked back in the history of Japan it would be apparent that for centuries civil war was a way of life in Japan, and in premodern times there were periods when Buddhist monks had their own armies for the protection of their monasteries and other properties.

None of this makes Buddhism sound like a religion which promotes peace and nonviolence among its adherents. Nor does Buddhism sound like a religion of peace when we recall that the Tibetan monks had large armies during the twelfth and thirteenth centuries. However, Ch'en reminds us that instances of Buddhist aggression are relatively few in the twenty-five hundred years of its existence, and that there is nothing in the history of Buddhist aggression to compare with the horrors of the Inquisition.[2] He also points out that there are many cases of warlike peoples who lost their zeal for warfare and conquest after being converted to Buddhism. An example is the Mongols.[3]

The Buddha placed great stress on the importance of not killing, and of choosing nonviolent means of resolving conflicts within and between nations. In his early sermons he listed the vocation of "soldier" as contrary to the Noble Path of "Right Livelihood," although later he admitted that there might be occasions when the sacrifice of some lives would be necessary in order to save others, so that being a soldier might not be completely unacceptable. Nevertheless, although many Buddhists do fight for their country, the traditional spirit of Buddhism is one of tolerance, nonviolence, and compromise.

The main thrust of Nichiren Shoshu of America is in the direction of regarding it as a religion which promotes world peace by means of working for a change in oneself, and by promoting the happiness of all mankind. Zen masters and Tibetan gurus have repeatedly indicated that Buddhism is a religion of peace, tranquillity, and compassionate understanding of others. During the Vietnam war, also, ministers of the Buddhist Churches of America frequently took the stand that being a conscientious objector was consistent with Buddhist principles.

## Buddhism and Ecology

The Buddhist attitude toward life is one which embraces not only respect for human life but also preservation of animal and plant life when compatible with human welfare. It is recognized that human survival would be difficult if not impossible without animal or plant food and that destruction of bacteria and certain other organisms is necessary to preserve health. However, the Buddhist believes in letting nature use its own resources to combat its problems, and if man uses the gifts of nature for his own well-being he must return these gifts to the maximum extent possible. The Buddhist also believes that man should not exploit nature's gifts beyond the point of need. All of this is consistent with a way of life designed to protect the environment from pollution, ravagement, and wanton waste.

The Buddhist attitude with respect to waste is reflected in the practice at one Zen center, where the toilet is not flushed until it has been used twice, and recycled paper is used for the quarterly publication of the center. It is also reflected in the Zen practice at meals of accepting only what one can eat, and the practice at some Zen monasteries of using tea for rinsing out the bowls from which the food has been eaten, then drinking the tea. More directly expressive of a Buddhist approach to ecology are the following excerpts from an article by Patterson:

> Each day, as the garbage in our dumps and lives gets deeper and deeper, new solutions to our environmental crisis are suggested until the weight of the suggestions is almost as great as the garbage. These solutions generally advocate either a social/political change or a technological approach. The problem is divorced from the individual. But the nature of the problem rests firmly *with* the individual. The environmental crisis came about because man . . . has been living out of harmony with nature. . . . One of the greatest contributing factors has been the assumption that we are separate from nature, from others such as grasshoppers, hippopotamuses, and people, and even ourselves.
>
> It is in the experience of oneness . . .that we can ultimately hope to find our solution. We must fully appreciate that the garbage, pollution, and ugliness in the environment is but a reflection of the garbage, pollution, and ugliness in our minds. The environment reflects our minds; our minds reflect the environment. . . . Just as it is obvious that technology is not the cause of the environmental crisis, but merely a lever for allowing a much greater expression of our irreverent attitudes toward nature, so too it is obvious that technology cannot be a solution. The real pollution is mind pollution perpetuated by industries, the mass media they support, and we who would support them both by overconsumption and irreverence. Pollution will cease when the mind is full of beauty and the necessities are found within.
>
> To reach this point, the many things we must be con-

cerned about have their focus in just one—our daily life. I cannot find the way for you, and you cannot find the way for me, but ... I can share with you a few of the experiences I have had which I consider related to ecological living—to daily life and my daily practice. ...

Several years ago, while standing in the middle of the yard, I was shaken for the first time in this way. I can only describe it as if I were hit by a powerful, violent blow over the head which 'said' I *had to garden*. I surrendered and became a gardener. Each day since, I have realized that from the beginning of this world, plants have supported our lives, and that it is fitting that we support theirs. This I call living in harmony with plants. The tending of plants has become a central focus of my life. In this way, also, I understand the ancient ones who shared the same house, the same living room with the animals they ate. As the animals supported their lives, so they supported the animals'. ...

A further experience had to do with excrement and said that it belonged to the mother earth. The plant I had eaten had now become part of me and yet there was this part that was left. This was organic matter useful to soil. In growing, the plant had used up part of the organic content of the soil, and now that I had eaten the plant, I had produced organic matter necessary for the soil. I realized that I should close this vital cycle that I had been breaking for so many years. If I wanted the soil to support my plants, I must support the soil, and give back what was hers.

So, composting also became a way of life. In addition to our excrement, all of the small scraps of unused organic matter were carefully saved to be composted together and returned to the soil. In a short time, this experience expanded to mean the recycling of everything recyclable, and the avoidance of those things which were considered to be unrecyclable. Paper is recycled to produce more paper or burned with the burnable to produce heat and light, and the ashes placed in the garden where the minerals can be reused by the plants. In this way, the garbage carried away from the house has been reduced to one small sack a week. ...

We are each a dynamic ongoing union of the four elements, and should take some time each day at mealtimes or in quiet meditation to celebrate and contemplate; wonder at the nature of this union. Such experience tells me that it is fitting to support the life of air, earth, fire, and water, and that they will support us for as long as is necessary.[4]

In keeping with the concept of the unity of all forms of life, in recent years American Zen Buddhists have been involving themselves increasingly in reforestation projects. Zen centers, also, have interested themselves in farming, using organic fertilizers and demonstrating the Buddhist's understanding of the principles of ecology. The above paragraphs were written before the fuel crisis became a matter of national and international concern. We might note, however, that the conservationist attitude of American Buddhists is one which encourages the conservation of fuel as well as other natural resources. It has been our observation that the cars driven by devoted practitioners of the Buddhist Way are most frequently compact models; that meditation halls tend to be chilly except in the summer; that electric bulbs used for general lighting in Zen and Tibetan centers are usually few, of low wattage, and turned off when not needed; and that Zen devotees sometimes make their own candles for use on the altar. All of this, then, suggests that the Buddhist approach to ecology is also one which, if adopted by others, might have helped to prevent a fuel shortage.

## Race Relations and Civil Rights

The Buddha did not deal specifically with problems of race relations or discrimination against ethnic minorities, since all of those to whom he preached were Indians. However, he did protest against the caste system in the India of his day. The status of the "untouchables" and lower caste Indians during the Buddha's life was analogous to the status of certain racial minority groups in the United States before the onset of the civil rights movement. Had the Buddha lived twenty-five hundred years later, there is little doubt that he would have been a civil rights advocate.

Buddhism (especially Mahayana Buddhism) contends that the Buddha nature is found in all sentient beings, and that all are of equal worth. It is repeatedly stressed that sex, race, nationality, creed, or social class do not alter this basic fact of equality of all mankind. In America, Buddhist priests frequently stress this idea of equality, and one might suppose that this would link Buddhism with the civil rights movement.

If one looks at the history of Buddhism, it is apparent that it has not always been consistent in carrying into action the belief in the equality of all mankind. The Buddha, himself, was reluctant to ordain women. Even today Buddhist nuns may be required to make more vows than are required for monks, and also to acknowledge the superiority of the male. One British female Zen priest who was trained in Japan reported being discriminated against by Japanese priests who resented her because she was a foreigner and a woman.[5] Some Oriental Zen masters who were interviewed hinted at a possible inferiority of Westerners. However, in the United States, we have not heard any Americans complaining of being discriminated against by Buddhists, and there is every indication that all ethnic groups—Jews and Christians, whites and blacks, Latins and Orientals—are treated with respect and friendliness by the Buddhist groups of which they become members.

## Buddhism, Alcoholism, and Drug Dependence

Theoretically, every Buddhist who has accepted the precepts should eschew the use of alcohol and consciousness-altering drugs, since these are specifically forbidden by the fifth precept. In practice, however, whereas virtually all Buddhist priests and scholars would agree that use of hallucinogenic and addictive drugs is contrary to this precept, there is considerable variety in interpretation of the precept as far as its implications for use of alcohol are concerned. Probably there would be unanimity in believing that alcoholism or habitual drunkenness would be breaking the precept, but beyond this there is little agreement. At monasteries alcohol is generally forbidden, but in nonmonastic settings the policy is usually more flexible, and many Buddhists interpret this precept as forbidding the imbibing of alcoholic beverages only to such an extent as would "becloud the mind."

It seems that the Buddhist Churches of America give scant attention to the fifth precept, and that Nichiren Shoshu of America does not forbid either drinking or drug use. However, judging from the testimonials given in Nichiren Shoshu meetings, there is little doubt that one of the frequent results of conversion to Nichiren Shoshu is abandonment of the drug habit. Of all the Buddhist groups in America, those focusing on meditation have been most attractive to young people from the drug scene, and it is these groups that have taken the strongest stand against drug use.

The psychological literature as well as the literature on Zen abounds in descriptions of the altered states of consciousness experienced under the influence of LSD-25 and other hallucinogenic drugs. Descriptions of these drug-induced states often compare them with the experience of satori or enlightenment which may result from Buddhist meditation. Frequently the opinion is expressed that, under certain circumstances, the LSD experience is a satori experience.[6]

The Zen-like quality of the LSD experience for some people is illustrated in the following report by Alan Watts:

> There is first a slowing down of the sense of passing time. This moment becomes of supreme importance, and one seems able to savor its nuances to the utmost. In this state of mind, the future-oriented strivings of ordinary people seem to be somewhat insane: ... missing the whole point of life. ...
>
> Next there are subtle changes in sense-perception. Colors become intensely bright and vivid. Sounds ... acquire astonishing resonance. Light seems to come from inside things ... and the whole world acquires that peculiar luminosity which is normally seen at dawn and at twilight. Both to sight and touch, objects seem to undulate or breathe. ... At this stage, and for some time later ... closing the eyes will reveal extraordinary visions of highly-colored, arabesque designs which, for me, have raised the question that I may be seeing patterns of energy related to the basic structure of my nerves.
>
> In the stage following, the "influence" passes into the thinking process. ... Here, the discriminating mind is confounded because it becomes completely clear that all so-called opposites imply each other and go together in somewhat the same way as the two sides of a single coin. Yes indeed, form is very much emptiness, and emptiness is very much form! And the same goes for "self" and "other," as also for what you *do* voluntarily and what *happens* to you involuntarily: it's all the same process. ...
>
> But here there is a danger point in the experience, especially for those who have not had previous training in Zen, Yoga, or some similar discipline. It may appear, on the one hand, that you are the helpless victim of everything that happens, a total puppet of fate. ... On the other hand, it may appear that you yourself, like God, are doing and are personally reponsible for everything that happens. Paranoia or megalomania may result from siding with either aspect of

this experience—in other words, from failing to see that these are two opposite ways of looking at the same state of affairs. . . .

But if this stage is passed without panic . . . the rest of the experience is total delight. . . . For there follows what, in Buddhist terms, would be called an experience of the world as *dharmadhatu,* of all things and events, however splendid or deplorable from relative points of view, as aspects of a symphonic harmony which, in its totality, is gorgeous beyond all belief. . . .

But, in my own experience, the most interesting thing seems to happen just at the moment when the chemical wears off and you "descend" from these exalted and ecstatic experiences into your ordinary state of mind. For here, in "the twinkling of an eye," there is the realization that so-called everyday or ordinary consciousness is the supreme form of awakening. . . . The *problem* vanishes, for the problem was the ever-impossible one of representing reality consistently in the forms of ideas and words, or of looking for something beyond and above this eternal here-and-now. This is where Zen language makes perfect sense. The ultimate meaning of Buddhism is MU!—or "The-sound-of-one-hand" —or of my old worn-out sandals.[7]

Daisetz Suzuki, writing on "Religion and Drugs," concedes the superficial similarity in the content of the experiences from hallucinogenic drugs and those resulting from religious practice. However, he contends that they are not equivalent because the drug-induced experience represents illusion and fantasy, whereas the religious experience reaches the *true man.* That is, what is crucial is not the experiences themselves but *the one* who does the experiencing.[8]

Illustrating his point, Suzuki says, "Deep in the inner recesses of religion is the *true man.* To be fully human means to become the *true man.* However much one may see before him, externally and objectively, a god-like world of wonder, and 'expanding his mind' induce a state of holy trance, such phenomena are all spurious and imaginary. They have nothing whatever to do with religion. This is because the *true man* is not present. It is not a question of what is seen or how it is being seen, but of the *true man* who is doing the seeing. Only when one becomes this *man* himself does one enter the realm of religion."[9]

Of those who have described the LSD experience as Zen-lik , as resembling satori, some have had no experience with Buddhi.. meditation; others have had some experience with such meditation but have not experienced kensho or satori. Most of those who have had more extensive experience with zazen or some other form of Buddhist meditation, and those who have had a true kensho experience resulting from meditation, see the LSD experience as but a weak and shallow imitation of the real thing. Alan Watts points out that the satori experience arrived at through LSD is remembered, but the "true feeling of it passes off," so that he prefers the simple practice of zazen.[10] Ray Jordan, before his kensho experience, had believed that the LSD experience was similar to Zen, and could be an aid to realizing prajna as well as in the development of meditational practice; but after a true kensho experience resulting from Zen practice he expressed the conviction that LSD and other hallucinogens are obstacles in the practice of Zen.[11]

Comparing the true kensho experience with his LSD experiences, Jordan found the true kensho experience to have greater vividness and clarity, with the LSD experiences like "shadows or indirect reflections" of the events experienced in the Zen sesshin during which kensho occurred.[12] He also found the Zen experience to have a greater relationship to life events which followed it, than was true of the LSD experience.[13] Finally, he made an observation similar to some of Suzuki's comments, saying, "I am convinced that some events which have sometimes occurred in conjunction with the use of psychedelics may be similar to kensho experiences as *experiences*. What is essential in kensho, however, is not the experiential events but the Reality."[14]

Virtually all Zen masters, Tibetan gurus, and teachers of Buddhist meditation of whatever sect in the United States, report that a large percentage of young adults coming as new students for training in meditation have done some experimenting with drugs. Most of this has involved marijuana and the hallucinogens—especially LSD— with very few having been on heroin or other hard drugs. Many wanting to meditate have had a glimpse of rapture or of a spiritual dimension to life through their drug experience, but have recognized it as shallow or transitory and are looking for something deeper and more permanent, divorced from any outside agent. Some who have not actually experimented with drugs have admitted an interest in doing so but have indicated their preference for an experience which is not based on an alteration of body chemistry.

*y* of four meditation centers in the United States, Tyler about fifty percent of those with a background of drug acted a Buddhist meditation center decided not to medi-Zen practice, apparently feeling that they either did not e up the drug habit or could not do so.[15] (How many of these ___ lly did continue with the drug practice, of course, is not known.) These same four centers reported that, of 446 former drug users who did undertake meditation, 441 (99%) stopped drug use. In three of the centers drug use was forbidden, and in the fourth members were "strongly urged" to discontinue the habit.[16] Unfortunately, there is no information on how many of those who discontinued the use of drugs after beginning meditation would have done so had they not undertaken the meditation experience.

In contacts with twenty Buddhist meditation centers, this writer found thirteen where drug use was specifically forbidden, and seven where it was strongly disapproved. Where it was forbidden, there were three centers which refused to accept students who reported any recent or deep involvement with drugs. In centers where drug usage was not actually forbidden, it was reported that most users who practiced meditation found the effect of the drug to be such that it was extremely difficult for them to maintain the self-discipline required by the program of meditation, so that the drug habit was usually abandoned. One Zen teacher commented that "probably 75-90% of the people stop the use of drugs after meditating regularly for some time."[17] Another expressed the opinion that "all those who persist in the practice of meditation inevitably discontinue drug use."[18]

The attitude of Zen Buddhists toward drug use is expressed in comments made by the abbot of a Korean Zen temple in the United States, who said,

> "Orthodox Buddhism frowns on the use of intoxicating substances willfully ingested. It is against the Fifth Precept... The aim of Buddhist meditation being the attainment of Mindfulness at all times leading to the great Awakening, Enlightenment, the use of any such agents would be a deterrent to this end. Buddhist Masters unanimously oppose the practice of drug use as tending to separate practice and will, and lead to clinging or attachment to a particular substance, seen by Buddhists as the very cause of Suffering....[19]

According to Kapleau, "the spiritual heights can no more be scaled by smoking pot and dropping acid than a mountain can be climbed by looking at a map of it while reclining in an easy chair drinking beer. It is the climbing that brings joy and strength—joy in the release from the bondage of self and mountain, top and bottom; strength to LIVE in this realization."[20]

Tyler agrees with various Zen masters in his expressed opinion that meditation is a promising approach for the prevention and cure of drug abuse.[21] Certainly it is an alternative which holds out the possibility of psychological growth rather than dependency.

*Poverty and Welfare*

Traditionally, Buddhism has been very much involved with social welfare, and in Buddhist countries the problems of poverty and unemployment have been prominent among the concerns of the Buddhist Church. Buddhist philosophy, also, has stressed simplicity of living with a minimum of waste, with the idea that the surplus would go for the support of the church and its projects, and to help those less fortunate than oneself. In the United States, however, many Buddhist centers are operating on a shoestring budget and are burdened with mortgage payments, so there is little surplus for the support of charitable enterprises. Recently several Zen centers have been concerning themselves with the question of how the Zen Way can be translated into a way of doing business so that the needs of all may be met. In at least one such center there are plans for organizing a labor union on such a basis that neither labor nor management will be motivated by greed and a wish to exploit the other.

Many members of Nichiren Shoshu of American come from disadvantaged groups, and this organization states that if money and a job are what one needs in order to attain happiness, these may be attained by diligent chanting. Whatever faith in the Gohonzon and zealous chanting may have to do with the practitioner's change in fortunes, fellow-members of Nichiren Shoshu offer encouragement and support, and lend assistance to the individual who needs food, a job, an apartment, or money for tuition. Hence, it may be said that they do concern themselves seriously with problems of poverty and welfare and do what they can to help.

In the more prosperous BCA churches, service projects of various types are often undertaken. These include projects such as running a drug clinic, supporting a pregnancy counseling program, conducting services in prisons and hospitals, or planning facilities and programs for senior citizens.[22] Tibetan Buddhist groups in the United States are contributing to the support of Tibetan refugees,[23] and the Sino-

American Buddhist Association offers free meals to senior citizens.[24]

All of this adds up to the fact that, although Buddhist groups in the United States may not be as systematically involved in charitable enterprises as their Asian counterparts, engaging in service to others is a part of the life of the American Buddhist, as it is for the Asian Buddhist.

## Law and Order

Because of the inaccuracies in crime statistics and the many variables related to the incidence of crime, any attempt at comparing crime rates in Buddhist and non-Buddhist countries would be meaningless, as would be any attempt at comparing the incidence of crime among Buddhists and non-Buddhists in the United States. However, it may be mentioned that virtually all Buddhist groups place considerable emphasis on keeping the precepts, and many place stress on being good citizens.

Particularly in BCA churches and other Buddhist churches of the congregational worship type, there are numerous organizations and programs with character education objectives. These include the Sunday School, Boy Scouts, Campfire Girls, athletic leagues, and youth service groups.

Nichiren Shoshu of America prides itself on its good citizenship record and the commendations it has received from the mayors of various cities where it has held its annual conventions. One member of the executive staff at national headquarters in Santa Monica said that, in the late 1960s, most of those joining NSA were "bums," but indicated that this no longer was the case. Several young men who are now law-abiding members of the establishment—and liking it that way—said they had at one time engaged in stealing, vandalism, and flouting of the law in many ways, but that Nichiren Shoshu had helped them to get on the right track. Nichiren Shoshu does not preach or punish, but creates an atmosphere which makes good citizenship and respect for the law seem like the most rewarding way to choose.

## Child-Rearing and the Buddhist Family

Buddhism has never placed much emphasis on the concept of family, or the concept of the specific roles of parents and children as determined by their Buddhist identity. Buddhism in America was imported principally from East Asia, where the family ethic was mostly Confucian in its orientation. Hence, although Sunday Schools were established in some of the Jodo Shinshu churches of America around the turn of the century, most Buddhists of Oriental ancestry did not regard Buddhism as contributing too significantly to a sense of "family." In fact, with Buddhism's characteristic tolerance for other religions and the Oriental's tendency to be pragmatic, many Buddhist parents encouraged their children to attend Christian Sunday Schools.

After World War II the situation began to change, at least in the Japanese-American community. The nisei, many of whom had attended Christian Sunday Schools as children, began to develop a new sense of identity which involved a blend of identification with their Japanese heritage and a wish to be thoroughly American. They saw the Buddhist background of their parents as a part of the heritage which they wanted for themselves and their children, but they wanted a Buddhism congruent with modern Western psychology and the American way of life. One result of this was a working out of a Sunday School curriculum strongly influenced by developments in the Sunday Schools of Christian churches, with much attention paid to translating Buddhism into parent-child and peer relationships. In addition, ministers of Buddhist churches in America began preaching sermons dealing with family relationships, young mothers had discussion sessions on child psychology, and members of BCA headquarters staff prepared leaflets on Buddhism in relation to successful marriage.

Soka Gakkai in Japan has always insisted that any convert to Nichiren Shoshu must bring the rest of his family into the fold. In the United States, where shakubuku is less aggressive than in Japan, not so much stress is placed on this. At the Nichiren Shoshu meetings which this writer attended, Japanese mothers frequently brought their young children, but Caucasian mothers almost never did so. In Ikeda's book, *The Family Revolution,* he deals with each individual's "human revolution" to create a meaningful family life. He does not, however, say anything about chanting or about Buddhism in connection with family life.[25]

Rissho Koseikai, another Nichiren group in Japan, has made extensive use of group counseling in dealing with problems of parent-child relations. It has also used this approach in its small American mission, with Buddhist principles being used as a guide to family relations.

In the Zen and Tibetan Buddhist groups in America, most members are non-Orientals who come from Jewish or Christian backgrounds. Often they have begun the practice of meditation because of personal problems of their own and without any thought of embracing Buddhism as a religion. When they finally do decide to "take the refuge," it is with a sense of doing so by means of exercising a free choice rather than because they have been pressured into it. Many of these have been quite hesitant to urge their children to become Buddhists, or even to encourage them to become involved with Buddhism, feeling that their children must be entirely free to choose for themselves. However, with the proliferation of Buddhist "communities," Buddhist parents who are members of these communities have often felt that they wanted to share with their children the feeling of "belongingness" which the Buddhist community has given them.

At some meditation centers, children and adolescents are given instructions in meditation techniques, and Sunday Schools have been started, but this is still on a very small scale. Of the meditation centers, Zen Center in Rochester has perhaps most successfully integrated the children into the Buddhist community while at the same time trying not to alienate them from their non-Buddhist peers.

Philip Kapleau's talk on "Suggestions for Bringing up Children According to the Teachings of Zen Buddhism" represents a breakthrough in attempting to cope with the problem of the family where parents are Zen Buddhists.[26] The principal point made in his talk was that Buddhism should not be forced on a child, but parents should provide a home environment that reflects the emotional and devotional qualities of Buddhism so the child will be ready for Buddhist practice when he has matured sufficiently.

Kapleau suggests that, in the preschool period, the environment of the child should include pictures, stories, and songs that will orient the child toward Buddhist imagery and teachings. He suggests also that mealtime chants be used.

During the elementary school years, Kapleau says, making a game of having the family do zazen together each evening can be a meaningful experience for all, and give the child a beginning in learning self-discipline. Then, in the preadolescent and adolescent years, the child will be ready for disciplined forms of exercise such as judo or hatha yoga, studies of Buddhist art, encouragement to think of the center of being as located in the area just below the navel, and more formal instruction in zazen. He believes that at the age of eighteen the young adult is ready to take the refuges and precepts in an initiation ceremony.

The way in which Buddhism becomes a meaningful part of life

for the children of Zen Center at Rochester is illustrated in the description of a festive celebration, in 1972, of the Buddha's birthday. On that occasion the center was gaily decorated with colorful paper models of birds, fish, and other animals. When all were gathered, everyone witnessed the ceremony of tea and flowers, in which the roshi offered a flower and then used sweet tea to bathe an image of the baby Buddha, following which flowers brought by others were gathered and placed before the Buddha. Then, in the context of a puppet theater, the children heard stories about the birth of the Buddha.[27] (The ceremony of bathing the Buddha on Buddha's birthday is traditional in most Buddhist temples and centers.)

## Buddhism and Health

The attainment of mental and physical well-being is not a major objective of Buddhism, but is recognized as an outcome of pursuing the Buddhist way of life—especially if that way involves the strict observance of the precepts, and the regular practice of Buddhist meditation.

Some Buddhists express disapproval of those whose principal motivation for the practice of Buddhist meditation is the attainment or maintenance of health. On the other hand, Yasutani Roshi designated "Zen for the improvement of health" ("Bompu Zen") as one of the "five varieties of Zen."[28] Chogyam Trungpa indicates that "basic sanity" is an acceptable objective for Buddhist meditation,[29] and Tarthang Tulku expresses an interest in using Tibetan Buddhism as a clinical psychological approach to relieve anxiety.[30] It is also reported that, before his death, Suzuki Roshi of Zen Center, San Francisco, was discussing the organization of a Zen mental health clinic. In addition, there is widespread agreement that a high percentage of Americans who become interested in Buddhism are drawn to it because of their hope for peace of mind and relief from anxiety, and most who stay with it feel that they have attained these objectives.

With physical illness so frequently having its psychosomatic components, it is difficult to evaluate the extent to which improved physical well-being resulting from Buddhist meditational practices may reflect the mitigation of anxiety or a lessening of hostility. Overlooking the psychosomatic aspects of sickness and health, the kind of life lived by the individual who is affiliated with the average Buddhist monastic or residential center is such as to favor the development of physical fitness. Plenty of outdoor exercise, abstention from alcohol and tobacco, a well-balanced diet, and regular hours of work and rest combine to produce a regimen which contributes to organic health. In summary, whether the problems of America be those associated with international conflict, crime, drug dependency, the generation gap, race relations or illness, Buddhism does speak to these problems and has significant contributions to make toward their solution.

## Buddhist Sectarianism and Fragmentation

Buddhist ideology and practices do have relevance to the problems of American society. However, Buddhists as a group are not making any significant impact as far as social action is concerned. Their ineffectiveness is probably due largely to the fact that Buddhists constitute a very small minority in the American population, with a large proportion of that minority representing a segment of still another relatively nonactivist minority. Another factor is Buddhism's noninvolvement with politics in the United States. Significant also is the fact that Buddhism in America is not a unitary movement, but is fragmented by sectarianism and internal conflict.

### Sectarianism, Personalism, and Racism

The Japanese missionaries who introduced Buddhism to the United States brought with them a sectarian type of Buddhism. The promotion of sectarianism has persisted over the years, and in some cases has been a deterrent to healthy growth as well as a block to unified action.

In the Zen and Tibetan sects a factor making for divisions within a given sect is the tendency for disciples of particular teachers to form exclusive enclaves. The syndrome of "my Roshi is better than your Roshi" or "my Rinpoche is better than your Rinpoche" often stands in the way of cooperative endeavor.

As yet there are relatively few Caucasian or black Buddhist priests or teachers as compared to the number of those of Oriental background. It seems that there is some prejudice against those who are not Orientals—a feeling that a non-Oriental cannot really understand Buddhism. One Caucasian Buddhist nun, commenting about a Caucasian Zen master, said, "I know he's good, but I feel that I must have a *Japanese* Roshi."

### Political Maneuvering and Power Struggles

In various parts of the country attempts have been made to combat the divisive effects of Buddhist sectarianism by organizing nonsectarian or intersectarian Sanghas, but with little success. Attempts have been made also to get different Buddhist groups together for joint projects or ritual observances, but usually political maneuvering and power struggles have resulted in abandonment of these efforts.

In most cities where there are Buddhists in any significant number, there are Buddhist Ministerial Associations. In meetings of these associations, Buddhist priests exchange ideas on problems of mutual concern but seldom do much in the way of really working together, although the degree of conflict and cooperation varies from one community to another. In one city visited, there was also an Association of Assistant Ministers of Buddhist Churches, and in this locality the conflict between ministers and their assistants was greater than the sectarian conflict.

## "Dharma Hoppers"

One observation often made about Americans interested in Buddhism is that they tend to be "Dharma hoppers," shopping around for a magic key to happiness and peace of mind, then dropping out when they discover that Buddhism is a "do-it-yourself kick." Many have tried several Buddhist sects, some have tried several Christian denominations before becoming Buddhists, and some have played around with Yoga, Krishna Murti, or Sufi. All of this does not make for the kind of solidarity needed for any concerted attack on the problems of society.

## Ecumenism, Cooperation, and "Peaceful Coexistence"

Despite the great deal of fragmentation that exists in Buddhist churches in America, there also are evidences of ecumenism. This is taking several forms: (1) establishment of nonsectarian or intersectarian churches and monasteries; (2) intersectarian sharing of resources, for example, Sunday School materials and visual aids; (3) exchange of priests or ministers on occasion; (4) integration of meditational-type approaches into ceremonial-type churches; and (5) joint services involving different sects and/or non-Buddhist groups. In each of these ways Buddhists of different sects do get together in comfortable interaction, coexistence, or union.

Is sectarianism really in conflict with Buddhist unity and a block to effective action? Some would say that it need not be.

An often-quoted Japanese Buddhist dictum says that many roads lead to the top of Mount Fuji. With few exceptions, most Buddhist groups in the Orient hold that Buddhism is Buddhism; that many paths lead to the attainment of its objectives; that different paths leading to the goals are preferred by different persons; but that any given chosen path is not necessarily superior to all other paths for all persons. This Oriental view of sectarianism is different from the view of most Westerners who, despite the ecumentical movement, are inclined to think of Heaven as reserved especially for Presbyterians, or Baptists, or Roman Catholics. But it is not beyond the grasp of some Western Christians and Buddhists.

Exemplifying Buddhists who can accommodate sectarianism within the context of tolerance and unity is Mary Farkas. Speaking as a Zen Buddhist while addressing a group of BCA Sunday School teachers, she said, "I do not see any conflict in the various views of Buddhists, any more than there is conflict in the hundred views of Fuji. The Dharmadatu has room for every way to be fully expressed without conflict. So shouting *Mu* and reciting *Namu Amida Butsu* are not in conflict. Let us each do our utmost. All the elements of Buddhism are beautiful, like the pieces we see in a kaleidoscope. Whatever pattern we twist it to, we can enjoy."[31]

Looking at the total scene, it is clear that Buddhism in America is fragmented and sectarian, but at the same time is tending toward ecumenism and synthesis with other groups. It is clear, also, that sectarianism does not always mean conflict; rather, it can mean comfortable, meaningful, enriching coexistence and interaction. More importantly, it can mean communication and understanding. And perhaps these are the necessary forerunners of cooperative social action.

# 10

# Buddhism, Psychology, and Psychotherapy

Buddhist scholars have repeatedly emphasized that Buddhism is a philosophy and a religion, and that it is not a psychological system. Kapleau dislikes being asked to provide psychological explanations of Zen concepts, and Suzuki warned that a term such as the "unconscious," when used by the Zen Buddhist, is not a psychological term in either a narrower or broader sense.[1] Nevertheless, one finds in Buddhist literature many terms included in the working vocabulary of the Western psychologist—terms such as self, ego, consciousness, the unconscious, and insight. The temptation exists, then, to attempt to translate these terms into modern psychological concepts as well as to use current Western psychological constructs in describing the methods, processes, and results of the Buddhist approaches to meditation. As witness to the irresistibility of this temptation, for more than two decades psychologists and psychiatrists have been writing on the psychological implications of Buddhism, especially Zen.[2] Until his death, C. J. Jung was fascinated by possible parallels between Buddhist beliefs and his own conceptual system.[3] Many of the articles on this subject have appeared in *Psychologia*, an English-language journal of Oriental psychology published in Japan, with authors including both Japanese and Westerners.

Since the 1920s the two comprehensive theories of human nature having the greatest influence on American psychology have been the Freudian and behavioristic views, with psychoanalytic thinking dominating clinical theory and practice and experimentalistic-positivistic-behavioristic approaches influencing the form and content of psychological research. In the early 1960s, however, a number of splinter groups outside of these two schools coalesced to form a significant third force, designated as "humanistic" psychology. This force has become institutionalized in the Association of Humanistic Psychology. Buddhism, with its basically humanistic orientation, has caught the imagination of this group of psychologists, and Buddhists are frequently invited to present papers at regional and national meetings of American psychologists.

Branching off from the humanistic psychology movement another group has emerged, which is known as the Association for Transpersonal Psychology. Its field is defined as "concerned with the empirical scientific study and responsible implementation of the findings relevant to: spiritual paths, becoming, meta-needs (individual and species-wide), ultimate values, unitive consciousness, peak experiences, B-values,[4] compassion, ecstasy, mystical experience, awe, being, self-actualization, essence, bliss, wonder, ultimate meaning, transcendance of the self, spirit, oneness, cosmic awareness, individual and species wide synergy, theories and practices of meditation, sacralization of everyday life, transcendental phenomena, cosmic self-humor and playfulness, and related concepts, experiences, and activities."[5] Both the *Journal of Humanistic Psychology* and the *Journal of Transpersonal Psychology* accept articles dealing with Buddhist psychology, and those affiliated with the sponsoring organizations consider religion as subjective experience to be a proper subject for scientific investigation. (It is conceded that this may require a broader conception of science than that usually accepted today.[6])

An important factor in the articulation of a Buddhist psychology comprehensible to Americans is the growing interest in such an endeavor on the part of Buddhist adherents. Among the disciples of Asian Zen masters and Tibetan lamas in America, probably psychologists represent the largest single professional group. The enthusiasm of these disciples has doubtless often infected their teachers, with a resulting dialogue which has helped to translate Eastern, esoteric concepts into terms meaningful to Westerners. Tarthang Tulku of the Tibetan Nyingmapa Meditation Center in Berkeley, working with a group of psychologists, opened the Nyingma Institute in the summer of 1973, where nearly sixty psychotherapists gathered for an eight-week program on the Nyingma approach to psychology and psychotherapy. Along analogous lines. Dr. Thich Thien-An, a Vietnamese Buddhist priest designated as president of the newly incorporated College of Oriental Studies in Los Angeles, has listed East-West Psychology as one of the five departments in which instruction is offered.[7] Also, Chogyam Trungpa, seeing Buddhist practice in America in terms of an approach to the development of basic sanity, seeks to interpret it in an idiom meaningful to the American psychologist and psychiatrist.

## CONSCIOUSNESS AND THE UNCONSCIOUS

The Theravadin view of consciousness is found in the *Abhidamma* (Sanskrit, Abhidarma), one of the three "baskets" of the *Pali Canon*, said to be the oldest recorded psychology.[8] As a psychological work rather than a metaphysical one, the Abhidamma seeks to provide a classification of human experience which will make clear the fact of impermanence and the illusory nature of the self.

Consciousness, regarded by the Buddhist as a characteristic of all sentient beings, is depicted in the Abhidamma as consisting of a series of momentary mental states comprised of unanalyzable elements or atoms known as *dhammas* (Sanskrit, dharmas). These unanalyzable elements compiled into groups of 79 to 174 by different Buddhist schools, are sometimes likened to the individual frames of a motion picture film, which when shown quickly and successively give the impression of continuous action.[9] At any moment in consciousness a multiplicity of elements is involved, with each of these elements conditioning others and being conditioned by others. They occur in temporary combinations which are constantly in the process of integration and disintegration.[10] Each element also represents both the result of a previous state and the cause of a future state of consciousness. The Abhidamma indicates that all phenomena have three elements: consciousness or awareness, the quality of consciousness or that which accompanies it, and physical form or corporeality. For each state of consciousness, fifty-two mental properties or concomitants are said to be possible, thus creating the potentiality of a great variety of mental events.[11]

There are many ways of classifying the elements of consciousness. For example, they may be classified as conditioned or unconditioned; defiled or undefiled; or according to whether they involve the material-sensory world, the world of pure form, the world of

formlessness, or the transcendental world.[12] One classification believed to have practical applicability as a means of helping the individual to realize the illusory nature of the "self" is a classification
in terms of five aggregates or "heaps" (*skandhas*) —form (matter),
feelings, perceptions, impulses or volitional reactions, and consciousness (awareness).[13]

Although an individual may be inclined to say, "I have an itchy
rash," "I have a headache," "I believe you," or "I enjoy the music,"
there is no "I" or "me" among the elments of consciousness listed
in the Abhidhamma. Rather, analyzing "I have an itchy rash" in
terms of the five aggregates, one would say, "The rash on the chest
is the *form* or matter; an uncomfortable itching is the *feeling*; the
*perception* involves sight, touch, and pain; the *volitional reaction* involves fear that the itching may portend something harmful, resentment at the discomfort, a wish to scratch, a greed for comfort and
well-being; and consciousness is *awareness* of all this." Being concerned with the processes or thoughts involved, the experiencer then
has no need to postulate a thinker—an "I" or a "self"—and one sets
up a habit of viewing all things impersonally with detachment.

There are three terms in Buddhist literature which are commonly translated as "mind" or consciousness: *citta, manas,* and *vijnana.* Of these, citta refers to consciousness in the form of any individual thought or mental event, and it is consciousness in this sense
which is analyzable into the dhammas or elements. Manas refers to
consciousness as it is involved with selecting, judging, and evaluating.
This is the mind which is said to create and control the dhammas,
the consciousness which represents understanding of the nature of
the world. It is subject to modification and represents consciousness
which is involved in the emergence of intuitive wisdom. Vijnana represents consciousness in the sense of "pure awareness"—the fifth of
the aggregates. In some Mahayana sects, this is the only type of con-
ciousness which is believed to be real, and which is believed to trans-
migrate from rebirth to rebirth.[14] If consciousness is considered in
these three aspects, it is perceived as both active and reactive, as well
as embracing what Western psychologists have referred to as consciousness, the unconscious, the subconscious, the preconscious, and what
Bucke has designated as "cosmic consciousness."[15]

Considering consciousness in its various aspects, Mahayana Buddhists have sometimes distinguished eight classes of consciousness.
The first six are the sense experiences involving sight, sound, smell,
taste, touch, and thought. The seventh is manas, and the eighth is

*alaya-vijnana,* or "store-consciousness." Kapleau states that, whereas the intellect creates the illusion of a subject "I" standing apart from an object world, it is not persistently conscious of this "I." In the stage of manas, however, this awareness of a discrete ego-I is constant. In addition, manas also acts as a conveyor of the "seed-essence" of sensory experience to the store-consciousness, "from which specific 'seeds' are reconveyed by manas to the six senses, precipitating new actions, which in turn produce other 'seeds'."[16]

The concept of alaya-vijnana or store-consciousness deserves further comment. A Mahayana group postulated that there is an over-personal consciousness which is the foundation of all acts of thought, and that the impressions of the whole of past experience (in this and previous lives) are "stored up" in it, comprising sort of an *unconscious*.[17] Although this concept is not too clearly articulated, the impression is conveyed that the existence of this store-consciousness is regarded as at least one source of the illusion of a permanent "self" or "soul." This concept appears to have much in common with Jung's concept of the "racial unconscious" or "collective unconscious."

The Theravadins as well as Mahayanists have made provision for the unconscious, with the Abhidamma postulating an "unconscious stream" into which an object may enter, representing a latent potentiality for conscious experience.

The above concepts are but a few of the many and very complex ideas about consciousness and the unconscious found in the Buddhist scriptures and commentaries. A more detailed and extended explication of these theories would seem to serve no purpose here, since American psychologists are not likely to adopt any of these theories to replace those of Freud or Jung with which they are more comfortable. As far as the concept of the unconscious is concerned, Buddhist psychologists are more likely to be Jungian than Freudian, because the concept of the collective unconscious can readily accommodate itself to the doctrines of karma and rebirth. Mahayanists, in general, seem to find the Buddhist concept of consciousness consistent with William James's idea of the "stream of consciousness," but some Theravadins would look upon the idea of a "stream" as an illusion analogous to that of apparent movement exemplified by neon signs.

Looking at the various Buddhist theories and classification schemes of consciousness and the unconscious, two facts emerge: (1) the Buddhist classification schemes with reference to consciousness are much more detailed and complex than any of the models suggested by Western psychologists; (2) within the Buddhist scheme are categories of consciousness which seem to cover the phenomena included in the "preconscious," the "personal unconscious," and the "collective unconscious," as these are known to Western psychologists. It should be noted, also, that, although modern psychology began as the scientific study of conscious experience and Gestalt psychologists have always been interested in the nature of perception, until the last decade American psychologists have had little interest in studying the nature of consciousness itself. With the growing popularity of Buddhist and yogic meditational practices, however, that situation is changing. An interest in studying the "altered states of consciousness" resulting from meditation has led to an interest in the scientific study of consciousness itself, and in this sense the Buddhist psychology of two thousand years ago is influencing American psychology of today.

## MEDITATION AND ALTERED STATES OF CONSCIOUSNESS

Reports of individuals who have engaged in Buddhist and yogic meditational practices make it clear that such practices do result in altered states of consciousness. Even the person who does not attain enlightenment experiences a deepening and expansion of awareness—a greater openness to experience and a change in its quality. Further changes are associated with the attainment of enlightenment, whether one calls it nirvana, satori, oneness with God, or mystical union. Goleman classifies meditation—specific states of consciousness as a subcategory of "altered states of consciousness," but includes under this rubric only those states attained through meditation that transcend normal conditions of sensory awareness and cognition.[18]

The experiential aspects of meditational states have been described in previous chapters of this book. Discussing the satori of Zen, Maupin notes that, "while intuiting totality, the individual is said to perceive objects more objectively than before, less distorted by personal motives."[19] Fingarette states that the "dwelling in voidness" of the mystic involves a complete openness to experience, unblocked by preconceived ideas or overly-rigid maintenance of logical forms.[20] Suzuki describes the results of satori in the following terms: "All our mental activities will now be working on a different key, which will be more satisfying, more peaceful, more full of joy than anything you ever experienced before. The tone of life will be altered. There is something rejuvenating in the possession of Zen. The spring flower will look prettier, and the mountain stream runs cooler and more transparent."[21]

William James considered mystic states as characterized by the subliminal or subconscious mind's breaking through into consciousness,[22] and Maupin sees the results of meditation in similar fashion.[23] Certainly much that is described as resulting from meditation is consistent with the concept of the individual who is not in the grip of conflicts and defenses, and who has relatively free access to material in the "preconscious." Yet, concepts such as intuitive awareness and experiencing of "voidness" cannot be readily subsumed under the conventional labels relating to consciousness and the unconscious. Suzuki suggests the term "cosmic unconscious" as a designation for the source of such transcendental experiences, but Bucke and Fromm prefer to speak of "cosmic consciousness."[24] Dean suggests "ultra-conscious" as a suitable label for the "supra-sensory, supra-rational region of the mind, whose existence has been known since antiquity."[25]

Support for the idea of a meditation-specific altered state of consciousness is found in physiological research on Zen priests, yogis, and persons engaging in transcendental meditation.[26] Quite consistently this research shows that brain waves of meditators are characterized by patterns of alpha activity not characteristic of any other state, in addition to certain changes in heart rate, blood pressure, and rate of breathing indicating alterations of functions controlled by the autonomic nervous system. More recently, research reported by Ornstein has suggested that meditation involves activation of the nondominant hemisphere of the cerebral cortex, in contrast to logical thinking, which involves the dominant hemisphere.[27]

## The "True Self"

It is perhaps in the concept of the "true self" or the "real self" that Buddhist thinking differs most from that of Western psychologists, and yet, even in this area, there seems to be some affinity between Eastern and Western thinking.

In Western psychology, it is common to think of the self in dualistic terms, with the self as subject being designated as the ego, and the self as object being referred to as the self. Symonds, especially, stressed the importance of differentiating between these two concepts, placing his view in direct opposition to that of Buddhist thinkers.[28] The views of Carl Rogers and C. J. Jung, however, are easier to reconcile with Buddhist theory.[29]

For Rogers the "self" or the "real self" is the self which embraces all of the significant sensory and visceral experiences of the organism. The self as perceived by the individual himself—the "concept of self"

—may be in essential agreement with the organically experienced self, or may be at variance with it. In Rogers's thinking, a communality between the real self and the concept of self is associated with adjustment, and a divergence between the two is associated with maladjustment.[30] The Buddhist notes that the individual identifies his concept of self as his *real* self, although, in fact, the self as an object of consciousness is a fiction.[31] Rogers would concede that there is never complete identity of the real self and the self-concept, but he would differ from the Buddhist theorist on the nature of the real self.

In the Rogerian view, the individual who has attained self-realization is characterized by naturalness, openness to experience, acceptance of others, trust of self, self-direction, flexibility, and so forth. These characteristics are seen by Sato as also characterizing "Zen people," with the "true self" of Zen being seen as the "limit" in this direction.[32] However, Sato states, there must be a "leap" to reach this limit, and the true self of Zen is not a substantial self, but "Void." The Rogerian self, he says, "may very well develop on the basis of the bottomless bottom of the True Self of Zen."[33] The "self" as postulated by Jung may be closer to the Buddhist concept of the real self than the Rogerian real self, although Jung contended that communication between himself and Japanese Zen scholars was not good enough for him to be sure that they were talking about the same concept.

In Jungian theory, the psyche is regarded as consisting of various interacting systems, chief of which are the *ego* or conscious mind, the personal unconscious containing material repressed or forgotten, and the collective or *transpersonal* (racial) unconscious containing the *archetypes*. Added to these are the *attitudes* of introversion and extraversion, the functions of thinking, feeling, sensing, and intuiting, and finally the self.[34]

In his earlier writings Jung considered the self as the total personality. However, in his later formulations he regarded it as an archetype representing man's striving for unity, and expressing itself through various symbols, including that of the *mandala* or magic circle. Rather than seeing the self as the total personality, he then saw it as the midpoint of personality around which other systems are constellated. He saw it also as the basic life goal—that which man strives for but seldom reaches, and which motivates him in his search for wholeness.

In terms of the personality structure, Jung saw the self as located between consciousness and unconsciousness.[35] This concept he developed following his studies of Oriental religions, with their stress on a striving for unity and oneness with the world through ritualistic and meditational practices.[36] There is little doubt that he was very much influenced by these studies, but his "self" does not quite correspond to the real self of the Buddhist, as he revealed in an interview with Japanese Professor Hisamatsu.

In the dialogue between Jung and Hisamatsu, Jung compared his concept of self with the concept of *atman,* the latter being seen as personality but at the same time as a superhuman atman. Hisamatsu felt that the concept of atman implied the existence of form and substance, and therefore could not be considered as the equivalent of the Buddhist "true self" with its characteristics of voidness.[37] Hence, although Jung's concept of self seems to have some elements in common with the Buddhist true self, the two are not identical.

## ENLIGHTENMENT AND THE "PEAK EXPERIENCE"

Among the writings of American psychologists, those of the late Abraham Maslow have probably done the most to bridge the gap between the psychologies of East and West. A pioneer in the "third force," he also was interested in transpersonal psychology and at the time of his death was actively involved in the study of mystical experiences and other transcendental experiences.

The two contributions for which Maslow is best known are his research on self-actualization and the "peak experience." Of these, the latter is of particular interest in relation to the experience of enlightenment, although self-actualization and the peak experience are interrelated and both related to what Maslow referred to as a "psychology of being."

In studying the nature of the peak experience, Maslow gave the following instuctions to his subjects:

> I would like you to think of the most wonderful experience of your life; happiest moments, ecstatic moments, moments of rapture, perhaps from being in love, or from listening to music or suddenly 'being hit' by a book or a painting, or from some great creative moment. First list these. And then try to tell me how you feel in such acute moments, how you feel differently from the way you feel at other times,

how you are at the moment a different person in some ways."[38]

Although no one individual reported the complete syndrome, Maslow indicated the following as the characteristics of cognition found in the generalized peak experience:

1. A tendency to perceive the object as a whole, as a complete unit, detached from relations, from possible usefulness, from expediency, and from purpose.

2. "Full" or "total" attention to the perception, with a sense of the whole cosmos being encompassed in the perception.

3. Perception of the object as if it were detached from or irrelevant to human concerns.

4. Intraobject richness.

5. Perception which is relatively ego-transcending, self-forgetful, egoless.

6. Feeling of the peak experience as a self-validating, self-justifying moment which carries its own intrinsic value with it.

7. Disorientation in time and space.

8. Evaluation of the peak experience as good and desirable, and never experiencing it as evil or undesirable.

9. Perception of the peak experience as more absolute and less relative than "normal" experience.

10. Cognition much more passive and receptive than active.

11. Emotional component having a special flavor of wonder, of awe, of reverence, of humility and surrender before the experience as before something great.

12. Perception of the world as a unity or perceiving one small part of the world as if it were for the moment all of the world.

13. Having simultaneously the ability to abstract without giving up concreteness and the ability to be concrete without giving up abstractness.

14. At the higher levels of maturation, the ability to fuse, transcend, or resolve many dichotomies, polarities, and conflicts.

15. A tendency to be godlike in the complete, loving, uncondemning, compassionate, and perhaps amused acceptance of the world and of the person, however bad he may look at more normal moments.

16. Perception which tends strongly to be idiographic and nonclassificatory.

17. A complete though momentary loss of fear, anxiety, inhibition, defense, and control, a giving up of renunciation, delay, and restraint.

18. As the essential Being of the world is perceived by the person, he becomes concurrently closer to his own Being—to being more perfectly himself.

19. In psychoanalytic terms, the peak experience may be seen as "a fusion of ego, id, super-ego and ego-ideal, of conscious and unconscious, or primary and secondary processes, a synthesizing of pleasure principle with reality principle, a regression without fear in the service of the greatest maturity, a true integration of the person at *all* levels."[39]

Summarizing, Maslow defines the peak experience as "an episode, or a spurt in which the powers of the person come together in a particularly efficient and intensely enjoyable way, in which he is more integrated and less split, more open for experience, more idiosyncratic, more perfectly expressive or spontaneous, or fully functioning, more creative, more humorous, more ego-transcending, more independent of his lower needs, etc. He becomes in these episodes more truly himself, more perfectly actualizing his potentialities, closer to the core of his Being."[40]

The characteristics of the peak experience summarized above (which on a more enduring basis are the characteristics of the self-actualizing person) have a ring of familiarity as being characteristic of the experience of satori, or enlightenment. Maslow, in fact, has expressed the opinion that probably the core religious experience of all mystics, including the enlightenment of the Buddha, may be subsumed under the classification of peak experiences.[41]

Also described by Maslow but not as thoroughly investigated as the peak experience are the "nadir-experience" and the "plateau experience." Like the peak experience, the sustained experience on the high plateau is a unitive experience. It is an experience of calm serenity rather than one involving a poignantly emotional, climactic autonomic response. Rather than being experienced as a symbolic "death and rebirth," it is likely to be expressed as pure enjoyment and happiness. Unlike the peak experience, also, it always has a noetic element, and is more under voluntary control than peak experiences.[42] Maslow points out that plateau-experiencing can be earned by long hard work, exemplified by the various "spiritual disciplines," all of which take time, work, study, and commitment.[43]

With relatively few Buddhist meditators really attaining "enlightenment," it seems to us that most who report long term benefits have attained what Maslow calls the "high plateau." (He suggests that, for older persons, this may be healthier than the more sudden peak-experience.[44])

## Psychological Processes Involved in Buddhist Meditation

Psychologists are generally agreed that meditation is primarily an exercise in the deployment of attention, and that it can be at least partially understood on the basis of factors related to the selectivity of sensation and perception, in addition to well-known facts about habituation and dishabituation.[45]

Although even within Buddhism and within a single sect of Buddhism there are multiple techniques of meditation used, all have in common the goal of making it possible for the individual to perceive the world and himself in ways which are new and fresh. In a sense, then, all of the techniques have as an end result the illumination of areas to which the person was once blind—the "opening up" or "expansion" of awareness. However, in one approach to meditation the new vision and expanded awareness are an "after-effect" of a "turning *off*" of awareness, whereas in another approach the expanded awareness is directly cultivated.

Ornstein sees the direct and indirect means of expanding awareness exemplified in two different basic techniques: (1) concentrative meditation in which there is a restriction of awareness to a single, unchanging source of stimulation for a definite period of time, and (2) those techniques which involve a deliberate attempt to open up awareness of the external environment.[46] Examples of the first type of technique are concentration on mantras, visual images, breathing, or koans. The techniques of "just sitting" found in *shikan-taza* and the "bare attention" characterizing the "mindfulness" of *vipassana* meditation would be examples of opening-up techniques. Most schools of Buddhist meditation to some extent use both groups of techniques, even though they may emphasize one type of technique over the other. For example, Tibetan Buddhists use multiple techniques of both types, as do T'ien-t'ai Buddhists. In vipassana, also, the meditator concentrates on his breathing but takes note of all mental processes that distract his attention—thinking, pressing, hurting, intending—so that in a sense he is using both techniques in a single type of practice.

Although one type of meditation technique is a direct opening-up technique, actually both techniques involve a restriction of input during meditation—by sitting motionless, cutting down on light and sound, taking care of all unfinished business before commencing a course of meditation, and so on. Of course, the serious cultivator of Buddhist meditation is expected to continue his meditation in whatever he is doing—while eating, walking, working. As Naranjo says, "Meditation is concerned with the development of a *presence,* a modality of being, which may be expressed or developed in whatever situation the individual may be involved."[47] Nevertheless, the meditator is not expected to make significant progress in meditation while dodging traffic, while arguing politics, or when worrying about the unpredictability of the stock market. So that awareness can be expanded and deepened in significant ways it is necessary that the senses and emotions not be bombarded. This requires a temporary detachment or removal from the confusion and concerns of the outside environment. For this reason, one does not usually find televisions and newspapers in Buddhist meditation centers. Indeed, when one enters a center he is frequently asked to remove shoes in order to cut down on noise, to refrain from engaging in unnecessary conversation, and to eat meals in silence.

## Concentrative Meditation

In concentrative meditation one focuses his attention on a single source of stimulation, attempting to exclude all else from awareness. He tries to keep the unchanging stimulus constantly in mind, as when he visualizes a lotus; or he repeats a sound again and again, as when he is chanting "Nam' myoho renge kyo" or "OM-AH-HUM." Ornstein regards this psychologically as an "attempt to recycle the same subroutine over and over again in the nervous system."[48] This leads to what Buddhism has called "emptiness" or "the void." Psychologists would call it a withdrawal of the senses or a "shutting off" of perception of the outside. This shutting off can be explained from the standpoint of physiological psychology on the basis of "habituation" (of which sensory adaptation is one form).

The phenomenon being discussed can be illustrated by an exercise which Tarthang Tulku sometimes assigns his students. The subject sits before a mirror looking into the eyes of his image, perceiving the image as a person *staring at him.* He continues to look steadily at the image, which may change in various ways, perhaps becoming a cyclops; but if the gaze is a steady one, eventually the image will disappear entirely. Analogous to this phenomenon are experimental observations which show that stabilization of a visual image causes it to disappear completely.

Studying brain wave changes evoked by stabilized images, Lehman, Beeler, and Fender found increased alpha waves from the occipital cortex when the image disappeared.[49] Analogously, Hochberg,

Triebel, and Seaman reported bursts of alpha activity during a "blankout" after exposure to a homogeneous visual field.[50] With findings such as these, it would seem not unreasonable to conclude that the experience of the void occurring as a result of koan concentration during zazen, and the existence of increased alpha activity during concentrative meditation might also be a manifestation of habituation resulting from a recycling of the same input over and over.[51]

Since concentrative meditation results in a turning off of all input processing for a period of time, this makes it possible for the individual to get away from the external environment. While the processing of input is "shut off," dishabituation occurs, so that when the same sensory input is introduced later, it is seen differently, or "anew." Ornstein suggests that this is like coming home again after being on a vacation, when everything looks new and fresh.[52]

## "Opening Up Awareness"

Both the aftereffects of the concentrative type of meditation and of the opening-up type can be interpreted in terms of the psychology of perception.

It is known by both the psychologist and the layman that the information we have about ourselves and the world comes to us through the sensory systems, but that our perceptions represent only a very small portion of the world of physical energy, with most of this energy being "filtered out" and never becoming a part of our conscious experience. The selective nature of our experience of awareness is partly a function of the limitations of our sense organs and the limitation in the "load" which the nervous system can process. However, it is a fact also that we attend to only a very small part of the stimulus field of which we *could* become aware, and that our senses discard and simplify much of the information which impinges on them. In addition, at the level of the central nervous system there is a further sorting of information along a limited number of dimensions.

To some extent the characteristics of potential stimulus objects will determine which ones come into awareness and how we perceive them, but so do our motivations, needs, and past experiences. To some degree attention—and therefore awareness—is involuntary. For example, if a bird were to fly against the windshield of a car, almost everyone would be aware that *something* had been hit. If suddenly confronted with tear gas, nearly everyone would be aware of a noxious stimulus. If one had been lost all day on the desert, he would be unlikely to overlook the presence of water. But not all awareness is involuntary. A housewife busy taking a burned roast from the oven may not hear the doorbell ringing until someone calls her attention to it. Most of us have chest pains every day which we do not notice because we are attending to other things, but if we looked for them we would notice them.

Meditation as expansion of awareness may be of two types: (1) it may occur on the basis of dishabituation, following an experience of "voidness" resulting from concentrative meditation; (2) it may result from a conscious and deliberate attempt to be aware of all that is going on in and around one, without dwelling on or clinging to anything. (Dwelling and clinging restrict awareness because they keep attention from moving on.)

*Non-attachment*

A third technique of meditation which is particularly important in connection with the opening up of awareness is an attitude of non-attachment. About non-attachment Ornstein says, "One major barrier to development of expanded awareness is that we continuously tune out those portions of the external environment that do not suit our needs at the moment.... In its effect on awareness, the practice of non-attachment can be considered as an additional way to remove the normal restrictions on input. If there are no desires, there is less of a bias at any one moment to 'tune' perception."[53]

*Affective and Autonomic Processes*

Virtually all descriptions of the enlightenment or satori experience include allusions to its emotional dimensions. We hear that a person experienced great happiness, joy, gratitude, and bliss. We are also told that practicing Buddhist meditation results in mitigation of anxiety, and a "calming down." Wallace and Benson report a reduction of basal metabolic rate in those engaging in transcendental meditation, and attribute this to control of the autonomic nervous system.[54] Kasamatsu and Hirai also report that the psychogalvanic skin response of Zen priests suggests a low level of emotional disturbance.[55] Studies of yogis indicate that meditation can result in the ability to exercise voluntary control over the functions of the autonomic nervous system, and modern bio-feedback research may soon give us a better understanding of these phenomena than we now have. At present, however, our understanding of the affective aspects of meditation is less complete than our understanding of its cognitive aspects.

## Buddhist Meditation and Psychotherapy

In interviews with Zen masters, Tibetan lamas, and the American disciples of various Buddhist priests and teachers, I have repeatedly been confronted with claims and listened to testimonials which point to the conclusion that countless Americans with emotional problems have been helped by their participation in Buddhist practices—especially the practice of "meditation" (or zazen, if this term is preferred by Zen practitioners). In addition, over a period of more than twenty years, both Japanese and American psychiatrists and clinical psychologists have been publishing articles and books in which the psychotherapeutic potentialities of Buddhist meditation (especially Zen) have been discussed. Unfortunately, Zen masters, Theravada meditation instructors, and Tibetan lamas apparently are rarely if ever members of the American Psychiatric Association or the American Psychological Association, and those American psychologists and psychiatrists who have themselves benefitted from Buddhist practices have seldom reported on their own experiences with meditation. Also, although some of them have used meditational techniques in their clinical practice, they have not published case studies in the professional literature nor done experimental studies with adequate controls. Some have reported on the use of meditation as a supplement to interview techniques or other Western approaches to psychotherapy. In the absence of controls, however, it is difficult to estimate the extent to which improvement is a function of meditation and the degree to which it is due to other aspects of the therapy.

### Therapeutic Potentialities of Buddhist Meditation

One of the few controlled studies showing changes resulting from meditation is that by Lesh, who reported that engaging in zazen improved the empathetic ability of a group of counseling psychologists in training, as compared with a control group.[56]

Humphreys had indicated earlier that a group of English subjects who practiced sitting meditation and breath concentration for several years increased in intuitive development, withdrew projections by which they had tended to distort reality, and showed greater serenity, ability to cope, and compassion. He said, "All who have made this experiment in the last few years have changed remarkably, passing of course through periods of depression and doubt, but finding these well suffered as the price of wider awareness, deeper understanding of external truths, and many a brief experience of things no words can usefully describe."[57]

Kondo stated that he instructed his neurotic patients to practice sitting meditation (shikan-taza) and breath concentration in addition to their psychoanalytically oriented interview sessions with him. After an initial exacerbation of symptoms the exercise seemed to aid progress in therapy. He commented that the sitting blocked use of activity as an escape mechanism to avoid facing problems, and that the eventual result was a more unified feeling of self and development of a calm vigor.[58]

Several psychiatrists have reported to me that use of transcendental meditation in conjunction with psychoanalytically oriented therapy has speeded up therapeutic progress, and some clinical psychologists have reported the very fruitful use of a Soto Zen-type meditation in conjunction with Gestalt therapy and psychodrama.

Stunkard notes that the effect of Zen is to clear away all the symbols which stand between a person and his experience, so that there is regression to preverbal stages of ego organization.[59] In line with this, Maupin suggests the possibility that the use of zazen may enable patients to deal with problems which are inaccessible to other kinds of psychotherapy, that is, problems related to preoedipal experience, in connection with which the verbal communication of therapy runs into difficulty.[60] Similarily, Fromm suggests that zazen might be helpful in the treatment of character disorders.[61] In reviewing the literature and talking with Buddhist Zen masters, teachers, and lamas, I have found no one who has recommended that Buddhist meditation be substituted for Western approaches to psychotherapy. Most who are sophisticated in Western psychology and Buddhist practice, however, would agree with Kasamatsu and Hirai to the effect that Zen and other types of meditation can serve as a useful adjunct to medical and psychological therapy.

The possible usefulness of meditation in the treatment of neurotics and individuals with character disorders seems not to be controversial—at least, it is agreed that its effects probably would not be harmful. When the question of the advisability of using it with the borderline psychotic is considered, however, the guidelines are by no means clear. Stunkard reminds us that enlightenment involves the loss of ego boundaries, and that the accounts of the enlightenment experience have a "psychotic ring."[62] (He does not suggest that there is any permanent loss of ego boundaries.) Personal communications from several apparently schizophrenic persons who have incorporated Buddhist concepts into their schizophrenic thinking, however, suggest that perhaps one should be cautious in using meditational techniques with persons whose ego boundaries are already weak. At the same time, there is evidence to show that a number of schizophrenic individuals have made satisfactory adjustments in the highly controlled and structured atmosphere of the Buddhist monastery.

## Regression in the Service of the Ego

Despite misgivings about the use of meditational techniques with those whose ego boundaries are weak, most who have studied the psychology of meditation in the Buddhist context regard satori or enlightenment as "regression in the service of the ego," or psychologically adaptive regression.[63]

Developmental psychologists have commonly expressed the theory that a breaking up of old patterns, with a consequent temporary regression, is necessary before there can be integration at a more mature level. (The most obvious illustration of this is the disorganization which tends to characterize the pubertal period, when the individual frequently engages in emotionally immature behavior which he has previously abandoned.) This concept seems relevant to the functional significance of the regression taking place in the enlightenment experience.

The reasons for classifying satori as a psychologically adaptive regression are summarized by Maupin as follows:

> First, discussions of satori repeatedly emphasize flexibility in the use of ego functions. One thinks when the situation requires it, and the intellectual mode may be abandoned when it is unnecessary. Secondly, other types of regressions which might be less adaptive—hallucinations, trances, ecstacies— are consistently rejected as spurious by the Zen master. Thirdly, the states of mind which become possible as a result of satori are clearly used for adaptive purposes. . . . Finally, the implied increase in energy, and decrease in conflict, inhibiting self-consciousness and anxiety, suggest that satori promotes adaptation.[64]

## Buddhist Meditation as Relaxation Therapy

Considerable importance is attached to learning relaxation in the early stages of Buddhist approaches to meditation. In Tarthang Tulku's summer program for psychologists, the principal goal for the first two weeks was that of relaxation. The lotus position is said to be conducive to relaxation while at the same time not encouraging the individual to go to sleep. The breathing exercises used in all systems encourage relaxation, and in the Nyingma system yogic exercises also foster relaxation. Speaking especially of the bodily adjustments of zazen, Sato has said that these have effects comparable to those of Jacobson's "progressive relaxation." These effects include a reduction in the quantity of mental activity, a lessening of anxiety by focusing on the "here and now," cathartic release of thoughts or emotions of which the individual was previously unaware, and a facilitation of free association.[65]

## Eastern and Western Approaches to Psychotherapy

Comparisons of Buddhist meditational approaches to therapy with Western psychotherapeutic approaches show parallels as well as differences.

Perhaps one of the most obvious analogies between Western psychotherapy and Eastern meditation is that of the therapist-patient relationship and the master-disciple relationship. Just as the therapist is expected to have undergone therapy as a part of his training, the master or guru must have an emotional understanding of the processes involved in meditation on the basis of his own experience.[66] Lederer comments that the master-disciple relation contains elements of resistance, transference, eventual insight, and resolution of transference as does the relation between patient and analyst.[67] Both types of relationships also require an ultimate dissolving of a dependency tie and rejection of the master or therapist as an authority figure.

Both Eastern and Western approaches to therapy have an ethical orientation. Freud implied that a healthy character develops from the greedy, cruel, and stingy into an active, independent orientation, and Fromm speaks of evolution from the receptive, through the exploitative, hoarding, marketing, to the productive orientation. The Theravada orientation to meditation involves a path of purification with abandonment of lust, greed, and anger, and the Mahayana groups stress the way of love and compassion which develops as a result of engaging in Buddhist practices. Neither Buddhism nor any Western approach to psychotherapy would be regarded as primarily an ethical system. The aim of all approaches in either group transcends that of ethical behavior. Yet all assume that the achievement of their aim brings with it an ethical transformation.[68]

Most Western forms of psychotherapy have as a major aim the attainment of "insight." Freudian psychoanalysis sees this as insight into the causes of neurotic behavior, attained through bringing to consciousness conflicts and memories which have been repressed into the unconscious.[69] Horney would perhaps see insight in terms of a clear perception and understanding of one's defenses.[70] For Adler it would be insight into the difference between the real goal and the fictitious goal.[71] For Rogers it would be insight into the nature of the "real self."[72] For the followers of Sullivan it would be insight into the "parataxic distortions."[73] All of these types of insight presumably result from making the unconscious conscious and involve the dispelling of illusions. Similarly, in Buddhism is found "insight," the "making conscious of the unconscious," and the dispelling of illusions. However, in Buddhist practice these terms have different connotations, although in both systems insight may be gradual or sudden.

Comparing the concept of insight in psychoanalysis and Zen, Lederer says that "where analysis aims to illuminate the unconscious with the clear light of reason, calling this insight, Zen strives to eliminate the intellect, as a noxious interference, from the otherwise free flow of the unconscious. Analysis heightens awareness of self; Zen ideally eliminates self-awareness."[74] Fromm mentions "insight into one's own nature" as a goal of Zen as well as a goal of psychoanalysis, but this insight in the Zen context implies insight into the nonduality of self and object. On the other hand, Fromm contends that, in Zen or psychoanalysis, being fully awake to reality means seeing the object without distortions by greed or fear; seeing it as it is, not as one wishes it or him to be or not to be; seeing without parataxic distortions.[75] Stunkard sees satori as involving no special insight, but does see Zen and psychoanalysis as both involving the abandonment of illusions or distortions of reality. In the case of Zen, however, he notes that the principal illusion to be uprooted is the idea of one's self as an enduring entity.[76]

"Insight," when used as a translation of vipassana, refers to the transcendental insight into, or analysis of, the nature of things—insight into the Buddhist "truths" concerning suffering, impermanence, and the impersonality of all existence.[77] When used by the Theravada Buddhist, it usually has a more precise and specific meaning than when used by the Mahayana Buddhist.

All forms of Buddhist meditation have discouraged discursive thinking—they have concerned themselves with concrete, real life experiences rather than thoughts about life, and in this sense are consonant with an existential approach to psychotherapy.[78] Naranjo notes, also, the parallel between the satipatthana method of "mindfulness" and the exercise of the "awareness continuum" in Gestalt therapy.[79] Both involve suppression of fantasy, minimization of conceptual activity and the elimination of reminiscences, with attention to awareness of the here and now.

So far, no mention has been made of behavior modification therapy in relation to Buddhist practice. This involves the application of principles of conditioning, with the use of positive reinforcement of desirable patterns and avoidance training in connection with undesirable patterns. This would seem to have little relevance to the Buddhist methods discussed here. However, as noted in chapter 6, the methods used by Soka Gakkai in Japan and Nichiren Shoshu of America do seem to utilize conditioning principles, and so perhaps do have some relationship to behavior modification therapy.

## BUDDHISM AND THE PSYCHOLOGY OF CREATIVITY

The testimonials found in *Zen Bow* and other Zen publications sometimes mention the freeing of creative potential among the benefits of zazen experienced. This writer, also, has found that during arid periods engaging in Zen meditation has seemed to hasten creative "breakthroughs" and sustain them. Of course, the very nature of Zen is such that a transcending of conventional logic is encouraged, so it should not be too surprising that creative expression is one of the outcomes of zazen. (Both creativity and zazen, also, involve the non-dominant hemisphere of the brain.)

If one examines what Western psychologists and psychiatrists have to say about the creative process, one finds a great deal that is similar to what writers on Zen have to say about the results of zazen. D. T. Suzuki, writing about the nature and aim of Zen, said,

Zen in its essence is the art of seeing into the nature of one's being, and it points the way from bondage to freedom.
... We can say that Zen liberates all the energies properly and naturally stored within us, which are in ordinary circumstances cramped and distorted so that they find no channel for activity. ... It is the object of Zen, therefore, to save us from going crazy or being crippled. This is what I mean by freedom, giving free play to all the creative and benevolent impulses inherently lying in our hearts.[80]

There is much in this statement that is similar to Maslow's ideas about "self-actualizing creativity,"[81] and Roger's thoughts concerning "psychological freedom" as a condition for creativity.

In satori one "experiences the universe as a totality of being of which oneself and all other objects are manifestations."[82] This type of experience has frequently been described as associated with the inspirational phase of the creative process.[83]

Writers on Zen have mentioned the expansion of awareness to embrace the intuitive, or the "ultraconscious."[84] Many writers on creativity, also, stress the importance of such expanded awareness in the creative process. Rogers speaks of "openness to experience."[85] Fromm talks about the "ability to see,"[86] and Kubie mentions accessibility of the materials of the preconscious as characterizing the creative individual.[87]

In describing the person who has experienced satori, Suzuki suggests that one perceives the world in all of its "suchness"—that one is able to abandon conceptualizations and abstractions, and relate to the world in terms of its concrete reality.[88] This perception, also, is such that everything stands out in all of its uniqueness, with greater clarity, but at the same time with an erasing of the distinction between subject and object. The enlightened individual also is more spontaneous, freer to express his feelings in their full richness and totality, than he was before satori. All of this is in keeping with thoughts about creativity mentioned by Maslow, Rogers, May, Fromm and others.[89] Of course it is similar also to the enlightenment experience resulting from other Buddhist approaches to meditation.

## EXPERIENTIAL REPORTS

Throughout this book, case material has been used to give an existential flavor to the descriptions. This material will not be repeated. However, included are partial reports of three psychologists who have engaged in meditational practice under a Zen master and/or a Tibetan lama.

*1a.* Psychology professor, female, beginning after twenty hours of concentrating on breathing and shikan-taza extending over three weeks; instruction by a Soto Zen priest but no dokusan, and most zazen taking place in a classroom with students, but five hours being in a Zen temple.

Monday—

"Last time shikan-taza did not seem to work too well, so today I concentrated on breathing as I inhaled and exhaled. I was aware of sounds which normally I would have ignored

—a student clearing his throat, a carpenter pounding nails next door, a car accelerating as it passed on the street in front of the building, a door closing in an adjoining room, and the inexorable dripping of the restroom faucet. But I didn't *think* about these sounds—I just *heard* them. Thoughts and pictures did drift through my mind—the worried look of the Catholic student who was 'turned off' on his religion, the Florida sunshine being enjoyed by my neighbor while I shivered in the sub-zero cold of the midwest, the white rats I must order for the experimental psychology class, the soot-encrusted snow that covers earth and trees and roofs—but each thought or image faded away into a comfortable nothingness. A part of me said, 'Don't suppress these thoughts; but don't *cling* to them either.' The time passed quickly.

Tuesday—

Today I concentrated on breathing again. Either it wasn't as noisy as yesterday, or I wasn't noticing. But the faucet was still dripping and I lost myself in a drop of water. Somehow, the dripping didn't annoy me, but each drop was perfection. I could feel myself as the drop of water suspended on the faucet, crystal-clear, then dropping in a transparent pear-shaped perfectness, to disappear into nothing and everything with a 'plop' into the basin. . . .

Friday—

Today I didn't try to meditate—just took a look at myself. What's happened to me in these last three weeks? Well, I had a couple of experiences that 'shook' me, when I wondered if I was flipping my lid. Losing myself in the drop of water was one of them. However, ignoring these experiences, I think I've been undergoing some changes. Some of them are a little hard to describe or explain. One thing I've noticed is that in the teaching I do after zazen, the generation gap seems to telescope until it is no more, and person-to-person communication is warm and meaningful. Aside from this, I think I can see myself expanding in awareness, experiencing a greater intensity of encounter, feeling greater empathy with the world, and feeling a greater freedom to be myself.[90]

*1b.* Same subject; two and one-half years later, after intermittent practice of zazen and vipassana meditation, and now having had two weeks of daily meditational practice under a lama of the Nyingma sect.

This has been an amazing two weeks. There have been problems, due in part to the fact that I had a fall about three weeks ago and wrenched my left knee, which means that cross-legged sitting has been very painful and quite distracting. During the second week I spent part of the time sitting on a chair, and this was very helpful. The practice has been quite varied, including relaxation exercises, concentration on breathing, mantras, visualization, attending to the heart beat, listening to external sounds, and integration of sensations and images from several senses. I have always believed that I was not a visualizer and was quite surprised to discover that I was able to produce very vivid imagery. I found the use of mantra very effective in promoting relaxation. After repeating mantra I very quickly go into a state of calm peacefulness in which any thoughts that appear just float gently in and out of consciousness. During a tongue exercise with visualization I had a marvelous sensory enjoyment associated with the feeling of the sliding of the tongue over the palate. In a visualization exercise involving a turning wheel, also, I had a feeling of intense pleasure. During these two weeks, I had experiences of peace and quietness, but also experiences of joy, love, and ecstasy, with the feeling that changes were taking place in me much more rapidly than ever before. With the variety of techniques used in this Nyingma approach, there is no chance of getting in a rut.

My first two days at the Nyingma Institute were tiring ones. The days were long, beginning with cleaning the living room at 6:30 every morning. However, commencing on the third day I always found myself feeling refreshed and relaxed after meditation. Three things seem to have happened to me during these two weeks: (a) Incidents and situations which previously would have annoyed me I am able to react to with a sense of detachment and equanimity; (b) life has taken on new colors and dimensions, and so has become more meaningful; (c) I have become more relaxed in all interpersonal relationships. I have not attained enlightenment, nor do I expect to do so, but have gained some inkling of the usefulness of this approach in expanding awareness and reducing tension.[91]

2. Consulting psychologist, male, a student of Tarthang Tulku; reporting on a month at Padma Ling Tibetan Nyingma Meditation Center.

Some generalizations about the experiences—
*By living in a high state of awareness one naturally learns thousands of little details about psychological processes.* . . . In terms of fields of psychology, the main area of learning is *perception.* You prove to yourself quickly that the mind filters reality, including all sense data. You begin to take *responsibility* for the interpretive role of your mind, realizing that you perceive only what you attend to and only within the mood, attitude and categories which make up your mental set. . . . In addition to perception, other areas of learning on psychological topics are: the dynamics of attention, projection, defensiveness, alienation, memory, mental strain . . . , fantasy, sexuality, body movements in relation to feelings, the operation of the five senses, emotions and emotional conflicts.

*By keeping an open, high awareness mind one can quickly have a number of therapeutic experiences, making dramatic progress on some deep and long standing emotional problems.* If you stay with a high state of awareness and don't repress or block the things the mind delivers, then previous experiences and psychological troubles will naturally surface, dreams will be remembered, etc. The emotions are watched as an unfolding drama. After a while, by simply listening to and watching these mental processes, emotions work themselves through or get transcended through the natural healing powers of the mind. . . .

*The role of the teacher was central but not unduly mystified or dependency creating.* Tarthang Tulku was central by helping me to discover his quality of mind (Buddha-mind) within me as a self-sufficient operational reality. . . . His role was central especially when I was blocked in some self-imposed dichotomy. . . . Rinpoche helped me recognize that Nyingma teachings are generic to all advanced psycho-spiritual experience of human beings. . . . and not necessarily in conflict with the prevalent Western traditions.

*The withdrawal of senses from their objects, as in visualization, brings the senses under conscious control and heightens sensory awareness and perceptivity....* Temporary withdrawal of senses from objects seems to have four results: (a) to give the sensory mechanisms practice and to create leverage on perceiving the object world; (b) to remind one that the perception of the so-called objective world is always mediated through the senses, thus reminding us to keep our glasses cleaned and ears unplugged; (c) to allow the mind a wider range of clear perception by reducing mental agitations and allowing perception to function more like photographic memory than like self-conscious linear thinking; (d) to heal the senses from the barrage of overstimulation in Western society.

*The body becomes more healthy by concentrating on holistic development rather than by concentrating on body work per se....*

*The experiences of personal development in Nyingma do not tend to inspire self-satisfaction or pride.* Even though progressing beyond the wildest dreams of various Western 'self-improvement' schemes, progress in Nyingma makes you aware mainly of the strength of the method (Vajrayana), the smallest amount of progress compared to the potential, and the small relevance of narrowly defined 'personal' happiness when others are suffering. As your personality-cognitive-emotional structure is capable of receiving it, visions unfold of the potential of mind as an appreciative, fully functioning, open system located in our bodies in one sense but also beyond bodies and clocks among all people.[93]

3. Clinical psychologist, male, who has had considerable experience with zazen and as a clinician has functioned within a Jungian context; reporting after six weeks of practice under the guidance of Tarthang Tulku at the Nyingma Institute.

On my second day at the Institute I met the lama who immediately asked me to work in the kitchen. I was a little taken aback but proceeded to do so. I discovered that I was not alone, Rinpoche's students worked diligently from early morning until late in the evening. One day I overheard Rinpoche talking to one of his students who was also working in the kitchen. He was saying, "When you work, be conscious of what you are doing, you work for yourself, you know." As the students carried out their tasks I began to notice that much of Rinpoche's teaching happens in everyday events and encounters. As time went by I saw that no work was considered menial, it was all an opportunity for practice.

With this in mind and while cleaning the kitchen floor, I became aware of my own thought processes. I was tempted to make it easy on myself by passing over those little corners of dirt and hard to get to places when the analogy to my own psychological situation hit me. I became aware how in my meditation as well as in everyday life I found little ways of not quite being honest with myself, not quite doing an exercise completely or avoiding little pains and pressures. I began to put more effort into my meditation practices and my bones ached as Rinpoche talked of the importance of relaxation. I felt as if I was working very hard, till one day Rinpoche said that external performance means little, we must be deeply honest. It's the inner work that makes the difference. At this point I felt invaded as if there was no longer even an inner refuge in which to hide. I started to get angry, and thought I could quit, I didn't have to work so hard. But the thought "you work for yourself, you know," kept going through my mind. As I began to more genuinely accept my task I began to learn about determination, and it seemed that simultaneously Rinpoche was saying things that became more and more relevant to my practice. . . .

My positive experiences did not remain consistently and when they did come I was anxious to deepen and increase them; as I attempted to do so they would disappear in a wisp. Here again Rinpoche's instructions were helpful. He described how in meditation there is a critical time when positive experience is about to begin, we get excited and try to grasp. But this is a time of skill, we must learn not to give up but not to grasp. There is a delicate vital balance that is needed. In the following days Rinpoche spoke about developing a gentle patience learning to be where you are. Each development seems to bring with it a new meaning of relaxation, a new befriending of whatever comes. "Everything comes in its own course, it feeds you naturally." "If you are dull, bored, tired, emotional, or feeling good, don't go beyond this. Accept what is there." If you try to get away or increase what is going on you lose it. . . .

As the work continued, physical exercises, deep massage, symbolic visualization, I had many experiences and felt deep emotions, childhood cries, archaic memories, physical sensations, visions, all seemed to form a bio-experiential whole. Everything we were doing seemed interconnected. The sensory practices seemed to work on the total person, physical, mental, emotional, spiritual, all working together.

I began to have vivid dreams; one of a large red mountain of glass crashing down and releasing a slowly rising ocean of water. After this I was anxious for a day or so and had great difficulty in meditating. The following night I had a dream of a hysterical woman who didn't want me for her doctor, because my medicine was new and exploratory and not all laid out in a textbook. The next day in a meditation I felt I was the hysterical woman but afterward was able to proceed in my meditation.

After this I was able to experience aspects of my "body" I had never felt before and sensed their interrelationships with my breathing and everyday activities. I felt myself beginning to deeply relax. Tensions seemed to unfold, leaving me in a pool of progressive comfort and heightened awareness. Everyday activities were smoother, more rewarding and had a glow as if my senses were beginning to nourish me.

Rinpoche's words again had some experiential basis. He was talking about how the food of relaxation is very rich and how we have been sped up so long, we don't even notice our tensions. . . .

In the last week Rinpoche's influence became instrumental in helping me see how easy it is to get attached to special modes of awareness. What I am beginning to realize is that an altered state of consciousness was not what one attains in Buddhist practice—it is rather the other way around. The everyday modes of life that are filled with craving and desire are the altered states—which continue through extraordinary experiences. But detachment and freedom from karma seem to occur in the simplicity of "ordinary life."[93]

## CONCLUSIONS

Considering Buddhist theory and practice in relation to psychology, it does not seem at all likely that the psychology of the Abhidamma will replace or even significantly modify that of the West. One influence it has already had, however, is the stimulation of a renewed interest in the psychology of consciousness on the part of American psychologists. The interest in the psychology of consciousness is related especially to the altered states of consciousness resulting from meditation, with such states now being studied both introspectively and from the standpoint of physiology. Buddhist meditational practices, also, have become recognized for their therapeutic potentialities. Because of the esoteric nature of these practices they cannot be effectively used by the therapist trained only in Western approaches to psychotherapy. However, as more psychologically sophisticated and qualified Zen masters, Theravada teachers, and lamas follow the example of Tarthang Tulku in setting up special courses for Western psychologists, we should see meditational techniques increasingly used by members of the helping professions in the United States.

With American psychologists being research-oriented, those interested in the effects of meditation are being intrigued by the possibilities of experimental studies of the outcomes of the expansion of awareness. For example, psychologists are speculating about the possibility that meditation could raise one's I.Q., and this, of course, is a question which could be studied experimentally. With the tools now available, it is also possible to study likenesses and differences in the results of different approaches to meditation and if it makes any difference whether the meditation is a part of a total way of life as in Buddhism, or whether it is a separate segment of life with no articulated relation to general life style as in the case of transcendental meditation. It is also possible to make studies of possible relationships between personality types and the specific approaches to meditation which are most effective. All of this will be of concern to psychologists in the future.

# 11

# Buddhism and the Christian Tradition in America

The literature on comparative religions is replete with theological and philosophical discussions of similarities and differences between Buddhist concepts and Judaeo-Christian thought. The authors of these discussions, however, are usually theologians and scholars and the concepts which they believe to be central to each religion may bear little relationship to what the average lay adherent conceives to be the essence of his religion. Actually, most Americans who leave Judaism or Christianity to become Buddhists do so not because of their preference for the beliefs of Buddhism over those of Judaism or Christianity, but either because the Judaeo-Christian establishment in its institutionalized form has failed to meet their personal needs and what they perceive to be the needs of society, or because the practices in the church seem cold, sterile, and lacking in dynamism (see chapter 13). Some converts to Buddhism, of course, are attracted to it on the basis of ideology; but these are relatively few, consisting principally of Caucasians who have joined the predominately Japanese Buddhist churches.

## COMPARING THE RELIGIONS

*Similarities between Buddhism and Christianity*

Aside from superficial similarities in forms and routines of worship, there are several basic similarities between Christianity and Buddhism.

To begin with, since their inception both religions have been regarded as universal religions—religions without a "chosen people." Both have been missionary religions, ever since their respective founders admonished the disciples to spread the gospel throughout the world.[1]

Buddhism and Christianity are alike also in that each is centered on a particular *person*—Buddha in the one case, and Jesus Christ in the other. In each religion, the person is referred to as the "Lord" and is considered the personification of Truth, the incarnate Logos: "I am the Way, the Truth, and the Life" was taught by Gautama the Buddha as well as by Christ.[2] Many of their teachings were similar, even to the use of similar parables, and both advocated a direct approach to salvation rather than the use of rituals.[3] In Christianity the doctrine of the second coming of Christ was articulated, and in Buddhism there developed a doctrine of the Buddha of the future, *Maitreya*, with both being associated with eschatology.[4]

Two other similarities worth noting are the teaching of a spiritual death and rebirth or renewal, and concepts of a Trinity. (The latter applies to Mahayana Buddhism, but not to the Theravada school.)

*Differences between Buddhism and Christianity*

There are numerous differences between Buddhism and Christianity, in both general and specific terms.

Buddhism has often been designated an "intellectual" religion, with Christianity being more of an "emotional" or "practical" religion.[5] Buddhism's statements about ultimates are always in terms of *negatives*, whereas Christianity is a religion of hope and love and faith.[6] Christianity is *socially* oriented, aiming toward service to others and believing in the importance of corporate worship; Buddhism is more oriented toward the *individual*. Christianity is a religion of *involvement*; Buddhism aims at *detachment*. However, if one looks at the meaning of each of these orientations, the behavioral differences associated with them are not as great as the labels would imply.

A basic difference in the attitudes of Christians and Buddhists is the greater tolerance of Buddhists for other faiths.[7] It would be impossible for a committed Christian to also be a committed Buddhist. However, the Buddhist sees all religions as having merit and would see no reason that a Buddhist should not also be a Taoist, Shintoist, Sufi, or Christian. If he were really a Buddhist, of course, he would place Buddhist interpretations on some Christian concepts, would be open-minded about others, and would reject some. He would not accept the doctrine of Jesus as the Son of God, but would accept Christ as a Buddha or bodhisattva, and recognize that the Truth is to be found not only in the Buddhist sutras, but in Christ's teachings as well.

Of the specific concepts on which Christian and Buddhist teachings are different, most frequently mentioned are those with reference to God and Creation, the self or "soul," monism versus dualism, the nature of Christ, the concepts of love, sin, and guilt versus suffering, the means to salvation, ethics, and spiritual techniques. Each of these will be briefly discussed.

*God.* Belief in God is a central concept in Christianity, with God conceived as (a) being the creator, (b) having "personal" characteristics (consciousness, activity, sensibility), and (c) being "holy."[8] In contrast, Buddhism categorically denies God as Creator, accepting only an impersonal law of causation which has no beginning.[9] Aside from denying the existence of a Creator-God, Buddhism—especially Mahayana Buddhism—takes no stand on the existence or nonexistence of God. Theravada Buddhism makes it clear that Sakyamuni Buddha was not in any way superhuman. In the Mahayana Trinity there seems to be room for a concept of God, although it is not the personal God of Christianity and no such concept is explicitly formulated.

*The soul.* Christianity emphasizes man's essence as being his unique, self-conscious individuality and as constituting his eternal soul which continues after death. It sees the soul as ultimately reaching the presence of God (Heaven) or being destined for eternal separation from God (Hell). The Buddhist doctrine of anatta or anatman is a doctrine of no-soul, but the doctrine of karma in some Mahayana sects provides for the possibility that rebirth may not only be as a person or animal on this earth, but as a deity in a heaven or a demon in a hell. (Some more liberal Buddhists regard karma as operating on this earth in this life, and also regard rebirth as a spiritual rebirth and renewal. For them, hell means anxiety or suffering and heaven means sensual bliss, with these states existing here and now. These concepts are actually not too different from those of some liberal Christians who do not believe in an afterlife.)

*Monism versus dualism.* Associated with the Buddhist-Christian divergence over the existence of God and the nature of the soul or self is the basic conflict of monism versus dualism. Buddhism regards Christianity as basically "dualistic," with God and self being seen as distinct and separate. In contrast, Buddhism says there are no separate entities of God and self—only one universal Truth. Popular Christianity sees God as being "somewhere" and the self also as being "somewhere." However, the experience of Christian mystics such as Eckhart, Saint Theresa, and Saint John of the Cross suggests that the Buddhist monistic outlook is not foreign to Christianity. There is also much in the Gospels and Epistles to suggest that some of Christ's earlier followers may have had monistic types of insight.[10]

*Christ.* Belief in the divinity of Christ and His saving grace is of course of central importance in Christianity, and unacceptable to Buddhists. However, Buddhists generally have a great reverence and admiration for Jesus Christ, which is not ordinarily matched by a Christian admiration and respect for the Buddha.

*Love and mercy.* The Bible uses three terms which are translated as "love"—*eros, philia,* and *agape*—with agape representing love's highest level wherein love of God and man are combined through practice. This love is represented in the two commandments given by Christ; it is selfless, redemptive, and universal.[11] Philia means charity or benevolence, and eros is humanistic love of family, friends, and others who are close.

Buddhist love (*metta*, Pali; *maitra*, Sanskrit), sometimes translated as "loving kindness," consists of mercy for all living things, which grows out of "compassion" (*karuna*). According to Buddhist thought, the experiencing of sorrow or grief from a realization of personal suffering then extends to sorrow for the suffering of all sentient beings, which finds its expression in compassion and mercy. All are united at the depth of one's self, and only when one experiences unity with the universe can he fully realize that others also bear the same burden of existential suffering. In Buddhism this is called "the feeling of compassion for the same suffering and the same sorrow."[12] In Western psychological terms it would probably be called the development of compassion through empathy. As far as behavior is concerned, what the Buddhist calls loving kindness might have elements of either philia or agape love, but differs from both in having as its starting point the individual's own human suffering.

*Sin, suffering, and salvation.* Basic in Christianity is the concept of original sin, or at least the idea of the inevitability of sin and guilt, with redemption occurring by the grace of God through Jesus Christ. Buddhism, on the contrary, is not concerned with sin. Rather man is seen as an ignorant sufferer who is released from suffering and attains enlightenment through his own efforts.[13] (A possible exception to the concept of salvation by self-effort is found in the Amidists' doctrine of "other-power," which allows for the concept of grace.)

*Ethics.* Both Buddhism and Christianity have an ethical orientation. Superficially, the orientation is similar, with the Buddhist precepts duplicating some of the Ten Commandments. However, although both the precepts and the commandments are ethical guides, they do not have the same significance for the Buddhist and the Christian.

For the Christian, obeying the commandments (given by God and His Son) is a duty and an obligation, and failure to do so constitutes sin, which one confesses and for which he asks forgiveness. The Christian is expected to actively apply the "Golden Rule" in his relationships with others and to take initiative in expressing Christian love through service.

For the Buddhist the precepts suggest an attitude, rather than constituting rules which must be obeyed. For example, the precept against killing suggests an attitude of respect for animal and human life rather than constituting a prohibition against eating meat or swatting a mosquito. The precept against the use of intoxicants is interpreted as suggesting that "beclouding the mind" by whatever means should be avoided, rather than being seen as specifically forbidding imbibing a martini before dinner. Observing the precepts also is regarded as helpful to the individual in preparing him for meditation which will further his progress toward self-actualization. However, ethical behavior is perceived as developing chiefly from the personality changes taking place as a result of meditation or other "practice," which will then find expression in compassion and loving kindness. Perhaps one way of describing the difference between the Christian and Buddhist attitude toward ethics would be to say that the Christian approach is more direct and involved, whereas the Buddhist approach is more indirect and detached.

*Spiritual techniques.* For the Christian, the principal spiritual technique is prayer, and prayer is the heart of all Christian liturgies. In contrast, it is claimed that the Buddhist does not pray, since there is no God who could respond, but that his spiritual technique is meditation.[14]

Anyone visiting a Buddhist temple in a Chinatown would notice worshipers placing offerings of fruits and flowers on an altar before an image of a Buddha or bodhisattva, kneeling before the altar and voicing petitions. At a Zen temple he might notice a Japanese or American priest genuflecting before an image of Avelokitesvara, intoning sentiments of gratitude. Are these not prayers? As far as the lay worshiper in the Chinatown temple is concerned, he is praying to Kuan-yin or Amit'o-fo and hopes for a response. As far as the priest is concerned, his words and actions are an expression of respect and gratitude, but not directed to any supernatural being, and not with anticipation of any response; therefore, what he is voicing is not prayer. For most Oriental lay Buddhists, prayer as the Christian knows it is a part of religious practice. For most American lay Buddhists, however, religious practice does not involve prayer.

## Becoming a Buddhist

What happens when a Christian becomes a Buddhist? He gives up his concept of God as Creator; he accepts man-made laws as such, but regards no laws as "divine" in nature. Since he has given up God, he also gives up prayer. Christ becomes for him a great teacher (or perhaps a bodhisattva), while Moses and the Old Testament prophets are significant persons in the history of a great people. But Christ is not seen as a deity, and the great figures of the Old Testament are perceived as being deluded in their belief in their inspiration and guidance by "God"; he has given up his belief in the resurrection and his belief in an "immortal soul," which will live on after death of the body.

Having given up what to him have been the underpinnings of his Christian faith, what does the neophyte Buddhist have in its place? He has a naturalistic belief in causation. He believes that he, and he alone, is responsible for his salvation; that his guide to conduct is to be found in the life and teachings of Gautama Buddha and his followers; that karma operates in this life and future incarnations. He believes that the "divine" is the "true self" or the "void" which represents a dissolving of the subejct-object dichotomy as he discovers his "Buddha-nature"; that this experience of the divine is attainable by the diligent practice of meditation.

### Approaches to Meditation and Contemplation

Mysticism has been a part of the tradition of all the major religions of the world, with the possible exception of Confucianism (if, indeed, Confucianism can be termed a religion). Mystics have been among the most highly respected and revered of the ancient Judaic sages and prophets, as well as among the Christian saints. Usually the transcendental mystical experiences reported by these persons have resulted from what Orientals would call "meditation" or *dhyana*.

Is the experience of the Christian mystic comparable to the Buddhist "enlightenment" experience? The reports of Christian mystics usually contain some references to union with God; yet one has the impression that dualism persists even in this experience. However, there appear to be some Christian mystics whose transcendent experiences have been identical with the satori experience of Zen, although interpreted in the Christian context. An example is that of Meister Eckhart, who describes the feeling of "breaking through" as follows:

> I transcend all creatures and am neither God nor creature: I am that I was and I shall remain now and forever. Then I receive an impulse which carries me above all angels. In this impulse I conceive such passing riches that I am not content with God as being God, as being all his godly works, for in this breaking-through I find that God and I are both the same. . . .[15]

Another example is that of St. Theresa, who says, "By highest point I mean when the faculties are lost through being closely united with God." She adds, "This complete transformation of the soul in God lasts but a short time and it is only while it lasts that none of the soul's faculties is able to see or to know what is taking place."[16]

### Two Approaches to Meditation

Chogyam Trungpa suggests that in the varied techniques of meditation which have developed in different religious traditions, there are two basic forms. The first is concerned with discovering the nature of existence; the second seeks to develop communication with an external higher Being, or God.[17]

In the first form of meditation, exemplified by the Buddhist approach, a central concept is that of "nowness." The meditator has no particular object or ambition, other than to see what is here and now. He tries to transcend concepts, to find out what *is*.[18]

The second type of meditation is based on devotion and prayer. Trungpa says,

This is well known in the Hindu teachings, where the emphasis is on going into the inward state of samadhi, into the depths of the heart. One finds a similar technique practiced in ... Christianity, where the prayer of the heart is used and concentration on the heart is emphasized. This is a means of identifying oneself with an external Being and necessitates purifying oneself. The basic belief is that one is separate from God, but there is a link, one is still a part of God. ... This practice makes use of emotions and devotional practices which are aimed at making contact with God or some particular saint. These devotional practices may also include the recitation of mantra.[19]

## Christian Mysticism and Contemplation

Zen adherents frequently object to having the term "Zen" translated as "meditation." In support of this position is the fact that, in the Christian context, meditation is defined as "mental prayer in its discursive form,"[20] and generally consists of a reflective pondering on a chosen theme. With zazen and other forms of Buddhist meditation aimed at eliminating discursive thinking, to use the same term for what seem to be contrasting approaches is perhaps misleading unless it is understood that the processes are different. In Christian practice, what is called "contemplation" corresponds more nearly to Buddhist "meditation" than does the usual Christian interpretation of the latter in terms of discursive thinking.

Parry proposes a classification of stages or types of prayer which includes both discursive meditation and contemplation, and puts them into a continuum. This classification lists as the three basic types of prayer the vocal prayer, the mental prayer, and the contemplative prayer. Each includes several subtypes.[21] Mental prayer and contemplation are related to the degrees of the spiritual life in Ascetical Theology known as the Purgative Way, the Illuminative Way, and the Unitive Way.

*Vocal prayer.* This would include vocally uttered prayers of adoration, thanksgiving, confession, and petition. In most cases such prayers would not be called "meditation," although when they reflect a realization of divine purpose and a "lifting up" of man, they might be considered as related to meditation.

*Mental prayer.* In this category are two types, representing two stages of spiritual progress—meditation of intellectual pondering, and the affective prayer.

"Intellectual pondering," corresponding to the Purgative Way in Ascetical Theology, has as its purpose the identification and elimination of bad habits. This approach uses imagination and intellect as its principal instruments.

"Affective prayer" represents the beginning of the Illuminative Way. In this approach the emotions and will are used. The individual becomes increasingly detached from persons and things, but develops an expansion of love for God, which results in an expanded ability to love his fellows. (In Buddhism, also, one notes an attitude of detachment resulting in increased ability to love.)

A form of prayer illustrating the use of vocal utterances and both stages of mental prayer is the "Jesus Prayer." This prayer form, developed by the Eastern Orthodox Church, involves practices called Hesychasm, which are said to open the heart to contemplation. The prayer consists of the words, "Lord Jesus Christ, have mercy on me, a sinner." In the beginning the prayer is repeated a number of times each day. Next the words are repeated silently an increased number of times during the day and night, possibly coordinating the words with the rhythm of breathing as a means of building concentration. In the final stage the prayer is taken down into the heart and "now lives with every heartbeat." (Some adherents of Shin Buddhism have used the nembutsu in a similar way.)

*Contemplative prayer.* Christian theologians and mystics distinguish between two types of contemplation: "acquired contemplation," which is the peak of Ascetical Theology, and "infused contemplation," which is the subject of Mysical Theology. Both constitute the Unitive Way. In the Christian context, acquired contemplation represents the highest level which an individual may attain by the maximal development of his natural powers. Infused contemplation is interpreted as the action of God, working in man, and represents the apex of Christian experience. It is said that in infused contemplation the barrier between God and man is broken down, although this point is approached in acquired contemplation.

There are two stages of acquired contemplative prayer. In the first stage, "the mind possesses truth and contemplates it by a direct and simple act and enjoys it without effort."[22] At this point there is only one reality—that which is perceived. In the second stage the reality of God is experienced "beyond any concept, theology, idea or title which the mind or imagination can frame."[23] Now, love breaks through—a love which is without concept or desire.[24]

As a contemplative penetrates ever deeper into the Darkness of Unknowing, he finally comes to what John Ruysbroeck has described as follows: "In this darkness there shines and is born an incomprehensible light, which is the Son of God, in Whom we behold eternal life. And in this light one becomes seeing; . . . in the idle emptiness in which the spirit has lost itself through fruitive love, and where it receives without means the brightness of God, and is changed without interruption into that brightness it receives."[25] At this point acquired contemplation has been left behind and the individual is in the realm of infused contemplation, leading to the experience of unity—what the Buddhist would call enlightenment.

## Christian Systems of Meditation

There are many systems of Christian meditation. The best known of these is the system of "Spiritual Exercises" devised by Saint Ignatius of Loyola, and used by several Roman Catholic orders as well as within the Anglican communion.[26] The exercises are divided into four weeks or stages. The first, corresponding to the Purgative Way, involves meditation upon sin and its consequences. The second, belonging to the Illuminative Way, focuses on Christ's life and teachings. The third stage (also of the Illuminative Way) is devoted to contemplation on the Passion. In the fourth stage, pertaining to the Unitive Way, the exercisant contemplates the Resurrection and Ascension. Then, to crown it all, Saint Ignatius gives an exercise which he calls, "Contemplation for Obtaining Love."[27]

In addition to the various Catholic approaches to meditation and contemplation, most of which make some use of visualization, there are several Protestant approaches. Notable examples are Martin Luther's method of contemplation and the Quaker system.

Luther's system involves reflection and meditation on the words of the Lord's Prayer, the Ten Commandments, the Psalms, or various words of Christ or Paul. Luther's method differs from that of Saint Ignatius in that he does not use visualization, but otherwise it is similar.[28]

The Quaker system involves a group practice in which "unregenerate man achieves spiritual regeneration by meditating upon the Light."[29]

## Modern Trends in Buddhism and the Western Religions

The meditational heritage of the so-called Oriental religions is widely recognized, but less attention is given to the equally rich meditational tradition of Judaism and Christianity. Although meditation has had a place in the history of most religions, in both the East and the West it has usually been considered an activity for monks and nuns. In Buddhist Asia it was frequently regarded as too difficult for the layman or impractical for one who had to earn his living. In the West it was in conflict with the work ethic—rejected on the basis of being unproductive. Even in the contemplative orders of Roman Catholicism, as monks and nuns involved themselves in teaching, social work, and community-oriented activities, meditation came to play a more minor role. In the parish church its role became almost nonexistent, although there are some indications of renewal of interest in the churches of America.

The type of Buddhism which has appealed most to Americans who are not of Oriental ancestry has been that involving meditation, and most of the Americans practicing Buddhist meditation are laymen. In many Zen centers in America, one finds a few Roman Catholic priests and nuns doing zazen. At a summer institute on Tibetan meditational practices an Episcopal priest was enrolled. In Unitarian-Universalist churches Zen groups have frequently been set up, and Dom Aelred Graham reported introducing meditational techniques to high school boys in a Catholic boys' school. Zen masters are increasingly being asked to conduct sesshins at Roman Catholic monasteries; a number of Protestant churches have become interested in conducting retreats in which meditational practices are employed. On the West coast, where Buddhism is strong, sometimes Buddhist-type practices are used in a Christian context. Nevertheless, despite these developments, neither Western nor Eastern types of meditation have as yet had much impact on the Christian Church in the United States.

## Mutual Influences between Buddhism and Christianity

A Christian visiting a Buddhist temple, either in Asia or the West, will find certain things which are familiar to him—the altar, flowers, candles, and something which symbolizes an object of worship on the altar. If one is of the Roman Catholic, Eastern Orthodox, or Episcopal persuasion, the incense, priestly robes, bowing, genuflecting, and chanting may not seem too strange. Some of the gestures made by the Buddhist priest may not seem too unlike those made by one's own parish priest. When the first Roman Catholic missionaries appeared in Japan, their external trappings were so similar to those of the Buddhists that many Japanese assumed Catholicism to be just another Buddhist sect. We have already noted certain parallels in Christian and Buddhist theology—can it be that they have a mutual heritage, or have influenced each other?

We know that cultural and commercial contacts between Asia and the West existed at least two thousand years before Christ and continued until the end of the fourth century A.D. By the end of the fourth century B.C., Buddhist missionaries were found in Athens, and during the next century Buddhists were travelling far from India to spread the Dharma. By the time of the Christian era Buddhist thought was quite familiar to all of the areas where the early Christian missionaries established their churches. By this time, also, pagan influences had become apparent in Buddhist forms of worship. The first images of the Buddha were made by the Greeks—a practice which would have shocked Sakyamuni Buddha. Pagan influences probably were responsible for some of the worship practices which developed in the Christian church, as well as their similarity to Buddhist practices. On the basis of Tibetan texts, also, it has been suggested that Jesus may have traveled to Tibet during his adolescence and early adulthood, although Christian historians generally do not accept this story.[30]

Coming to more modern times, and Buddhism in America, we have already seen some of the ways in which Buddhism has adapted itself to the American way of life. The influence of American Protestantism on the Buddhist Churches in America should also be mentioned. When the first Japanese Buddhist Churches were established in Hawaii, one way in which they tried to avoid being labeled as "heathen" was to model their external forms after those of Protestant Christianity. This practice was continued after the Shin churches began to be established on the mainland. As we have seen, this involved imitation of church furnishings, form of church government, type of liturgy, Sunday School, auxiliary organizations, Sunday services, and so on. It also involved scheduling of a Sunday sermon. (The Buddha himself established a tradition of preaching, but this had largely dropped out of the picture until modern times.)

Except for the arousal of an interest in meditation, and introduction of lesson materials on comparative religions into some of the Christian Sunday Schools and young people's groups, Buddhism appears to have had little impact on twentieth-century Christianity in America.

## What Can Christianity Learn From Buddhism?

Maslow, in a discussion of religion in relation to peak experiences, postulates that there are two kinds of religious persons—those who have deep and transcendent (core-religious) experiences easily and often, and those who have never had them or who repress or suppress them.[31] He suggests that the capacity to have the core-religious experience is associated with personal growth and fulfillment.[32] He states also that there is a negative relation between organization and religious transcendent experience,[33] and that familiarization and repetition produce a lowering of the intensity and richness of consciousness.[34] What he is saying, then, is that a rich religious experience cannot be associated with a religious setting involving a high degree of organization and a stress on ritual. If we recall, also, that Maslow associates the peak experience with self-actualization, which he regards as a basic human need, this would suggest that perhaps churches need a freer structure and more provision for meditation as well as other types of personal involvement if they are to continue as viable institutions. It would explain also the fact that it is the meditational and evangelistic types of Buddhist groups that are growing most rapidly in this country.

In considering what Christianity can learn from Buddhism, two answers might be given: a *point of view* and an approach to religious *practice*. This first of these is exemplified by Dom Aelred Graham in his book, *Zen Catholicism*. Father Graham notes that, over the centuries, Christianity has become overlaid with a legal superstructure and credal formularies, so that the time has come for the Western world to get to the heart of its own tradition. He suggests that Buddhist insights might help in that enterprise. Commenting that the modern world has become a little weary of prophets and needs the light that comes from the seers, he raises the question concerning whether the "Buddhist insight, and the particular concern of the Enlightened One for truth—for reality as distinct from appearances, as distinct from verbal statements—has not something to contribute in greatly helping Christians to realize their own inheritance, their own tradition."[35]

Swearer expresses the opinion that Christianity could benefit from consideration within its own tradition of certain Buddhist ideas and attitudes: that man can transcend the "frailties flesh is heir to" without appealing to any power beyond himself; that freedom from ignorance is a viable approach to freedom from hatred, greed, and lust; that appreciation of the relative nature of the world may combat the static tendency toward stereotyping and prejudiced pigeon-holing; that the Noble Eightfold Path provides a practical means of transcending suffering; that every act of a person's life has an effect or consequence in his life; and that the lives of individuals play a critical role in shaping and sustaining society.[36]

Neither of these writers is suggesting that Christians become Buddhists, but both are indicating that there are aspects of Buddhism which can deepen and enrich the lives of Christians and can help them to become more reflective religious persons.

With reference to religious *practice,* the history of Buddhism in America points to the conclusion that the Christian church must give more attention to the individual spiritual experience and revive the practice of meditation and contemplation if it is to flourish. Further, meditation and contemplation must be for the layman as well as the monk and nun. Also, it would seem that some of the meditational methods used in Zen, Satipatthana, and Tibetan Buddhism, with certain modifications and adaptations, may be more productive in terms of spiritual enrichment than the systematic methods which have developed within the Christian tradition. This is supported by Father William Johnston, a Jesuit, who has developed a Christianity-oriented Zen practice which he calls "Christian Zen."[37]

# part 3

# The American Buddhist

# 12

# Who Are the American Buddhists?

Are Buddhists a rare breed in America, or have they become so numerous as to no longer be considered unique? How many Buddhists are there in the United States?

Are Buddhists in America mostly Orientals, or are there significant numbers of Caucasian and black American Buddhists? Are American Buddhists mostly men, or are women also attracted to Buddhism? How about age? Are they mostly young, or are there also middle-aged and elderly American Buddhists?

Where do American Buddhists come from? Do they tend to belong to any one social class? What kinds of occupations do they pursue? What about their educational backgrounds and their past religious affiliations or commitments?

What sorts of people are these Buddhists? Hippies? Yippies? Fugitives from the drug scene? Nonconformists? Rebels? Mentally ill? Escapists?

The present chapter is concerned with answers to such questions. This sort of study, of course, does not lend itself to the comprehensive accumulation of demographic data, which in some cases would have been refused and often would have been resented as an intrusion on privacy. Nichiren Shoshu of America does gather such data and that organization's membership statistics for 1970 were available.[1] The

Nyingma Meditation Center has reported a survey of those practicing at that center in 1973.[2] Raw data from a questionnaire formulated by Miss M. Koren and administered to members of the Zen Center of Los Angeles were made available to this writer, and members of the California Bosatsukai (Los Angeles) were identified in terms of occupation when they were introduced to this reporter. Supplementing the above was other information more selective in nature, including articles in newsletters,[3] published biographies of American Buddhists,[4] interviews with Oriental Buddhist monks, ministers, and teachers working with Americans, conversations with many American Buddhists, interviews with professors whose students have been converted to Buddhism, and testimonials given at Nichiren Shoshu meetings.

Even a cursory consideration of the question concerning the nature of the American Buddhist in terms of his background and personality reveals immediately that the answer will be different depending on what kind of Buddhism we are talking about. Rather than attempting any breakdown according to sect, however, we shall consider the picture in terms of the three major styles of Buddhism most prevalent in the United States: the "evangelistic" style of Nichiren Shoshu; the "meditational" style of Zen, Tantric Buddhism, Satipatthana, and T'ien T'ai; and the "church" style Buddhism exemplified especially by the Buddhist Churches of America but also characteristic of Jodo-shu, Nichiren-shu, Buddha's Universal Church, and others.

### How Many Buddhists?

Whether one is counting Buddhists in China, Japan, Southeast Asia, Europe, or America, the figures which emerge are less than satisfactory. It is not too difficult to count Buddhist monks and nuns, but the task of estimating the number of lay adherents in any country is an almost hopeless one, mainly because there are no generally accepted criteria of what constitutes a lay Buddhist. For example, in figures reported by the Chinese Buddhist Association between 1930 and 1947, the number of Buddhist devotees in China was estimated at about 1 percent of the population.[5] Yet, according to Welch, probably 90 percent of the population occasionally resorted to Buddhist rites or worshipped at Buddhist temples and 99 percent were influenced by Buddhist contributions to Chinese thought and behavior. Undoubtedly, if figures had been reported for China in 1960, the number of Buddhists reported would have been less than 1 percent. In contrast, statistics reported in Japan for 1960 class about 80 percent of the population as Buddhist adherents, with most of these also being Shinto adherents.[6] Was Japan that much more Buddhist than China? Probably not. The most likely explanation for the difference is that in China a lay Buddhist was considered to be one who had accepted the Three Refuges and five precepts, whereas in Japan a man was considered a Buddhist on the basis of practice, financial support, and where he planned to be buried, rather than on the basis of any vows taken or personal commitment.

What is a Buddhist in America? Is he one who has taken the Three Refuges? If so, making an educated guess, there probably are not more than fifty thousand Buddhists in the United States.[7] Is he one who has either taken the Three Refuges or gone through some other Buddhist ceremony of commitment (such as receiving the gohonzon)? Then the number might be as high as 300,000, or even more. Is he one who participates in some form of Buddhist practice, such as zazen, but may or may not have made any formal commitment to Buddhism and may or may not have renounced his former religious commitments? If so, the figure might rise to as many as 500,000 adherents, or perhaps more. Then, of course, one could add to this figure the countless numbers of college and university students who have been influenced in one way or another by the courses in Buddhism which they have taken, and the reading which they have done on Buddhist philosophy.

On the basis of the above remarks, it is obvious that one cannot say exactly how many Buddhists there are in America. However, for the sake of being able to describe the American for whom Buddhism has become a meaningful part of life, we shall think of Buddhists as including three groups, which may or may not overlap: (1) those who have made a formal commitment to Buddhism and/or have been accepted as "disciples" by a Buddhist priest, minister, or teacher; (2) those considered by Buddhist churches as "members," on the basis of continuing interest and regular financial support; (3) those who have engaged in Buddhist "practice" (for example, meditation, sutra study, chanting) on a regular basis for a year or more.

## Geographic Origins

A map showing the location of Buddhist groups in the United States would reveal the greatest concentration on the West Coast, with the East Coast ranking next, and other concentrations being in and around urban centers. It would also show some Buddhist centers in rural or mountain areas in various parts of the country. A map showing the home towns of known Buddhists born in America would show the same sort of distribution—the greatest number in California and Washington state, many in the New York-New Jersey-Pennsylvania area, quite a few in such urban centers as Chicago, but few in Iowa, the Dakotas, Nebraska, Kansas, Idaho and other states with a predominately rural population or without large urban centers, as well as few in the deep south. There are no states without Buddhist residents. However, if the origins of all Buddhists in America were indicated there would still be a significant number from various points in Asia.

## Personal Characteristics

*Age.* As a generalization, one can say that there are non-Oriental Buddhists in the United States ranging from adolescence to old age. However, the largest group tends to be in the twenty-one to thirty-five year age range. The only exception to this is in the Buddhist "church" groups, where worship involves sitting in pews, repeating a liturgy, and listening to a sermon. Most non-Oriental members of the latter are men who married Japanese women either after World War II or during the Korean conflict, and so are likely to be in the forty to fifty-five year age bracket.

Nichiren Shoshu issued the following figures regarding age distribution as of 1970: 20 or younger—17%; 20 to 30—35%; 31 to 40—15%; 51 to 60—6%; 61 and older—3%.[8] (On the basis of observations made while attending Nichiren Shoshu meetings in several localities, it was this writer's impression that the majority of the middle-aged members were women of Japanese ancestry. These women invariably participated in the chanting with faith and commitment, as well as great enthusiasm. There always were a few non-Oriental older persons present, but for the most part they tended to be observers rather than participants, frequently seated themselves in the fringe areas of the room, and often seemed embarrassed and uneasy.)

In "meditational" Buddhism, also, the greatest concentration is in the group of young adults under 35. At Zen Center in Los Angeles the age range of a sample of twenty-five (out of eighty) was from 18 to 41, with a median age of 28.32. At Zen Center in San Francisco, most are young, although some are over 40. At First Zen Institute, new members are mostly between 20 and 30, but there are older members who have been with the group for thirty years or more. In most of the Tibetan groups there is a wide age range, but with the greatest concentration in the late 20s and early 30s. At the Sino-American Buddhist Association, also, members are young. Of the meditational groups visited, only three had a membership consisting predominately of middle-aged people, and one of these, California Bosatsukai of Los Angeles, has been in existence for many years.

In the groups which have taken the form of churches, those devotees of Oriental ancestry range in age from preschoolers to senior citizens. Most of these churches have Sunday School classes for children and various programs for young people, as well as activities for adults. Those involved in the programs of the church, however, tend to be either under 15 or over 25, with relatively few teenagers and young adults being interested. The usual pattern is for youngsters to drop out in high school and college, but to return when they are married and have children of Sunday School age. (The exception to this is Buddha's Universal Church, which has a large choir that appeals to adolescents, and has many teen-agers in the Amitabha play.)

*Sex.* Nichiren Shoshu in 1970 reported 59% female members and 41% males.[9] This predominance of females over males is mostly due to the many Japanese housewives in the membership. Without these, the membership would be split about equally between men and women.

In most of the meditational groups there are more males than females. At Zen Center of Los Angeles, the sample of 25 included 19 males (76%). First Zen Institute reported "mostly males."[10] At several other Zen groups the number of males exceeded females, but this was not always so. The same was true of the Tibetan groups (the Tibetan Nyingma Meditation Center reported 60% males).[11] At the Sino-American Buddhist Association in 1971, the group of 55 most active "cultivators" included 23 males (42%) and 32 females (58%).[12]

In the Buddhist Churches of America and other churches of that type, membership figures are in terms of households, so there is no breakdown according to sex. However, at church services usually at least two-thirds of those attending are women. (At the Japanese services these tend to be older women, for the most part, but at the English-language services they are younger women.) Furthermore, the Women's Association is the most active organization in the church.

*Marital status.* Nichiren Shoshu statistics for 1970 show 47% married, 40% single, 9% divorced, and 4% widowed.[13] For those who are married, it is not indicated whether or not both husband and wife are members of Nichiren Shoshu.

At Zen Center of Los Angeles, in the sample studied, 40% were married and 40% had children. Other Zen groups as well as Tibetan groups usually have more single than married members, and it seems that the number of divorced women has been greater than one would expect on the basis of statistical probability. In several Zen groups, monks and nuns were permitted to marry, and sometimes married each other. Among young married couples, it is not unusual for both husband and wife to practice Zen, and a fair number of marriages take place in Zen groups. In the Chinese groups and Theravada groups, where monks and nuns must be celibate, there are no married couples among bhikkhus and bhikkhunis, of course. Among the lay disciples of Ch'an Master Hsuan Hua at the Sino-American Buddhist Association, most are single, but there are some married couples.[14] In a highly disciplined group like this, it is difficult to maintain ascetic discipline and also discharge responsibilities of spouse and parent.

In the church-type group, the adult members are more likely to be married than single, with unmarried young adults frequently drifting away.

*Racial and ethnic characteristics.* Nichiren Shoshu membership figures for 1970 show 41% Caucasians, 30% Orientals, 13% Latin-Americans, 12% Afro-Americans, and 4% "Other."[15] If one combined Caucasians with Latin-Americans, and Orientals with Afro-Americans, with the status of "other" being unknown, there would be 54-58% whites and 42-46% nonwhites. However, if Orientals, Latin-Americans, Afro-Americans, and "others" are considered as minority groups, and the 6% of the Jews in the organization are added to these, one would find 65% of the membership of Nichiren Shoshu being drawn from minority groups. In visiting various Buddhist groups over the country, I noticed many more blacks and Chicanos in Nichiren Shoshu than in any other Buddhist group.

In the Zen groups, most are Caucasian with a few blacks and Orientals. (At Zen Center of Los Angeles, 98% were Caucasian.) The same is true of the Tibetan groups, with the exception of monasteries for Tibetan lamas. In the majority of the Chinese groups most are Chinese, with a few Caucasians. However, in the Chinese meditational groups, about two-thirds are Caucasian and there sometimes are a few blacks.

In the church type groups, about 95% are Orientals, less than 1% black, and the remainder Caucasian.

## Religious Background

Nichiren Shoshu gives the following breakdown in terms of family religious background of its members: Roman Catholic, 30%; Protestant, 30%; Buddhist, 25%; Jewish, 6%; other, 4%; atheist 5%. Among the Protestants, Baptists comprised 40%; Methodists, 19%; Presbyterians, 9%; Episcopalians, 8% Lutherans, 7%; and all others a total of 17%.[16]

Several comments may be made about the Nichiren Shoshu figures: (1) the majority of the members of Japanese ancestry come from Buddhist backgrounds, so that joining Nichiren Shoshu has been not so much a matter of changing religions as changing sects; (2) the equal representation of Roman Catholics and Protestants indicates some under-representation of Protestants in terms of the number of Roman Catholics and Protestants in the United States; (3) since the Baptist churches comprise the largest group of Protestant bodies in America and the Methodists rank second, their relative representation in this group is about as expected, but the number of Lutherans is low in terms of statistical expectation; and (4) the small number of Jews in the group is about as expected, perhaps a little higher than would be anticipated.

In the sample from Zen Center of Los Angeles, 28% were Jewish, 12% had been Roman Catholics, 52% had been Protestants, and 8% had professed no religious beliefs before their involvement with Zen. This is not a typical picture, however. Most persons who have done either formal or informal surveys of Zen groups have reported a relatively high representation of Jews and Catholics. The same is true for the Tibetan groups: in both one finds former Methodists, Presbyterians, Baptists, Lutherans, and Episcopalians, but few from the fundamentalist-revivalist churches. The Nyingma Center reported that 45% had been involved with Christianity, 34% had practiced yoga, and 26% had practiced Zen. No figures were given for those who were of Jewish background.[17]

In the church type of Buddhist group, where the membership is mostly Oriental, most members have always been Buddhists. No systematic information is available on the religious background of non-Oriental members, but the impression is that most of these tend to fall into one of three groups: (1) those who were not much interested in religion before they became Buddhists, (2) those who always had a liberal orientation to religion, and (3) those who sampled several Christian denominations before deciding to embrace Buddhism.

## Educational and Occupational Status

Nichiren Shoshu has not issued any statistics on the educational background of its members. It has a growing group of college and university students in its membership. Aside from these, however, most of the members seem to have no more than a high school education and many have less than this. This is true also of the older, issei members of the BCA churches, but the nisei and sansei members frequently are college graduates.

Among the non-Oriental members of meditational groups, most have had some college work. Many have dropped out of college and then have returned to complete their degrees after starting on their Buddhist practice. (Often this is with the encouragement of a Zen master, Tibetan lama, or other religious counselor.) Quite a few have completed some graduate work and some have graduate or professional degrees. Many have done some studying of Oriental languages, and/or philosophies.

Nichiren Shoshu's occupational statistics for 1970 show 27% housewives, 19% students (high school and college), 10% professional, 10% clerical, 9% blue collar, 6% unskilled and 4% executive.[18] ("Professional" here includes entertainment professions.) In meeting with several of these groups during 1971 and 1972, this writer noticed both high school and college students, two engineers, one teacher, always some Japanese housewives, small shop owners, some artists and musicians, typists and file clerks, bookkeepers, clerks in department stores, waitresses, policemen, truck drivers, construction workers, taxi drivers, warehouse clerks, a bank guard, and others in comparable social brackets. There were large contingencies of unemployed, hoping for help in getting jobs. It seemed that the Orientals represented a wider range in social class status than did the non-Orientals who, except for the college student group, had an especially large representation in what would be called the "lower middle-class."

The majority of the meditation centers include a large group of college students, with some centers having close to 50 percent. There are also a good many professional men and women in these groups: physicians, psychologists, professors, public school teachers, social workers, dentists, architects, artists, writers, medical technicians, physiotherapists, musicians, dancers, actors, recreation workers, and photographers. There are bankers, business executives, and salesmen, as well as electricians, radio operators, clerks, and waitresses. Although many occupations are represented, the majority are middle-class or upper middle-class, and most members of these groups come from family backgrounds where parents are teachers, doctors, lawyers, engineers, or professional people of some kind. Among those living in Zen, Tibetan, or T'ien T'ai residential centers, or belonging to a Buddhist community, many are working at any job available for enough money to live on and perhaps to make it possible to spend a few months in a monastery. These are obviously not career jobs but consist of doing housework, babysitting, or typing; taking on house-painting jobs; and working as gas station attendants, janitors, or construction workers.

For those Buddhist groups of the church type in which the membership is primarily Oriental, there is no information about the occupations of the members, but one would assume that they would conform to the occupational pattern for the Japanese-Americans or Chinese-Americans in the area, and that virtually all occupational groups would be represented. With respect to those non-Oriental members with Japanese wives, there seems to be no consistent pattern. Those who have no family connection with the Orient are most frequently professional men and women.

## Personality Factors

So far our picture of American Buddhists does not seem to differ very much from a cross section of middle-class and upper middle-class Americans except that it might include a higher percentage of intellectuals and college graduates and a higher percentage of Oriental-Americans than would be found in the general population.

If one were to spend an evening with a group of young American Buddhists, their conversation at first would not seem too different from that of any other group of Americans of the same age. But soon the outsider would realize that these were not in all ways typical young Americans. They are especially friendly, warm, polite, and considerate; loyal to their leader, whether he is present or absent; not inclined to be lax or complain in a work situation. One would observe the sense of "oneness" and "community" in the group, and the unmistakable devotion to the ideals of the Buddhist way. He would also sense that these were happy young people—happy not only because Buddhism was effecting changes in their personal lives, but because they perceived in the Buddhist approach to life one which could hold out hope for society.

Perhaps an observer of American Buddhists would be troubled because it would seem that some of these young people were trying to make the problems of society go away by withdrawing from them. This might seem especially true for those who have chosen the monastic life. However, one would realize that most American Buddhists were functioning within society most of the time, and that time spent in monastic retreats helped them to gain perspective and function more effectively in their usual environment.

What were these non-Oriental Americans like before they became Buddhists?

Reverend Kodani of the Senshin Buddhist Church in Los Angeles feels that those Caucasians who become seriously interested in the True Pure Land sect tend for the most part to be well integrated, mature individuals with a deep understanding of Buddhism. Most of the ministers in the Shin Buddhist group whom I have met would agree with this assessment, although they would grant that a few are individuals with severe personal problems that have not been resolved.

Many middle-aged Buddhists whom I have met—especially if they became Buddhists in the pre-World War II years—appear to be persons who, over a long period of time, have been liberal in their political and religious views, broad in their interests, and conservative in their personal habits. In this group also, however, are some who have come to Buddhism for help with problems of a personal and social nature.

Are there any common patterns in the young adults who have been turning to Buddhism in the past ten to fifteen years? Do they show any similarities in childhood experiences, emotional characteristics, interests, attitudes, and ways of trying to cope with life problems? An examination of their life stories does show some frequently recurring patterns.

Often today's American Buddhist felt a sense of "rootlessness" as a child. Frequently he belonged to a family that was always moving, so that no place ever seemed like home. (A number are Army children.) Many of these young Buddhists travelled abroad as children or adolescents, which gave them exposure to other cultures and perhaps contributed to an attitude of receptiveness for something other than the American way. Often the moving around in childhood was continued in a pattern of drifting in adolescence and early adulthood—drifting from one school to another, in and out of the university, from one job to another, one state to another, in and out of various religious or quasi-religious groups such as Bahai, Krishna, and Yoga—always with a restlessness that never found the anchor it was seeking. Sometimes the rootlessness had its source in patterns within the family—perhaps an unavailable or overly strict father, or a vague and inconsistent mother; perhaps loss of a parent at a crucial point in development. Whatever the cause, however, its result was the same. The restlessness had often taken the form of drifting in and out of the drug scene. In fact, not infrequently it was this experience which had given the future Buddhist his first glimpse of a more beautiful world, which now he hoped to be able to find on a more solid, permanent, satisfying basis.

Many young Buddhists have always had an interest in religions —especially Oriental religions. Often they have taken courses in Buddhism or comparative religions at a university, and usually have personal libraries well stocked with paperbacks on Zen, Yoga, Hinduism, Taoism, and other non-Western schools of thought. Sometimes their interest in religion in the past has taken the form of considering the possibility of becoming a rabbi, Roman Catholic priest, or Protestant minister—or perhaps entering a convent. But both Judaism and Christianity have been examined and found wanting.

In the survey made by Miss Koren at Zen Center of Los Angeles, the reasons given for rejecting Christianity or Judaism were quite varied, and included the following: (1) it requires blind faith and doesn't stand up intellectually; (2) there is a gap between the values identified with the Judaic and Christian traditions and the behavior patterns displayed by those who claim to believe in these values; (3) Christianity or Judaism is a religion which was *forced* on the individual—not a system of belief which he chose; (4) it is oriented toward sin and punishment, especially punishment in the world to come; and (5) it is too much concerned with empty ritualism and not enough with helping the individual with his life problems. Other criticisms of Judaism and/or Christianity were on the basis of their dualism, lack of faith in the self, commercialism, and their being "too emotionally geared."

Several professors from colleges where students have dropped out of college to enter Buddhist monasteries have made two comments about these students: (1) they are idealists who are disillusioned because they see society as corrupt, and see no way of dealing with the "value vacuum" by remaining in the society; (2) frequently they are individuals who have either become anxious because of the excessive permissiveness in our society and feel the need of "authority," which they find in a relationship with a guru, or who because of disillusionment with either too strict or too permissive authority figures, are seeking self-discipline.

Several Zen masters and Tibetan lamas have commented about

the need for affiliation which characterizes many of their students and disciples—a need which expresses itself in a wish to live together and to form a community.

A number of life histories have shown the young adult who becomes a Buddhist as being confused and depressed. With depression being essentially a turning inward of hostility with a resultant feeling of worthlessness, it is not surprising that for many of these ascetic practices have a strong appeal. Psychosomatic disorders, dependency problems, borderline psychotic states, difficulties in getting along with others, and a host of other psychological problems are found among those who seek help in some form of Buddhism. Frequently the individual has been involved in psychotherapy of some sort, sometimes without much success in alleviating his anxiety or changing his relationships with others. Often it is these problems and the suffering associated with them which are the motivating factors leading the individual to Buddhism.

## American versus Asian Buddhists

How do American practicing Buddhists differ from Asian Buddhists? A number of Japanese clergymen and roshis, two Tibetan rinpoches, a Ceylonese bhikkhu, and a Chinese T'ien T'ai monk attempted to answer this question. The answers differed, but there were some points on which virtually all agreed.

A member of the headquarters staff of BCA stated that the Caucasian members tended to be "less involved" than Japanese members, and to make less substantial financial contributions. By less involved he meant, in part, less involved in the activity programs of the church. Since many of these programs are oriented toward the perpetuation of Japanese culture in America (judo, kendo, folk dancing, flower arrangement groups, and so on), and most Caucasian members of these churches are men who became Buddhists principally to please their Japanese wives, this situation is understandable.

When speaking of those who do not have Japanese spouses, and who express an interest in becoming "Shin" Buddhists, ministers describe them as eager and earnest—perhaps more so than the Japanese members—very intelligent, and highly versed in Buddhology, but without any real grasp of the essence of Buddhist experience nor much interest in a deepening of religious experience. The approach of Shin Buddhism often seems to them too passive, and they express a wish to meditate or *do* something. The Japanese are more ready to take an experiential rather than an intellectual approach to Buddhism and to try to deepen that experience.

Americans who take the Three Refuges in one of the meditational groups are frequently described as "reacting against established society," and as having to be led back to that society. In contrast, for the Oriental, Buddhism and its institutions are viewed as an essential part of society. Teachers of Zen, Satipatthana, T'ien T'ai meditation and Tantric practice comment that American seekers who come to them have read so many books on Buddhism that they are thoroughly confused. Dualistic thinking is firmly entrenched, delusions are confused with reality, and it is very difficult for the American to break the habit of conceptual thinking. In contrast, Asian Buddhists have grown up with a way of thinking which makes a denial of dualism much easier. The gurus agree, also, that Americans tend to be impatient—to want "instant enlightenment"—and to be discouraged if perfect bliss does not come immediately, although some will settle for "basic sanity" as release from suffering. In contrast, the Oriental tends to be more patient—more content with the "slow and gradual" path to Nirvana.

On the basis of personal observations, it seems that much of the above would apply also in the case of American and Japanese members of Nichiren Shoshu. Young Americans chant vigorously and enthusiastically for desired benefits, are excited by the dynamic concept of "human revolution," and have been interested in discussions of Nichiren's philosophy, but seem less ready than their Japanese counterparts to think in terms of deepening their religious practice.

# 13
# Why Buddhism?

Whether one is in New England or Florida, Michigan or Ohio, Houston or San Francisco, it is apparent that in the 1970s Buddhism is a real presence on the American scene, and that Americans in significant numbers are turning their backs on Western religions to accept the Buddhist Way. Why this growing interest in a religion which superficially seems alien to American society?

It would appear that the growth of Buddhism in America cannot be understood solely in the context of our Hellenic tradition and the intellectual ferment of the day, nor can it be entirely accounted for as an extension of the Buddhist missionary movement which started with Sakyamuni Buddha and spread through China, Korea, Southeast Asia, and Europe. Rather, it must be thought of as the result of the conflux of many factors, including the evangelical-revivalist Protestant tradition and widespread disillusionment with Christianity and Judaism in having failed to respond adequately to the ills of society. In addition, its growth is related to the needs and motivations of the particular individuals who choose to become Buddhists and with which this chapter is principally concerned.

## REASONS FOR BECOMING BUDDHISTS

What is the appeal of Buddhism and what are the reasons that American Buddhists have chosen this alternative from among those available? The reasons for choosing Buddhism are many, of course, but there are a few which are especially significant.

## Familial-Cultural Affinity

Probably most of the American Buddhists of Oriental ancestry have chosen Buddhism because the members of their families and many of their closest friends are Buddhists, and Buddhism has been a part of their lives since infancy. For them being Buddhists does not require rejection of a family tradition, nor the choosing of a religion. Buddhism is something which is *there*.

For many of the second-, third-, and fourth-generation Americans of Chinese or Japanese ancestry who attend schools where Orientals are a minority, there may be a culture conflict and encounter with religious discrimination which makes adherence to Buddhism no longer the easy thing to do. This is especially true if community prejudices are strong, if parents do not have strong feelings about their Buddhism, if the majority of Orientals are Christians, or if Buddhist parents feel that there are economic and social advantages to be gained by encouraging their children to attend Christian churches. In communities like Cleveland, Ohio, and Seabrook, New Jersey, for example, when boys and girls reach high school age and there are strong peer-group pressures to conform to its standards, the young Buddhists are likely to repudiate any affiliations which suggest that they are not 100 percent American. They want nothing to do with a foreign language (other than a European one), foreign customs, or a foreign religion. Some may attend Christian churches, especially if they have Christian boyfriends or girlfriends; others drop all religious affiliations. Many of today's young adult nisei whose parents experienced the discriminations and injustices of the war years report that, as children, they were urged to attend Christian Sunday Schools because their parents felt that no young person of Japanese ancestry could possibly gain acceptance in American society unless he were a Christian.

A large percentage of the Oriental-Americans who leave Buddhism in adolescence, or who have been sent by their Buddhist parents to Christian Sunday Schools, are permanently lost as members of the Buddhist community, although the Buddhist values which they encountered in the family will continue to influence them throughout life. However, a significant number of those who have dropped out in adolescence return as young adults, especially if they have married within their own ethnic group. Also, a goodly number who, as children, never had any membership relationship to a Buddhist church or temple, as young adults abandon the Christian Church and become devout Buddhists.

Young Japanese-American adults who have left Christianity for Buddhism frequently report that their Buddhist heritage is a part of their identity, and that to deny it is to fragment the self, to deny being a whole person. This is true especially if their relationships with their parents have been warm and happy ones. They report that they always had some feelings of discomfort and tension associated with their affiliation with Christianity, whether or not they experienced any theological conflict. (Social psychologists would perhaps explain this on the basis of Rosenberg's "consistency" theory or Festinger's "cognitive dissonance" theory of attitude formation and change.[1]) Sometimes these individuals have returned to Buddhism with a deeper and clearer understanding of its meaning. Several erstwhile Protestants from Buddhist families have become ministers in BCA, and are among those doing the most outstanding job of working with Buddhist young people.

## The Intellectual, Scientific Appeal

Among Americans—both Orientals and non-Orientals—are many who have difficulty with wholehearted commitment to Christianity, in part on the basis of dogma which they feel they cannot accept. The concepts of God as Creator, existence of a personal God, the virgin birth, the deity of Christ, the Resurrection, the validity of miracles, the Second Coming, the power of prayer, salvation by faith, the existence of Heaven and Hell, the infallibility of the Scriptures all are rejected.

Some of those rejecting Biblical concepts end up in the ranks of the atheists, and some identify themselves as agnostics. Some stay quietly within their churches or suppress their doubts. Many join or shift to churches where the nature of Christian Truth is interpreted in symbolic terms which they find acceptable. Some of these may find themselves reasonably comfortable in a church home with a liberal Presbyterian, Congregational, or Methodist minister who places a strong emphasis on the "social gospel" of Christianity. Others, if they do not just let Christianity go by default, will join the Unitarian-Universalist communion. Then there will be some who, while rejecting Christianity as stretching credulity too far, feel a need for a religion which they can find intellectually acceptable and scientifically sound. For these, Buddhism sometimes seems to be the answer. For them, the Buddha's admonition to accept nothing on authority has a strong appeal, as does Buddhism's nontheistic interpretation of creation and its naturalistic concept of man's place in the universe.

The American Buddhist who has chosen Buddhism on an intellectual basis or because it seems scientifically sound is more likely to join a Theravada or Zen group than one where the emphasis is on "salvation by faith," or one where there is widespread belief in the existence of demons and ghosts, heavens and hells. If one chooses a church of the Pure Land or True Pure Land sect, he usually rejects a literal interpretation of Buddha's Pure Land or the Western Paradise, and accepts an interpretation of the Pure Land as synonymous with nirvana, to be attained in this life.

## Appeal of a Rational Cure for a Sick Society

Many young people who turn from Christianity to embrace Buddhism do so because, in their idealism, they see the Christian Church as having failed to cure the ills of society. They perceive church members as hypocrites who mouth acceptance of the Ten Commandments and then break them with regularity. (Of course, some of these same idealists may again be disillusioned when they see their favorite roshi becoming a little tipsy during the cocktail hour.) Buddhism seems to make sense to them as an approach to the elimination of war, poverty, racism, prejudice, environmental pollution, intemperance, and drug abuse. (And if it doesn't work, they can always withdraw from the miserable world and take refuge in the peace and quiet of the monastery.)

## Appeal of Pageantry, Symbolism, and the Esoteric

For many Christians and Jews, the church and synagogue have become drab and unexciting. The robes worn by the priest, minister, or rabbi—if, indeed, he wears any robes at all—are not as elaborate as they used to be, nor as colorful. Altars have been stripped of all of the "nonessentials." Ambiguous language is being removed from rituals. Some symbols remain, of course, but often they are not recognized as symbols and few people are curious about them or remember what they mean. One wonders how many are aware of the meaning of flowers and candles on the altar, and of burning incense. How many Christians recall (if they ever knew) the meaning of IHS? And how many Jews know the meaning of the Star of David?

In contrast to all of this, Buddhism seems colorful, glamorous, mysterious, and full of rich symbolism. True, BCA churches look very much like the church or synagogue down the street, and the minister of any of these Buddhist churches is clad in robes as drab as those of his Protestant or Jewish counterpart, except on festival days. But the altar is resplendent with gleaming gold ornaments and flanked by Oriental drums and gongs; the chanting is in a foreign language, incomprehensible, but obviously with deep significance; and the meaning of symbols such as bowing, prostration, gassho, incense, candles, and flowers is constantly being brought to attention. Aside from these, there is an air of mystery. In Zen temples and others of the meditational type, the motionless robe-clad figures sitting cross-legged in the dimness of a zendo enhance the aura of esoteric mysticism. However, those who are drawn to Buddhism because they see it as colorful, glamorous, and mysterious are likely not to stick with it after the sense of pageantry and mystery wears off, unless by this time they have experienced some tangible benefits.

## Do It Yourself Appeal

Attractive to many Americans is the Buddha's thought that man can assure his own salvation, through his own efforts, and this is one aspect of the meditational approach which makes it so appealing. Especially for individuals with problems centering around dependence or trust, the idea that one can attain salvation without having to trust some supernatural being and without having to depend on anyone other than oneself makes the jiriki type of Buddhism one which would appeal to many.

## Wish to Transcend the Ordinary

There are some who are drawn to Buddhism by a wish to go beyond the satisfactions, pleasures, and sensory experiences of everyday life. They want to see what most men cannot see, to hear music that is beautiful beyond what can be imagined, to experience taste that is more wonderful than ambrosia, to have wisdom beyond that of the most honored sages, and to experience joy of such magnitude that the ordinary man cannot even conceive of it. Furthermore, they want to have this experience here and now and not in some distant "heaven" where one hopes to go after death. Persons with this kind of drive for earthly bliss have frequently had a brief and watered-down glimpse of it through experimenting with psychedelic drugs. Often they have read and reread Philip Kapleau's descriptions of enlightenment experiences, and are looking for shortcuts to nirvana.[2] What they want is perfect bliss, and their approach to it is through Zen.

## Need for a Wise and Benevolent Authority Figure

For many who become Buddhists, a relationship with a Zen Master, Ch'an Master, or Rinpoche represents the culmination of a long search for closeness with an authority figure who is firm but benevolent; who guides but does not steer; who helps, but encourages independence; who releases his disciple when the disciple is ready, but does not abandon him. Those with this sort of motivation usually are individuals who have grown up with excessive permissiveness, parental inconsistency, or with authority figures so rigid and strict that rebellion against authority took place before the individual was mature enough to assume responsibility for himself. For one who is motivated by this need, the essence of Buddhism is found in the relationship between the disciple and his master.

## Need to Rebel against the Establishment

In the case of the non-Oriental who chooses Buddhism, becoming a Buddhist means rejecting establishment religions—most often the religion of the parents. Some parents are happy to have their children choose any religion, and others can accept their children's affiliation with Buddhism by thinking of it as a philosophy, or system of meditation, or an approach to therapy. However, most Christian or Jewish parents are quite upset when they learn that their children have abandoned the religion of their fathers to take up a religion which belongs to an entirely different tradition. For most young people, parents are symbolic of the establishment, and a denial of the parents' religion then becomes a means of rebelling against them as well as against the society of which they are a part.

## Need for Relief from Suffering

Probably the majority of non-Orientals who become practicing Buddhists do so because of an overriding need for relief from suffering. Sometimes the suffering is physical, but more often it is emotional and often psychosomatic. The individual practicing meditation, chanting, or any kind of Buddhist "self-cultivation" is motivated by a need for symptomatic relief, mitigation of anxiety and depression, reduction of hostility, sometimes even relief from the suffering associated with poverty and hunger. (In some instances feelings of guilt will go away only when meditation is coupled with self-punishment in the form of ascetic practices.) The individual wants peace, tranquility, prosperity, health, and happiness in place of tension, conflict, turmoil, anxiety, illness, poverty, and misery.

## Need for a Richer, Fuller, More Effective Life

A good many who take up Buddhist practice—especially meditational practice—do so not because they are "suffering" but because they feel that it will open up new dimensions of experience for them, enrich their lives, give them more energy, and generally make them more effective persons. Often individuals with this type of motivation do not actually become Buddhists, but practice within the context of a different religion. As noted in chapter 11, monks in Roman Catholic monasteries are increasingly using Zen methods to deepen their own religious experience. Of course, Catholicism is full of mantras and mudras, and the practice of visualization while meditating makes the Tantric approach also one which has much to offer within the Christian context. Even those who are not particularly religious may practice Buddhist meditation because they believe it is good for them mentally and physically—that it keeps them well and functioning at an optimal level.

## Seeking for Truth

It does not seem that many persons become interested in Buddhism because of an overriding desire to discover the nature of ultimate Truth. However, quite a few who remain with Buddhism and become deeply involved report a visceral experience that shouts to them "This is *It*! This is Reality! This is *Truth*!" This conviction, they claim, keeps them as devoted followers of the Buddha.

## How People Happen to Become Buddhists

How Americans happen to be Buddhists is illustrated by the following excerpts from the life stories of various Buddhists or potential Buddhists.[3]

It was three o'clock on a Saturday afternoon in August, in a suburb of Los Angeles. Marjorie Takahashi, a pretty young nisei housewife whose thirty-year-old sansei husband was an up-and-coming lawyer in a Los Angeles firm dealing mostly with the Japanese-American community, was driving her eight-year-old daughter, Sally, to the local Buddhist church. The children of the Sunday School were to practice the "Bon-Odori" (Bon Dance), in which children and adults of the church would all participate next week, during O-Bon (festival of departed spirits). The car stopped at the curb in front of the handsome, split-level grey stone home of the wealthy Yamaguchis, where

Sally expected to pick up her friend, Thelma, who was nine. Surprised that Thelma was not waiting on the sidewalk, Sally jumped from the car and ran to the front door, where she rang the bell. A uniformed Latin-American maid answered her ring. No, the maid said, Miss Thelma wasn't there—she'd gone swimming. The Bon dance practice? She didn't know about that, but she'd heard that Thelma and her parents were going to attend the Presbyterian church: the mister thought it would be good for his business if he mingled more with Anglos.

Climbing back in the car, Sally reported to her mother, who made no comment, but sighed as she started the car. This was getting to be more and more of a problem in the church. Both she and her husband, Tom, came from devout Buddhist families. Her brother-in-law was in Japan studying for ordination as a BCA minister, and her father was a member of the church's Board of Directors. She hadn't been too regular in her church attendance during her college years at U.C.L.A. Even now she couldn't get her husband to go too frequently, but she was active in the Junior Fujinkai, and Tom contributed generously to the church. He was conscientious about burning incense on the family altar, too. Both of them wanted Sally and her four-year-old brother to be Buddhists.

Sally thought about the fun Thelma was having at the swimming pool. It was a hot day, and the cool water would feel good. She wondered, too, what Thelma would do in the Presbyterian Sunday School. Sensing that her friend would not be at the Bon-Odori, she wondered if Thelma would have any place to wear the new silk kimono which her grandmother had sent her from Japan. She, Sally, would miss her chum at the Hanamatsuri parade next spring, too, and she felt a pang at the thought that her erstwhile companion would not get to bathe the baby Buddha. She wondered, also, when the minister would think that she, Sally, was old enough to take the Three Refuges.

Sally was destined to be a Buddhist, like her parents and grandparents before her.

Julie Mathews, a thin, sallow girl of twenty with long blond hair and thick glasses, sat before the gohonzon in a Chicago living room, joining twenty others as she chanted, "Nam' myoho renge kyo, nam' myoho renge kyo, nam' myoho renge kyo." While chanting, she rolled her Buddhist rosary between her palms. When the chanting stopped, the leader asked for testimonials. Smoothing her blue jeans, Julie got to her feet to tell her story.

Julie, a university sophomore, described herself as one who, a year before, had been "filled with paranoid hate." She had believed that her home situation was intolerable, that nobody understood her, that everyone treated her unfairly. And she had believed that she couldn't do anything about her life other than to complain and express resentment, so she was depressed all the time. Then a boyfriend attending the University of Illinois had told her about Nichiren Shoshu. He kept urging her to try chanting, insisting she would find that it worked. But she was suspicious of anything she didn't understand —thought the "magic formula" was just a gimmick. She chanted a few times when she felt she hadn't studied enough for a test, but didn't do gongyo because she thought it was too hard. Her friend didn't give up, so finally she committed herself. She felt that there had been a real "human revolution" in herself, and said that for the first time she knew the meaning of social responsibility. Now she felt happy and fulfilled, and life was really worth living.

"Why am I here?" The young man at San Francisco's Zen Center answered the visitor's question. "It's the anxiety, and with the world the way it is, you can't learn to live in it."
"Are you getting less anxious?" the visitor asked.
"Yes, I suppose so," he said, "but I have a long way to go."
"Will you return to the world?"
"Yes, but I'm not ready yet."

A former businessman and journalist, the middle-aged American roshi originally became involved with Zen in his search for relief from suffering, and for the attainment of satori. A tense, miserable man with ulcers and a host of allergies, he had read numerous books on Zen philosophy and attended Suzuki's lectures at Columbia, but none of this had brought him any real relief. Finally he decided to quit his business and go to Japan in search of a Zen master who could guide him in his practice. This led to hard practice in several monasteries under three roshis, and after five years he had his first satori experience. His kensho deepened with further practice, and finally he returned to the United States as a Zen priest, to start an American Zen Center. His allergies were gone, his ulcers healed, and his fears and anxieties had withered.[4]

Phil Loomis, a New York University graduate student in philosophy, began attending the services at the Temple of Enlightenment on Sunday mornings. Soon he joined the evening meditation group and was meditating regularly, enjoying the feeling of freedom which it gave him. A man who had never resolved his problems of dependency in relation to his mother, he felt he was finally becoming a man through acceptance of the Buddha's idea that each person must be responsible for his own salvation.

Frieda Golden was a thirty-five-year old physicist who, from adolescence, had rejected the idea of a personal God and was dissatisfied with the concept of God as Creator. A Chinese fellow student in graduate school had introduced her to Buddhism and she found it more congenial to her views than Judaism. She had never taken the Three Refuges and was not a member of any Buddhist organization, but regarded herself as a Buddhist and always listed herself as such in biographical directories.

## BENEFITS RECEIVED FROM BUDDHIST PRACTICE

Controlled research dealing with the psychological and physical changes resulting from Buddhist practice is still sparse, but will doubtless increase as humanistic psychologists become more interested in Buddhist psychology (see chapter 10). This section deals not with such research, but mainly with self-assessments of those participating in Buddhist practice, whether or not they actually have committed themselves to Buddhism as a religion. It must be remembered, of course, that these are mostly persons who have stayed with their Buddhist practice for an extended period of time, and that those who dropped out probably did not experience the benefits reported by the persons who are continuing the practice.

### BCA and Other Buddhist Churches

Our contacts with non-Orientals in the church-type Buddhist groups have been too scanty and too superficial to be very meaningful. For the most part, these persons do not feel that Buddhism meets any particular personal need, nor has changed them in any way. They do find it intellectually stimulating and satisfying, and enjoy the contacts with other Buddhists. Some feel that they are no longer at a dead end with respect to doing something for society but are involved in an approach which could work.

### Nichiren Shoshu of America

Nichiren Shoshu gives the following summary of the greatest benefits of chanting, as reported by its members in 1970: purpose of living, 22%; improvement of character, 21%; improved human relations, 19%; improved health, 18%; financial gains, 17%; better grades in school, 3%.[5] These figures are supported by testimonials given in Nichiren Shoshu meetings, for example:

A young woman said, "I felt that everybody was against me, but now my former enemies buy me presents."

A young man reported, "I was really a bum, stealing from grocery stores, swiping hubcaps from cars, allergic to work of any kind, stoned on pot most of the time, shacking up with a different dame every night. Now I'm a reformed character—have a good job and a wonderful wife, don't touch pot or acid, and I'm all for law and order. I like it that way."

A thirty-year-old housewife testified, "I was so down that most days I didn't even bother to get out of bed. The house was filthy and my husband had to get his own meals. There didn't seem to be any point in living, and I took all the aspirin that we had in the house. But it wasn't enough to do the job. Then a friend talked me into getting out of bed and going to a Nichiren Shoshu meeting. She wanted me to start chanting, but it was too much trouble. She started coming over to the house every morning and hauled me out of bed so we could chant together. After the chanting we'd have coffee. Pretty soon I began feeling better. Now I'm chanting regularly and I look forward to every day. My house is neat and clean, I'm doing all of the cooking now, and I've started taking guitar lessons. Life is wonderful, and it's all because of the Gohonzon."

A middle-aged woman said, "I used to have so much trouble with arthritis—kept myself doped up with medicine—and sometimes I couldn't even walk. Then I joined Nichiren Shoshu and started chanting. Now I'm in good health and don't even have to take an aspirin."

A college student reported, "I was doing so poorly in my courses that I was in danger of flunking out. It seemed to me that there wasn't any point in staying in school. Besides, the tuition had gone up and my kid brother was ready for college, and my dad couldn't afford to send two of us. Actually, he really couldn't afford to send either of us to college, because my mom had fallen and broken her hip, and the hospital bills were terrific, so that both my brother and I were going to have to get jobs. I didn't have any money and I couldn't find a job, and my grades were terrible. I was feeling pretty low. Then Mr. Williams had a seminar about True Buddhism on our campus, and I started chanting. The first thing that happened was that my grades started to improve. Then I found a part-time job at the state hospital. And now I have a scholarship for the fall. All of this happened after I began chanting."

*Meditational Buddhism*

Americans who have been involved in intensive meditational practice frequently have undergone personality changes which have been noticed by friends and members of the family. Among the changes most often observed by others are increased warmth and friendliness, spontaneity, improved disposition, more efficient functioning, and serenity.[6]

Probably most of those practicing Buddhist meditation have not really experienced enlightenment, or else their enlightenment experience was a relatively shallow one, but many report that they have experienced altered states of consciousness with expanded awareness, clarity of vision, the beginning of a breaking down of dualistic thinking, and perceptual intensification, all accompanied by a feeling of great joy and boundless gratitude. They report also such benefits as alleviation of anxiety and depression, better physical health, a sense of purpose and direction, improved concentration, better self-control, awakening of creativity, a reduction in ego-centeredness, and a withering of excessive attachment to material things. Some report that the close relationship with the master or teacher is the most meaningful relationship they have ever had.

# part 4

# Conclusions and Speculations

# 14

# What Future for Buddhism in America?

If Buddhism in America had its beginning with the founding of the Theosophical Society, then it has existed for about a century. If it began when Soyen Shaku made his two impressive talks in Chicago, then it is eighty years old. If one looks at such time spans in the context of the rapidity with which religious "fads" usually come and go in the United States, Buddhism cannot be called a fad. However, when we compare the eight to ten decades of the propagation of Buddhism in America with the more than twenty-five hundred years of its existence in Asia, and with the lengthy Judaeo-Christian tradition which was brought from Europe to America by our founding fathers, it is obvious that Buddhism is a new religion for the non-Orientals of North America.

Looking at the various forms in which it manifests itself, it is clear that Buddhism in America does not really have an American style, but appears as an Oriental anachronism in a Western society. Some of the values which it espouses are consonant with those of the Judaeo-Christian tradition, but others are inconsistent with it. In many ways, also, the ideology and practices of Buddhism are in conflict with the dominant values of our technological, materialistc, secular society.

We have estimated that possibly a half million Americans are participating regularly in Buddhist practice of some sort, whether or not they actually call themselves Buddhists. This seems like quite a large group, and actually, it may be larger. However, when we recall that a substantial proportion of the Buddhists in America are of Asian background, the number does not seem too impressive. In addition, when we remember that probably 90 percent or more of all Buddhists in America are on the West Coast, and most of the remainder are on the East Coast or in urban centers, the picture becomes one which reveals that Buddhism is known very little if at all in most parts of the country. In rural areas, except for the West Coast, almost nothing is known of Buddhism; throughout most of the South and Midwest, also, it does not exist, aside from an occasional meditation group in a college community and a few Buddhist churches or centers in large metroplitan areas such as Chicago and Minneapolis.

What is the future for Buddhism in America? Has it already reached its apogee, signaling an inevitable decline? Will it ever become a significant force in rural America, or the "Bible Belt" of the deep South and Midwest? Will it show a steady and significant growth? If Buddhism does survive in America, what kind of Buddhism will it be? If it does not survive, will there be remnants of its influence found in other religious traditions? Can there be a creative synthesis of Buddhism and the cultural society in America?

Needleman, in discussing the future of the "new religions" in California and how they may influence society, points out that even if we were able to predict numbers of adherents over a given period of time, we could not assess their possible impact on society unless we knew whether or not they were *real* Buddhists, or *real* Hindus, or whatever.[1] In other words, the impact of one hundred Buddhists who each year made contributions to BCA, but did not engage in any religious practices at home, largely ignored the precepts, and went to church once a year for the Hanamatsuri celebration might be quite different from that of one hundred Zen adepts who earnestly practiced zazen with regularity and faithfully followed the bodhisattva way in their approach to the problems of society. Needleman asks if we are really capable of distinguishing between those who merely adopt the terminology of a new teaching without its changing anything essential in their inner lives, and those who are sincerely struggling to live by the teaching.[2]

Related to the point raised by Needleman that predictions mean nothing when they are in numerical terms only, and exclude consideration of the quality of religious experience, is Swearer's delineation of three ways in which Buddhism can influence the West—by appropriation, transformation, and dialogue.[3]

Swearer indicates that the Buddhist presence is manifested in "appropriation" when an individual actually becomes a Buddhist, identifies himself as such, and accepts the Buddhist way of life. "Transformation" takes place when the individual creatively integrates certain Buddhist concepts and practices into his life, thereby changing his life and outlook, although he does not actually become a Buddhist. "Dialogue" refers to exchanges between Buddhists and non-Buddhists, for purposes of increasing understanding, with the interchanges sometimes resulting in enrichment for the parties involved, and sometimes resulting in the adoption by non-Buddhists of selected Buddhist practices which are engaged in within a secular setting or in the context of some other religion.[4] (An example of the latter would be the case of the Roman Catholic priest who starts a Zen-type meditation group for Catholic youth.) In predicting the future of Buddhism in America, then, we would have to consider each of these possible modes of Buddhist influence, as well as the influence which persons in each of these categories might have on the future of Buddhism.

When one takes on the role of observer and reporter, the picture which emerges never conforms perfectly to objective reality as viewed by the non-Buddhist. Selectivity of attention, the bias of the observer, and errors of interpretation all serve to introduce distortions. In addition, the dynamic, constantly changing scene is such as to render any observation obsolescent as soon as it is made. The experiences of this observer, during the three years involved in the present study, have been such as to provide strong support for the Buddhist doctrine of "impermanence" as a basic fact of life. Yet, when one changes from the role of observer-reporter to that of prognosticator, one is moving into an area where the uncertainties and sources of error are infinitely greater. As observer, one is dealing with that which he preceives to be occurring or to have occurred. As predictor, he is evaluating a complicated past and present in relation to an equally complex and most indefinite future.

In the scientific laboratory the experimenter works in a controlled setting, manipulating independent variables so as to produce changes in dependent variables. He notes the cause-effect relationships between the variables he is studying, and makes hypotheses based on his understanding of these relationships. But even in a scientific laboratory, one can do little more than say, *"If this* condition obtains, *probably that* will happen." When one moves out of the relatively controlled atmosphere of the laboratory, and attempts to predict the future status of any development within sociey, he is moving into a situation in which the independent variables are not only uncontrollable but also interacting, in which many new variables will emerge, and in which prognostication is highly speculative. Nevertheless, despite the hazards in such an undertaking, we shall attempt in this chapter to analyze some of the factors which appear to be related to the status of Buddhism in American sociey, and venture a few guesses about possible future developments.

## Contingency Variables

Among the factors which will determine the future of Buddhism in America are the following: economic, social, political, ideational, and technological factors within the society; methods of propagating the Dharma and modifications within Buddhism itself; developments within Judaism and the Christian Church; meditational movements and techniques of a secular nature; continued success of meditational approaches to psychotherapy; growth of the movements of humanistic and transpersonal psychology. Each of these is briefly discussed below.

### Factors within the Society

To some extent, the growth of Buddhism in the past decade has been associated with the emergence of the so-called counter culture of young people—on the one hand spoiled by permissive parents, and on the other hand rebelling against the technocratic, materialistic, computerized society which has taken the fun and excitement out of life while at the same time failing to make substantial progress in the solution of problems related to war, race relations, crime, pollution, inflation, unemployment, alchoholism, and so on.[5] Many of these adolescents and young adults who have found their way into the zendo or the Tibetan meditation center have wandered away to try some other road to the attainment of nirvana, but some have remained to become members of the Sangha or lay disciples of a guru or Zen master. The nature of this counter culture is changing, but Roszak believes that the generational revolt will increase in the years to come and will continue until at least around 1984.[6] Of course, it is possible that involvement with Buddhist practices will not be part of the life style of dissenting youth in the years to come, but Buddhism represents one path which may be chosen.

Both within the "hippie" group and among those whose life style is of a more conventional stripe are many who view our technological civilization as having a structure based on greed. To these, the stress which Buddhism places on destruction of the ego seems to hold promise for showing the way for attainment of a better world. Eden, a British Buddhist who is a relative newcomer to Buddhism, says, "The outcome of hatred, greed and fear must eventually be conflict in which weapons are used which can destroy all life on this planet, while unbridled consumption of raw materials and energy which our economic system demands, coupled with a soaring birth rate and low death rate raises the spectre of economic collapse and mass famine even if Armageddon can somehow be avoided."[7]

For Eden, the appeal of Buddhism is a rational one and lies in four factors, as follows:

(a)  Buddhism identifies clearly the nefarious activities of the ego and demonstrates the turmoil and suffering which is caused for as long as we cling to our egocentric experience of life.

(b)  There are remarkable parallels between the intuitive knowledge of the cosmos revealed in many Buddhist texts and the findings of modern science. . . .

(c)  Buddhism is essentially practical, offering various systems of mind training which ultimately can help the individual to live his life in harmony with Reality and not in conflict with it. . . .

(d)  Buddhism is not burdened with the concept of God who in many people's minds is still essentially a superpolitical figure making demands and issuing threats in the same way as any ruler on earth. . . .[8]

With some choosing Buddhism as an antidote to the effects of technocracy and a means of alleviating the ills of society, its future would be expected to be negatively related to progress made in finding other solutions to these problems. These other possible solutions would involve the areas of politics, economics, science, social planning, and education—the use of technology to destroy its own evils. The prospects that this will happen in the foreseeable future seem very slight, so that people will continue to seek for solutions in nontechnological ideologies, among them Buddhism.

*Methods and Modifications within Buddhism*

Several factors within Buddhism itself are related to its perpetuation and possible growth in the future, as well as to the forms which it will take. Among these are Buddhist missionary efforts, modifications in practices to meet the needs of Westerners, and emphasis on training American monks and teachers.

*Buddhist missionary efforts.* Since the beginning of the twentieth century, the planned propagation of Buddhism in America has been largely under the leadership of teachers and priests from the Orient, whose mission has been to spread the Dharma in the West. Many of these have had to communicate through interpreters. With the multiplicity of Oriental religions and pseudo-religious groups in America —especially on the West coast—it would seem that continued growth of Buddhism will require missionary efforts outside of the areas where the followers of this or that guru are trying to outshout each other. This will require efforts which will involve communication at a level and in a form which those receiving the message can understand.

Continued concentration of missionary activities in California— especially the San Francisco Bay area—would seem to be self-limiting. On the other hand, it is doubtful if a Zen center or Tibetan Buddhist monastery in Mississippi or in a small town in South Dakota would generate many sincere followers of the Buddhist way. University towns and some as yet untouched urban centers would be areas in which Buddhist missionaries might find a friendly reception.

Nichiren Shoshu of America has been successful in part because it has recognized the importance of communicating at a level which is appropriate for the group toward which its message is beamed. The college student is interested in the philosophy of Nichiren Shonin, as it relates to world peace, but the waitress and unemployed factory worker would rather hear about how chanting and faith in the gohonzon can bring in more dollars and improve the individual's financial security. Other Buddhist groups could benefit by application of the lesson which Nichiren Shoshu has learned.

Eden, speaking from the standpoint of the Buddhist "convert," reminds his fellow Buddhists of the fact that it is all too easy to forget how strong are the influences of the prejudices and misconceptions which people have grown up with. He says,

> We must start our discussions at the level at which the "average" intelligent person is thinking, at the level at which his environment has conditioned him; this may necessitate initially eschewing all mention of Buddhism to avoid arousing prejudices which could block receptivity. The hopes, fears, beliefs and outlook of the individual, however confused, petty or irrelevant must be the starting point from

which the possibility of a new way of experiencing life is revealed. The most careful and detailed map is useless unless the map reader can first identify his own position on it.[9]

What we are saying, then, is that the future of Buddhism in America will be dependent in part on continuation of missionary efforts, but in new areas and in an idiom which will convey its message to a wider spectrum of society.

*Westernization of Buddhist practices.* Buddhism in the United States has never been a Buddhism which really fits with the American life style. Many for whom Zen has some appeal will shake their heads regretfully, saying, "I just can't sit in the lotus position." When told that it is all right to sit on a chair if the lotus posture is impossible, they say, "But that would make me feel conspicuous," or "I hate to admit that I can't do it."

In addition to the problem of sitting in a cross-legged position (which the nonmeditational sects have resolved by the use of pews or folding chairs), there is the fact that chants, responses, or mantras are usually in Japanese, Chinese, Korean, Tibetan, Vietnamese, Pali, or Sanskrit—all unfamiliar to most Westerners. Some argue that English does not lend itself to chanting and that if chanting is used as a meditational vehicle, putting the chants into a comprehensible language would be distracting and encourage discursive thinking. Nevertheless, some Buddhist leaders have contended that Buddhism must fit in with the American way of life if it is to have a meaningful place in that life. They have taken the position that translating sutras into English, drinking coffee instead of green tea, eating American food, and wearing western-type clothing does not compromise the basic nature of Buddhism and helps to make it something which can fit into the life of the American adherent rather than stand out as something apart.

Undoubtedly, without the Oriental trappings, Buddhism would not appeal to some who are drawn to it. However, for many who see the Oriental as glamorous and mysterious, the attraction of Chinese or Japanese Buddhism diminishes as the novelty wears off. It would seem that, on a long-term basis, more modification of practices to meet the needs of a Western society would be indicated, without, however, obscuring the uniqueness of Buddhism.

*Development of an American Sangha.* Traditionally, the members of the Sangha are the leaders of the Buddhist community and teachers of the Dharma. In the middle 1970s most of the ministers of Buddhist churches, priests in Chinatown temples, Zen masters, Theravada monks, and lamas are Orientals, with only a handful of Western-ers among them. In several Zen and Tibetan groups provision has been made for living in a monastic or semimonastic setting, and there has been ordination of American monks and nuns. Some of these are now serving as teachers, and more will be doing so.

Humphreys has noted that several attempts have been made to establish an English branch of the Theravada Sangha in London, so far without success because of the difficulty in keeping the Vinaya rules in London.[10] At present there are a Sinhalese and a Thai Sangha in London, but few Englishmen have been ordained and few would wish to even try to keep the rules of the Order under the difficult circumstances of living in the West. Much the same situation as that outlined by Humphreys exists in the United States. So far, the Ma-hayana Buddhists have been much more flexible and practical than the Theravadins in setting up conditions which make it possible for dedicated young Americans to join the Sangha and assume functions of teaching and religious leadership while discharging other roles in society. Several Zen masters serving as abbots of monasteries have even permitted monks and nuns to marry each other.

The growth of Buddhism in America will depend in part on the growth of an American Sangha which, in turn, will depend on adap-tations to the characteristics of a modern Western society.

## Developments within Judaism and the Christian Church

Almost all of the great religious traditions have valued medita-tion as an approach to transcendental mystical experience. Generally speaking, however, this has been regarded as an activity for saints and holy men, and has been considered to be beyond the capacities of ordinary human mortals. In the Western religions of modern times, practically its only remnants have been in the meditative practices of some of the Roman Catholic monasteries and convents. Even there, however, in the twentieth century less and less time has been spent in contemplative practices. In the synagogue and most Protestant churches there has been concern with liturgy and with the social problems of society, but usually a complete lack of any meditative dimension to religious experience.

Since the publication of Suzuki's books on Zen, there has been a steady increase of interest in Zen meditation on the part of Roman Catholic priests and nuns. This interest was stimulated especially by the works of Father Thomas Merton, Dom Aelred Graham, and Father William Johnston.[11] Its outcome has been the now fairly widespread practice of inviting Zen masters to visit monasteries for the purpose of giving instruction in zazen, and in the fairly frequent presence of nuns and Catholic priests in Zen centers and Tibetan Buddhist meditation groups. As yet, however, meditational practice has not been widely adopted by Roman Catholic groups as a part of church-sponsored devotional activity.

As far as Protestant and Jewish groups are concerned, except for some practice of zazen in Unitarian and other liberal Protestant groups, there has been little official interest in meditation as a form of religious experience. On the basis of the reactions of young Americans who have left the Christian Church or Judaism to "take the refuge" in a Zen center or Tibetan Buddhist meditation center, it is apparent that many are seeking a religion in which there is a meditational dimension. At least some of these would not leave their own religious heritage if a more enriching religious experience were available within the context of Judaism or Christianity. Hence, one factor which might retard the growth of Buddhism as a separate body would be the incorporation of Buddhist-type meditational practice within the structure and program of Christian and Judaic institutions.

## Secular Meditational Movements

In recent years, the transcendental meditation (TM) movement has had a phenomenal success in America. What effect this has had on the development of Buddhist meditational groups is not known. Undoubtedly, many who have involved themselves in the practice of TM would not consider Buddhist meditation, because the latter is non-Christian, because it involves a disciplined way of life, or because it is too difficult. Some have said that they would have tried Zen, if TM had not been available. On the other hand, some who have tried TM have then become interested in a "deeper," more demanding practice, and for this they have come to Buddhism. In short, the continued existence of centers for the teaching and practice of transcendental meditation or other meditational practices in a secular setting could either retard the growth of meditational Buddhism or stimulate its further growth. The evidence available presently would seem to point to the latter.

## Meditation and Psychotherapy

Among the sixty psychological practitioners who enrolled in the Nyingma Institute Human Development Training Program during the summer of 1973, most had previously participated in either transcendental meditation or some form of Buddhist meditation, and had experienced personal benefit. Probably a third of the group, in addition, had used meditation therapeutically in their professional practice, mostly in conjuction with other forms of therapy, such as Gestalt therapy. Those who attended the program for the full eight weeks were certified as teachers of Nyingma meditation techniques, and presumably planned to use these techniques in their therapeutic practice. Most psychotherapists using Buddhist and other meditational techniques in the middle 1970s have become interested in such approaches on the basis of theoretical considerations and/or their own personal experiences with meditation. Their continued interest in these approaches, however, will depend in part on how successful they are, and in part on what other approaches to psychotherapy appear on the scene.

## Humanistic and Transpersonal Psychology

The meditational sects of Buddhism have always attracted a goodly number of professional men and women—teachers, social workers, lawyers, priests, psychologists, psychiatrists, and others. Of these, psychologists have probably shown the greatest increase in interest in recent years. As noted in chapter 10, this is associated with interest in "peak experience" studied intensively and extensively by Abraham Maslow, who postulated that the Buddha's enlightenment might be classified under this rubric, and therefore be understood psychologically. Maslow and other psychologists interested in peak experiences as "transpersonal" experiences formed the core of a group of psychologists identifying themselves as humanistic psychologists, transpersonal psychologists, or both. With psychology in the United States being a science committed to the use of scientific methodology in research, the interest which psychologists have displayed in Buddhist meditation has given Buddhism something of an aura of respectability in the scientific community and in other professional groups. However, future interest among such groups—and especially among psychologists—would seem to be related to continued interest displayed by humanistic and transpersonal psychologists and their continued acceptable standing within the American Psychological Association.

## PREDICTIONS OR SPECULATIONS?

Each of the above contingency factors contains in it elements of uncertainty, so that predictions can be little more then speculations in which hunches and intuition will probably play a more prominent role than scientifically determined trends based on hard facts. Nevertheless, this observer will make a few educated guesses, accepting the risk that these guesses may be wrong.

As far as the general picture is concerned, indications are that there will be an acceleration of interest in Buddhism for a few more years, followed by a period of slower growth.

As the issei population decreases, the church type of Buddhist sect will have an increasingly difficult time in keeping the interest of the third- and fourth-generation Japanese-American members. Unless there are moves away from the "Presbyterian Buddhism" format in these churches and more incorporation of meditation in them, they will have little chance of gaining non-Oriental members or of maintaining their total membership figures at their present levels. It appears unlikely that these churches will report significant growth in the next decade.

In the meditational types of Buddhist groups, the present mushroom growth will continue for a while and then slow down, except possibly in the Tibetan groups which may continue their rapid growth for a longer period. In any event, there will be continued interest in Zen, Theravada, and Tibetan Buddhist meditation. In all likelihood the nature of the membership in these groups will change, with more intellectuals being involved, and fewer hippies.

It is difficult to predict the future of Nichiren Shoshu in America. It might be expected, however, that interest would lag in the college group but be maintained among the members of minority groups and the disadvantaged. A slowing down of recruitment will be inevitable if the large numbers are not to get out of hand. A change in emphasis from chanting for personal benefit to a deepening of spiritual life may result in the loss of some members, but at the same time it could result in greater stability and commitment of those remaining.

Of the three modes of Buddhist influence in the United States mentioned by Swearer, that of appropriation seems most uncertain, in the future. The likelihood that seriously committed Buddhists will ever even approach the number of Christians and Jews in America is so slight as to be almost nonexistent. Also, there seems little probability that there will be many Buddhists in the deep south or the rural midwest in the foreseeable future. Yet it is almost certain that Americans will continue to "take the refuge" and that Buddhist groups will continue on American soil, although how many and in what sects may be uncertain.

Although how many acknowledged Buddhists will rise to be counted in the years to come cannot be estimated, we can confidently predict an increase in the absorption of Buddhist concepts and practices in such ways as to change our existing institutions and ways of life. The continuation of meditational practices and integration of meditation into certain ones of the Christian churches seems inevitable, and Buddhist ideas about suffering, impermanence, and nonself have already been widely accepted. Meditation as a method of psychological treatment has found acceptance by the scientific community, which as yet shows no signs of abandoning it. Greater attention to the psychology of consciousness also seems destined for the next decade. Many influenced by Buddhism will be more comfortable with quietness, and content with a simpler life style. Transformation of existing institutions and modes of living, then, will be a conspicuous aspect of the Buddhist influence in the years to come, as will be an increase in dialogue between Buddhists and their Christian or Jewish neighbors.

In summary, then, we can say that the influence of Buddhism in America has been and will continue to be greater than membership figures would lead us to expect, and it is here to stay.

*OM AH HUM!*

# Notes

## Introduction

1. F. H. Littell, "World Church Membership," in *Britannica Book of the Year* (Chicago: Encyclopedia Britannica, 1973), p. 600.
2. Christmas Humphreys, *Buddhism* (Baltimore: Penguin, 1959), p. 229.
3. Personal communication.
4. Donald K. Swearer, *Buddhism in Transition* (Philadelphia: Westminster Press, 1970), p. 13.
5. Robert N. Bellah, "Epilogue: Religion and Progress in Modern Asia," in *Religion and Progress in Modern Asia*, ed. Robert N. Bellah (Glencoe, Ill.: The Free Press, 1965), p. 193.
6. Humphreys, *Buddhism*, p. 230.
7. Christmas Humphreys, *The Buddhist Way of Life* (London: Allen and Unwin, 1969), chaps. 25, 26.
8. Zen is a type of Buddhism stressing meditation rather than doctrine. See chapter 5.
9. Humphreys, *The Buddhist Way of Life*, chap. 25.

## Chapter 1 / The Buddha, the Dharma, and the Sangha

1. Swami Prabhavananda and Frederick Manchester, trans., *The Upanishads: Breath of the Eternal* (New York: Mentor, 1957).
2. Robert E. Hume, trans., *The Thirteen Principal Upanishads*, rev. ed. (London: Oxford University Press, 1931).
3. A. L. Basham, *The Wonder that was India* (New York: Grove Press, 1954), pp. 243-45.
4. Hume, *Thirteen Principal Upanishads*, p. 6.
5. Ibid., p. 9.
6. For details of the Buddha's life see the account given in Dwight Goddard, ed., *A Buddhist Bible* (Boston: Beacon Press, 1938), pp. 3–21.
7. These teachings are found in Goddard, ed., *A Buddhist Bible*, pp. 22–60; 645–56.

8. T. O. Ling, ed., *A Dictionary of Buddhism* (New York: Scribner's, 1972), p. 207.
9. Procedures for keeping the mind and body under disciplined control are found in Goddard, ed., *A Buddhist Bible*, pp. 634–42.
10. Ling, *Dictionary of Buddhism*, pp. 20, 22, 108.
11. Christmas Humphreys, *The Buddhist Way of Life* (London: Allen and Unwin, 1969), pp. 90–95.
12. John Walters, *The Essence of Buddhism* (New York: Crowell, 1964), p. 134.
13. Mahayana Buddhists accept five additional precepts.
14. In the United States, Buddhist weddings are fairly common.
15. In the Jodo Shin sect, monks are permitted to eat meat, and frequently do so if it is available. In virtually all sects, although a monk may be forbidden to take animal life for food or to eat meat if the animal was killed specifically to provide food for him, he may in most instances eat meat if it is offered to him.
16. "The Zen Priest," *Time*, 71 (May 26, 1958): 65.
17. Informational pamphlets published by Zen Mountain Center, Tassajara, Cal.; Mt. Baldy Zen Center, Mt. Baldy, Cal.; and Hui-Neng Zen Temple, Easton, Pa.
18. Edward Conze, *Buddhism: Its Essence and Development* (Oxford: Bruno Cassirer, 1951), pp. 89–90.
19. Richard H. Robinson, *The Buddhist Religion* (Belmont, Cal.: Dickenson, 1970), chap. 3.
20. Ibid., pp. 37–38.
21. Beatrice Lane Suzuki, *Mahayana Buddhism* (New York: Macmillan, 1969), p. 22.
22. Kenneth K. S. Ch'en, *Buddhism, The Light of Asia* (Woodbury, N. Y.: Barron's Educational Series, 1968), p. 133.
23. Conze, *Buddhism: Its Essence and Development*, Chapter 4.
24. Suzuki, *Mahayana Buddhism*, p. 36.
25. Ibid., p. 21.
26. Ibid., pp. 34–35.
27. Ibid., pp. 35–36.
28. Ibid., p. 33.
29. Ibid., pp. 52–63.
30. Christmas Humphreys, *Buddhism* (Baltimore: Penguin, 1951), p. 79.
31. Suzuki, *Mahayana Buddhism*, p. 35.
32. Ibid., p. 35.
33. Ch'en, *Buddhism*, p. 62.

34. Suzuki, *Mahayana Buddhism*, p. 35.
35. Ibid., p. 35.
36. Ibid., pp. 8–9.
37. John Blofeld, *The Tantric Mysticism of Tibet* (New York: Dutton, 1970), chap. 2.
38. Conze, *Buddhism: Its Essence and Development*, p. 181.
39. Ch'en, *Buddhism*, p. 81.

## Chapter 2 / THE HISTORY AND NATURE OF BUDDHISM IN AMERICA

1. More detailed histories of specific Buddhist denominations and sects are given in subsequent chapters.
2. Christmas Humphreys, *Buddhism* (Baltimore: Penguin Books, 1951), pp. 71–73.
3. Soyen was Shaku's Buddhist name and he was usually called by this name, with no surname appended.
4. *The Buddhist Churches of America* (San Francisco: Buddhist Churches of America, 1971).
5. The first Pure Land sect to be established in America was from the "western" branch of the True Pure Land sect. Later the Pure Land sect (Jodo Shu) and the "eastern" branch of the True Pure Land sect established missions in California.
6. Nichiren Shu is a Japanese sect founded in the thirteenth century. It is based on the Lotus Sutra and emphasizes repetition of "Namu Myoho Renge Kyo" (Hail to the Lotus of the Wonderful Law), to obtain benefits.
7. Japanese version of Chinese Chen Yen or "True Word" sect— a syncretistic esoteric sect stressing repetition of special words and formulas, and use of symbolic gestures.
8. Sanskrit term for "monk."
9. A modern Japanese organization of believers in Nichiren Buddhism—one of Japan's socalled "new religions." This organization, although having no clergy, is regarded as a "church," and it specializes in use of the small discussion group.
10. An orthodox Nichiren sect which has burgeoned in Japan as a layman's organization called *Soka Gakkai*. (See chapter 6.)
11. *Wind Bell*, 9 (Fall-Winter, 1970–71).
12. Thick, straw mats which cover the floor in most Japanese homes as well as the floors of Japanese temples in areas where shoes may not be worn.

## Chapter 3 / AMIDA'S PURE LAND AND THE BUDDHIST CHURCHES OF AMERICA

1. "Buddha on 94th Street," *Newsweek*, 29 (June 9, 1947) : 82–83.
2. Ejitsu Hojo and Takeo Tomita, "Looking forward to the 75th Anniversary of Buddhist Churches of America," *Buddhist Churches of America Newsletter* (March, 1972), p. 1.
3. Christmas Humphreys, *Buddhism* (Baltimore: Penguin, 1951), pp. 161–65.
4. E. Dale Saunders, *Buddhism in Japan* (Philadelphia: University of Pennsylvania Press, 1964), p. 195.
5. William K. Bunce, *Religions in Japan* (Rutland, Vt.: Tuttle Publishing Co., 1955), p. 74.
6. Beatrice Lane Suzuki, "The Conception of the Bodhisattva according to the Shin Sect," *Hawaiian Buddhist Annual* (1951), p. 5.
7. Shugaku Yamabe, "Amida as Saviour of the Soul," *Eastern Buddhist* 1 (2).
8. Richard H. Robinson, *The Buddhist Religion* (Belmont, Cal.: Dickenson Publishing Co., 1970), p. 65.
9. Japanese form of T'ien T'ai sect, advocating universality of salvation or attainment of Buddhahood. Its teachings are based on the Lotus Sutra.
10. Saunders, *Buddhism in Japan*, p. 189.
11. Ibid.
12. Robinson, *The Buddhist Religion*, p. 103.
13. Saunders, *Buddhism in Japan*, p. 199.
14. Bunce, *Religions in Japan*, p. 87.
15. Shojun Bando, "Shinran's Indebtedness to T'an-luan," *Eastern Buddhist*, n. s., 4 (May, 1971) : 72–87.
16. Ibid.
17. *Satori* is Japanese term for "enlightenment."
18. Bando, "Shinran's Indebtedness to T'an-luan," p. 83.
19. Ibid.
20. Ibid., p. 87.
21. Hogen Fujimoto, "The Saga of the Birth of BCA," *Buddhist Churches of America Newsletter* (March, 1972), p. 3.
22. Ibid.
23. *Buddhist Churches of America* (San Francisco: Buddhist Churches of America, 1971).
24. *The Altar*. Pamphlet published by Eastern Canada Buddhist Association, Toronto (no date given).

25. The Buddhist rosary is a circle of beads joined together on a string. It originally consisted of 108 beads, and Tibetan Buddhists still carry a string of this length. The number 108, according to one theory, is supposed to correspond to the number of human defilements. Nowadays, for the sake of convenience, the number of beads is becoming less and less, but is usually one-half, one-third, or one-fourth of the original number, except for one big bead which symbolizes the Buddha, and two smaller beads in between which symbolize the compassion and wisdom of the Buddha. There is ordinarily a tassle extending from the large bead, and this has no purpose other than decoration.

26. Ensei H. Nekoda, *A Guide to Creative Thinking in the Sunday School* (San Francisco: Buddhist Churches of America, n.d.).

27. Ibid., p. 6.

28. *Buddhist Churches of America* (San Francisco: Buddhist Churches of America, 1971).

29. D. T. Suzuki, *Shin Buddhism* (New York: Harper and Row, 1970), p. 83.

## Chapter 4 / ZEAL FOR ZEN

1. These observations were made in 1972. A year later it was announced that the group, with a Korean priest, would relocate in Philadelphia.

2. "Circumambulation of Mt. Tamalpais—Buddha's Birthday, 1969," *Wind Bell*, 9 (Summer 1970) : 8–9.

3. The Four Vows are: Sentient beings are countless, I vow to save them all; tormenting passions are innumerable, I vow to uproot them all; the gates of the Dharma are manifold, I vow to pass through them all; the Buddha's way is peerless, I vow to realize it.

4. Philip Kapleau, *The Three Pillars of Zen* (New York and Tokyo: John Weatherhill, 1965), p. xv.

5. Christmas Humphreys, *Buddhism* (Baltimore: Penguin, 1951), p. 182.

6. Ibid., p. 181.

7. Daisetz T. Suzuki, *The Field of Zen* (London: The Buddhist Society, 1969), p. 13.

8. William K. Bunce, *Religions in Japan* (Rutland, Vt. and Tokyo: Charles E. Tuttle, 1955), pp. 82–92.

9. A koan is a formulation, in baffling language, pointing to ulti-

mate truth. Example: You know the sound of two hands clapping. What is the sound of one hand?

10. Kyung Beo Seo, "A Study of Korean Zen Buddhism Approached through the Chodangjip" (Ph.D. diss., Temple University, 1969).

11. Discourses or sermons by the Buddha.

12. See illustrations in Kapleau, *Three Pillars of Zen*, pp. 317–20.

13. Referred to as the "hara."

14. The stick is wielded differently in the Rinzai and Soto sects.

15. Kapleau, *Three Pillars of Zen*, p. 336.

16. Ibid., pp. 46–49.

17. Ibid., p. 329.

18. In Rinzai temples, dokusan is sometimes referred to as *sanzen*, although the latter is a more inclusive term, covering several kinds of individual contacts with the roshi.

19. Daisetz T. Suzuki, "The Heart of Zen." In *Zen Buddhism, Selected Writings of D. T. Suzuki*, ed. William Barrett. (New York: Doubleday, 1956), chap. 4.

20. Humphreys, *Buddhism*, p. 185.

21. Ibid., p. 186.

22. D. T. Suzuki, "Heart of Zen," p. 84.

23. Ibid., pp. 103–8.

24. Humphreys, *Buddhism*, p. 183.

25. Daisetz T. Suzuki, *The Field of Zen* (London: The Buddhist Society, 1969), p. 31.

26. Ibid., pp. 28–29.

27. Humphreys, *Buddhism*, p. 184.

28. Ibid., pp. 134, 184.

29. Philip Kapleau, "Practical Instructions to the Dying," *Zen Bow* 3 (May/June + Sept/Oct 1970) : 10.

30. For another translation see ibid., pp. 5–6, 11.

31. Daisetz T. Suzuki, "The Zen Doctrine of No Mind," *Zen Buddhism*, ed. William Barrett, p. 163.

32. Ibid., p. 163.

33. Ibid., p. 166.

34. Ibid., p. 163.

35. Beatrice Lane Suzuki, *Mahayana Buddhism* (New York: Macmillan, 1957), p. 63.

36. Alan W. Watts, *The Way of Zen* (New York: Random House, 1957), p. 42.

37. B. L. Suzuki, *Mahayana Buddhism*, p. 41.

38. Watts, *Way of Zen,* p. 61; B. L. Suzuki, *Mahayana Buddhism,* p. 42.
39. B. L. Suzuki, *Mahayana Buddhism,* pp. 42, 43, 45.
40. Daisetz T. Suzuki, "The Zen Doctrine of No-Mind," pp. 186–226.
41. *Wind Bell* 9 (Summer 1970) ; 9 (Fall-Winter 1970–71).
42. A "Dharma heir" is one who has been authorized by his Zen Master to be a teacher of Zen and to pass on to future generations of Zen students the teachings of the Master; "Dharma brothers" are disciples of the same Zen Master.
43. Alan W. Watts, *Beat Zen, Square Zen, and Zen* (San Francisco: City Light Books, 1959).
44. John Kerouac, *The Dharma Bums* (New York: Viking Press, 1958).
45. Stephen Mahoney, "The Prevalence of Zen," *The Nation,* 187 (Nov. 1, 1958) : 311–12.
46. Ibid., p. 312.
47. Erich Fromm, D. T. Suzuki, and Richard De Martino, *Zen Buddhism and Psychoanalysis* (New York: Harper and Row, 1970).
48. Dom Aelred Graham, *Zen Catholicism* (New York: Harcourt, Brace and World, 1963).
49. Dom Aelred Graham, *Conversations: Christian and Buddhist* (New York: Harcourt Brace Jovanovich, 1968).
50. Thomas Merton, *Zen and the Birds of Appetite* (New York: New Directions, 1968) ; *Mystics and Zen Masters* (New York: Farrar, Strauss and Giroux, 1961).
51. *Meal Chants* (Mt. Baldy, Cal.: Mt. Baldy Zen Center, n. d.).
52. See especially *Zen Bow,* Vol. 5, No. 1 (Jan/Feb. 1972).
53. Philip Kapleau, ed., *The Wheel of Death* (New York: Harper and Row, 1971).
54. Peter Fingesten, "Beat and Buddhist," *Christian Century* 76 (Feb. 25, 1959) : 226–27.
55. Ibid.
56. Christian Humphreys, "A Western Approach to Zen," *The Middle Way* 46 (May 1971) : 10–16.
57. Ibid., pp. 11–12.
58. Ibid., pp. 13–16.
59. Van Meter Ames, *Zen and American Thought* (Honolulu: University of Hawaii Press, 1962), p. 3.
60. Ibid., p. 5.
61. Ibid., p. 8.
62. Ibid., p. 278.

## Chapter 5 / FROM TIBETAN PEAKS TO BERKELEY HILLS— TANTRISM IN AMERICA

1. Robert B. Ekvall, *Religious Observances in Tibet: Patterns and Function* (Chicago: University of Chicago Press, 1964), p. 16.
2. Christmas Humphreys, *Buddhism* (Baltimore: Penguin, 1964), p. 190.
3. Kenneth K. S. Ch'en, *Buddhism, the Light of Asia* (Woodbury, N.Y.: Barron, 1968), p. 189.
4. Ekvall, *Religious Observances in Tibet*, chap. 2.
5. John Blofeld, *The Tantric Mysticism of Tibet* (New York: E. P. Dutton, 1970), p. 131.
6. Ibid., chap. 2.
7. Ibid., chap. 5.
8. Chogyam Trungpa, *Meditation in Action* (Berkeley, Cal.: Shambala, 1970).
9. Blofeld, *Tantric Mysticism*, Chaps. 3–5.
10. Ibid., pp. 85–86.
11. Ibid., pp. 87–90.
12. "The Vajra Guru Mantra," *Crystal Mirror* 2 (Summer 1972): 17.
13. Lama Anagarika Govinda, *Foundations of Tibetan Mysticism* (London: Rider, 1959), p. 19.
14. "The Vajra Guru Mantra," *Crystal Mirror*, p. 17.
15. Ibid., p. 17.
16. Govinda, *Foundations*, p. 27.
17. Ibid, p. 27.
18. "The Vajra Guru Mantra," *Crystal Mirror*, pp. 17–38.
19. Ibid., p. 17.
20. Ibid., p. 21.
21. Ibid., p. 24.
22. Ibid., p. 30.
23. Blofeld, *Tantric Mysticism*, p. 91.
24. Edward Conze, *Buddhism: Its Essence and Development* (Oxford: Bruno Cassirer, 1951), p. 187.
25. Ibid., pp. 40–41, 84.
26. Humphreys, *Buddhism*, p. 41.
27. Blofeld, *Tantric Mysticism*, p. 41.
28. Ibid.
29. Chogyam Trungpa, *Born in Tibet* (London: George Allen and Unwin, 1966); Marco Pallis, *The Way and the Mountain* (London: Kennikat, 1968).

30. Blofeld, *Tantric Mysticism*, pp. 64–65.
31. Ibid., p. 65.
32. Conze, *Buddhism*, p. 189.
33. Ibid.
34. Ibid., p. 190.
35. Ibid.
36. Material on the history of Tibetan Buddhism is taken mostly from K. S. Ch'en, *Buddhism, the Light of Asia* (Woodbury, N. Y.: Barron, 1968), pp. 190–205; and from Sir Charles Bell, *The Religion of Tibet* (Oxford: Oxford University Press, 1931).
37. Jacob Needleman, *The New Religions* (Garden City, N. Y.: Doubleday and Co., 1970), p. 8.
38. Trungpa, *Born in Tibet*, p. 252.
39. Ibid.
40. *Garuda* (Spring 1972), pp. 53–54, 61.
41. Ibid., p. 58.
42. In Tibetan Buddhism, wrathful deities do not depict divine wrath; rather, they represent the energy devoted to battle against passion and delusion. See Blofeld, *Tantric Mysticism*, pp. 110–11.
43. *Garuda III* (1973), pp. 83–91; Vajradhatu, *Naropa Institute* (informational leaflet) (Boulder, Col.: Vajradhatu, 1974).
44. Ibid., p. 4.
45. Ibid.
46. Ibid.
47. Ibid.
48. Chogyam Trungpa, *Meditation in Action* (Berkeley, Cal.: Shambala, 1970), p. 51.
49. Ibid., p. 52.
50. Ibid., pp. 52–53.
51. Ibid., p. 56.
52. Chogyam Trungpa, "Cutting Through," *Garuda* (Spring 1972): 3–6.
53. Ibid., p. 5.
54. Ibid., p. 6.
55. *Tibetan Nyingmapa Meditation Center* (informational leaflet).
56. Needleman, *New Religions*, pp. 178, 183.
57. *Crystal Mirror* (Berkeley, Cal.: Dharma Press, 1971), p. 81.
58. Ibid., p. 59.
59. Ibid.
60. Ibid.

61. Ibid., p. 60.
62. Ibid.
63. Ibid., p. 61.
64. Needleman, *New Religions,* p. 191.
65. Guru Padmasambhava (The Lotus-born Teacher) is the great saint and teacher who brought Buddhism to Tibet in the 8th century, A.D. Deeply revered by all Tibetans, he is often called the "Second Enlightened One."
66. *Crystal Mirror* (Berkeley, Cal.: Dharma Press, 1971), pp. 62–63.
67. Ibid., p. 63.
68. Ibid., p. 64.
69. Ibid., pp. 64–65.
70. William K. Bunce, *Religions in Japan* (Rutland, Vt., and Tokyo: Tuttle, 1955).
71. E. Dale Saunders, *Buddhism in Japan* (Philadelphia; University of Pennsylvania Press, 1964), p. 161.
72. Bunce, *Religions in Japan,* p. 69.
73. Ibid., pp. 70–71.
74. Ch'en, *Buddhism,* p. 178.
75. Shoyu Hanayama, "Various Types of Buddhism," in *A Guide to Buddhism* (Yokohama: International Buddhist Exchange Center, 1970), p. 86.
76. *Service Order* (Los Angeles: Koyasan Buddhist Temple, n.d.).
77. H. Byron Earhart, *A Religious Study of the Mount Haguro Sect of Shugendo* (Tokyo: Sophia University, 1970).
78. Ibid.
79. Ibid., p. 8.
80. Ibid., p. 5.
81. Ibid., p. 29.
82. Ibid.
83. Ibid.
84. Ibid., p. 106.
85. Ibid.
86. "Shugendo," mimeographed material (San Francisco: Kailas Shugendo, n. d.).
87. "Shugen Shugyo according to Kailas Shugendo," mimeographed (San Francisco: Kailas Shugendo, n. d.).
88. Neville Warwick, "Tantracism," mimeographed (source not given).

Chapter 6 / NICHIREN SHOSHU IN AMERICA:
A RELIGION OF PEACE THROUGH HAPPINESS

1. *Daishonin* means "great saint."
2. "The Power of Positive Chanting," *Time* 93 (January 17, 1969) : 51.
3. Risshu is a nondenominational school concerned mostly with the rules of behavior for monks and nuns.
4. Robert L. Ramseyer, "The Soka Gakkai," in Richard K. Beardsley, ed., *Studies in Japanese Culture: 1* (Ann Arbor: University of Michigan Press, 1965), pp. 141–92.
5. David L. Hasselgrave, "A Propagation Profile of Soka Gakkai" (Ph.D. diss., University of Minnesota, 1965), p. 3.
6. Ibid., p. 5.
7. Ibid., p. 6.
8. Ibid., p. 70.
9. Kazuhiko Nagoya, "Japan's New Political Party," *Atlas* 9 (Feb. 1965) : 11.
10. James W. White, *The Sokagakkai and Mass Society* (Stanford, Cal.: Stanford University Press, 1970), p. 35.
11. Ibid., p. 36.
12. Ibid., pp. 131–32.
13. Ibid.
14. Ibid.
15. Hasselgrave, "Propagation Profile."
16. Kishi Nobusaka, "Political Movements in Japan," *Foreign Affairs* 44 (October 1965) : 90–99.
17. Hasselgrave, "Propagation Profile."
18. "Buddhists in Japan: Profit in Purity," *Economist* 208 (July 13, 1963) : 134.
19. White, *Sokagakkai,* p. 83.
20. Hasselgrave, "Propagation Profile."
21. William Helton, "Political Prospects of Soka Gakkai," *Pacific Affairs* 38 (Fall-Winter 1965-66) : 231–44.
22. White, *Sokagakkai,* p. 93.
23. George M. Williams, ed., *N.S.A. Seminar Report, 1968–71* (Santa Monica, Cal.: World Tribune Press, 1972), p. ii.
24. Ibid., Appendix 3.
25. Guy C. McCloskey, personal correspondence.
26. *World Tribune,* numerous issues.

27. Ibid.
28. *World Tribune* (August 15, 1969).
29. Williams, *Seminar Report*, p. 40.
30. B. F. Skinner, "Some Contributions of an Experimental Analysis of Behavior to Psychology as a Whole," *American Psychologist* 8 (1953) : 69–78.
31. A. H. Maslow, *Motivation and Personality* (New York: Harper and Row, 1954).

Chapter 7 / CHINESE BUDDHISM FOR AMERICANS

1. William Theodore de Bary et al., *Sources of Chinese Tradition* (New York: Columbia University Press, 1960), p. 306.
2. Arthur E. Wright, *Buddhism in Chinese History* (Stanford, Cal.: Stanford University Press, 1959), chapter 5.
3. Ibid., p. 115.
4. Ibid.
5. *Buddhism in Taiwan* (Taipei: Bohedrum Publications, n. d.), p. 25.
6. Ibid.
7. Jerrold Schecter, *The New Face of Buddha* (Tokyo: John Weatherhill, 1967), p. 45.
8. Holmes Welch, *Buddhism under Mao* (Cambridge, Mass.: Harvard University Press, 1972).
9. Holmes Welch, *The Practice of Chinese Buddhism* (Cambridge, Mass.: Harvard University Press, 1967), p. 398.
10. Ibid., pp. 398–400.
11. August K. Reischauer, "Buddhism," in *The Great Religions of the Modern World*, ed. Edward J. Jurji (Princeton, N. J.: Princeton University Press, 1947).
12. Welch, *Chinese Buddhism*, p. 398.
13. Richard H. Robinson, *The Buddhist Religion* (Belmont, Cal.: Dickenson Pub. Co., 1970), pp. 82–83.
14. Kenneth K. S. Ch'en, *Buddhism, the Light of Asia* (Woodbury, N. Y.: Barron's Educational Series, 1964), pp. 160–61.
15. Ibid., pp. 161–62.
16. Ibid., p. 162.
17. *Buddhism in Taiwan*, p. 30.
18. Lu Kuan Yu, *The Secrets of Chinese Meditation* (New York: Samuel Weiser, 1964), chap. 2.
19. *Buddhism in Taiwan*, p. 28.

20. Ch'en, *Buddhism*, pp. 159–60.
21. *Buddhism in Taiwan*, p. 28.
22. Ibid., pp. 33–37.
23. Mariann Kaye Wells, "Chinese Temples in California" (Master's thesis, University of California, 1962).
24. Ibid., p. 5.
25. Ibid., p. 19.
26. Ibid., pp. 19–24.
27. Ibid., pp. 25–28.
28. Ibid., pp. 25-28.
29. Conversation with Dr. Frederick Hong.
30. Idem.
31. Paul F. Fung and George D. Fung, tr., *The Sutra of the Sixth Patriarch on the Pristine Orthodox Dharma* (San Francisco: Buddha's Universal Church, 1964).
32. Welch, *Chinese Buddhism*, pp. 279–81.
33. "International Buddhist Translation Institute Established," *Vajra Bodhi Sea* 4 (Sept. 1973) : 38–40.
34. What the Chinese Buddhist translates as "genuflection" is a *k'ou t'ou* consisting of kneeling and placing the head on the floor.
35. Yu, *Secrets*, p. 47.
36. Ibid.
37. Ibid.
38. Ibid., chap. 4.
39. Ibid., p. 159.
40. Ibid., p. 158.
41. Ibid.
42. Ibid.
43. Ibid.
44. Ibid., p. 159.
45. Ibid.

Chapter 8 / SATIPATTHANA COMES WEST:
THE OLD WISDOM SCHOOL IN AMERICA

1. Edward Conze, *Buddhism: Its Essence and Development* (Oxford: Bruno Cassirer, 1951), chap. 4.
2. Mary Farkas, "The Practice of the Hinayana," *Zen Notes* 16, pt. 4 (1969), pages unnumbered.
3. M. O'C. Walshe, *Why Buddhism? Why Theravada?* (Kandy, Ceylon: Buddhist Publication Society, 1971), p. 8.

4. Ibid., p. 14.
5. Christmas Humphreys, *Buddhism* (Baltimore: Penguin Books, 1951), pp. 234–37.
6. S. G. F. Brandon, ed., *A Dictionary of Buddhism* (New York: Harper and Row, 1959).
7. Farkas, "Practice of the Hinayana."
8. Ibid.
9. Ibid.
10. Ibid.
11. Ibid.
12. Ibid.
13. Ibid.
14. Conze, *Buddhism*, p. 117.
15. Brandon, *Dictionary of Buddhism*.
16. Kosho Yamamoto, *Buddhism in Europe* (Tokyo: The Karinbunko, 1967), p. 11.
17. Humphreys, *Buddhism*, pp. 224–25.
18. Yamamoto, *Buddhism in Europe,* pp. 33–39.
19. Kenneth K. S. Ch'en, *Buddhism, the Light of Asia* (Woodbury, N. Y.: Barron's, 1968), pp. 117–24.
20. Ibid., pp. 118–19.
21. H. R. Perera, *Buddhism in Ceylon,* Wheel Pub. No. 100 (Kandy, Ceylon: Buddhist Publication Society, 1966), p. 70.
22. Ibid., pp. 70–71.
23. Ibid., pp. 71–72.
24. Ch'en, *Buddhism,* pp. 119–20.
25. Donald Swearer, ed., *Secrets of the Lotus* (New York: Macmillan, 1971), p. 92.
26. Edward Conze, *Buddhist Meditation* (London: George Allen and Unwin, 1956), p. 17.
27. Phra Maha Singhathon Narsapo, *Buddhism: An Introduction to a Happy Life* (Bankok: The Preachers' Association, n. d.).
28. Nyanoponika Thera, *The Heart of Buddhist Meditation* (New York: Samuel Weiser, 1973).
29. Conze, *Buddhist Meditation,* p. 16.
30. Nyanoponika, *Heart of Buddhist Meditation.*
31. Mahasi Sayadaw, *Practical Insight Meditation* (San Francisco: Unity Press, 1972).
32. Ibid.
33. Ibid., p. 2.

34. Henepola Gunaratana, *Come and See* (Washington, D.C.: Washington Buddhist Vihara, 1972).
35. Nyanoponika, *Heart of Buddhist Meditation,* p. 28.
36. Ibid., p. 44.
37. Ibid., pp. 45–46.
38. Ibid., p. 46.
39. Ibid., chap. 5.
40. Sujata, personal communication.
41. Gunaratana, *Come and See.*
42. Conze, *Buddhism,* p. 100.
43. Ibid., pp. 11–101.
44. Ibid., p. 101.
45. Ibid., p. 105.
46. Farkas, "Practice of the Hinayana."
47. Informational booklet, Washington Buddhist Vihara, Washington, D.C.
48. Gunaratana, *Come and See.*
49. Informational flyer, Stillpoint Institutes, Denver, Colorado.

## Chapter 9 / BUDDHISM AND THE PROBLEMS OF AMERICAN SOCIETY

1. Soyen Shaku, "Arbitration Instead of War," *The World's Parliament of Religions* (Chicago: Parliament Pub. Co., 1893; reprinted in *Zen Notes* 17, pt. 8 (1970), pages unnumbered.
2. Kenneth K. S. Ch'en, *Buddhism, the Light of Asia* (Woodbury, N. Y.: Barron's, 1968), p. 281.
3. Ibid., p. 281.
4. Ronn Patterson, "At Home," *Wind Bell* 9 (Summer 1970), pp. 22–25.
5. Jiyu Kennett, "All is One and All is Different," *The Journal of the Zen Mission Society,* 2 (December 1971), pp. 3–11.
6. Wilson van Dusen, "LSD and the Enlightenment of Zen," *Psychologia* 4 (1961): 11–16; G. Ray Jordan, Jr., "Reflections on LSD, Zen Meditation and Satori," *Psychologia* 5 (1961): 124–30; Arthur H. Rogers, "Zen and LSD: an Enlightening Experience," *Psychologia* 7 (1964): 150–51.
7. Alan Watts, "Ordinary Mind is the Way," *The Eastern Buddhist,* n. s. 4 (October 1971): 134–36.
8. Daisetz Suzuki, "Religion and Drugs," *The Eastern Buddhist,* n. s. 4 (October 1971): 128–33.

9. Ibid., p. 130.
10. Watts, "Ordinary Mind," p. 136.
11. Ray Jordan, "Psychedelics and Zen: Some Reflections," *The Eastern Buddhist,* n.s. 4 (October 1971) : 138–40.
12. Ibid., p. 138.
13. Ibid., p. 139.
14. Ibid., p. 140.
15. Bruce C. Tyler, "Meditation and its Effect on Drug Use," unpublished manuscript, 1972.
16. Ibid., p. 1.
17. Ibid., p. 2.
18. Ibid.
19. Ibid., pp. 1–2.
20. Philip Kapleau, "Acid, Pot and Zen," *Zen Bow* 2 (May/June/July 1969) : 3.
21. Tyler, "Meditation," pp. 4–8.
22. *Buddhist Churches of America Newsletter,* monthly issues.
23. Nyingmapa Tibetan Meditation Center, Information Bulletin.
24. *Vajra Bodhi Sea,* various issues.
25. Daisaku Ikeda, *The Family Revolution* (Santa Monica, Cal.: World Tribune Pub. Co., 1970).
26. Philip Kapleau, "Growing Up with Zen Buddhism," *Zen Bow* 5 (March/April 1972) : 4–8.
27. "The Buddha's Birthday 1972," *Zen Bow* 5 (June 1972) : 1–2.
28. Philip Kapleau ,*The Three Pillars of Zen* (Tokyo and New York: Weatherhill, 1965), p. 42.
29. Personal interview.
30. Personal interview.
31. Mary Farkas, "How Sectarian Should Sunday School Education Be?" *Zen Notes* 19 (May 1972) : 1.

Chapter 10 / BUDDHISM, PSYCHOLOGY, AND PSYCHOTHERAPY

1. Daisetz T. Suzuki, *Zen Buddhism* (New York: Anchor Books, 1956), p. 188.
2. Stanley R. Dean, "Beyond the Unconscious: The Ultraconscious," *Psychologia* 8 (1965) : 145–50; Edward W. Maupin, "Zen Buddhism: A Psychological Review," *Journal of Consulting Psychology* 26 (1962) : 13–20.; Akira Onda, "Zen and Creativity," *Psychologia* 5 (1962) : 13–20; Koji Sato, "Zen from a Personalogical Viewpoint," *Psychologia* 11 (1968) : 3–24.

3. Carl G. Jung and Shin-ichi Hisamatsu, "On the Unconscious, the Self and the Therapy," *Psychologia* 11 (1968) : 25–32.
4. B-value is a term Maslow uses for "Being-values," characterizing the self-actualizing person.
5. Anthony J. Sutlich, "Association for Transpersonal Psychology," *Journal of Transpersonal Psychology* 4 (1972) : 95.
6. Abraham H. Maslow, *Religions, Values, and Peak Experiences* (New York: Viking Press, 1970), chap. 2.
7. Informational booklet, College of Oriental Studies Graduate School, Los Angeles.
8. Edward Conze, *Buddhism: Its Essence and Development* (New York: Harper and Row, 1959), p. 106.
9. S. G. F. Brandon, ed., *A Dictionary of Buddhism* (New York: Harper and Row, 1959), p. 106.
10. Kenneth K. S. Ch'en, *Buddhism, the Light of Asia* (Woodbury, N. Y.: Barron's, 1968), p. 223.
11. Brandon, *Dictionary*, p. 76.
12. Conze, *Buddhism*, p. 107.
13. Brandon, *Dictionary*, pp. 273–75.
14. Ibid.
15. Richard R. Bucke, *Cosmic Consciousness*, 17th ed. (New York: Dutton, 1954) .
16. Philip Kapleau, *The Three Pillars of Zen* (New York: John Weatherhill, 1965), p. 327.
17. Conze, *Buddhism*, pp. 168–69.
18. Daniel Goleman, "The Buddha on Meditation and States of Consciousness," *Journal of Transpersonal Psychology* 4 (1972) : 2.
19. Maupin, "Zen Buddhism," p. 324.
20. H. Fingarette, "The Ego and Mystic Selflessness," *Psychoanalysis and Psychoanalytic Review* 45 (1958) : 16.
21. Daisetz T. Suzuki, *Introduction to Zen Buddhism* (London: Rider, 1949), p. 97.
22. William James, *The Varieties of Religious Experience* (New York: Longmans, Green, 1928) .
23. Maupin, "Zen Buddhism."
24. Daisetz T. Suzuki, "Lectures on Zen Buddhism," in *Zen Buddhism and Psychoanalysis*, Erich Fromm, D. T. Suzuki, and Richard De Martino (New York: Harper and Row, 1960), pp. 16–17; Bucke, *Cosmic Consciousness*; Erich Fromm, "Psychoanalysis and Zen Buddhism," in *Zen Buddhism and Psychoanalysis*, Erich Fromm, D. T. Suzuki, and Richard De Martino

(New York: Harper and Row, 1960), p. 134.

25. Dean, "Beyond the Unconscious," p. 145.

26. Robert Keith Wallace and Herbert Benson, "The Physiology of Meditation," in *Altered States of Awareness*, ed. Timothy T. Tayler (San Francisco: W. H. Freeman, 1972), pp. 125–31.

27. Robert E. Ornstein, *The Psychology of Consciousness* (San Francisco: W. H. Freeman, 1972).

28. Percival Symonds, *The Ego and the Self* (New York: Appleton-Century-Crofts, 1951).

29. Carl R. Rogers, "Some Observations on the Organization of Personality," *American Psychologist* 2 (1947): 358–68; Carl J. Jung, *Collected Works*, vol 17, *The Development of Personality* (New York: Pantheon Press, 1954).

30. Carl R. Rogers, *Client-Centered Therapy* (Boston: Houghton Mifflin, 1951), p. 532.

31. Maupin, "Zen Buddhism," p. 363.

32. Koji Sato, "Psychotherapeutic Implications of Zen," *Psychologia* 1 (1958): 213–18.

33. Ibid., p. 215.

34. Calvin S. Hall and Gardner Lindzey, *Theories of Personality* (New York: Wiley, 1957), chap. 3.

35. Ibid.

36. Ibid.

37. Jung and Hisamatsu, "On the Unconscious."

38. Abraham H. Maslow, *Toward a Psychology of Being* (Princeton: Van Nostrand, 1962), p. 67.

39. Ibid., chap. 6.

40. Ibid., p. 91.

41. Abraham H. Maslow, *Religion, Values, and Peak Experiences* (New York: Viking Press, 1970), chap. 3.

42. Ibid., p. xiv.

43. Ibid., pp. xv–xvi.

44. Ibid., p. xvi.

45. Robert E. Ornstein, "The Techniques of Meditation and their Implication for Modern Psychology," in *On the Psychology of Meditation*, Claudio Naranjo and Robert E. Ornstein (New York: Viking Press, 1971), p. 142.

46. Ibid.

47. Claudio Naranjo, "Meditation: Its Spirit and Techniques," in *On the Psychology of Meditation*, Naranjo and Ornstein, p. 8.

48. Ornstein, *Psychology of Meditation*, Chap. 1.

49. D. Lehmann, G. W. Beeler, and D. H. Fender, "EEG Responses

during the Observation of Stabilized and Normal Retinal Images," *Electroencephalography and Clinical Neurophysiology* 22 (1967) : 136–42.

50. J. E. Hochberg, W. Triebel, and G. Seaman, "Color Adaptation under Conditions of Homogeneous Visual Stimulation (Ganzfeld)," *Journal of Experimental Psychology* 41 (1951) : 153–59.

51. Ornstein, *Psychology of Meditation*, pp. 167–68.

52. Ibid., p. 192.

53. Ibid., p. 203.

54. Wallace and Benson, "Physiology of Meditation," p. 130.

55. Akira Kasamatsu and Tomio Hirai, "An Electroencephalographic Study on the Zen Meditation (Zazen)," *Folia Psychiatrica Neurologica Japanica* 20 (1966) : 315–36.

56. Terry V. Lesh, "Zen Meditation and the Development of Empathy in Counselors," *Journal of Humanistic Psychology* 10 (1970) : 39–78.

57. Christmas Humphreys, *Zen Comes West* (New York: Macmillan, 1960), p. 205.

58. Akihisa Kondo, "Zen in Psychotherapy," *Chicago Review* 12, pt. 2 (1958) : 57–64.

59. Albert Stunkard, "Some Interpersonal Aspects of an Oriental Religion," *Psychiatry* 14 (1951) : pp. 419–31.

60. Maupin, "Zen Buddhism," p. 377.

61. Fromm, "Psychoanalysis and Zen Buddhism."

62. Stunkard, "Interpersonal Aspects," p. 426.

63. Lesh, "Zen Meditation"; Maupin, "Zen Buddhism."

64. Maupin, "Zen Buddhism," p. 326.

65. Sato, "Psychotherapeutic Implications," pp. 213–18.

66. Stunkard, "Interpersonal Aspects."

67. Wolfgang Lederer, "Primitive Psychotherapy," *Psychiatry* 23 (1959) : 263.

68. Fromm, "Psychoanalysis and Zen Buddhism."

69. Sigmund Freud, *An Outline of Psychoanalysis* (New York: Norton, 1939).

70. Lederer, "Primitive Psychotherapy," p. 263.

71. Alfred Adler, *The Practice and Theory of Individual Psychology* (New York: Harcourt, Brace and World, 1927).

72. Carl R. Rogers, *Counseling and Psychotherapy* (Boston: Houghton Mifflin, 1942).

73. Harry Stack Sullivan, *The Interpersonal Theory of Psychiatry* (New York: Norton, 1953).

74. Lederer, "Primitive Psychotherapy," p. 263.

75. Fromm, "Psychoanalysis and Zen," p. 83.
76. Stunkard, "Interpersonal Aspects."
77. Brandon, *Dictionary.*
78. Norma Haimes, "Zen Buddhism and Psychoanalysis," *Psychologia* 15 (1972) : 25.
79. Naranjo, "Meditation."
80. Daisetz T. Suzuki, *Zen Buddhism* (New York: Doubleday, 1956), p. 3.
81. Harold H. Anderson, ed., *Creativity and its Cultivation* (New York: Harper, 1959), chap. 7.
82. Ibid., Chap. 6.
83. Maupin, "Zen Buddhism," pp. 362–78.
84. Dean, "Beyond the Unconscious."
85. Anderson, *Creativity,* chap. 6.
86. Ibid., chap. 7.
87. Lawrence S. Kubie, *Neurotic Distortion of the Creative Process* (Lawrence, Kan.: University of Kansas Press, 1958).
88. Daisetz T. Suzuki, *Zen Buddhism.*
89. Anderson, *Creativity.*
90. Private communication.
91. Private communication.
92. James Schultz, "Early Experiences at Padma Ling," *Crystal Mirror* 2 (Summer 1972) : 74–79.
93. Stanton Marlon, "The Human Development Training Program," *Gesar News* 1 (Summer 1973) : 11–13.

## Chapter 11 / Buddhism and the Christian Tradition in America

1. Masaharu Anesaki, "How Christianity Appeals to a Japanese Buddhist," in *Christianity: Some Non-Christian Appraisals,* ed. David W. McKain (New York: McGraw-Hill, 1964), p. 96.
2. Ibid., p. 99.
3. Robert Linssen, *Living Zen* (London: George Allen and Urwin, 1958), pp. 212–14.
4. Anesaki, "How Christianity Appeals to a Japanese Buddhist," p. 103.
5. Ibid., p. 91.
6. Fumio Masutani, "A Comparative Study of Buddhism and Christianity," in *Christianity,* p. 133.
7. Anesaki, "How Christianity Appeals to a Japanese Buddhist,"

p. 103; also Daisetz T. Suzuki, "Mysticism: Christian and Buddhist," in *Christianity*, p. 118.

8. Winston L. King, *Buddhism and Christianity* (Philadelphia: Westminster Press, 1962, pp. 19–20.

9. Linssen, *Living Zen*, pp. 224–25.

10. William Johnston, *Christian Zen* (New York: Harper and Row, 1971), chap. 3.

11. Masutani, "Comparative Study," pp. 142–52; King, *Buddhism and Christianity*, p. 67.

12. Masutani, "Comparative Study," p. 152.

13. King, *Buddhism and Christianity*, p. 105; Linssen, *Living Zen*, pp. 229–32.

14. Dom Aelred Graham, *Conversations: Christian and Buddhist* (New York: Harcourt Brace Jovanovich, 1968), pp. 165–77.

15. C. de B. Evans, *The Work of Meister Eckhart* (London: Watkins, 1921), p. 221.

16. Edith Schlosser, "Christian Mysticism," in *Approaches to Meditation*, ed. Virginia Hanson (Wheaton, Ill.: Theosophical Publishing House, 1973), p. 117.

17. Chogyam Trungpa, "Meditation," in *Approaches to Meditation*, p. 120.

18. Ibid., pp. 121–22.

19. Ibid., pp. 120–21.

20. *Oxford Dictionary of the Christian Church*.

21. John Brian Parry, "Christian Meditation and Contemplation," in *Approaches to Meditation*, pp. 45–51.

22. Ibid., p. 48.

23. Ibid., p. 50.

24. Ibid., pp. 45–50.

25. Ibid., p. 50.

26. Saint Ignatius of Loyola, *The Spiritual Exercises of Saint Ignatius of Loyola*, trans. W. H. Longridge (London: A. R. Mowbray and Co., 1930).

27. Ibid., p. ix.

28. Rudolph Otto, *Mysticism East and West* (New York: Collier Books, 1962), Appendix IV.

29. Hal Bridges, *American Mysticism from William James to Zen* (New York: Harper and Row, 1970), p. 24.

30. Linssen, *Living Zen*, p. 208.

31. Abraham Maslow, *Religions, Values, and Peak Experiences* (New York: Viking Press, 1970), p. 29.

32. Ibid.
33. Ibid., p. 33.
34. Ibid., p. 34.
35. Graham, *Conversations*, p. 120.
36. Donald Swearer, "The Appeal of Buddhism: A Christian Perspective," *Christian Century* (1971): 1289–93.
37. William Johnston, *Christian Zen*.

## Chapter 12 / WHO ARE THE AMERICAN BUDDHISTS?

1. George M. Williams, *NSA Seminar Report 1968–71* (Santa Monica: World Tribune Press, 1972), Appendix 3.
2. "A Survey of Center Students," *Crystal Mirror* 3 (1974): 127–36.
3. See especially *Zen Bow* (Rochester, N. Y.: Zen Center), *Zen Notes* (New York: First Zen Institute), and *Zen Notes* (Chicago: Zen Buddhist Temple).
4. Especially *Vajra Bodhi Sea* (San Francisco: Sino-American Buddhist Association), and Philip Kapleau, *The Three Pillars of Zen* (New York: John Weatherhill, 1965).
5. Holmes Welch, *The Practice of Chinese Buddhism, 1930–1950* (Cambridge, Mass.: Harvard University Press, 1967), p. 393.
6. *Statistical Handbook of Japan, 1962* (Tokyo: Bureau of Statistics, Office of the Prime Minister, 1962).
7. The figures given are "educated guesses" at best, not to be taken as authoritative.
8. Williams, *NSA Report*, Appendix 3.
9. Ibid.
10. Personal correspondence with Mary Farkas.
11. "A Survey of Center Students," p. 128.
12. *Vajra Bodhi Sea*, January, 1971.
13. Williams, *NSA Report*, Appendix 3.
14. *Vajra Bodhi Sea*, biographies published in almost each issue.
15. Williams, *NSA Report*, Appendix 3.
16. Ibid.
17. "A Survey of Center Students," p. 128.
18. Williams, *NSA Report*, Appendix 3.

## Chapter 13 / WHY BUDDHISM?

1. Leon Festinger, *A Theory of Cognitive Dissonance* (New York: Harper and Row, 1957); also Milton Rosenberg, "A Structural

Theory of Attitude Dynamics," *Public Opinion Quarterly* 24 (1960) : 319–40.

2. Philip Kapleau, ed., *The Three Pillars of Zen* (New York and Tokyo: Weatherhill, 1965) , Part III.
3. Unless otherwise indicated, these stories were obtained in the author's interviews with Buddhists.
4. Kapleau, *Three Pillars of Zen*, pp. 208–29.
5. George M. Williams, *NSA Seminar Report, 1968–1971* (Santa Monica, Cal.: World Tribune Press, 1972) , Appendix 3.
6. *Zen Bow* 4 (July/August 1970) :4.

CHAPTER 14 / WHAT FUTURE FOR BUDDHISM IN AMERICA?

1. Jacob Needleman, *The New Religions* (Garden City, N. Y.: Doubleday, 1970), p. 227.
2. Ibid.
3. Donald Swearer, "Three Modes of Buddhism" (unpublished paper) , 1972.
4. Ibid.
5. Theodore Roszak, *The Making of a Counter-Culture* (Garden City, N. Y.: Doubleday, 1969) , chap. 1.
6. Ibid., p. 40.
7. Philip M. Eden, "Buddhism's Future in the West," *The Middle Way* 47, pt. 3 (1972) : 103.
8. Ibid., p. 104.
9. Ibid., pp. 105–6.
10. Christmas Humphreys, "Ananda Metteyya," *The Middle Way* 47 (1972) : 133–36.
11. Thomas Merton, *Zen and the Birds of Appetite* (New York: New Directions, 1968) ; also *Mystics and Zen Masters* (New York: Dell, 1969) ; Dom Aelred Graham, *Zen Catholicism* (New York: Harcourt, Brace and World, 1963) ; also *Conversations: Christian and Buddhist* (New York: Harcourt Brace Jovanovich, 1968) ; William Johnston, *Christian Zen* (New York: Harper and Row, 1971) ; also *Still Point: Reflections on Zen and Christian Mysticism* (New York: Fordham University, 1970) .

# Glossary

(Note: Sanskrit words are marked Skt.; Pali, P.; Japanese, J.; Chinese, Ch.; Tibetan, T.; and Korean, K. No diacritical marks have been used.)

*Abhidhamma* (P.) ; *Abhidharma* (Skt.) : the third of three "baskets" (Tipitaka) of Buddhist literature, the other two being the vinaya and the sutras. The Abhidhamma is a philosophical and psychological analysis of mental phenomena and their interrelationships.

*alaya-vijnana* (Skt.) : store consciousness, where all the impressions and experiences of man are stored. The alaya-vijnana persists and is subject to repeated births and deaths.

*Amitabha* (Skt.) ; *Amida* (J.) ; *Amit'o* (Ch.) : Buddha of Infinite Life; presiding Buddha of the Western Paradise or Pure Land.

*anatta* (P.) ; *anatman* (Skt.) : doctrine of egolessness; absence of a permanent self or soul.

*anicca* (Skt.) : doctrine of the impermanence of all things.

*arahant* (P.) ; *arhat* (Skt.) : one who has put an end to rebirth, the goal of monastic discipline in Theravada Buddhism.

*ariyan* or *aryan* (P.) : a saint.

*atman* (Skt.) ; *atta* (P.) : breath, self, soul, inner essence of man.

*Avalokitesvara* (Skt.) : bodhisattva of compassion.

*bhikkhu* (P.) ; *bhikshu* (Skt.) : Buddhist monk.

*bhikkhuni* (P.) ; *bhikshuni* (Skt.) : Buddhist nun.

*bija mantra* (Skt.) : seed syllables.

*bodhi* (Skt.) : enlightenment, awakening.

*bodhicitta* (Skt.) : enlightened mind; aspiring to enlightenment.

*bodhisattva* (Skt.) : one who is destined to be a Buddha.

*causation, chain of*: doctrine that all physical and psychical phenomena are conditioned by antecedent physical or psychical factors, and that the whole of existence is an uninterrupted flux of phenomena, without beginning or end; doctrine of dependent origination.

*Ch'an* (Ch.) : Chinese meditational sect; Zen.

*Chen-re-zi* (T.) : Avalokitesvara.

*Chen Yen* (Ch.) : True Word school; Chinese esoteric Buddhism— "secret" school.

*Chiao* (K.) : Korean Buddhist sect emphasizing sutra study.

*chih*: see Chih-Kuan.

*Chih-kuan* (Ch.) : A T'ien-t'ai meditational technique, consisting of concentration (*chih*) followed by contemplative insight (*kuan*).

*Ching T'u* (Ch.) : Chinese Pure Land sect.

*Chogye* (K.) : Korean sect combining Zen and sutra study.

*Citta* (P., Skt.) : mind, consciousness.

*daimoku* (J.) : repetition of the words *namu myoho renge kyo* (hail to the Lotus sutra of the mystical law), an invocation believed by Nichiren Buddhists to have magical powers.

*daishonin* (J.) : great saint; frequently used as a designation for Saint Nichiren.

*dharani* (Skt.) : especially in Tibetan Buddhism, written mantras often visualized in the form of a circle.

*dharma* (Skt.) ; *dhamma* (P.) : a term with a variety of meanings: when capitalized it usually means either universal Law or the teachings of the Buddha; without a capital it usually refers to the elements of human existence.

*dhyana* (Skt.) : in Buddhist meditation, stages toward enlightenment.

*dokusan* (J.) : individual regularly scheduled interviews with a Zen master.

*dukkha* (P.) ; *duhkha* (Skt.) : suffering, ill, pain—one of the attributes of existence.

*eko* (J.) : term used by T'an-luan to designate interaction of Amida and man through Amida's vow power and man's faith.

*enlightenment*: in the Buddhist context, refers to the experiencing of one's true nature and therefore awakening to the nature of all existence.

*four vows*: vows repeated by the Zen Buddhist at the conclusion of zazen.

*gassho* (J.) : Oriental gesture of respect, hands raised to level of chest with palms together.

*gatha* (Skt.) : hymn.

*Gelugpa* (T.) : reformed Tibetan Buddhist sect constituting the established church and referred to as the Yellow Hat sect.

*Gohonzon* (J.) : mandala serving as the object of worship in Nichiren Buddhism.

*Gongyo* (J.) : chanting of the Lotus sutra, as practiced by Nichiren sects.

*Guru* (Skt.) : a spiritual teacher.

*han* (J.) : small group.

*Higashi Hongwanji* (J.) : Eastern Hongwan Temple—head temple for one of the two branches of True Pure Land Buddhism in Japan.

*Hinayana* (Skt.) : lesser Vehicle—Theravada Buddhism.

*Hompa Hongwanji* (J.) or *Nishi Hongwanji* (J.) Western Hongwan Temple—head temple for one of the two branches of True Pure Land Buddhism in Japan.

*hua-t'ou* (Ch.) : a device used in Ch'an meditation, in which the individual rids himself of thoughts by concentrating on mind before it hears, sees, feels, or is stirred by thought.

*Hua-yen* (Ch.) : A Chinese Buddhist sect based on the Garland sutra, affirming the principles that the absolute and phenomenological are interfused, and that all phenomena are interrelated.

*jhana* (P.) : dhyana; in samatha meditation usually refers to the trance stages leading to enlightenment.

*Jina* (Skt.) in Vajrayana, each of five Buddhas representing different aspects of Divine Wisdom—*Vairocana* (brilliance), *Akshobhya* (imperturbability), *Ratna Sambhava* ("jewel born"), *Amitabha* (infinite light and life), and *Amoghasiddhi* (unfailing success).

*jiriki* (J.) : self-power.

*jobutsu* (J.) : self-realization or enlightenment through practices of Nichiren Shoshu.

*Jodo Shinshu* (J.) : True Pure Land sect of Buddhism.

*Jodo Shu* (J.) : Pure Land sect in its Japanese form.

*Kargyutpa* or *Kargyupa* (T.) : semi-reformed Tibetan Buddhist sect of the Red Hat group.

*karma* (Skt.) : law of cause and effect; doctrine that one's present life and circumstances are the product of his past thoughts and actions, and that his present actions in this life will affect his mode of existence in future lives.

*karuna* (Skt.) : compassion.

*keisaku* (J.) : narrow, paddle-like stick used to strike meditators in zazen, as an aid to awakening the mind.

*kensho* (J.) : enlightenment; see also satori.

*kinhin* (J.) : walking Zen meditation.

*koan* (J.) : a riddle-like formulation of a problem which cannot be solved by logical reasoning, but only by awakening a deeper level of mind beyond the discursive intellect. (Example: What is the sound of one hand clapping?)

*komeito* (J.) : Clean Government Party, a Japanese political party originally constituting the political arm of Soka Gakkai.

*kosen-rufu* (J.) : conversion of the world to Nichiren Shoshu Buddhism.

*kuan*: see Chih-kuan.

*Kuan-yin* (Ch.) : Avalokitesvara bodhisattva, depicted in China as the Goddess of Mercy.

*Kwannon* or *Kannon* (J.) : Avalokitesvara bodhisattva.

*Kyojong* (K.) : Korean sect formed from unification of twelve Chiao sects and now forming one component of the Chogye sect.

*kyosaku* (J.) : keisaku. Kyosaku is the term used in Soto Zen, whereas keisaku is used in Rinzai Zen.

*Mahayana* (Skt.) : greater Vehicle—one of the two major schools of Buddhism, sometimes known as the Northern School; the major school of Buddhism in China, Japan, and Tibet.

*maitri* (Skt.) ; *metta* (P.) : loving-kindness.

*Maitreya* (Skt.) ; *Metteyya* (P.) : name of the Buddha who is yet to come.

*mandala*: mystic circle or diagram, cosmogram; in Buddhism, usually depicts a Buddha in the center, surrounded by and related to other Buddhas, bodhisattvas, and possibly other creatures.

*Manjusri* (Skt.) : the bodhisattva of wisdom.

*mantra* (Skt.) : mystic syllables, the pronunciation of which generates great powers.

*Mappo* (Skt.) : Latter Day of the Law, i.e., the present degenerate era.

*Mara* (Skt.) : The tempter, in the Buddhist tradition.

*min-on* (J.) : musical groups, in Nichiren Shoshu.

*mokugyo* (J.) ; *mu-yü* (Ch.) : wooden fish—a wooden percussion instrument which is struck to mark the tempo and rhythm of chanting.

*mondo* (J.) : a question and answer session in which a Zen student asks his master a question about Buddhist doctrine, with the master giving a logically nonsensical response which evokes an answer from the deeper levels of the student's intuitive mind.

*mudra* (Skt.) : symbolic movements of hands, fingers, or body.

*nembutsu* (J.) : repetition of the syllables *Namu Amida Butsu* (hail to Amitabha Buddha), to invoke the power of faith in the vow power of Amida Buddha.

*Nichiren Shoshu* (J.) : sect of Nichiren orthodox Buddhism.

*Nichiren Shu* (J.) : sect of Nichiren Buddhism.

*nirvana* (Skt.) ; *nibanna* (P.) : literally, the "void"; dissolution of dualities, with realization of the selfless "I" and accompanying inner peace and freedom when one experiences enlightenment.

*Nyingmapa* (T.) : oldest of Tibetan Buddhist sects; one of three sects of the Red Hat school.

*Obaku* (J.) : earliest Japanese Zen sect.

*Ojuzu* (J.) : beads; Buddhist rosary.

*Pali Canon*: the canon of Theravada Buddhist literature, written in the sacred language of Pali; the Tipitaka.

*paramita* (Skt.) : term used in Mahayana Buddhism to indicate certain "perfections" or virtues, the cultivation of which leads to enlightenment.

*prajna* (Skt.) : intuitive wisdom.

*rinpoche* (T.) : Tibetan religious guide and teacher—the equivalent of "roshi" in Zen.

*Rinzai* (J.) : Zen sect emphasizing koan study.

*Rissho Koseikai* (J.) : Society for the Establishment of Righteousness and Friendly Intercourse—one of the new religions of Japan; a religious organization of laymen, which makes extensive use of the discussion group.

*Risshu* (J.) : a Japanese nondenominational Buddhist school concerned mostly with the rules of behavior for monks and nuns.

*roshi* (J.) : Zen master.

*Sakyapa* (T.) : semi-reformed Tibetan Buddhist sect of the Red Hat group, almost indistinguishable from Yellow Hats.

*samadhi* (Skt.) : concentration.

*samatha* (P.) : an approach to Theravada meditation which involves calming down and induction of trance states through one-pointed concentration.

*samsara* (Skt.) : the cycle of rebirth.

*sangha* (Skt.) : community of monks and/or nuns; third of the three "jewels" of Buddhism, the other two being the Buddha and the Dharma.

*sansen ichinen* (J.) : three thousand worlds in a single moment.

*sanzen* (J.) : formal appearance before a roshi; includes *dokusan*, but also other types of individual and group contacts between disciples and masters.

*satipatthana* (P.) : mindfulness.

*satori* (J.) : enlightenment (usually indicates a deeper level of enlightenment than kensho) .

*sesshin* (J.) : an extended period of zazen, lasting from a few days to several months.

*shakubuku* (J.) : conversion technique involving forceful persuasion; used by Nichiren Shoshu.

*shikantaza* (J.) : just sitting—meditational technique used in Soto Zen.

*Shin Buddhism*: Jodo Shinshu.

*Shingon* (J.) : Japanese school of esoteric Buddhism; Japanese form of Chen Yen.

*shonin* (J.) : saint.

*Shugendo* (J.) : Japanese esoteric sect involving mountain practice.

*sila* (Skt.) : moral conduct.

*skandha* (Skt.) : Buddhist term for the five heaps or aggregates that make up the personality: body, senses, perceptions, volitions, and consciousness.

*Soka Gakkai* (J.) : Value Creation Society—organization of lay members of Nichiren Shoshu.

*Sonjong* (K.) : Korean Zen sect formed from unification of nine Zen sects; now represents Zen component of the Chogye sect.

*Soto* (J.) : Zen sect emphasizing practice involving shikantaza rather than koan study.

*stupa* (Skt.) : a dome, sometimes housing relics of the Buddha, serving as a focus for popular piety.

*sunyata* (Skt.) : emptiness; the void.

*sutra* (Skt.) ; *sutta* (P.) : sermons or discourses of the Buddha—one of the "three baskets" of Buddhism.

*Tantra* (Skt.) : sutras of a so-called mystical nature, forming the basis for the "secret" practices of esoteric Buddhism. Tantric Buddhism utilizes the mandala, and such practices as mantra, mudra, and visualizations.

*tariki* (J.) : other-power.

*tathata* (Skt.) : suchness.

*teisho* (J.) : lecture by a Zen master.

*Tendai* (J.) : Japanese sect based on scriptures and treatises of T'ien t'ai school of Chinese Buddhism; stresses universality of salvation (attainment of Buddhahood).

*thanka* (T.) : Tibetan temple banner.

*Theravada* (Skt.) : Southern school of Buddhism based on the *Pali Canon*, most prevalent in South and Southeast Asia; Hinayana.

*Threefold Refuge*: commitment made by Buddhists to take refuge in the triple jewel (*tri-ratna*) of the Buddha, the Dharma, and the Sangha.

*T'ien t'ai* (Ch.) : See Tendai; also chih-kuan.

*Tipitaka* (P.) : the "three baskets" of the *Pali Canon*; includes the *Abhidamma*, the *suttas*, and the *vinaya*.

*trikaya* (Skt.) : Mahayana trinity, consisting of the three forms of the Buddha's body—the Body of the Law, the Body of Bliss, and the Body of Transformation.

*tri-ratna*: See Threefold Refuge.

*tulku* (T.) : incarnate lama.

*upasaka* (Skt.) : devout layman who has taken the "three refuges."

*upasika* (Skt.) : female equivalent of upasaka.

*Vairocana* (Skt.) : Sun Buddha—one of the five Jinas.

*Vajrayana* (Skt.) : a late development of Mahayana Buddhism, which includes the teachings and practices of Tantric groups.

*vihara* (P.) : Buddhist temple in Ceylon and Thailand.

*vinaya* (P.) : one of the three baskets of the *Pali Canon*, containing rules for the Sangha.

*vipassana* (P.) : insight meditation of Theravada Buddhism.

*yamabushi* (J.) : literally translated "mountain people," yamabushi are practitioners of Shugendo.

*zazen* (J.) : sitting Zen meditation.

*Zen* (J.) : Japanese meditational school.

*zendo* (J.) : Zen meditation hall.

# Selected Bibliography

BOOKS AND ARTICLES

Ames, Van Meter. *Zen and American Thought*. Honolulu: Univ. of Hawaii Pr., 1962.

Bando, Shojun. "Shinran's Indebtedness to T'an-luan." *Eastern Buddhist*, n. s. 4 (May, 1971) : 72–87.

Barrett, William, ed. *Zen Buddhism: Selected Writings of D. T. Suzuki*. Garden City, N. Y.: Doubleday, 1956.

Basham, A. L. *The Wonder that was India*. New York: Grove Pr., 1954.

Bellah, Robert N., ed. *Religion and Progress in Modern Asia*. Glencoe, Ill.: The Free Press, 1965.

Blofeld, John. *The Tantric Mysticism of Tibet*. New York: Dutton Company, 1970.

Bloom, Alfred. *Shinran's Gospel of Pure Grace*, Tucson. Univ. of Arizona Pr., 1964.

Bridges, Hal. *American Mysticism from William James to Zen*. New York: Harper and Row, 1970.

*The Buddhist Churches of America*. San Francisco: Buddhist Churches of America, 1971.

Bunce, William K. *Religions in Japan*. Rutland, Vt.: Tuttle Publishing Co., 1955.

Chang, Garma C. C., tr. *The Hundred Thousand Songs of Milarepa*. New York: Harper and Row, 1970.

Ch'en, Kenneth K. S. *Buddhism in China, a Historical Survey*. Princeton, N. J.: Princeton Univ. Pr., 1964.

_____. *Buddhism, the Light of Asia*. Woodbury, N. Y.: Barron's Educational Series, 1968.

Conze, Edward. *Buddhism, Its Essence and Development*. New York: Harper and Row, 1951.

_____. *Buddhist Meditation*. London: George Allen and Unwin, 1966.

_____. *Buddhist Thought in India*. Ann Arbor: Univ. of Michigan Pr., 1967.

————, tr. *Buddhist Wisdom Books.* London: George Allen and Unwin, 1958.

————, Horner, I. B.; Snellgrove, D.; and Waley, A., eds. *Buddhist Texts through the Ages.* Oxford: Cassirer, 1954.

Cox, Richard H., ed. *Religious Systems and Psychotherapy.* Springfield, Ill.: Charles C Thomas, 1973.

Cowell, E. B.; Muller, F. Max; and Takakusu, J., trs. *Buddhist Mahayana Texts.* Oxford: Clarendon Pr., 1894.

Dai, Bingham. "Zen and Psychotherapy." *Voices* 5 (Fall/Winter, 1969–70) : 118–24.

Dean, Stanley R. "Beyond the Unconscious: The Ultraconscious." *Psychologia* 8 (1965) : 145–50.

deBary, William Theodore, ed. *The Buddhist Tradition in India, China and Japan.* New York: Random House, 1969.

"Drugs and Buddhism"—A Symposium. *Eastern Buddhist,* n. s. 4 (Oct. 1971) : 128–52.

Earhart, H. Byron. *A Religious Study of the Mount Haguro Sect of Shugendo.* Tokyo: Univ. of Chicago Pr., 1964.

Ekvall, Robert B. *Religious Observances in Tibet*: *Patterns and Function.* Chicago: Univ. of Chicago Pr., 1964.

Evans-Wentz, W. Y. *The Tibetan Book of the Dead.* London: Oxford Univ. Pr., 1964.

————. *The Tibetan Book of the Great Liberation.* London: Oxford Univ. Pr., 1960.

————. *Tibet's Great Yogi Milarepa.* London: Oxford Univ. Pr., 1928.

Fromm, Erich; Suzuki, D. T.; and De Martino, Richard. *Zen Buddhism and Psychoanalysis.* New York: Harper and Row, 1960.

Fung, Paul F. and Fung, George D., trs. *The Sutra of the Sixth Patriarch on the Pristine Orthodox Dharma.* San Francisco: Buddha's Universal Church, 1964.

Gard, Richard. *Buddhism.* New York: George Braziller, 1962.

Goddard, Dwight, ed. *A Buddhist Bible.* Boston: Beacon Press, 1938.

Goleman, Daniel. "The Buddha on Meditation and States of Consciousness." *Journal of Transpersonal Psychology* 4 (1972) : 1–44; 5 (1973) :151–70.

Govinda, Lama Anagarika. *Foundations of Tibetan Mysticism.* London: Rider, 1959.

Graham, Dom Aelred. *Conversations*: *Christian and Buddhist.* New York: Harcourt, Brace Jovanovich, 1968.

————. *Zen Catholicism*: *A Suggestion.* New York: Harcourt, Brace and World, 1963.

Guenther, H. V. *Buddhist Philosophy in Theory and Practice*. Baltimore: Pelican Books, 1972.

————, tr. *The Life and Teachings of Naropa*. London: Oxford Univ. Pr., 1963.

————. *The Tantric View of Life*. Berkeley, Cal.: Shambhala, 1969.

Hanson, Virginia, ed. *Approaches to Meditation*. Wheaton, Ill.: Theosophical Publishing House, 1973.

Helton, William. "Political Prospects of Soka Gakkai." *Pacific Affairs* 28 (Fall-Winter 1965–66) : 231–44.

*A History of Fifty Years of the Tri-State Buddhist Church*. Denver: Tri-State Buddhist Church, 1967.

Hume, Robert E., tr. *The Thirteen Principal Upanishads*, rev. ed. London: Oxford Univ. Pr., 1931.

Humphreys, Christmas. *Buddhism*. Baltimore: Penguin Books, 1951.

————. *The Buddhist Way of Life*. London: Allen and Unwin, 1969.

————. *Zen Buddhism*. New York: Macmillan, 1949.

Ikeda, Daisaku. *The Complete Works of Daisaku Ikeda*. Vols. 1-4. Tokyo: The Seikyo Press, 1967–71.

Inaba, Shuken and Funabashi, Issai. *Jodo Shinshu*. Kyoto: Otani Univ. Pr., 1961.

Johansson, Rune E. A. *The Psychology of Nirvana*. London: George Allen and Unwin, 1960.

Johnston, William. *Christian Zen*. New York: Harper and Row, 1971.

————. *Still Point: Reflections on Zen and Christian Mysticism*. New York: Fordham Univ. Pr., 1970.

Kapleau, Philip, ed. *The Three Pillars of Zen*. New York and Tokyo: Weatherhill, 1965.

————, ed. *The Wheel of Death*. New York: Harper and Row, 1971.

Kern, H., tr. *Saddharma-Pundarika or the Lotus of the True Law*. Oxford: Clarendon Pr., 1884.

King, Winston L. *Buddhism and Christianity*. Philadelphia: The Westminster Press, 1962.

Lesh, Terry V. "Zen Meditation and the Development of Empathy in Counselors." *Journal of Humanistic Psychology* 10 (1970): 39–78.

Ling, T. O., ed. *A Dictionary of Buddhism*. New York: Scribner, 1972.

Linssen, Robert. *Living Zen*. London: George Allen and Unwin, 1958.

LuKuan Yu. *The Secrets of Chinese Meditation*. London: Rider and Company, 1964.

McFarland, H. Neill. *Rush Hour of the Gods*. New York: Macmillan, 1967.

McKain, David W. *Christianity: Some Non-Christian Appraisals.* New York: McGraw-Hill, 1964.

Mahasi Sayadaw. *Practical Insight Meditation.* San Francisco: Unity Pr., 1972.

Maslow, Abraham H. *Religions, Values and Peak Experiences.* New York: Viking Pr., 1970.

Masutani, Fumio. *A Comparative Study of Buddhism and Christianity.* 2nd ed. Tokyo: Bukkyo Dendo Kyokai, 1967.

Maupin, Edward W. "Zen Buddhism: A Psychological Review." *Journal of Consulting Psychology* 26 (1962) : 362–78.

Merton, Thomas. *Mystics and Zen Masters.* New York: Dell, 1969.

————. *Zen and the Birds of Appetite.* New York: New Directions, 1968.

Mi-pham, Lama. *Calm and Clear.* Berkeley, Ca.: Dharma Publishing, 1973.

Murata, Kiyoaki. *Japan's New Buddhism: An Objective Account of Soka Gakkai.* New York and Tokyo: John Weatherhill, 1969.

Murphy, Gardner and Murphy, Lois B., eds. *Asian Psychology.* New York: Basic Books, 1968.

Murti, T. R. V. *The Central Philosophy of Buddhism.* London: George Allen and Unwin, 1970.

Naranjo, Claudio and Ornstein, Robert E. *On the Psychology of Meditation.* New York: Viking Pr., 1971.

Needleman, Jacob. *The New Religions.* Garden City, N. Y.: Doubleday, 1970.

Nyanoponika, Thera. *The Heart of Buddhist Meditation.* New York: Samuel Weiser, 1973.

Onda, Akira. "Zen and Creativity." *Psychologia* 5 (1962) : 13–20.

Otto, Rudolph. *Mysticism East and West.* New York: Collier Books, 1962.

Prabhavananda, Swami and Manchester, Frederick. *The Spiritual Heritage of India.* New York: Doubleday, 1963.

————, trs. *The Upanishads: Breath of the Eternal.* New York: Mentor Books, 1957.

Robinson, Richard H. *The Buddhist Religion.* Belmont, Ca.: Dickenson Publishing Company, 1970.

Roszak, Theodore. *The Making of a Counter-Culture.* Garden City, N. Y.: Doubleday, 1969. Chapter 1.

Sangharakshita. *The Three Jewels.* London: Rider and Company, 1967.

Sato, Koji. "Psychotherapeutic Implications of Zen." *Psychologia* 1 (1958) :213–18.

Saunders, E. Dale. *Buddhism in Japan*. Philadelphia: Univ. of Pennsylvania Pr., 1964.

Schecter, Jerrold. *The New Face of Buddha*. Tokyo: John Weatherhill, 1967.

Seo, Kyung Beo. "A Study of Korean Zen Buddhism Approached Through Chodangjip." Ph.D. dissertation, Temple University, Philadelphia, 1969.

Streng, Frederick. *Emptiness—A Study of Religious Meaning*. Nashville: Abingdon Pr., 1967.

Stcherbatsky, Th. *Buddhist Logic*. Two volumes. New York: Dover, 1962.

————. *The Conception of Buddhist Nirvana*. The Hague: Mouton, 1970.

Stunkard, Albert. "Some Interpersonal Aspects of an Oriental Religion." *Psychiatry* 14 (1951):419–31.

Suzuki, Beatrice Lane. *Mahayana Buddhism*. New York: Macmillan Company, 1959.

Suzuki, Daisetz T. *The Field of Zen*. London: The Buddhist Society, 1969.

————. *Mysticism, Christian and Buddhist*. New York: Harper and Row, 1957.

————. *Shin Buddhism*. New York: Harper and Row, 1970.

Swearer, Donald K. *Buddhism in Transition*. Philadelphia: Westminster Pr., 1970.

————, ed. *Secrets of the Lotus*. New York: Macmillan, 1971.

Tannisho Kenkyukai. *Perfect Freedom in Buddhism: An Exposition of the Words of Shinran*. Translated by Takuwa Shinji. Tokyo: Hokuseido Pr., 1968.

Thien-An, Thich. *Zen Buddhism and Nationalism in Vietnam*. Los Angeles: International Buddhist Meditation Center, 1970.

Trungpa, Chogyam. *Born in Tibet*. London: George Allen and Unwin, 1966.

————. *Cutting through Spiritual Materialism*. Berkeley, Ca.: Shambhala, 1973.

————. *Meditation in Action*. Berkeley, Ca.: Shambhala, 1970.

Walters, John. *The Essence of Buddhism*. New York: Crowell Publishing Company, 1964.

Watts, Alan W. *Psychotherapy East and West*. New York: Random House, 1961.

————. *The Way of Zen*. New York: Pantheon Books, 1957.

Welch, Holmes. *Buddhism Under Mao*. Cambridge, Mass.: Harvard Univ. Pr., 1972.

————. *The Buddhist Revival in China.* Cambridge, Mass.: Harvard Univ. Pr., 1968.

————. *The Practice of Chinese Buddhism, 1900-1950.* Cambridge, Mass.: Harvard Univ. Pr., 1967.

Wells, Mariann K. "Chinese Temples in California." Master's thesis, Univ. of California, Berkeley, 1962.

White, James W. *The Sokagakkai and Mass Society.* Stanford, Ca.: Stanford Univ. Pr., 1970.

Williams, George M. *N.S.A. Seminar Report, 1968–1971.* Santa Monica, Ca.: World Tribune Pr., 1972.

————. *N.S.A. Seminars: An Introduction to True Buddhism.* Santa Monica, Ca.: World Tribune Pr., 1974.

Wright, Arthur E. *Buddhism in Chinese History.* Palo Alto, Ca.: Stanford Univ. Pr., 1959.

Yang, C. K. *Religion in Chinese Society. A Study of Contemporary Social Functions of Religion and Some of their Historical Factors.* Berkeley, Ca.: Univ. of California Pr., 1961.

## JOURNALS AND BULLETINS PUBLISHED BY AMERICAN BUDDHIST CENTERS

(Most Buddhist churches or centers publish newsletters or journals. The following constitute a representative sample.)

*Buddhist Temple of Chicago Bulletin.* Chicago: Buddhist Temple of Chicago (monthly).

*Crystal Mirror.* Berkeley, Ca.: Nyingma Tibetan Meditation Center (annual).

*Garuda.* Boulder, Col.: Karma Dzong (annual).

*Gesar.* Berkeley, Ca.: Nyingma Tibetan Meditation Center (quarterly).

*International Buddhist Meditation Center Newsletter.* Los Angeles: International Buddhist Meditation Center (monthly).

*The Journal of the Zen Mission Society.* Mt. Shasta, Ca.: Shasta Abbey (quarterly).

*Matava Buddhist Temple Newsletter.* Saginaw, Mich.: Matava Buddhist Temple.

*Mount Baldy Zen Center Newsletter.* Mount Baldy, Ca.: Mount Baldy Zen Center (quarterly).

*N.S.A. Quarterly.* Santa Monica, Ca.: Nichiren Shoshu Academy.

*Rinzai-ji Newsletter.* Los Angeles: Cimarron Zen Center (quarterly).

*Suchness.* Chicago: American Buddhist Association (quarterly).

*Vajra Bodhi Sea.* San Francisco: Sino-America Buddhist Association.

*Washington Buddhist.* Washington, D.C.: Washington Buddhist Vihara (bimonthly).

*Wheel of Dharma.* San Francisco, Ca.: Buddhist Churches of America (monthly).

*Wind Bell.* San Francisco: Zen Center (quarterly).

*World Tribune.* Santa Monica, Ca.: Nichiren Shoshu of America (triweekly).

*ZCLA Journal.* Los Angeles: Zen Center of Los Angeles (quarterly).

*Zen Bow.* Rochester, N. Y.: Zen Center (quarterly).

*Zen Notes.* New York: First Zen Institute of America (monthly).

## OTHER JOURNALS

*The Eastern Buddhist.* Kyoto: The Eastern Buddhist Society.

*Journal of Humanistic Psychology.* San Francisco: Association of Humanistic Psychology.

*Journal of Transpersonal Psychology.* Palo Alto, Ca.: Association of Transpersonal Psychology.

*The Middle Way.* London: The Buddhist Society.

# Index

## About the Author

EMMA MCCLOY LAYMAN is Professor Emeritus of Psychology at Iowa Wesleyan College, where she is currently a lecturer on Asian history and culture. She headed the Department of Psychology there from 1960 to 1975, also serving as the director of the East Asian Institute, director of International Studies, and chairman of the Social Science Division. Prior to 1960, she was the chief psychologist at Children's Hospital in Washington, D.C., supervisory clinical psychologist at Brooke Army Hospital, associate professor of psychology at the University of North Carolina, and supervisor of psychological services for the Iowa Board of Social Welfare.

Dr. Layman graduated from Oberlin College and subsequently obtained her M.A. from New York University and her Ph.D. from the University of Iowa. She has been both president and director of the International Council of Psychologists. *Buddhism in America* is Dr. Layman's third book.